TOEIC
TEST
PREP

Other Titles of Interest from LearningExpress

Grammar Success in 20 Minutes a Day

Reading Comprehension Success in 20 Minutes a Day

TOEFL iBT: The English Scores You Need

Vocabulary for TOEFL iBT

Vocabulary and Spelling Success in 20 Minutes a Day

Writing Success in 20 Minutes a Day

TOEIC
TEST
PREP

LEARNINGEXPRESS®

NEW YORK

Library of Congress Cataloging-in-Publication Data:
TOEIC test prep.—1st ed.

    p.   cm.

   ISBN 978-1-57685-757-1

  1. Test of English for International Communication—Study guides.   2. English language—Examinations—Study guides.   3. English language—Textbooks for foreign speakers.

  PE1128.T65535 2010

  428.2'4—dc22

                                             2010006387

Printed in the United States of America

9 8 7 6 5 4 3 2 1

First Edition

ISBN: 978-1-57685-757-1

Regarding the Information in This Book
We attempt to verify the information presented in our books prior to publication. It is always a good idea, however, to double-check such important information as minimum requirements, application and testing procedures, and deadlines with your local law enforcement agency, as such information can change from time to time.

For more information or to place an order, contact LearningExpress at:
  2 Rector Street
  26th Floor
  New York, NY 10006

Or visit us at:
  www.learnatest.com

CONTENTS

HOW TO USE THIS BOOK ▶

This book was written to help ensure your success with the TOEIC. It includes test taking tips, descriptions of the four test sections, practice questions, and four full-length practice exams.

Studying this material will help you to know what to expect when you take the test. For many of us, test taking is stressful enough without adding any surprises. In this book, you will learn what to expect from each section of the test, what kinds of questions are asked, and how much time you will have. You will also see examples for each type of question.

You will have four opportunities to take full-length practice exams modeled on the actual TOEIC within this book, plus an additional practice exam online. Consider taking the diagnostic exam before reading Chapters 4 through 7. This will allow you to see how well you can answer different questions from the TOEIC listening, reading, speaking, and writing sections now as you begin preparing for the actual TOEIC. When you finish the book, take practice exams 1 through 3 and the online practice exam for additional practice and to see how much you have improved.

This book is accompanied by audio files, which can be accessed at **http://www.learnatest.com/ SpeakingGuides/TOEIC_Test_Prep**. Every time you must listen to an audio file within a set of practice questions or during a practice exam, you will see this icon: 🎧 . The information next to this icon will indicate which audio file you should listen to. Make sure your computer has speakers; otherwise you will need to use headphones.

The complete transcripts for all audio files are included in the appendix of this book, in case you do not have access to a computer or headphones. If you do not have access to these, ask someone who speaks English fluently to read the material to you face-to-face or into a tape recorder. Be sure your reader speaks clearly at a normal, conversational pace.

1 ▶ TEST OF ENGLISH FOR INTERNATIONAL COMMUNICATION (TOEIC)

There are several tests of English proficiency. What sets the TOEIC, or Test of English for International Communication, apart from the others is its strong business theme. It is focused on real-life situations in the international workplace and so is tailored to adult business professionals who want to certify that their English meets the daily tasks of professional business communication. TOEIC test scores are used by businesses, schools, and governments all over the world to hire, recruit, and promote adult speakers of English as a second language. An employer can look at a non-native English speaker's TOEIC test scores to gauge his or her everyday English skills. Employers can also use it to set language standards and create training programs for their workers.

The test is most commonly taken by businesspeople who use or plan to use English in real-life work settings. They often work for hotels, hospitals, or restaurants, or use their English frequently in international business meetings or conventions. The test is taken by candidates for managerial, sales, and technical positions in international business, commerce, and industry. Other test takers are simply preparing to enter the workforce or seeking to improve their qualifications for new jobs.

Although the test is especially suited to establishing employment credentials, TOEIC scores can also be used as a qualification for placement in university programs or courses. The test is often used in instructional settings, where it serves as an assessment tool to measure a broad range of English language skills and place students in appropriate classes. Individual test takers can also use their TOEIC scores to monitor their own competence in and progress with their English language skills.

WHY TAKE THE TOEIC?

The TOEIC is widely accepted as a measure of English skills. It can help you:

- improve your professional resume
- track your progress in English acquisition
- show employers you are ready for success at the next professional level
- know your own strengths and limitations
- qualify for educational opportunities and placement
- build your confidence
- qualify for a new position

How to Register for the TOEIC

The TOEIC is given in public sessions, at language schools, and at organizations around the world. You can register for the test online through the testing website, www.ets.org/toeic, using most major credit cards. The test fee for public testing sessions in the United States is $75. You can also register for these sessions by mail by filling out a paper application, which can be downloaded from the same website.

For public testing sessions outside the United States you must contact your local testing office about registration. There is a link on the testing website that offers contact information for testing offices in over 75 countries around the world. If there is no information for your country, or you need a different testing location, you can complete an information request form. The testing service can make special arrangements to administer the test in these circumstances.

There are 12 public testing sessions each year in the United States, one per month. A regularly updated calendar of the testing dates can be found on the Internet. The registration deadline for these tests is 5:00 P.M. Eastern Time the Thursday a week before the test. After you register for the test, you will not be able to cancel the registration or change your test date. A test may be canceled if fewer than five people register for it.

After you submit your online registration, you will receive a confirmation that the registration was received. This confirmation is not the same as a test ticket. The test ticket will be e-mailed later with a date, time, and location. It usually takes less than a week for the test provider to process your registration and send the test ticket. You will need the ticket and a photo ID to check in for the test. Passports, driver's licenses, state ID cards, military ID cards, and national ID cards are the recommended forms of identification. Before you register for the test, you should make sure that you will have a valid form of identification on the day of the test; otherwise, you cannot be admitted to the testing session.

Institutional testing sessions are arranged by language schools and employers. Anyone who wants to take the test in this venue should talk to his or her instructor, coordinator, or supervisor. When a test is administered by a company or school, registration processes and fees are set by that institution.

Where the TOEIC Is Given

In the United States, tests are administered regularly in public sessions in 23 states.

- California—Berkeley, Costa Mesa, Fullerton, Irvine, La Jolla, Los Angeles (two locations),

Northridge, Rosemead, Sacramento, San Diego, San Francisco, San Jose, Torrance
- Colorado—Denver
- District of Columbia—Washington
- Florida—Fort Lauderdale, Miami
- Georgia—Tucker
- Hawaii—Honolulu
- Idaho—Lewiston
- Illinois—Chicago
- Kansas—Manhattan
- Kentucky—Covington
- Massachusetts—Boston
- Michigan—Ann Arbor, Battle Creek, Novi
- Minnesota—St. Paul
- New Jersey—Closter, Fort Lee, Union City
- New York—New York City (two locations)
- Ohio—Columbus
- Oklahoma—Edmund, Oklahoma City, Stillwater, Tahlequah
- Oregon—Lake Oswego, Portland
- Pennsylvania—Philadelphia
- Tennessee—Nashville
- Texas—Austin, Dallas, Houston, Wichita Falls
- Utah—Salt Lake City
- Washington—Seattle

There is also a public testing site in Hato Rey, Puerto Rico. The addresses of these testing sites can be found on the TOEIC website.

To find testing locations outside the United States, you will need to get the contact information for the international testing offices. There are offices in the following countries:

Colombia	Netherlands
Costa Rica	New Zealand
Croatia	Nicaragua
Dominican	Nigeria
Republic	Panama
Ecuador	Paraguay
Egypt	Peru
El Salvador	Philippines
France	Poland
Germany	Portugal
Greece	Puerto Rico
Guatemala	Qatar
Honduras	Russia
Hong Kong	Saudi Arabia
Hungary	Singapore
India	Spain
Indonesia	Switzerland
Ireland	Syria
Israel	Taiwan
Italy	Thailand
Japan	Tunisia
Jordan	Turkey
Kenya	Ukraine
Korea	Uruguay
Kuwait	United Arab
Laos	Emirates
Latvia	United Kingdom
Lebanon	Uzbekistan
Malaysia	Venezuela
Mexico	Vietnam
Morocco	West Bank/Gaza
Nepal	Yemen

Argentina	Bolivia
Australia	Brazil
Austria	Cambodia
Bahrain	Canada
Belgium	Chile
Belize	China

These offices can give you information about international testing locations. If you need a different testing location or information about another country, you need to fill out an information request form to see if you can make special testing arrangements.

Format of the TOEIC

The TOEIC is broken into two separate tests that can be taken together or separately. Each of these two tests is further divided into two skill sets: the Listening and Reading Test; and the Speaking and Writing Test. You must register for each test individually. The Listening and Reading Test contains eight different types of questions and the Speaking and Writing Test contains nine types of questions. This book helps you familiarize yourself with the different types of questions as well as the test format.

The Listening and Reading Test is a two-and-a-half-hour test, given in paper-and-pencil format. It is broken into a timed 100-question listening section and a timed 100-question reading section. Test takers have 45 minutes to complete the listening portion and 75 minutes to complete the reading section. This is a multiple choice test with a separate answer sheet. You should practice filling in bubbles for the answers on a separate answer sheet if you are not already familiar with the process. The selections should be filled in darkly and completely with a #2 pencil.

The Listening and Reading Test is administered in paper-and-pencil multiple choice format.

The Speaking and Writing Test is taken on a computer. The speaking portion is 20 minutes long and requires the test taker to complete 11 speaking tasks, which are recorded for scoring. The writing portion of the test takes one hour to complete and requires the test taker to complete eight writing tasks on a standard QWERTY keyboard. If you are planning to take the Speaking and Writing Test, you should practice using the standard QWERTY (English-language) keyboard.

The Speaking and Writing Test is administered using a computer.

You can use the sample tests in this book to practice with the test format. It is important to thoroughly familiarize yourself with the format and question types before test day.

Types of Questions on the Tests

There are 17 question types on the TOEIC test. Eight different kinds of questions are used on the Listening and Reading Test, and nine kinds of question are used on the Speaking and Writing Test. This section provides a brief breakdown of the kinds of questions you can expect to see. The rest of this book provides you with more detailed descriptions, more examples, and more thorough explanations of the question types on each section of the test. It is very important to be familiar with the kinds of questions you will see, so that you do not waste valuable test time trying to determine what kind of answer is expected.

Question Types on the Listening Portion

On the listening portion of the Listening and Reading Test, you will see:

- questions that ask you to choose the best description of a picture
- questions that ask you to choose the best response to a question or statement
- questions about a recorded dialogue you will hear
- questions about a short talk or message you will listen to

Here are four descriptions of questions you might see on the listening portion of the TOEIC test.

1. **Photograph Description.** For these questions you will look at a picture in your test book, then hear four statements about that picture. When you hear the statements, select the one that best describes what you see in the picture. Then, mark the letter of that statement on your answer sheet. The statements will not be printed in your test book and will be spoken one time. There are 40 photograph description questions.

Example

You will see:

You will hear:
Now, listen to the four statements:
 a. He had a terrible accident.
 b. The freeway is crowded.
 c. The bus is late.
 d. The cars are for sale.

The best description of the picture is *The freeway is crowded*, so you would mark answer choice **b** on your answer sheet.

2. **Question Response.** For this type of question, you will hear a question or statement and three responses spoken in English. Then, you will select the best response to the question or statement and mark the letter of your answer choice on your answer sheet. The questions will not be printed in your test book and will be spoken one time. There are 30 question response items on the test.

Example

You will hear:
How often do we have staff meetings?
You will also hear:
 a. today
 b. four
 c. once a month

For this question you would mark choice **c** on the answer sheet, because the answer *once a month* best answers a question about the frequency of meetings.

3. **Conversations.** In this section, you will hear several conversations between two people. You will be asked to answer three questions about each conversation. The conversations will not be printed in your test book and will be spoken only once. There are ten conversations and three questions about each conversation, for a total of 30 questions.

4. **Short Talks.** These questions are similar to the conversation questions, except there is only one speaker. You will listen to someone speaking and answer a few written questions about what you heard. The talks will not be printed in your test book and will be spoken only one time. There are 30 questions about the short talks.

Question Types on the Reading Portion

On the reading portion of the Listening and Reading Test, you will see:

- questions that ask you to choose the best word to complete a sentence
- questions that ask you to choose the best word to complete a text
- questions about a single text you will read
- questions that you must use two pieces of text (usually a block of text and an item in a different, real-world format) to answer

Here are four descriptions of questions you might see on the reading portion of the TOEIC test.

1. **Incomplete Sentences.** In this kind of question, you will read a sentence with a word missing. There will be four answer choices for the missing word. You must choose the best word to complete the sentence and mark the corresponding letter of that answer choice on your answer sheet. There are 40 incomplete sentence questions on the test.

   Example

   Yesterday's meeting _____ because the director was sick.
   a. cancelled
   b. is cancelled
   c. is cancelling
   d. was cancelled

   For this question, you would mark choice **d** on your answer sheet because *was cancelled* correctly completes the sentence.

2. **Text Completion.** The text completion questions are similar to the incomplete sentence questions, except the sentences flow together into a single block of text. This means that you will have to read several sentences together to be able to choose the missing word. You will then fill in the correct letter of the answer choice on your answer sheet. There are 12 text completion questions on the test.

3. **Single Passage.** These are reading comprehension questions. You will read a passage and answer questions about what you read. Some of the questions will refer to texts in real-world formats, like advertisements or websites. The number of questions about each passage will vary. There are 28 single passage questions on the test.

4. **Double Passage.** These are also reading comprehension questions, but the questions are taken from two texts that are to be read together. You will read two passages, some of which will be in real-world formats, and answer questions about what you read. Some of the questions will require that you combine information from both passages. The number of questions about each pair will vary. There are 20 double passage questions on the test.

Question Types on the Speaking Portion

On the speaking portion of the Speaking and Writing Test, you will perform six kinds of speaking tasks:

- You will be asked to read a text aloud.
- You will be asked to describe a picture.
- You will respond to questions about your life and opinions.
- You will answer questions aloud using written information that is provided.
- You will listen to a problem and propose a solution to the problem.
- You will express an opinion aloud.

Here are six descriptions of questions you might see on the speaking portion of the TOEIC test.

1. **Read a Text Aloud.** For these questions, you will be asked to read two short texts aloud. The readings will be recorded and scored on clarity, pronunciation, and emphasis.

2. **Describe a Picture.** For this type of question, you will orally compose three to five detailed sentences describing a picture. What you say will be recorded for scoring. There is only one picture description on the speaking portion of the test. You will have 30 seconds to prepare the response and 45 seconds to speak about the picture.

3. **Respond to Questions.** For this portion of the test you will be asked three questions—two simple and one more complicated—on a single topic. You will have 15 seconds to answer the first two questions and 30 seconds to answer the third. Your responses will be recorded for scoring.

   Example

   You will hear: Where do you usually get the news?

   You will hear: How often do you get news from this source?

   You will hear: Do you think it is important to stay up-to-date on world events, and if so, why?

4. **Respond to Questions Using Information Provided.** For these questions, a text in real-world format, such as a webpage, advertisement, or order form, will appear on the computer screen. You will read the information and listen to questions about it. You will then use the information on the screen to answer questions. There will be three questions about the information; you will have 15 seconds to answer the first two and 30 seconds to answer the third.

5. **Propose a Solution.** This speaking task requires that you listen to a speaker talk about a problem. You will then offer a solution to the problem. You will have 30 seconds to prepare for your response and 60 seconds to speak.

6. **Express an Opinion.** The final question on the speaking portion of the test asks you to express an opinion about a given topic. You will hear a spoken prompt. You will then have 15 seconds to think and prepare, and 30 seconds to orally compose a response.

   Example

   You will hear: People have different understandings of what kinds of conversations are appropriate in work environments. Some people talk with their coworkers about all aspects of their lives and others keep their personal lives private. Do you think it is appropriate to talk about personal problems at the office? Give reasons and examples to support your opinion.

Question Types on the Writing Portion

On the writing portion of the Speaking and Writing Test, you will perform three kinds of writing tasks:

- write sentences describing pictures
- compose responses to written requests for information
- produce a well-organized opinion essay

Here are three descriptions of questions you might see on the writing portion of the TOEIC test:

1. **Write a Sentence Based on a Picture.** These questions are different from the picture questions in the other sections of the test in that you will not only have to describe the picture, but

you must also incorporate two given words or phrases into the one-sentence description. You will have to write a single complex sentence for each item. You have eight minutes to complete the five picture questions.

Example
You will see:

waiting for, so

A sentence that includes *waiting for* and *so* and also talks about the picture might read something like: *The people are waiting for the plane to take off so they can get out of their seats.*

2. **Respond to a Written Request.** For these questions, you must read a document that asks you to respond with information or questions about a topic. There are two questions of this type on the test. You will have ten minutes to respond to each prompt.

3. **Opinion Essay.** There is one complete essay to write. It will be about 300 words in length and will express a well-supported opinion. You will have 30 minutes to plan and write an organized three to five paragraph essay.

Scoring

Since your score indicates a proficiency level; it is impossible to fail the TOEIC test; different proficiency levels are necessary for different jobs, tasks, and placements. The proficiency levels that the test provide as part of your score come with descriptions of the strengths and weaknesses typical of someone using English at that level.

The Listening and Reading Test is scored by calculating the correct number of answer choices. The raw number of correct answers is converted to a scaled score, which compares an individual's raw score with the raw score of other test takers. This makes allowances for the difficulty level of any particular test administration.

The test score you receive on the Listening and Reading Test is based only on the number of questions you answer correctly; there is not a penalty for incorrect answers. The scaled scores for this test range from 5 to 495. A proficiency level is assigned based on the scaled score. A score report provides three scores: a listening score, a reading score, and a total score. Each of these corresponds to a proficiency level, which is listed with a description. There are three possible proficiency levels and descriptions for the listening section and four possible levels and descriptions for the reading section. A document also exists that translates these descriptions into real-life situations and tells what specific tasks someone at this level can usually do successfully in a work environment.

A test taker will usually receive a score report about seven days after completing a public session of the Listening and Reading Test. If the test is administered through a private organization, the scores are sent to that organization, whose responsibility it is to distribute the scores to individual test takers.

There are two separate scores for the Speaking and Writing Test, one for speaking and one for writing, but no total score. Each speaking and writing item is scored on a scale of zero through three, zero through four, or zero through five, according to a rubric. The item scores are then calculated into overall scaled scores that indicate proficiency levels in the domains of speaking and writing. The proficiency levels on these tests also come with proficiency level descriptors that give details about the strengths and weaknesses typical of speakers and writers at each level. It is worth noting that the Speaking and Writing Test is scored by people, not machines, so scores usually do not arrive as quickly as those for the Listening and Reading Test.

The Speaking Test items are scored using rubrics on a scoring scale between zero and three on the first nine questions, and between zero and five on the final two questions. The rubrics generally take into account pronunciation, intonation and stress, grammar, vocabulary, cohesion, relevance, and completeness. These scores are converted into an overall speaking score that ranges from zero through 200. Different scores on this scale are correlated with eight levels of speaking proficiency. There is a description of the typical skills and abilities of speakers at each proficiency level provided on the score report.

The Writing Test items are scored similarly. They use rubrics with scores ranging from zero to three on the first five questions, zero to four on the next two questions, and zero to five on the final question. Writing questions are generally scored on grammar, vocabulary, organization, complexity and variety of sentences, relevance to the prompts, and support for ideas. These item scores are then calculated into an overall writing scale score between zero and 200. Different scores on this scale correspond with nine levels of writing proficiency. Detailed descriptions of the strengths and weaknesses typical of writers at each of the nine proficiency levels are provided on the score reports.

The score reports for all four tests contain a great deal of information about a test taker's language skills. The reports not only give scores, but attempt to explain, using proficiency level descriptors, exactly what the scores mean. These descriptions can provide valuable information for test takers, schools, and employers. Other chapters of this book go into greater detail about the scoring of each section.

2 ▶ THE LEARNINGEXPRESS TEST PREPARATION SYSTEM

The LearningExpress Test Preparation System, developed exclusively for LearningExpress by leading test experts, gives you the discipline and attitude you need to succeed on the TOEIC. Like all good things, TOEIC-related skills do not come easily. You do have to work for them. But you don't have to work alone. The LearningExpress Test Preparation System is here to help. In just ten easy-to-follow steps, you will learn everything you need to prepare for the exam and help you perform your best. You'll be in control. Being a "good test-taker" requires more than just knowing your material. It means being prepared.

Here is how the LearningExpress Test Preparation System works: Ten easy steps lead you through everything you need to know and do to get ready to master your exam. Each step includes both reading about the step and one or more activities. It is important that you do the activities along with the reading, or you won't be getting the full benefit of the system.

Step 1: Know the Potential Test-Taking Blockers
Step 2: Get Information
Step 3: Conquer Test Anxiety
Step 4: Make a Plan
Step 5: Learn to Manage Your Time
Step 6: Learn to Use the Process of Elimination
Step 7: Know When to Guess
Step 8: Reach Your Peak Performance Zone
Step 9: Get Your Act Together
Step 10: Do it!

If you have several hours, you can work through the whole LearningExpress Test Preparation System in one sitting. Otherwise, you can break it up and do just one or two steps a day for the next several days. It is up to you—remember, you are in control.

Step 1: Know the Potential Test-Taking Blockers

Activities: Think about tests you had difficulty with in the past. Then look at the list of test-taking blockers and see how many of them applied to you back then. Now make your own list from the suggestions for correcting them, place it on your desk or refrigerator, and start making changes.

For example, if you were a negative thinker, write, "Think Positive: I WILL succeed on the TOEIC!"

Test-Taking Blockers

Test taking is challenging because of the many pitfalls that can keep you from doing your best.

- Having a negative attitude: Thinking that you will do poorly can actually cause you to do poorly. Think positive. Stand in front of a mirror and say, "I will do well on the TOEIC!" Post signs around your home and car that say, "I WILL succeed!"
- Not taking ownership of your career: Teachers don't fail students; students fail on their own.

Take ownership of your career. While others may help you, it ultimately remains up to you to succeed on the TOEIC.

- Not preparing for the exam: Don't be overconfident. Even straight-A students can perform poorly if they have not prepared.
- Preparing at the last minute: Everyone is pressed for time these days, but you need to make adequate time to prepare for your exam. Weeks are better than days, and days are better than hours. Squeezing several weeks of studying into one night only increases test anxiety. Save that last night for a quick review and a good night's sleep.
- Not practicing: The more you practice TOEIC-style questions, the better you'll be at answering the ones on the official TOEIC. Use and reuse the practice exams in this book. You will increase your comfort level and keep getting better at answering, listening, reading, speaking, and writing questions.

Step 2: Get Information

Activities: Read Chapter 1, "About the Test of English for International Communication (TOEIC)," and find out about the test.

Knowledge is power. Therefore, first, you have to find out everything you can about the TOEIC. Once you have your information, the next steps will show you what to do with it.

Why do you have to take this exam? One of the major objectives of TOEIC is to measure your ability to use English in everyday workplace activities. For many people, this test is a gateway to the best employment opportunities. Globalization and technology require you to have English listening, reaching, speaking, and writing skills for in-person, telephone, and e-mail communication.

Step 3: Conquer Test Anxiety

Activity: Take the Test Anxiety Quiz on page 14.
Having complete information about the exam is the first step in getting control of the exam. Next, you have to overcome one of the biggest obstacles to test success: test anxiety. Test anxiety can not only impair your performance on the exam itself; it can even keep you from preparing! In this step, you will learn stress management techniques that will help you succeed on your exam. Learn these strategies now, and practice them as you complete the exams in this book so that they will be second nature to you by exam day.

Combatting Test Anxiety

The first thing you need to know is that a little test anxiety is a good thing. Everyone gets nervous before a big exam, and if that nervousness motivates you to prepare thoroughly, so much the better. Many well-known people throughout history have experienced anxiety or nervousness—from performers such as actor Sir Laurence Olivier and singer Aretha Franklin to writers such as Charlotte Brontë and Alfred Lord Tennyson. In fact, anxiety probably gave them a little extra edge—just the kind of edge you need to do well, whether on a stage or in an examination room.

Stop here and complete the Test Anxiety Quiz on page 14 to find out whether your level of test anxiety is something you should worry about.

Stress Management before the Test

If you feel your level of anxiety rising in the weeks before the test, here is what you need to do to bring the level down again:

- **Get prepared.** There's nothing like knowing what to expect and being prepared for it to put you in control of test anxiety. That's why you are reading this book. Use it faithfully, and remind yourself that you are better prepared than most of the people taking the test.

- **Practice self-confidence.** A positive attitude is a great way to combat test anxiety. This is no time to be humble or shy. Stand in front of the mirror and say to your reflection, "I'm prepared. I'm full of self-confidence. I'm going to ace this test. I know I can do it." If you hear it often enough, you will come to believe it.

- **Fight negative messages.** Every time someone starts telling you how hard the exam is or how it is almost impossible to get a high score, start telling them your self-confidence messages. If the someone with the negative messages is you, telling yourself you don't do well on exams or you just can't do this, don't listen.

- **Visualize.** Imagine yourself conquering the TOEIC. Visualizing success can help make it happen—and it reminds you of why you are working to prepare for the TOEIC.

- **Exercise.** Physical activity helps calm down your body and focus your mind. Besides, being in good physical shape can actually help you do well on the exam. Go for a run, lift weights, go swimming—and do it regularly.

Stress Management on Test Day

There are several ways you can bring down your level of test anxiety on test day. They will work best if you practice them in the weeks before the test, so you know which ones work best for you.

- **Deep breathing.** Take a deep breath while you count to five. Hold it for a count of one, then let it out for a count of five. Repeat several times.

- **Move your body.** Try rolling your head in a circle. Rotate your shoulders. Shake your hands from the wrist. Many people find these movements very relaxing.

- **Visualize again.** Think of the place where you are most relaxed: lying on the beach in the sun, walking through the park, or whatever makes you feel good. Now close your eyes and imagine

TEST ANXIETY QUIZ

You need to worry about test anxiety only if it is extreme enough to impair your performance. The following questionnaire will provide a diagnosis of your level of test anxiety. In the blank before each statement, write the number that most accurately describes your experience.

0 = Never
1 = Once or twice
2 = Sometimes
3 = Often

_____ I have gotten so nervous before an exam that I simply put down the books and didn't study for it.

_____ I have experienced disabling physical symptoms such as vomiting and severe headaches because I was nervous about an exam.

_____ I have simply not showed up for an exam because I was scared to take it.

_____ I have experienced dizziness and disorientation while taking an exam.

_____ I have had trouble filling in the little circles because my hands were shaking too hard.

_____ I have failed an exam because I was too nervous to complete it.

_____ **Total: Add up the numbers in the blanks above.**

Your Test Stress Score

Here are the steps you should take, depending on your score. If you scored:

- **Below 3**, your level of test anxiety is nothing to worry about; it's probably just enough to give you that little extra edge.
- **Between 3 and 6**, your test anxiety may be enough to impair your performance, and you should practice the stress management techniques in this section to try to bring your test anxiety down to manageable levels.
- **Above 6**, your level of test anxiety is a serious concern. In addition to practicing the stress management techniques listed in this section, you may want to seek additional, personal help. Call your local high school or community college and ask for the academic counselor. Tell the counselor that you have a level of test anxiety that sometimes keeps you from being able to take the exam. The counselor may be willing to help you or may suggest someone else you should talk to.

you are actually there. If you practice in advance, you will find that you only need a few seconds of this exercise to experience a significant increase in your sense of well-being.

When anxiety threatens to overwhelm you right there during the exam, there are still things you can do to manage the stress level.

- **Repeat your self-confidence messages.** You should have them memorized by now. Say them silently to yourself, and believe them!
- **Visualize one more time.** This time, visualize yourself moving smoothly and quickly through the test answering every question correctly and finishing just before time is up. Like most visualization techniques, this one works best if you have practiced it ahead of time.
- **Find an easy question.** Skim over the test until you find an easy question, and answer it. Getting even one question answered gets you into the test-taking groove.
- **Take a mental break.** Everyone loses concentration once in a while during a long test. It is normal, so you shouldn't worry about it. Instead, accept what has happened. Say to yourself, "Hey, I lost it there for a minute. My brain is taking a break." Close your eyes and do some deep breathing for a few seconds. Then you will be ready to go back to work.

Try these techniques ahead of time, and see if they work for you!

Step 4: Make a Plan

Activity: Construct a study plan.

Maybe the most important thing you can do to get control of yourself and your exam is to make a study plan. Too many people fail to prepare simply because they fail to plan. Spending hours poring over sample test questions the day before the exam not only raises your level of test anxiety, but also will not replace careful preparation and practice over time.

Don't fall into the cram trap. Take control of your preparation time by mapping out a study schedule. On pages 24 and 25 are two sample schedules, based on the amount of time you have before you take the TOEIC. If you are the kind of person who needs deadlines and assignments to motivate you for

a project, here they are. If you are the kind of person who doesn't like to follow other people's plans, you can use the suggested schedules to construct your own.

Even more important than making a plan is making a commitment. You can't review everything you learned in for the TOEIC in one night. You need to set aside some time every day for study and practice. Try for at least 20 minutes a day. Twenty minutes daily will do you much more good than two hours on Saturday—divide your test preparation into smaller pieces of the larger work. In addition, making study notes, creating visual aids, and memorizing can be quite useful as you prepare. Each time you begin to study, quickly review your last lesson. This act will help you retain all you have learned and help you assess whether you are studying effectively. You may realize you are not remembering some of the material you studied earlier. Approximately one week before your exam, try to determine the areas that are still most difficult for you.

Don't put off your study until the day before the exam. Start now. A few minutes a day, with half an hour or more on weekends, can make a big difference in your score.

Learning Styles

Each of us absorbs information differently. Whichever way works best for you is called your dominant learning method. If someone asks you to help them construct a bookcase they just bought that may be in many pieces, how do you begin? Do you need to read the directions and see the diagram? Would you rather hear someone read the directions to you—telling you which part connects to another? Or do you draw your own diagram?

The three main learning methods are visual, auditory, and kinesthetic. Determining which type of learner you are will help you create tools for studying.

Visual learners need to see the information in the form of maps, pictures, text, or math problems. Outlining notes and important points in colorful highlighters and taking note of diagrams and pictures may be key in helping you study.

Auditory learners retain information when they can hear directions, the spelling of a word, a math theorem, or poem. Repeating information aloud or listening to your notes on a tape recorder may help. Many auditory learners also find working in study groups or having someone quiz them beneficial.

Kinesthetic learners must do! They might need to draw diagrams, write directions or build a model. Rewriting notes on index cards or making margin notes in your textbooks also helps kinesthetic learners to retain information.

Mnemonics

Mnemonics are memory tricks that help you remember what you need to know. The three basic principles in the use of mnemonics are imagination, association, and location. Acronyms (words created from the first letters in a series of words) are common mnemonics. One acronym you may already know is **HOMES**, for the names of the Great Lakes (**H**uron, **O**ntario, **M**ichigan, **E**rie, and **S**uperior). **ROY G. BIV** reminds people of the colors in the spectrum (**R**ed, **O**range, **Y**ellow, **G**reen, **B**lue, **I**ndigo, and **V**iolet). Depending on the type of learner you are, mnemonics can also be colorful or vivid images, stories, word associations, or catchy rhymes such as "Thirty days hath September . . ." created in your mind. Any type of learner, whether visual, auditory, or kinesthetic, can use mnemonics to help the brain store and interpret information.

Step 5: Learn to Manage Your Time

Activities: Practice these strategies as you take the practice exams in this book.

Steps 5, 6, and 7 of the LearningExpress Test Preparation System put you in charge of your exam by showing you test-taking strategies that work. Practice these strategies as you take the sample tests in this book, and then you will be ready to use them on test day.

First, you will take control of your time on the exam. The TOEIC has a time limit, which may give you more than enough time to complete all the questions—or may not. It is a terrible feeling to hear the examiner say, "Five minutes left," when you are only three-quarters of the way through the test. Here are some tips to keep that from happening to you.

- **Follow directions.** If the directions are given orally, listen to them. If they are written, read them carefully. Ask questions before the exam begins if there's anything you don't understand.
- **Pace yourself.** Glance at your watch every few minutes, and compare the time to how far you have gotten in the test.
- **Don't rush.** Though you should keep moving, rushing won't help. Try to keep calm and work methodically and quickly.

Step 6: Learn to Use the Process of Elimination

Activity: Complete worksheet on Using the Process of Elimination (see page 18).

After time management, your next most important tool for taking control of your exam is using the process of elimination wisely. It is standard test-taking wisdom that you should always read all the answer choices before choosing your answer. This helps you find the right answer by eliminating wrong answer choices. And, sure enough, that standard wisdom applies to your TOEIC, too.

Key Words

Often, identifying key words in a question will help you in the process of elimination. Words such as *always*, *never*, *all*, *only*, *must*, and *will* often make statements incorrect.

Words like *usually*, *may*, *sometimes*, and *most* may make a statement correct.

Even when you think you are absolutely clueless about a question, you can often use the process of elimination to get rid of at least one answer choice. If so, you are better prepared to make an educated guess, as you will see in Step 7. More often, you can eliminate choices until you have only two possible answers. Then you are in a strong position to guess.

Try using your powers of elimination on the questions in the worksheet on page 18, Using the Process of Elimination. The questions are designed to show you how the process of elimination works. The answer explanations for this worksheet show one possible way you might use the process to arrive at the right answer.

Step 7: Know When to Guess

Activity: Complete worksheet on Your Guessing Ability (see page 19).

Armed with the process of elimination, you are ready to take control of one of the big questions in test taking: Should I guess? The answer is Yes. Some exams have what's called a "guessing penalty," in which a fraction of your wrong answers is subtracted from your right answers—but the TOEIC doesn't work like that. The number of questions you answer correctly yields your raw score. So you have nothing to lose and everything to gain by guessing.

The more complicated answer to the question "Should I guess?" depends on you—your personality and your "guessing intuition." There are two things you need to know about yourself before you go into the exam:

1. Are you a risk-taker?
2. Are you a good guesser?

You will have to decide about your risk-taking quotient on your own. To find out if you are a good guesser, complete the Your Guessing Ability worksheet on page 19.

Step 8: Reach Your Peak Performance Zone

Activity: Complete the Physical Preparation Checklist.

To get ready for a challenge like a big exam, you have to take control of your physical, as well as your mental, state. Exercise, proper diet, and rest in the weeks prior to the test will ensure that your body works with, rather than against, your mind on test day and during your preparation.

Exercise

If you don't already have a regular exercise program going, the time during which you are preparing for an exam is actually an excellent time to start one. And if you are already keeping fit—or trying to get that way—don't let the pressure of preparing for an exam fool you into quitting now. Exercise helps reduce stress by pumping feel-good hormones called endorphins into your system. It also increases the oxygen supply throughout your body, including your brain, so you will be at peak performance on test day.

A half hour of vigorous activity—enough to raise a sweat—every day should be your aim. If you are really pressed for time, every other day is okay. Choose an activity you like and get out there and do it. Jogging with a friend always makes the time go faster, or take a portable music player.

But don't overdo it. You don't want to exhaust yourself. Moderation is the key.

Diet

First of all, cut out the junk. Go easy on caffeine and nicotine, and eliminate alcohol from your system at least two weeks before the exam. What your body

USING THE PROCESS OF ELIMINATION

Use the process of elimination to answer the following questions.

1. Ilsa is as old as Meghan will be in five years. The difference between Ed's age and Meghan's age is twice the difference between Ilsa's age and Meghan's age.
Ed is 29. How old is Ilsa?
   a. 4
   b. 10
   c. 19
   d. 24

2. "All drivers of commercial vehicles must carry a valid commercial driver's license whenever operating a commercial vehicle."

   According to this sentence, which of the following people need NOT carry a commercial driver's license?
   a. a truck driver idling his engine while waiting to be directed to a loading dock
   b. a bus operator backing her bus out of the way of another bus in the bus lot
   c. a taxi driver driving his personal car to the grocery store
   d. a limousine driver taking the limousine to her home after dropping off her last passenger of the evening

3. Smoking tobacco has been linked to
   a. increased risk of stroke and heart attack.
   b. all forms of respiratory disease.
   c. increasing mortality rates over the past ten years.
   d. juvenile delinquency.

4. Which of the following words is spelled correctly?
   a. incorrigible
   b. outragous
   c. domestickated
   d. understandible

Answers

Here are the answers, as well as some suggestions as to how you might have used the process of elimination to find them.

1. **d.** You should have eliminated choice **a** right off the bat. Ilsa can't be four years old if Meghan is going to be Ilsa's age in five years. The best way to eliminate other answer choices is to try plugging them in to the information given in the problem. For instance, for choice **b**, if Ilsa is 10, then Meghan must be 5. The difference between their ages is 5. The difference between Ed's age, 29, and Meghan's age, 5, is 24. Is 24 two times 5? No. Then choice **b** is wrong.

   You could eliminate choice **c** in the same way and be left with choice **d**.

2. **c.** Note the word not in the question, and go through the answers one by one. Is the truck driver in choice **a**, "operating a commercial vehicle"? Yes, idling counts as "operating," so he needs to have a commercial driver's license. Likewise, the bus operator in choice **b** is operating a commercial vehicle; the question doesn't say the operator has to be on the street. The limo driver in choice **d** is

operating a passenger in it. However, the driver in choice **c** is not operating a commercial vehicle, but his own private car.

3. **a.** You could eliminate choice **b** simply because of the presence of the word all. Such absolutes hardly ever appear in correct answer choices. Choice **c** looks attractive until you think a little about what you know—aren't fewer people smoking these days, rather than more? So how could smoking be responsible for a higher mortality rate? (If you didn't know that mortality rate means the rate at which people die, you might keep this choice as a possibility, but you would still be able to eliminate two answers and have only two to choose from.) And choice **d** is plain silly, so you could eliminate that one, too. You are left with the correct choice, **a**.

4. **a.** How you used the process of elimination here depends on which words you recognized as being spelled incorrectly. If you knew that the correct spellings were outrageous, domesticated, and understandable, then you were home free.

YOUR GUESSING ABILITY

The following are ten really hard questions. You are not supposed to know the answers. Rather, this is an assessment of your ability to guess when you don't have a clue. Read each question carefully, as if you were expected to answer it. If you have any knowledge of the subject, use that knowledge to help you eliminate wrong answer choices.

1. September 7 is Independence Day in
   a. India.
   b. Costa Rica.
   c. Brazil.
   d. Australia.

2. Which of the following is the formula for determining the momentum of an object?
   a. $p = MV$
   b. $F = ma$
   c. $P = IV$
   d. $E = mc^2$

3. Because of the expansion of the universe, the stars and other celestial bodies are all moving away from each other. This phenomenon is known as
   a. Newton's first law.
   b. the big bang.
   c. gravitational collapse.
   d. Hubble flow.

4. American author Gertrude Stein was born in
   a. 1713.
   b. 1830.
   c. 1874.
   d. 1901.

5. Which of the following is NOT one of the Five Classics attributed to Confucius?
   a. *I Ching*
   b. *Book of Holiness*
   c. *Spring and Autumn Annals*
   d. *Book of History*

6. The religious and philosophical doctrine that holds that the universe is constantly in a struggle between good and evil is known as
   a. Pelagianism.
   b. Manichaeanism.
   c. neo-Hegelianism.
   d. Epicureanism.

7. The third Chief Justice of the U.S. Supreme Court was
   a. John Blair.
   b. William Cushing.
   c. James Wilson.
   d. John Jay.

8. Which of the following is the poisonous portion of a daffodil?
   a. the bulb
   b. the leaves
   c. the stem
   d. the flowers

9. The winner of the Masters golf tournament in 1953 was
   a. Sam Snead.
   b. Cary Middlecoff.
   c. Arnold Palmer.
   d. Ben Hogan.

10. The state with the highest per capita personal income in 1980 was
   a. Alaska.
   b. Connecticut.
   c. New York.
   d. Texas.

Answers

Check your answers against the following correct answers.
   1. c.
   2. a.
   3. d.
   4. c.
   5. b.
   6. b.
   7. b.
   8. a.
   9. d.
   10. a.

How Did You Do?

You may have simply gotten lucky and actually known the answer to one or two questions. In addition, your guessing was probably more successful if you were able to use the process of elimination on any of the questions. Maybe you didn't know who the third Chief Justice was (question 7), but you knew that John Jay was the first. In that case, you would have eliminated choice **d** and, therefore, improved your odds of guessing right from one in four to one in three.

According to probability, you should get two-and-a-half answers correct, so getting either two or three right would be average. If you got four or more right, you may be a really terrific guesser. If you got one or none right, you may be a really bad guesser.

Keep in mind, though, that this is only a small sample. You should continue to keep track of your guessing ability as you work through the sample questions in this book. Circle the numbers of questions you guess on as you make your guess; or, if you don't have time while you take the practice tests, go back afterward and try to remember which questions you guessed at. Remember, on a test with four answer choices, your chance of guessing correctly is one in four. So keep a separate "guessing" score for each exam. How many questions did you guess on? How many did you get right? If the number you got right is at least one-fourth of the number of questions you guessed on, you are at least an average guesser—maybe better—and you should always go ahead and guess on the real exam. If the number you got right is significantly lower than one-fourth of the number you guessed on, you would be safe in guessing anyway, but maybe you would feel more comfortable if you guessed only selectively, when you can eliminate a wrong answer or at least have a good feeling about one of the answer choices.

Remember, even if you are a play-it-safe person with lousy intuition, you are still safe guessing every time.

needs for peak performance is simply a balanced diet. Eat plenty of fruits and vegetables, along with protein and carbohydrates.

Make sure to eat a healthy breakfast the day of the exam. Be sure to include protein, complex carbohydrates, and some fat. Complex carbohydrates, such as whole-grain toast or oatmeal, help you feel energized throughout the day.

Rest

You probably know how much sleep you need every night to be at your best, even if you don't always get it. Make sure you do get that much sleep, though, for at least a week before the exam. Moderation is important here, too. Extra sleep will just make you groggy.

If you are not a morning person and your exam will be given in the morning, you should reset your internal clock so that your body doesn't think you are taking an exam at 3 A.M. You have to start this process well before the exam. The way it works is to get up half an hour earlier each morning, and then go to bed half an hour earlier that night. Don't try it the other way around; you will just toss and turn if you go to bed early without having gotten up early. The next morning, get up another half an hour earlier, and so on. How long you will have to do this depends on how late you are used to getting up.

Step 9: Get Your Act Together

Activity: Complete the Final Preparations worksheet.

You are in control of your mind and body; you are in charge of test anxiety, your preparation, and your test-taking strategies. Now it is time to take charge of external factors, like the testing site and the materials you need to take the exam.

Find Out Where the Test Is and Make a Trial Run

The testing agency will notify you when and where your exam is being held. Do you know how to get to the testing site? Do you know how long it will take to get there? If not, make a trial run, preferably on the same day of the week at the same time of day. Make note, on the Final Preparations worksheet on page 23, of the amount of time it will take you to get to the exam site. Plan on arriving at least 10 or 15 minutes early so you can get the lay of the land, use the bathroom, and calm down. Then figure out how early you will have to get up that morning, and make sure you get up that early every day for a week before the exam.

Gather Your Materials

The night before the exam, lay out the clothes you will wear and the materials you have to bring with you to the exam. Plan on dressing in layers; you won't have any control over the temperature of the examination room. Have a sweater or jacket you can take off if it is warm. Use the checklist on the Final Preparations worksheet on page 23 to help you pull together what you will need.

Don't Skip Breakfast

Even if you don't usually eat breakfast, do so on exam morning. A cup of coffee doesn't count. Don't eat doughnuts or other sweet foods, either. A sugar high will leave you with a sugar low in the middle of the exam. A mix of protein and complex carbohydrates is best: Cereal with milk, or eggs with whole-grain toast, will do your body a world of good.

Step 10: Do It!

Activity: Prove your TOEIC skills!

Fast forward to exam day. You are ready. You made a study plan and followed through. You practiced your test-taking strategies while working through this book. You are in control of your physical, mental, and emotional states. You know when and where to show up and what to bring with you. In other words, you are better prepared than most of the other people taking the TOEIC with you. You are psyched.

Just one more thing. . . . When you are done with the exam, you deserve a reward. Plan a celebration. Call your friends and plan a party, or have a nice dinner for two—whatever your heart desires. Give yourself something to look forward to.

And then do it. Go into the exam, full of confidence, armed with test-taking strategies you have practiced until they are second nature. You are in control of yourself, your environment, and your performance on the exam. You are ready to succeed. So do it. Go in there and ace the exam. And look forward to TOEIC!

Getting to the Exam Site

Location of exam site: _____

Date: _____

Departure time: _____

Do I know how to get to the exam site?   Yes _____   No _____   (If no, make a trial run.)

Time it will take to get to exam site _____

Things to Lay Out the Night Before

Clothes I will wear   _____

Sweater/jacket   _____

Watch   _____

Photo ID   _____

Four #2 pencils   _____

Other Things to Bring/Remember

_____   _____

_____   _____

_____   _____

_____   _____

Schedule A: The 30-Day Plan

If you have at least a month before you take the TOEIC, you have plenty of time to prepare—as long as you don't waste it! If you have less than a month, turn to Schedule B.

TIME	PREPARATION
Days 1–2	Skim over written materials about the TOEIC. Go to the ETS website for answers to commonly asked questions. Read Chapter 1.
Day 3	Take the diagnostic exam in Chapter 3.
Day 4	Score the diagnostic exam. Based on this exam, identify your strongest and weakest areas.
Days 5–6	Read Chapter 4, Listening Comprehension Review.
Day 7	Complete the practice questions in Chapter 4. Review your answers.
Days 8–9	Read Chapter 5, Reading Comprehension Review.
Day 10	Complete the practice questions in Chapter 5. Review your answers.
Days 11–12	Read Chapter 6, Speaking Review.
Day 13	Complete the practice questions in Chapter 6. Review your answers.
Days 14–15	Read Chapter 7, Writing Review.
Day 16	Complete the practice questions in Chapter 7. Review your answers.
Days 17–19	Take Practice Exam 1. Score yourself and review any questions you missed.
Days 20–22	Take Practice Exam 2. Review your answers.
Days 23–25	Take Practice Exam 3. Look closely at the answer explanations.
Days 26–28	Complete the online practice test. Review your instant score feedback.
Day 29	Review any areas you are still weak in.
Day before the exam	Relax. Do something unrelated to the exam and go to bed at a reasonable hour.

Schedule B: The 10-Day Plan

If you have two weeks or less before you take the exam, you may have your work cut out for you. Use this 10-day schedule to help you make the most of your time.

TIME	PREPARATION
Day 1	Read Chapter 1. Take the diagnostic exam in Chapter 3 and score it using the answer key at the end. Identify which skill areas need the most work, based on your exam score.
Day 2	Read through Chapter 4, Listening Comprehension Review, and Chapter 5, Reading Comprehension Review. Take both practice question sets and score yourself.
Day 3	Read through Chapter 6, Speaking Review, and Chapter 7, Writing Review. Complete all practice questions and look at the answer explanations.
Day 4	Take the first practice exam in Chapter 8 and score it.
Day 5	If your score on the first practice exam shows weaknesses on the four areas you studied, review them.
Day 6	Take the second practice exam in Chapter 9 and score it. Review all questions that you missed.
Day 7	Take the third practice exam in Chapter 10 and score yourself.
Day 8	Review any areas that you are not entirely comfortable with.
Day 9	Take the online practice exam and review your instant score feedback.
Day 10	Use your last study day to brush up on any areas that are still giving you trouble.
Day before the exam	Relax. Do something unrelated to the exam and go to bed at a reasonable hour.

CHAPTER

3 ▶ DIAGNOSTIC EXAM

By taking this diagnostic exam before you begin studying for the TOEIC, you will get an idea of how much you already know and how much you need to learn. This diagnostic exam consists of questions modeled after the official TOEIC Listening, Reading, Speaking, and Writing sections.

1.	a	b	c	d		46.	a	b	c	d		91.	a	b	c	d
2.	a	b	c	d		47.	a	b	c	d		92.	a	b	c	d
3.	a	b	c	d		48.	a	b	c	d		93.	a	b	c	d
4.	a	b	c	d		49.	a	b	c	d		94.	a	b	c	d
5.	a	b	c	d		50.	a	b	c	d		95.	a	b	c	d
6.	a	b	c	d		51.	a	b	c	d		96.	a	b	c	d
7.	a	b	c	d		52.	a	b	c	d		97.	a	b	c	d
8.	a	b	c	d		53.	a	b	c	d		98.	a	b	c	d
9.	a	b	c	d		54.	a	b	c	d		99.	a	b	c	d
10.	a	b	c	d		55.	a	b	c	d		100.	a	b	c	d
11.	a	b	c			56.	a	b	c	d		101.	a	b	c	d
12.	a	b	c			57.	a	b	c	d		102.	a	b	c	d
13.	a	b	c			58.	a	b	c	d		103.	a	b	c	d
14.	a	b	c			59.	a	b	c	d		104.	a	b	c	d
15.	a	b	c			60.	a	b	c	d		105.	a	b	c	d
16.	a	b	c			61.	a	b	c	d		106.	a	b	c	d
17.	a	b	c			62.	a	b	c	d		107.	a	b	c	d
18.	a	b	c			63.	a	b	c	d		108.	a	b	c	d
19.	a	b	c			64.	a	b	c	d		109.	a	b	c	d
20.	a	b	c			65.	a	b	c	d		110.	a	b	c	d
21.	a	b	c			66.	a	b	c	d		111.	a	b	c	d
22.	a	b	c			67.	a	b	c	d		112.	a	b	c	d
23.	a	b	c			68.	a	b	c	d		113.	a	b	c	d
24.	a	b	c			69.	a	b	c	d		114.	a	b	c	d
25.	a	b	c			70.	a	b	c	d		115.	a	b	c	d
26.	a	b	c			71.	a	b	c	d		116.	a	b	c	d
27.	a	b	c			72.	a	b	c	d		117.	a	b	c	d
28.	a	b	c			73.	a	b	c	d		118.	a	b	c	d
29.	a	b	c			74.	a	b	c	d		119.	a	b	c	d
30.	a	b	c			75.	a	b	c	d		120.	a	b	c	d
31.	a	b	c			76.	a	b	c	d		121.	a	b	c	d
32.	a	b	c			77.	a	b	c	d		122.	a	b	c	d
33.	a	b	c			78.	a	b	c	d		123.	a	b	c	d
34.	a	b	c			79.	a	b	c	d		124.	a	b	c	d
35.	a	b	c			80.	a	b	c	d		125.	a	b	c	d
36.	a	b	c			81.	a	b	c	d		126.	a	b	c	d
37.	a	b	c			82.	a	b	c	d		127.	a	b	c	d
38.	a	b	c			83.	a	b	c	d		128.	a	b	c	d
39.	a	b	c			84.	a	b	c	d		129.	a	b	c	d
40.	a	b	c			85.	a	b	c	d		130.	a	b	c	d
41.	a	b	c	d		86.	a	b	c	d		131.	a	b	c	d
42.	a	b	c	d		87.	a	b	c	d		132.	a	b	c	d
43.	a	b	c	d		88.	a	b	c	d		133.	a	b	c	d
44.	a	b	c	d		89.	a	b	c	d		134.	a	b	c	d
45.	a	b	c	d		90.	a	b	c	d		135.	a	b	c	d

136.	ⓐ	ⓑ	ⓒ	ⓓ
137.	ⓐ	ⓑ	ⓒ	ⓓ
138.	ⓐ	ⓑ	ⓒ	ⓓ
139.	ⓐ	ⓑ	ⓒ	ⓓ
140.	ⓐ	ⓑ	ⓒ	ⓓ
141.	ⓐ	ⓑ	ⓒ	ⓓ
142.	ⓐ	ⓑ	ⓒ	ⓓ
143.	ⓐ	ⓑ	ⓒ	ⓓ
144.	ⓐ	ⓑ	ⓒ	ⓓ
145.	ⓐ	ⓑ	ⓒ	ⓓ
146.	ⓐ	ⓑ	ⓒ	ⓓ
147.	ⓐ	ⓑ	ⓒ	ⓓ
148.	ⓐ	ⓑ	ⓒ	ⓓ
149.	ⓐ	ⓑ	ⓒ	ⓓ
150.	ⓐ	ⓑ	ⓒ	ⓓ
151.	ⓐ	ⓑ	ⓒ	ⓓ
152.	ⓐ	ⓑ	ⓒ	ⓓ
153.	ⓐ	ⓑ	ⓒ	ⓓ
154.	ⓐ	ⓑ	ⓒ	ⓓ
155.	ⓐ	ⓑ	ⓒ	ⓓ
156.	ⓐ	ⓑ	ⓒ	ⓓ
157.	ⓐ	ⓑ	ⓒ	ⓓ

158.	ⓐ	ⓑ	ⓒ	ⓓ
159.	ⓐ	ⓑ	ⓒ	ⓓ
160.	ⓐ	ⓑ	ⓒ	ⓓ
161.	ⓐ	ⓑ	ⓒ	ⓓ
162.	ⓐ	ⓑ	ⓒ	ⓓ
163.	ⓐ	ⓑ	ⓒ	ⓓ
164.	ⓐ	ⓑ	ⓒ	ⓓ
165.	ⓐ	ⓑ	ⓒ	ⓓ
166.	ⓐ	ⓑ	ⓒ	ⓓ
167.	ⓐ	ⓑ	ⓒ	ⓓ
168.	ⓐ	ⓑ	ⓒ	ⓓ
169.	ⓐ	ⓑ	ⓒ	ⓓ
170.	ⓐ	ⓑ	ⓒ	ⓓ
171.	ⓐ	ⓑ	ⓒ	ⓓ
172.	ⓐ	ⓑ	ⓒ	ⓓ
173.	ⓐ	ⓑ	ⓒ	ⓓ
174.	ⓐ	ⓑ	ⓒ	ⓓ
175.	ⓐ	ⓑ	ⓒ	ⓓ
176.	ⓐ	ⓑ	ⓒ	ⓓ
177.	ⓐ	ⓑ	ⓒ	ⓓ
178.	ⓐ	ⓑ	ⓒ	ⓓ
179.	ⓐ	ⓑ	ⓒ	ⓓ

180.	ⓐ	ⓑ	ⓒ	ⓓ
181.	ⓐ	ⓑ	ⓒ	ⓓ
182.	ⓐ	ⓑ	ⓒ	ⓓ
183.	ⓐ	ⓑ	ⓒ	ⓓ
184.	ⓐ	ⓑ	ⓒ	ⓓ
185.	ⓐ	ⓑ	ⓒ	ⓓ
186.	ⓐ	ⓑ	ⓒ	ⓓ
187.	ⓐ	ⓑ	ⓒ	ⓓ
188.	ⓐ	ⓑ	ⓒ	ⓓ
189.	ⓐ	ⓑ	ⓒ	ⓓ
190.	ⓐ	ⓑ	ⓒ	ⓓ
191.	ⓐ	ⓑ	ⓒ	ⓓ
192.	ⓐ	ⓑ	ⓒ	ⓓ
193.	ⓐ	ⓑ	ⓒ	ⓓ
194.	ⓐ	ⓑ	ⓒ	ⓓ
195.	ⓐ	ⓑ	ⓒ	ⓓ
196.	ⓐ	ⓑ	ⓒ	ⓓ
197.	ⓐ	ⓑ	ⓒ	ⓓ
198.	ⓐ	ⓑ	ⓒ	ⓓ
199.	ⓐ	ⓑ	ⓒ	ⓓ
200.	ⓐ	ⓑ	ⓒ	ⓓ

Listening

You will now begin the listening section. You will be asked to demonstrate how well you understand spoken English. The entire listening section should take approximately 45 minutes. There are four parts, and directions are given for each part. Mark your answers on the answer sheet on pages 29 and 30.

When directed by the 🎧 icon, listen to the audio file at **http://www.learnatest.com/SpeakingGuides/ TOEIC_Test_Prep**. Or, if you do not have access to a computer, the complete transcripts are included in the appendix of this book. In that case, ask someone who speaks English fluently to read the material to you face-to-face or into a tape recorder. Be sure your reader speaks clearly at a normal, conversational pace. It is highly recommended, however, that you use the audio files for a more authentic TOEIC experience.

Directions: 🎧 For each question in this part, you will hear four statements about a picture. When you hear the statements, you must select the one statement that best describes what you see in the picture. Then, find the number of the question on your answer sheet and mark choice **a**, **b**, **c**, or **d** as your answer. The statements are available in audio files or written transcripts in the appendix of this book.

1.

Now, listen to Track 1.

2.

Now, listen to Track 2.

3.

Now, listen to Track 3.

4.

Now, listen to Track 4.

5.

Now, listen to Track 5.

6.

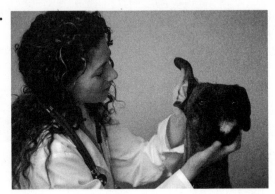

Now, listen to Track 6.

7.

Now, listen to Track 7.

8.

Now, listen to Track 8.

9.

Now, listen to Track 9.

10.

Now, listen to Track 10.

Directions: 🎧 You will hear a question or statement and three responses spoken in English. The questions and statements are available in audio files or written transcripts in the appendix of this book. Select the best response to the question or statement and mark choice **a**, **b**, or **c** on your answer sheet.

11. **Now, listen to Track 11.**
Mark your answer on the answer sheet.

12. **Now, listen to Track 12.**
Mark your answer on the answer sheet.

13. **Now, listen to Track 13.**
Mark your answer on the answer sheet.

14. **Now, listen to Track 14.**
Mark your answer on the answer sheet.

15. **Now, listen to Track 15.**
Mark your answer on the answer sheet.

16. **Now, listen to Track 16.**
Mark your answer on the answer sheet.

17. **Now, listen to Track 17.**
Mark your answer on the answer sheet.

18. **Now, listen to Track 18.**
Mark your answer on the answer sheet.

19. **Now, listen to Track 19.**
Mark your answer on the answer sheet.

20. **Now, listen to Track 20.**
Mark your answer on the answer sheet.

21. **Now, listen to Track 21.**
Mark your answer on the answer sheet.

22. **Now, listen to Track 22.**
Mark your answer on the answer sheet.

23. **Now, listen to Track 23.**
Mark your answer on the answer sheet.

24. **Now, listen to Track 24.**
Mark your answer on the answer sheet.

25. **Now, listen to Track 25.**
Mark your answer on the answer sheet.

26. **Now, listen to Track 26.**
Mark your answer on the answer sheet.

27. **Now, listen to Track 27.**
Mark your answer on the answer sheet.

28. **Now, listen to Track 28.**
Mark your answer on the answer sheet.

29. Now, listen to Track 29.

Mark your answer on the answer sheet.

30. Now, listen to Track 30.

Mark your answer on the answer sheet.

31. Now, listen to Track 31.

Mark your answer on the answer sheet.

32. Now, listen to Track 32.

Mark your answer on the answer sheet.

33. Now, listen to Track 33.

Mark your answer on the answer sheet.

34. Now, listen to Track 34.

Mark your answer on the answer sheet.

35. Now, listen to Track 35.

Mark your answer on the answer sheet.

36. Now, listen to Track 36.

Mark your answer on the answer sheet.

37. Now, listen to Track 37.

Mark your answer on the answer sheet.

38. Now, listen to Track 38.

Mark your answer on the answer sheet.

39. Now, listen to Track 39.

Mark your answer on the answer sheet.

40. Now, listen to Track 40.

Mark your answer on the answer sheet.

Directions: 🎧 You will hear conversations between two people. You will be asked to answer three questions about what the speakers say in each conversation. Select the best response to each question and mark that choice—**a**, **b**, **c**, or **d**—on your answer sheet. The conversations are available in audio files or as written transcripts in the appendix of this book.

Now, listen to Track 41.

41. Now, listen to Track 42.

What does the man want to do?

  a. He wants a new job.

  b. He wants to travel.

  c. He wants to meet people who have been in this country for a while.

  d. He wants to volunteer his time.

42. Now, listen to Track 43.

What does the woman suggest will be discussed in future conversations?

  a. the man's volunteering

  b. her own volunteering

  c. travel

  d. other countries

43. Now, listen to Track 44.

Where will the man meet people?

  a. in another country

  b. in the library

  c. at the town hall

  d. in class

Now, listen to Track 45.

44. Now, listen to Track 46.

What problem is the woman having?

a. Many students in her class were sick.

b. She is taking an evening class and is tired.

c. Her teacher was late for class.

d. Her class was canceled because there was no teacher.

45. Now, listen to Track 47.

What can we assume the woman would have preferred?

a. a note on the door informing the class the teacher was absent

b. a make-up exam

c. a higher grade

d. to have left after fifteen minutes

46. Now, listen to Track 48.

Why does the woman think it's likely the instructor was ill?

a. He was coughing.

b. He looked terrible.

c. He didn't show up for class, and students had been ill before that.

d. She felt sick herself and assumed the teacher was ill as well.

Now, listen to Track 49.

47. Now, listen to Track 50.

Why does the woman not take the first two pieces of advice the man offers her?

a. She is shy and does not know computers well.

b. She does not have the education to conduct interviews.

c. She is worried about her English.

d. She does not think the advice is very good.

48. Now, listen to Track 51.

Why can we assume the woman takes the man's final piece of advice?

a. She can do what he suggests in less time.

b. His final piece of advice would mean the best results.

c. She finds the other advice impractical.

d. It does not involve talking to customers or working with computers.

49. Now, listen to Track 52.

What does the woman hope to find out?

a. whether she is really good with computers

b. how well customers like her company's new product

c. whether she can overcome her shyness

d. how to do product research so that she can get a promotion

Now, listen to Track 53.

50. Now, listen to Track 54.

What is implied about the accountant's daughter?

a. She borrowed her father's car without asking.

b. She was speeding.

c. She was not careful with her father's car.

d. She is not careful with money.

51. Now, listen to Track 55.

What is bothering the accountant?

a. He will have to pay for damage his daughter inflicted on his car.

b. His car mechanic charges him too much money.

c. His insurance costs will go up because his daughter was in an accident.

d. His daughter was hurt in a car accident.

52. Now, listen to Track 56.

What did the accountant's daughter hit?

a. a car

b. a cat

c. a garbage can

d. a garage door

Now, listen to Track 57.

53. Now, listen to Track 58.

What good news does the woman give to the man?

a. The broken printer has been fixed.

b. The boss liked his sales report, and this might lead to a promotion.

c. He can take some time off because he is tired.

d. The deadline for the sales report has been extended.

54. Now, listen to Track 59.

Why did the man have trouble finishing his sales report?

a. He stayed up late and could not concentrate.

b. His printer stopped working correctly.

c. He was too tired.

d. He started the sales report too late.

55. Now, listen to Track 60.

How does the man feel after finishing his sales report?

a. worried that it is not good

b. proud that he did a good job

c. proud that he stayed up so late to finish it

d. tired

Now, listen to Track 61.

56. Now, listen to Track 62.

What does the man enjoy about France?

a. the travel

b. the food

c. the art galleries

d. the music

57. Now, listen to Track 63.

Who has been to France before?

a. the man

b. the woman

c. neither the man nor the woman

d. both the man and the woman

58. Now, listen to Track 64.

Why is the woman traveling to France?

a. for a wedding

b. to enjoy good food

c. to study

d. to enjoy the art galleries

Now, listen to Track 65.

59. Now, listen to Track 66.

Why does the woman hate Mondays?

a. She cannot stay in and read.

b. She cannot sleep in.

c. She thinks two days off is too little.

d. She dislikes the weekend.

60. Now, listen to Track 67.

What does the woman like to do on weekends?

a. read

b. go shopping

c. go boating

d. go to concerts

61. Now, listen to Track 68.

What argument does the man use to show the woman Mondays are not so bad?

  a. They get two days off, and they have to return one day, so it might as well be Monday.

  b. Mondays give us a chance to enjoy reading.

  c. It is good to have a job and make money.

  d. Mondays are a good day to start a productive week and get work done.

Now, listen to Track 69.

62. Now, listen to Track 70.

Why does the man want to go back to school?

  a. to improve his English

  b. to qualify for a visa

  c. to get a better job

  d. to impress his employer

63. Now, listen to Track 71.

What problem does the woman's cousin have?

  a. student loans

  b. homework

  c. night school

  d. instructors

64. Now, listen to Track 72.

Why does the man decide to go to night school?

  a. He wants to keep working and he does not want loans.

  b. He has heard that there will be less homework in night class.

  c. The night classes have easier instructors.

  d. It's the only time he has to study.

Now, listen to Track 73.

65. Now, listen to Track 74.

What will the woman be doing to support her local political party?

  a. distributing fliers

  b. canvassing door to door and talking to voters

  c. raising money

  d. talking on the telephone to voters

66. Now, listen to Track 75.

Why does the man not vote?

  a. He is not a citizen.

  b. He does not believe in voting.

  c. No party representative has talked to him.

  d. He is not informed about the issues.

67. Now, listen to Track 76.

Why does the woman want to take part in politics?

  a. She wants to run for office.

  b. She wants to convince people to vote.

  c. She likes meeting new people.

  d. She wants to support certain issues.

Now, listen to Track 77.

68. Now, listen to Track 78.

What does the woman need to do about her new computer?

  a. turn on the monitor

  b. plug in the mouse

  c. get technical support

  d. read the manual

69. Now, listen to Track 79.

What solution does the man offer the woman?

a. He will come by her office to help.

b. He will buy her a new computer.

c. He will call technical support.

d. He will install new anti-virus software.

70. Now, listen to Track 80.

Does the man think the computer is the problem?

a. Yes, he thinks the computer has a virus.

b. No, he thinks the woman needs to learn how to use the computer.

c. Yes, he thinks files have been lost.

d. No, he thinks the computer is not plugged in.

Directions: 🎧 You will hear some talks given by a single speaker. You will be asked to answer three questions about what the speaker says in each talk. Select the best response to each question and mark choice **a**, **b**, **c**, or **d** on your answer sheet. The talks will not be printed in your test book and will be spoken only one time.

Now, listen to Track 81.

71. Now, listen to Track 82.

What is the purpose of the workshop?

a. to let employees relax

b. to give employees a chance to sell products to customers

c. to create a marketing campaign

d. to improve the company by improving cooperation

72. Now, listen to Track 83.

For whom is the workshop?

a. volunteers

b. executives

c. employees

d. only employees who are new to the company

73. Now, listen to Track 84.

Who will be in each group?

a. employees from the same department

b. several mentors

c. employees from different departments and a mentor

d. executives and employees

Now, listen to Track 85.

74. Now, listen to Track 86.

Where is this speech taking place?

a. a classroom

b. a business meeting

c. a conference

d. a library

75. Now, listen to Track 87.

Who is Mr. Smith?

a. a speaker and author

b. a personal trainer

c. a sales executive

d. someone from Japan

76. Now, listen to Track 88.

Why is the topic of the talk *creativity*?

a. Creativity is important to personal development.

b. Creativity creates wonderful art.

c. Creativity is important to every part of a business.

d. Creativity is often overlooked.

Now, listen to Track 89.

77. Now, listen to Track 90.

What are the three goals of the conference?
a. skill building, networking, and learning
b. having fun, making money, and learning
c. lecturing, traveling, and sales
d. selling, promoting, and advertising

78. Now, listen to Track 91.

How can participants take part?
a. volunteer to give a speech
b. donate money
c. fill out a registration sheet
d. take part in next year's conference

79. Now, listen to Track 92.

How is the conference organized?
a. into lectures
b. into workshops, discussions, and lectures
c. into team events
d. into sales pitches

Now, listen to Track 93.

80. Now, listen to Track 94.

How would you describe this speech?
a. an announcement of changes
b. an announcement of an illness
c. an announcement of a retirement
d. a workshop

81. Now, listen to Track 95.

Where is this talk most likely to take place?
a. a library
b. a classroom
c. an office
d. a conference

82. Now, listen to Track 96.

What is one change that is announced?
a. More tests will be assigned.
b. New topics will be covered.
c. A term paper is now due on a different date.
d. More term papers will be assigned.

Now, listen to Track 97.

83. Now, listen to Track 98.

What is happening in this talk?
a. An announcement is being made on an airplane.
b. A delay is being announced.
c. Safety instructions are being given.
d. A lecture is being given.

84. Now, listen to Track 99.

When can passengers use mobile devices?
a. only when the plane is on the ground
b. only when the plane has landed in London
c. only after the plane has taken off
d. after the safety demonstration

85. Now, listen to Track 100.

What entertainment is offered on the flight?
a. dinner
b. music
c. a movie
d. none

Now, listen to Track 101.

86. Now, listen to Track 102.

Where is this conversation likely taking place?
a. a school cafeteria
b. a classroom
c. a boardroom
d. a conference

87. **Now, listen to Track 103.**

What is the speaker discussing?

a. a period in history

b. the importance of science

c. the importance of art

d. conflict

88. **Now, listen to Track 104.**

What was Romanticism a reaction to, according to the speaker?

a. reason

b. pollution

c. artists and writers

d. foreign countries

Now, listen to Track 105.

89. **Now, listen to Track 106.**

Why is there a delay?

a. a mechanical failure

b. a safety issue

c. schedule problems

d. bad weather

90. **Now, listen to Track 107.**

What options are presented to passengers?

a. get a refund or wait

b. exchange tickets

c. rent a car

d. take a plane

91. **Now, listen to Track 108.**

What will be offered to passengers?

a. immediate taxis

b. information as it becomes available

c. a written apology

d. immediate transportation by train

Now, listen to Track 109.

92. **Now, listen to Track 110.**

Where does the speaker get his information?

a. only from callers to the station

b. from the Internet

c. satellites

d. partly from callers to the station and partly from a helicopter crew

93. **Now, listen to Track 111.**

What problems are there on the roads?

a. malfunctioning traffic lights and accidents

b. pedestrians and a marathon

c. construction, congestion, and a stalled car

d. rush-hour traffic

94. **Now, listen to Track 112.**

What does the speaker request?

a. listeners stay calm in bad traffic

b. listeners call in with more information

c. listeners avoid bad traffic areas

d. listeners stay home until traffic improves

Now, listen to Track 113.

95. **Now, listen to Track 114.**

What is the speaker's current job?

a. public speaker

b. attorney

c. executive

d. congressperson

96. **Now, listen to Track 115.**

What is the speaker trying to do?

a. raise money for a political campaign

b. generate votes

c. convince his listeners that education is important

d. change the legal system

97. Now, listen to Track 116.

What does the speaker think he can change in the community?

a. jobs, taxes, and crime

b. his job and funding for local politicians

c. education, healthcare, and crime

d. laws in the community

Now, listen to Track 117.

98. Now, listen to Track 118.

What is the best way to describe this short conversation?

a. a weather report

b. an emergency announcement

c. an advice segment

d. a cancellation list

99. Now, listen to Track 119.

What is being forecast?

a. a flood

b. an earthquake

c. the first snowstorm of the season

d. bad wind in the southern states

100. Now, listen to Track 120.

What should viewers do?

a. prepare for bad weather

b. wait and see

c. call the television station

d. drive to their destination to avoid bad weather

Reading

You will now begin the Reading section. You will be asked to read a variety of texts and answer several different types of reading comprehension questions. The entire Reading section should take approximately 75 minutes. There are three parts; directions are given for each one. Mark your answers on the answer sheet on pages 29 and 30.

Directions: A word or phrase is missing in each of the sentences below. Four answer choices are given below each sentence. Select the answer that best completes the sentence. Then mark choice—**a**, **b**, **c**, or **d**—on your answer sheet.

101. Please sit in the _____ that has been assigned to you by conference staff.

a. train

b. airplane

c. seat

d. lecture

102. When taking a seat in the airplane, please _____ off your cell phones and mobile devices.

a. turn

b. turned

c. turning

d. turns

103. _____ seen the movie, he wanted to see even more films by the same director.

a. Have

b. Having

c. Has

d. Though

104. When we throw confetti on New Year's Eve, the pieces of paper fall _____ to the ground.
a. greatly
b. through
c. quickly
d. reasonably

105. Panda bears _____ bamboo shoots in the wild, and therefore must be brought this type of food when in captivity.
a. eat
b. eating
c. ate
d. having eaten

106. _____ the professor was late, the class had to stay late so he could finish his prepared lecture.
a. Though
b. Since
c. But
d. Nor

107. The day was _____ and warm, so we decided to go swimming.
a. rainy
b. sunny
c. stormy
d. saturated

108. When _____ down, please take care to tuck your feet under you so that other people don't trip on the way to their seats.
a. sit
b. having sit
c. sitting
d. sat

109. The conference was about to start and everyone fell _____, anticipating the guest speaker.
a. awake
b. asleep
c. numb
d. silent

110. When washing dishes, _____ them carefully to avoid leaving soap residue on your dinnerware.
a. having rinsed
b. rinsing
c. rinsed
d. rinse

111. Be sure to _____ the quarterly report prior to the conference call this afternoon.
a. reveal
b. review
c. revive
d. revoke

112. _____ we were late for the lecture, we were still able to get the complete notes we needed for the exam.
a. But
b. Only
c. Neither
d. Although

113. He decided to _____ in the marathon because he wanted to raise money for cancer research.
a. running
b. run
c. ran
d. rue

114. When baking a cake, mix together softened butter and sugar first, then stir _____ to combine the two.
   a. certainly
   b. rapidly
   c. surely
   d. distractedly

115. When he was _____ for mayor, he made a lot of promises about education.
   a. run
   b. ran
   c. jogging
   d. running

116. She had to prepare a sales _____ for the annual meeting this year.
   a. career
   b. report
   c. marathon
   d. job

117. Professionals who prepare a _____ resume have a greater chance of getting a job than those who do not have a resume.
   a. strong
   b. sent
   c. posted
   d. blue

118. He started _____ every day because he heard it was the best way to lose weight.
   a. exercise
   b. exercising
   c. breathe
   d. exercises

119. The accountant was very _____ because his computer files were lost and he could not do his job.
   a. mild
   b. upset
   c. nice
   d. professional

120. Could you please _____ me to the airport tomorrow?
   a. driving
   b. dive
   c. drive
   d. drove

121. Please open this package _____, as I think it might be very fragile.
   a. careful
   b. slow
   c. care
   d. carefully

122. I think a virus just erased five _____ on this computer.
   a. notebooks
   b. files
   c. printers
   d. Internet

123. We _____ on a holiday to France next year to look at some of the places where famous authors lived.
   a. going
   b. will go
   c. go
   d. went

124. He _____ all his books using notebooks and pens because he did not trust computers.
- **a.** is writing
- **b.** wrote
- **c.** write
- **d.** writes

125. Pizza is my favorite food because it is so _____ that I want to eat it all the time.
- **a.** delicious
- **b.** disgust
- **c.** greasy
- **d.** horrible

126. _____ so cold outside that I had to wear three sweaters under my jacket today.
- **a.** It's
- **b.** Its'
- **c.** It
- **d.** Its

127. Rather _____ seeing the movie later in the evening, we saw an earlier film and went out for dinner.
- **a.** then
- **b.** than
- **c.** when
- **d.** where

128. _____ car seems to be making a strange noise—should I drive you back to work?
- **a.** You're
- **b.** Your
- **c.** You
- **d.** Us

129. _____ is very little chance of convincing customers to buy our product in this way, so let's find a new way of selling.
- **a.** Their
- **b.** They
- **c.** Theirs
- **d.** There

130. Your ability to complete this project successfully could _____ your ability to land that promotion.
- **a.** affect
- **b.** effects
- **c.** effect
- **d.** affects

131. He _____ care whether we finish the report on time, so we shouldn't rush.
- **a.** doesn't
- **b.** don't
- **c.** do
- **d.** do not

132. Eating _____ meat can lower your cholesterol levels and may help you lose weight.
- **a.** less
- **b.** fewer
- **c.** lesser
- **d.** few

133. We decided to run an _____ for the new product in the local newspaper this week.
- **a.** add
- **b.** ad
- **c.** aesthetic
- **d.** commercial

134. The new workshop is supposed to be very helpful, so we should all _____ part in it.
- **a.** taking
- **b.** taken
- **c.** take
- **d.** takes

135. After looking for some time, he found his _____ toys under the chair.
- **a.** cats
- **b.** cot
- **c.** cat
- **d.** cat's

136. My employer told me that my best skills are _____, working, and learning.
- **a.** listen
- **b.** listens
- **c.** listening
- **d.** listened

137. When _____ the room to give your speech, look right at the audience and then walk confidently up to the stage.
- **a.** enter
- **b.** has entered
- **c.** entered
- **d.** entering

138. He _____ so ill that he has not been able to come to work for more than a month.
- **a.** been
- **b.** has
- **c.** has been
- **d.** be

139. This suit is a little _____ in the waist, so I am thinking of taking it to a tailor for alterations.
- **a.** loose
- **b.** lose
- **c.** looses
- **d.** loses

140. He liked the movie _____, so he went back and saw it again and again until he knew parts of it by heart.
- **a.** a lot
- **b.** lots
- **c.** lot
- **d.** alot

Directions: Read the texts that follow. A word or phrase is missing in some of the sentences. Four answer choices are given below each sentence. Select the best answer to complete the text. Then mark choice **a**, **b**, **c**, or **d** on your answer sheet.

Questions 141 through 144 refer to the following memorandum:

Memorandum

To: Employees of the Wong Advertising Agency

From: Wong Advertising Agency President Donald Wong

Date: November 15, 2009

Subject: Our Holiday Party

I would like to wish all our employees a very happy holiday season. As many of you (**141**) _____, we hold a holiday party for our staff members each year. This year, the theme of our party will be "Holidays in Hawaii," and festivities will be held at the Delta Hotel on Main Street. Please (**142**) _____ a costume or outfit appropriate to the theme. Hula skirts, Hawaiin shirts, and other outfits are all appropriate, but please remember our company dress code.

Allie's Party Rentals on Water Street has costumes (**143**) _____ , if anyone would like to rent one. I have arranged for a company discount of 10% at the store for every employee.

I would also like to extend a warm invitation to all friends and family of The Wong Advertising Agency. When attending this year's holiday party, please feel (**144**) _____ to bring spouses, friends, and children. However, please RSVP and include the total number of guests so that we can order the appropriate amount of refreshments. If you have any questions, Marie Clay in Human Resources is organizing the event and will be more than happy to answer any queries you might have.

Happy holidays to all our employees and friends.

141. a. know
  b. knowing
  c. knew
  d. now

142. a. chosen
  b. choosing
  c. chase
  d. choose

143. a. for rent
  b. rental
  c. rents
  d. rent

144. a. gratis
  b. free
  c. no charge
  d. able

Questions 145 through 148 refer to the following essay.

Kangaroos are large animals native to Australia. Kangaroos belong to a species known as marsupials, which carry their young in pouches. Although many smaller marsupials are on the endangered list, kangaroos are thriving. They are not harvested or (**145**) _____ hunted, although some are killed as pests or are killed for meat in some areas. In the wild, kangaroos can (**146**) _____ four to six years.

Kangaroos are known for hopping. In fact, kangaroos are the only large animals that hop as a primary means of locomotion. These animals can hop at up to 70 km/h (44 mph). Kangaroos hop (**147**) _____they have very long rear feet and small front paws, making crawling and walking difficult.

All kangaroos eat a vegetarian diet, although some species prefer fungi or grasses (**148**) _____ shrubs. Most species are active at night, although kangaroos have few natural predators and are not nocturnal to avoid enemies. Most kangaroos can cover large distances, largely to find food and water.

145. a. extensively
  b. badly
  c. quickly
  d. largely

146. a. life
  b. live
  c. lifes
  d. lives

147. a. because of
  b. although
  c. because
  d. even though

148. a. with
  b. to
  c. then
  d. than

Questions 149 through 152 refer to the following.

Good evening, and welcome to our panel discussion. Today, we will be discussing how to get organized.

Remaining organized in the workplace is crucial, since the only way to manage multiple projects and deadlines is to manage time and information effectively. Many people think, "If only I (**149**) _____more time, I could easily stay organized." However, organization is a skill you (**150**) _____ learn; even if you have limited time, you can still manage all your work and personal responsibilities effectively.

To get organized, you need to keep all your papers and information in one place. At the very (**151**) _____, you should have only three places where you keep information and papers that you haven't looked at or worked with: your e-mail inbox, your inbox tray, and a planner or notebook.

Work to empty these three containers each day. Convert each piece of paper into an action step on your calendar or a piece of information you have filed away in a filing system.

You will also need a planner or calendar to keep track of appointments and to-do items and lists. In your planner, you will want to write anything and everything you need to take care of, so that you forget nothing. I personally like a zippered planner with lots of dividers. A lot of information and scraps of paper (152) _____ in my planner, but the zipper keeps everything organized and in one place.

149. a. had
  b. have
  c. having
  d. has

150. a. able
  b. can
  c. will
  d. must

151. a. most
  b. least
  c. fewest
  d. less

152. a. put
  b. placing
  c. place
  d. get placed

Directions: In this part you will read a selection of texts, such as magazine and newspaper articles, letters, and advertisements. Each text is followed by several questions. Select the best answer for each question and mark choice **a**, **b**, **c**, or **d** on your answer sheet.

Questions 153 through 156 refer to the following menu.

Appetizers

French Onion Soup $5
Brochette $6
Vegetable plate (served with pita bread and
   hummus dip) $5

Lunch

Soup and sandwich (sandwich choices are
   vegetable or ham and cheese) $8
Sandwich (served on either whole wheat or
   white home-style bread with vegetables
   or ham and cheese) $6
Soup (chicken noodle is the house specialty;
   ask your server about the soup of the
   day) $5
Noodle stir-fry with sweet-and-sour sauce
   (includes vegetables and either tofu
   or chicken) $8
Small Greek or Caesar salad $5
Large Greek or Caesar salad $7

In addition, we have a daily lunch special—
   please ask your server for today's special.

Desserts

Ice Cream (served in a dish or cone) $3
Pie (we make our pies from scratch, four
   different flavors each day) $4

Drinks

Coffee $2
Soda $2
Tea $2
Hot Chocolate (made with milk, whipped
   cream, and real cocoa) $3

153. What sort of establishment is this menu most likely from?
- **a.** a four-star fine-dining restaurant
- **b.** a catering business
- **c.** a formal restaurant with lots of dinner options
- **d.** a casual diner specializing in lunch

154. What meals change daily?
- **a.** pie, soup, and lunch special
- **b.** lunch special and dinner
- **c.** drinks
- **d.** breakfast and lunch

155. What sort of bread products are available for sandwiches?
- **a.** buns and wraps
- **b.** multigrain bread and sourdough
- **c.** white and whole wheat
- **d.** gluten-free and white

156. What is special about the establishment's pie?
- **a.** It is made by hand and is offered in a variety of flavors.
- **b.** It is expensive.
- **c.** It is served with ice cream.
- **d.** It is served hot.

Questions 157 through 160 refer to the following article.

Investing in real estate is a great opportunity for those who want to generate a passive income. Anyone can get started in real estate investing, simply because so many products and services exist to help homebuyers purchase and pay for property. Investors can use these same services and mortgage products to develop their businesses.

There are many ways to get started in real estate. You can act as a real estate scout, gathering information for other investors. This is a low-risk way to get started with no money down. You can also buy homes to rent or lease. Another option is to buy homes, renovate them, and resell them at a profit. This is sometimes called *property flipping*.

If you want to get started today, you may want to read more about real estate investing. There are many wonderful online resources, as well as books about the subject. Research as much as you can before you get started. This way, you will know all the best ways to maximize your profits. You may also join a local investment club to learn more about real estate investing from other investors in your area.

157. How many options does the author give to someone just getting started in real estate?
- **a.** two
- **b.** three
- **c.** four
- **d.** five

158. Who can invest in real estate?
- **a.** anyone
- **b.** professional investors
- **c.** real estate agents
- **d.** mortgage lenders

159. What does the author suggest that potential investors do first?
- **a.** talk to a mortgage specialist
- **b.** research real estate investing
- **c.** save money for real estate
- **d.** buy a house

160. According to the author, what is the best way to invest in real estate without taking on large risks?
- **a.** research loans
- **b.** save money
- **c.** become a real estate scout
- **d.** talk to other investors to learn more

Questions 161 through 164 refer to the following e-mail.

Hi Allen,

I just wanted to check to see whether you are still on board for David's party next week. Anyway, we thought it would be fun to surprise him for his birthday on Friday. He always picks up Betty from work and I was thinking that when he comes up to accounting to get her on Friday, we could all hide behind the partition that divides Betty's desk from the rest of the office. That way we could really surprise him.

When he walks in, we'll jump out and shout, "Surprise!" Then we'll have cake and refreshments. I'll take care of those. As I told you at lunch, we won't be exchanging presents. All I need you to do is NOT tell David about the party. Also, I have a card for David here in my office. If you could sign it, that would be great. I'll take care of all the organizational details.

Cheers,

Bob

161. Who is the party for?
   a. Allen
   b. David
   c. Bob
   d. Betty

162. What is the point of the party?
   a. David and Betty are having a baby
   b. David and Betty are getting married
   c. David's birthday surprise
   d. David has a new job

163. What is Bob's responsibility?
   a. Signing the card
   b. Yelling "surprise"
   c. Getting David to visit Betty so that the party can happen
   d. Organizing the party and getting refreshments

164. What is Allen's responsibility?
   a. To get balloons
   b. To not spoil the surprise and to sign the card
   c. To get the cake
   d. To buy a gift

Questions 165 through 168 refer to the following article.

Public speaking is an important skill to develop, but almost everyone is frightened to speak in front of an audience. In fact, many studies have shown that public speaking is the most common fear people have—they tend to fear public speaking more than they fear death! If you are terrified of speaking in front of a group, there is hope for you. There are many good ways to overcome a terror of giving speeches.

Many professional speakers find that they get less nervous simply by giving many speeches, so practice seems to be a key way of reducing speaker stress. There are local groups known as Toastmasters that help people to develop their public speaking skills. These supportive groups are one place where you can give speeches and get encouragement and feedback. They're a great place to practice that sales presentation or thank you speech.

There are other ways of minimizing your fears. Some speakers find it useful to picture audience members naked. This helps to reduce the intimidation factor of most audiences! Some professional speakers practice speeches before a mirror and many strongly advocate writing down and memorizing key points or entire speeches so that you will never be at a loss for what to say next.

165. What does the author suggest is the best way to get over the fear of public speaking?
   a. practice
   b. get support from speakers on Internet groups
   c. read about public speaking
   d. talk to professional speakers

166. Why is it important to get over a fear of public speaking?
   a. Fear is bad for your health.
   b. Fear makes you look weak.
   c. Public speaking is an important skill.
   d. Public speaking makes you stronger.

167. What resources are available for public speakers?
   a. books
   b. toastmasters clubs
   c. online chat groups
   d. PowerPoint presentations

168. How can speakers remember what they want to say?
   a. get comfortable with public speaking
   b. develop better memory
   c. write down their presentations
   d. picture audience members naked

Questions 169 through 172 refer to the following article.

Volunteerism is a great way to build your resume, improve your communication skills, and make a positive difference. No matter who you are, your skills are in demand somewhere. Many nonprofit organizations and small businesses rely on the generosity of volunteers to help them help others. Volunteers organize projects, work with those who need help, and help manage organizations. Volunteer work helps charities and charitable groups help far more people.

Volunteers benefit from offering their time, as well. Volunteering time often means more experience and more letters of recommendation for a resume. As they help others, volunteers often build their skills, meet interesting people, and get the satisfaction that comes from helping others.

It is easy to volunteer. All you really need is some time. There are groups that match volunteers with organizations that need help. If there is a specific skill that you would like to develop or share, this is often a good way to find a group in need of your services. You can also contact individual charity groups and ask about their volunteer opportunities. Homeless shelters, animal shelters, the Red Cross, community groups, hospitals, schools, and many other organizations all rely on volunteer help.

169. Who can volunteer?
   a. anyone
   b. people who are legally adults
   c. those who have lots of free time
   d. those who do not have jobs

170. What are the career benefits of volunteering?
   a. letting your employer see that you are a caring person who deserves a raise
   b. learning to budget your time
   c. building your skills, improving your resume, and getting letters of recommendation
   d. You may be hired by a group that takes you on as a volunteer.

171. What does the text suggest a potential volunteer do if there is a specific skill the volunteer wants to develop?
   a. find an organization looking for volunteers through the phone book
   b. find a group that pairs volunteers and charitable organizations
   c. ask friends whether they volunteer somewhere
   d. look in the newspaper

172. What skills do businesses need in a volunteer?
   a. speaking skills
   b. listening skills
   c. all skills
   d. compassion

Questions 173 through 176 refer to the following label.

This product contains enough medication to seriously harm a child. Always keep this and any other medications well out of reach of children. Do not use this product if the security cap is broken. Always close the childproof cap of the bottle after using the product.

   Do not use this medicine if you are pregnant, breastfeeding, or have high blood pressure. If your symptoms persist for more than three days, consult a physician. Never take more than four pills in any 24-hour period. In the event of accidental overdose, do not induce vomiting. Drink a glass of milk and contact your local poison control center immediately.

   Store this product in a cool, dry place.

   In rare cases, this medication may cause allergic reactions or side effects in some patients. If you notice a rash, itching, difficulty breathing, or swelling in the throat area, discontinue this medication immediately and get immediate medical attention. If you experience stomach upset after using this product, take this product with meals.

173. Why does the label warn users to keep the product away from children?
   a. The medicine may not be effective on children.
   b. Children do not understand how to open the bottle.
   c. Children may be harmed by eating the medicine.
   d. The medicine is designed for adults only.

174. What measures has this manufacturer taken to prevent children from accidentally eating the medicine?
   a. a childproof lock
   b. a seal that cannot be broken
   c. a bottle that cannot be opened
   d. an unpleasant taste

175. What form does this medicine take?
   a. liquid
   b. syringe
   c. cream
   d. pills

176. What should someone NOT do if they have taken too much of this medicine?
   a. lie down
   b. vomit
   c. eat food
   d. apply an ointment

Questions 177 through 180 refer to the following article.

The public library is a resource available to everyone, but today few people take advantage of the materials and programs that libraries have to offer. Today's public libraries are much more than just collections of books. Most libraries offer online resources, reading rooms, after-school programs, volunteer opportunities, audio books, music, and classes. The library is no longer a place just to find books. Today, it's a place to find information of all types. It's also a place to meet people and pursue any interest.

   If it's been a while since you have been at your local library, maybe it's time to find that library card. Log on to your local library's website—just about every library now has one. Most library websites let you get audio and video content, renew books, and even get a library tour. It's a great place to get familiar with your library again.

Libraries have become great communities, and you don't have to be a bookworm to enjoy them.

177. What is this text trying to convince people to do?
a. volunteer at their library
b. avoid reading in the public library
c. take advantage of the public library
d. take a class at their public library

178. What is the main argument of this text?
a. Libraries have changed and become more diverse.
b. Libraries should be quiet.
c. Libraries should be better funded.
d. We should go online.

179. What does the text suggest people should do if they have not been in their libraries for a while?
a. buy a book
b. visit a library website to learn more
c. read a book
d. get a librarian to offer a library tour

180. Who can enjoy libraries, according to this article?
a. students
b. bookworms
c. volunteers
d. everyone

Questions 181 through 185 refer to the following resume and letter.

Albert Sanders
123 Genoa Drive
New York, New York
(506) 555-5566
asanders@mailpail.biz

Education
BA (Philosophy), Columbia University, USA, 1998
MA (Culture Studies), Stanford University, USA, 2005

Work Experience
Research Assistant, Stanford University, 2004–2005
- Assisted professors at the Stanford University Culture Studies Department by compiling research and conducting primary research at the library
- Assisted with general office tasks

Manager, California Newcomers Association, 2005–Present
- Helped the association compile information and statistics about members through voluntary polls and surveys
- Met with new Americans to discuss needs and challenges
- Compiled research about members' cultures

Allen Doe, CEO
Massachusetts Museum
123 Museum Drive
Alvertson, Massachusetts

Dear Mr. Sanders:

Thank you for your interest in our company. Unfortunately, the only vacancies we currently have are for cultural assistants to help us develop school programs and brochures. This is, however, an entry-level position. If you are interested in a position as a cultural assistant, please contact me at (708) 555-6766.

     I wish you good luck in your search. We were very impressed with your resume and are sorry that we have so few opportunities at present.

Sincerely,

Allen Doe

181. What is taking place, based on these two communications?
   a. Allen Doe is advertising new career opportunities.
   b. Allen Doe is sending out form rejection letters.
   c. Allen Doe is holding open interviews.
   d. Albert Sanders is applying for a job.

182. If Allen Doe has positions available, why does he express regret?
   a. He cannot find anyone to fill the positions he has.
   b. The only positions available are entry-level.
   c. The positions are all filled.
   d. He does not have the money to hire new workers.

183. Why might the jobs available not be right for Albert Sanders?
   a. He might qualify for better jobs.
   b. The jobs are far away from where he lives.
   c. The jobs start right away.
   d. He is competing with a lot of other applicants for the jobs.

184. If Albert takes the job, what will he be doing?
   a. reading books about culture
   b. creating brochures and programs for students
   c. acting as a research assistant
   d. completing general office tasks

185. What skills does Albert seem to have developed most?
   a. answering phones
   b. giving speeches
   c. creating presentations for clients
   d. research

Questions 186 through 190 refer to the following article and letter.

New York Resident Criticizes Youth
By A. Priors

New York – Delia Rodriguez has lived in New York City for 40 years and her neighborhood has changed a lot over time. What Rodriguez dislikes most is the way that young people have changed. "When I was young," Delia Rodriguez told our reporter, "we were taught to respect our elders. Now some of these young kids yell or race by on their skateboards."

     Delia is worried that the change in youth today may be making her less safe. "When I walk down the street and see these youngsters dressed in low-cut pants and short skirts, I just hold my purse tighter. I wouldn't be surprised if I were robbed one day." Recently, Delia added a security system to her home, noting that she is worried about robberies.

I was upset by your recent article ("New York Resident Criticizes Youth" by A. Priors). I think Delia Rodriguez is very biased, and the reporting in the article is very one-sided. Mrs. Rodriguez is basing her opinions on stereotypes. She should get to know the younger people in her neighborhood – she might find out that some younger people are really nice.

Sincerely,
Mosand Rogers, age 14

186. What is Delia Rodriguez worried about?
   a. too many children
   b. reporter bias
   c. crime
   d. stereotypes

187. Why might Mosand have been interested in the article?
   a. She lives in the same neighborhood.
   b. She is a young person.
   c. She is worried about crime, too.
   d. She dresses inappropriately.

188. What has Delia Rodriguez done as a result of her worries?
   a. She has a new purse.
   b. She has moved.
   c. She has written a newspaper story.
   d. She has installed a security system in her home.

189. Why might Mosand think the article is "very one-sided"?
   a. Mosand thinks young people dress well.
   b. Delia Rodriguez does not talk to young people.
   c. Only Delia Rodriguez's opinions are written about.
   d. The reporter writes about Delia Rodriguez's security system.

190. What is Mosand's advice to Delia?
   a. read a book
   b. volunteer
   c. write an article that is fairer
   d. get to know some young people

Questions 191 through 195 refer to the following advertisement and e-mail.

Acme Grocery Store

All prices in effect February 17–26

Wow! Check out our produce section. Fresh cherries, this week only $0.99/pound. Salad kits only $3. Eat fresh produce and get healthy. Check out our other deals this week:

Apples: $1.99/pound
Cheery Oat Flakes cereal: $4
Milk: $1/ liter
Apple juice (generic brand): $2/750 ml
Peanut butter: $1

Acme wants to be your grocery store and we'll do what it takes to make that happen!

To whom it may concern,

I am writing this e-mail today because I am very upset about the inaccuracies in your latest flyer. When I visited your store, I found that many of the items I wanted had different prices than the prices advertised in your flyer. Cherries were $3.99/pound, not $0.99/pound as advertised. Milk was $2 a liter not $1 a liter, as advertised. Apple juice was $2 per 150 ml not per 750 ml, as advertised. When I spoke to your manager about it, I was treated very rudely. If Acme wants to be my grocery store, as you claim in your ad, you will have to do better than this! I will be shopping at Savings Grocery Store from now on.

Steve

191. Why is Steve writing this e-mail?
  a. The store has changed its policies.
  b. The store does not stock his favorite items.
  c. The store ran out of stock.
  d. There were inaccuracies in an advertisement.

192. What did Steve do first when he noticed a problem?
  a. He called the store owner.
  b. He spoke to the manager.
  c. He told other customers.
  d. He decided to shop somewhere else.

193. What is Steve's long-term solution to the problem?
  a. He has decided to shop somewhere else.
  b. He has decided to tell everyone he knows.
  c. He will complain in the newspaper.
  d. He will talk to the manager again.

194. Why was Steve not happy with the manager's response?
  a. The manager was rushed for time.
  b. The manager was rude.
  c. The manager was not available.
  d. The manager was not knowledgeable.

195. When was the sale available?
  a. January
  b. February
  c. March
  d. April

Questions 196 through 200 refer to the following press release and fax.

For immediate release
Contact: Sam Johns
Atlantic Flights Airlines
Fax: (555) 555-5500
Tel: (555) 555-5555

Atlantic Flights Airlines in LA

January 5, 2010 (Los Angeles)—Atlantic Flights Airlines is now open for business. We are pleased to announce that we will be offering three flights in and out of LAX daily at low-cost to and from London, England, Sydney, Australia, and New York City.

Currently, we are the only airline to offer generous preferential discounts to seniors and students. In the coming months, we will offer a special points reward system, which will allow seniors and student travelers to save even more.

We want traveling to be affordable and enjoyable for everyone, and our customers seem very happy with the results. Our CEO, Mark Wilson, has expressed his interest in keeping Atlantic Flights Airlines unique. "We want people to enjoy flying with our airline and we want everyone to get the incredible experience that all travelers—regardless of budget—deserve."

Dear Mr. Johns:

I am a reporter with the *Daily News*. After reading your press release, I would like to schedule an interview with you, if possible, for an upcoming article I am writing about budget travel for students. I am especially interested in your student discount and possible reward program. Please contact me at 555-6565.

Sincerely,
Peggy Simms

196. Why is Peggy contacting Sam?

    a. She wants to research airplanes.

    b. She wants to conduct an interview.

    c. She wants a job.

    d. She wants to take a trip.

197. What is Peggy's job?

    a. volunteer

    b. businessperson

    c. airline attendant

    d. reporter

198. What is Peggy writing about?

    a. the airline industry

    b. Toronto

    c. Sydney

    d. low-cost vacations

199. What is Peggy most likely to ask about in her interview?

    a. airline safety

    b. destinations

    c. student discounts and travel

    d. airline industry standards

200. To what audience is Peggy targeting her article?

    a. business travelers

    b. elderly travelers

    c. students

    d. children

Speaking

This section tests your skills for the TOEIC Speaking Test. It includes 11 questions that measure different aspects of your speaking ability. The test lasts approximately 20 minutes.

For each type of question, you will be given specific directions, including the time allowed for preparation and speaking. It is to your advantage to say as much as you can in the time allowed. It is also impor-

tant that you speak clearly and that you answer each question according to the directions.

Directions: In this part of the test, you will read aloud the text on the screen. You will have 45 seconds to prepare. Then you will have 45 seconds to read the text aloud. Use a stopwatch or clock to keep track of your time.

201. Buying your first home can be a challenge, but there are many people and services to help you. Your real estate agent, for example, can help you find a home that suits your needs and budget and will guide you through the process of buying the home. A mortgage professional will help you get the loan you need to buy your home. Many banks have workshops and offer free services to first-time homebuyers, too. These seminars and workshops cover all the basics and help you understand what you need to do to buy your home. It can seem challenging to buy a property, but it can be done.

202. London Spa Services provides all the modern technology and tools you need for looking your best. Spa services include full hair services, makeup application, massage, and many relaxation services that help you ease away stress and look your best. You may want to book a waxing appointment or a nail appointment for a special occasion. Maybe you would like to buy a gift certificate to treat that someone special to a little pampering. London Spa Services has the professionals, the products, the services, and the facilities to make it happen. At London Spa Services, we are ready to help you feel and look your best.

Directions: In this part of the test, you will describe the picture on your screen in as much detail as you can. You will have 30 seconds to prepare your response. Then you will have 45 seconds to speak about the picture. Use a stopwatch or clock to keep track of your time.

203.

Directions: In this part of the test, you will answer three questions. For each question, begin responding immediately after you hear a beep. No preparation time is provided. You will have 15 seconds to respond to each of the first two questions, and 30 seconds to respond to the third. Use a stopwatch or clock to keep track of your time.

Imagine that you have applied to get a computer for work and the IT department needs to understand your computer needs. They will ask you questions about your computer use.

204. How well do you understand and use computers?

205. What sort of computer do you prefer?

206. What do you use your computer for most often?

Directions: In this part of the test, you will answer three questions based on the information provided. You will have 30 seconds to read the information. Then, you will have 15 seconds to respond to the first two questions, and 30 seconds to respond to the third question. Use a stopwatch or clock to keep track of your time.

Hello, I'm interested in eating dinner at your restaurant, but I have a few questions before I make my reservation.

Mimi's Restaurant Dinner Menu

Salmon plate (served with rice and a selection of vegetables) $16

Vegetarian stir-fry (made with grilled vegetables and tofu) $11

Seafood pasta (noodles served in a cream sauce with scallops, shrimp, and lobster) $18

Steak dinner (steak done to your specifications, served with potatoes and salad) $30

Roast duck (roasted duck breast served with beets and rice) $18

Kid-friendly options are available for children 12 years or younger; all include ice cream for dessert

    Burger and French fries $9

    Fish and chips $9

    Sandwich $9

207. Are there vegetarian options available for me?

208. What are your prices like?

209. Our son is nine years old. Is there food that is appropriate for him?

Directions: In this part of the test, you will be presented with a problem and asked to propose a solution. You will have 30 seconds to prepare. Then you will have 60 seconds to speak. Use a stopwatch or clock to keep track of your time.

210. Reply as though you work at the recruiting company.
As you reply, be sure to:
- explain how the speaker can use your services
- offer additional help in her job search

Now, listen to Track 130.

Directions: In this part of the test, you will give your opinion about a specific topic. Be sure to say as much as you can in the time allowed. You will have 15 seconds to prepare. Then you will have 60 seconds to speak. Use a stopwatch or clock to keep track of your time.

211. Some people believe that natural medicine is best because it has been used for a long time, while others think that the latest medical technology is the best way to stay healthy. What is your opinion about natural medicine and modern medicine? Give your reasons for your beliefs.

Writing

This is the TOEIC Writing Test. This test includes eight questions that measure different aspects of your writing ability. The test lasts approximately one hour. For each type of question, you will be given specific directions, including the time allowed for writing.

Directions: In this part of the test, you will write ONE sentence that is based on a picture. With each picture, you will be given TWO words or phrases that you must use in your sentence. You can change the forms of the words and you can use the words in any order.

Your sentence will be scored on

- the appropriate use of grammar
- the relevance of the sentence to the picture

You will have eight minutes to complete this part of the test. Write your answer on the lines provided on your answer sheet. Use a stopwatch or clock to keep track of your time.

212.

hiking, map

_____

_____

213.

field, summer days

_____

_____

214.

cities, lunchtime

_____

_____

215.

summer days, barbecue food

_____

_____

216.

celebrate, outdoors

_____

_____

Directions: In this part of the test, you will show how well you can write a response to an e-mail.

Your response will be scored on:

- the quality and variety of your sentences
- vocabulary
- organization

You will have 10 minutes to read and answer each e-mail. Use a stopwatch or clock to keep track of your time.

> From: Bob in Marketing
> To: Sarah in Accounting
> Subject: Welcome Party
> Sent: January 1, 2010
>
> Hi,
>
> I would like to organize a welcome party for Anne, the new receptionist in the accounting department. I was thinking that Friday might be a good day, before everyone leaves for the weekend. What do you think? Could you help out with organizing the party?
>
> Cheers,
>
> Bob

Reply to the e-mail as though you worked at the company and wanted to help with the party. Suggest at least two things you could do to help organize the party.

217. _____

_____

_____

_____

_____

_____

Directions: In this part of the test, you will show how well you can write a response to a letter.

Your response will be scored on:

- the quality and variety of your sentences
- vocabulary
- organization

You will have 10 minutes to read and answer each letter. Use a stopwatch or clock to keep track of your time.

> RRR Banking
> Los Angeles, CA
>
> Dear Mr. Washington,
>
> I understand that you spoke with my associate, Anderson, about a stolen bank card. I believe that a new card was issued to you. We appreciate your business here at the bank and I wanted to know whether there was anything else I could do to be of assistance.
>
> Sincerely,
>
> Mark Jones
> Customer Manager

Reply to the letter, thanking Mark for his concern and offering at least one suggestion for RRR Banking about how they can improve their customer service.

218. _____

_____

_____

_____

_____

_____

Directions: In this part of the test, you will write an essay in response to a question that asks you to state, explain, and support your opinion about an issue. Typically, an effective essay will contain a minimum of 300 words.

Your response will be scored on:

- whether your opinion is supported with reasons and/or examples
- grammar
- vocabulary
- organization

You will have 30 minutes to plan, write, and revise your essay. Use a stopwatch or clock to keep track of your time.

Many people think that the best way to learn a new language is to attend a class. Others believe that speaking a language is the most effective way to build a language skill. What are the best ways to learn a language, in your opinion? Create an essay, outlining your ideas and your reasons for your opinions.

219.

Answers

1. c. The man is attaching a name tag, likely for an event where he will be meeting others. While there are seats in the background, there is no indication that the man needs to be seated soon, so choice **b** is incorrect. There is also no indication that the man is speaking and not just attending an event, so choice **a** is incorrect. While the man is preparing for an event, it is impossible to determine how far in advance he is preparing, so choice **d** is inaccurate as well.

2. c. The location is outdoors, so choice **a** is incorrect. The woman is not speaking, so choice **b** is incorrect. There is no indication what day of the week it is, so choice **d** is also incorrect.

3. a. There is no indication that the woman is watching her weight, so choice **b** is incorrect. There is no indication what she will or will not buy and it is impossible to tell what food product she has in her hand, so choice **c** and choice **d** are also incorrect.

4. a. There is no indication that the woman is taking part in a business meeting—we do not see what she is doing, so choice **b** is incorrect. She is smiling, not speaking, so choice **c** is incorrect. Choice **d** is incorrect because we cannot hear what she may be listening to and we do not see her working.

5. a. It is impossible to tell whether the women have met in a store or whether they are sisters, so choice **b** and choice **c** are incorrect. The women in the picture are smiling, not talking, so choice **d** is incorrect.

6. c. There is no way to determine whether the dog requires shots or not. While choice **b** and choice **d** may be true in a general sense, they are not in any way connected to the picture.

7. b. There is no indication why the man is looking at a graph, so choice **a** is not correct. The photo shows information displayed on the computer monitor, so choice **c** and choice **d** are also incorrect.

8. d. Choice **a** generalizes too much—different businesses use different tools. The tools depicted are not generally about being professional and are not necessarily for a meeting, so choice **b** and choice **c** are also incorrect.

9. b. There is nothing in the picture that tells the viewer whether the couple is married or on a vacation, so choice **c** is incorrect. The two people are holding a surfboard, not surfing, so choice **a** is incorrect. While choice **d** may be true if the pair plan on surfing at the same time, there is no indication that they will do this right now.

10. a. While choice **b** may be factually true, the girl is not picking up the dog. There is nothing to suggest that the girl cannot take the picture, so choice **c** is incorrect. While there is a window box in the picture, no one in the picture is looking at it or moving towards it, so choice **d** is also incorrect.

11. b. The person responding offers directions to the washrooms, which is what the person posing the question has asked for. Choice **a** refers to another type of office area (the cafeteria), and choice **c** asks an unrelated question.

12. a. The person responding agrees to the meeting time and confirms the time. Choice **b** asks an irrelevant question and choice **c** gives directions that are not related to the question.

13. a. The person responding agrees to do as asked. Choice **c** expresses an intention that is not related to the question and choice **b** asks a question that is not related to the report.

14. c. The person responding offers the office hours being requested. Although choice **a** is relevant in explaining when one might visit, it does not answer the question directly. Choice **b** asks an unrelated question.

15. b. The person responding offers a solution to the fact that a deadline will arrive soon. Choice **a** asks a question that does not answer or add to the original comment. While choice **c** is about the same topic as the original statement, it is not a relevant response.

16. c. The person responding agrees to eat lunch in the park. Choice **a** asks an unrelated question and choice **b** asks the speaker to do something completely unrelated.

17. a. The person responding makes an offer to help the person who has with computer problems. Although choice **b** and choice **c** might be questions related to computer problems, they are more likely to be follow-up questions asked by the speaker rather than answers someone might give to the speaker.

18. b. The person responding tells the first speaker where to find the executive assistant. Choice **a** gives directions to the wrong spot and choice **c** asks for directions to something else.

19. a. The person responding agrees to create an appointment and poses a relevant follow-up question about time. Choice **b** is not a relevant response for someone asking something and choice **c** is a response more appropriate to another request.

20. b. The person responding agrees to return for lunch when the eatery is less full. Choice **a** is not relevant to the topic of lunch and choice **c** is incorrect because appointments are not usually made for lunches.

21. c. The person responding offers a solution for finding resources for a project. Choice **a** is incorrect because it is about an airport, whereas the original comment is about a project. Choice **b** is an irrelevant question.

22. c. It is the only answer to provide a time for when the reports are due. Choice **a** asks an unrelated question and choice **b** mentions lunch, which is not relevant to the subject being discussed.

23. b. The person responding explains what type of clothing is appropriate for the event. Although choice **a** and choice **c** are about the same topic—clothing—they do not answer the question in a relevant, direct way.

24. c. The person responding explains where the car is parked. Although choice **a** might be a problem if one cannot find a parked car, it does not answer the question. Choice **b** suggests an unrelated course of action.

25. c. The person responding offers a solution for finding a car. Although choice **a** is about a similar topic, it states facts that are not helpful. Choice **b** suggests a course of action not related to the main topic.

26. b. The person responding accepts a newspaper and offers thanks. Eggs are not relevant to the conversation, so choice **a** is incorrect. Choice **c** asks a question that is not relevant.

27. a. The person responding offers a solution that allows the speaker to understand how to use a fax. Although the other two responses also have to do with office machines, they are not relevant. Choice **b** makes a request that is different from the initial request and choice **c** suggests that the person responding does not need the printer, which is not relevant to the speaker's request for help.

28. **c.** The person responding offers help with the copy machine when requested to do so. Choice **b** asks an unrelated question and choice **a** is an unrelated complaint by the person responding.

29. **b.** It tells the person asking the question the name of the catering company. Choice **a** asks an unrelated question and choice **c** is an unrelated complaint from the person responding.

30. **c.** It tells the person asking the question a detail about the conference. Choice **a** responds to a question by asking another, unrelated, question. Choice **b** tells the speaker an unrelated fact about the person responding.

31. **a.** The person responding tells the speaker how the letter will get to the accountant. Choice **b** is more appropriate for an offer of some sort. Choice **c** is a statement that the person responding would prefer to send something, which is not relevant to the question.

32. **a.** The person responding tells the questioner when the auditor is next available. Choice **b** would only be appropriate if the questioner had asked whether the auditor is available. Choice **c** offers directions to the office, even though the speaker has not indicated these are needed.

33. **b.** The person responding offers a reasonable explanation for the vice-president's mood. Choice **a** is more appropriate if the person asking the question were waiting to see the vice-president, and there is no indication of this. Choice **c** is an off-topic remark.

34. **c.** The person responding tells the questioner where the coat was purchased. Although choice **b** may refer to clothing, it states an opinion instead of answering the question. Choice **a** states a preference that is not relevant to the conversation.

35. **c.** It explains who will order food. Choice **b** asks for directions that are not relevant to the original question. Choice **a** offers a reassurance that there is plenty of time to order food, which is not relevant to the question.

36. **a.** The person responding makes a suggestion for a place to meet. Choice **b** asks a question that is not relevant to meeting places. While choice **c** states a suggestion, perhaps of when not to meet, it does not answer the question.

37. **b.** Choice **b** is correct. It offers a concrete suggestion for meeting a changed deadline. Choice **a** suggests an idea for lunch, that is not relevant to a new deadline. Choice **c** asks a question that does not relate to the subject being discussed.

38. **a.** The person responding agrees to go to a concert. Although a car may be important to go to the concert, choice **b** is a question that does not relate directly to the original question. Choice **c** is a comment about work and is not related to the concert being discussed.

39. **b.** The person responding suggests a time for the party. Choice **a** does not offer a response to the question. Choice **c** is a suggestion about the location of the party, which is not what the speaker asks about.

40. **c.** The person responding offers a concrete reason for throwing a party. Choice **a** refers to a woman, not the man being discussed in the question. Choice **b** is an acceptance of an invitation, which is not a relevant response to someone asking about the reason for a party.

41. d. The man says "I think I'm going to volunteer." He does not mention a new job or travel, so choices **a** and choice **b** are incorrect. Although he will be meeting new people, choice **c** is incorrect because he will be meeting people who are new to this country and the man does not say he wants to volunteer specifically to meet new people.

42. a. The woman says, "I look forward to hearing about the people you meet." Choice **b** is incorrect since the woman does not mention her own volunteering. Choice **c** and choice **d** are not mentioned in this conversation.

43. b. The man says, "I was thinking of volunteering at my local library." While the people he meets will be from other countries, he will be meeting them locally, so choice **a** is incorrect. The town hall and the classroom are not mentioned, so choice **c** and choice **d** are incorrect.

44. d. The woman says, "My instructor didn't show up for my evening class yesterday." Choice **c** is incorrect because the instructor did not show up at all, not even after thirty minutes. Choice **a** is incorrect because that is a possible reason the woman gives for her instructor being late—it is not the reason she is annoyed. She does not mention being tired, so choice **b** is incorrect.

45. a. The woman says, "I hope next time there's a note on the class door if he's late." She does not mention a missed exam or her grades, so choice **b** and choice **c** are incorrect. She does not complain about having to wait thirty minutes, so choice **d** is incorrect.

46. c. The woman says, "That's possible. Many of us in the class have had the flu." She does not say that the instructor had any symptoms before being absent, so choice **a** and choice **b** are incorrect. She does not mention she was ill herself, so choice **d** is incorrect.

47. a. The woman says, "I'm shy" and "I'm not good with computers." She does not mention that she is worried about her language skills, so choice **c** is incorrect. She does not say that she can't do interviews—just that she is shy—so choice **b** is incorrect. She does not say that the advice is bad, so choice **d** is incorrect.

48. d. She claims shyness and lack of computer skills as the reasons not to take the other advice and says that she'll try the third piece of advice. The man does not suggest a particular option will take less time or will be more effective, so choice **a** and choice **b** are incorrect. The woman does not say at any time that the man's advice is impractical, so choice **c** is incorrect.

49. b. The woman says her project is "about whether our customers enjoy our new perfume." She already believes that she lacks computer skills and is shy, so she is not trying to find these things out, and therefore choice **a** and choice **c** are incorrect. The woman does not mention a promotion, so choice **d** is incorrect.

50. c. The woman says, "His daughter drove the car into a garbage can," implying that the daughter was not watching where she was going. No mention is made of whether the girl asked her father's permission or whether she was speeding, so choice **a** and choice **b** are incorrect. Her attitude about money is not discussed, so choice **d** is incorrect.

51. a. The woman says, "he'll have to pay for the damage" after the accident. There is no mention of the accountant's mechanic or his insurance, so choice **b** and choice **c** are incorrect. The man specifically mentions that "no one was hurt," so choice **d** is incorrect.

52. c. The woman says, "His daughter drove the car into a garbage can." There is no mention of a cat or garage door in the conversation, so choice **b** and choice **d** are incorrect. The daughter was driving the car; she did not hit it. Therefore, choice **a** is incorrect as well.

53. b. The woman says, "I heard the vice-president say it was really good" and "that should be good news for your promotion." She does not mention that the printer problem is resolved, so choice **a** is incorrect. There is no indication that the man can take time off, so choice **c** is incorrect. The man has already handed in the report, so choice **d** is incorrect.

54. b. The man says, "it was really hard to do; my printer broke." He does not mention that he could not focus, so choice **a** is incorrect. He mentions that he is tired now, not while he was working on the project, so choice **c** is incorrect. He does not mention when he began the sales report, so choice **d** is incorrect.

55. d. The man says, "I'm so tired today" because "I was up late working on the final sales report." He does not mention being proud, so choice **b** and choice **c** are incorrect. He does not mention being worried, so choice **a** is incorrect.

56. c. The man says, "I loved the art galleries most." The woman, not the man, says she loved the food and the travel, so choice **a** and choice **b** are incorrect. No one mentions music, so choice **d** is incorrect.

57. d. The man says, "I studied art there six years ago" and the woman says, "I studied there for three years." Choice **a** and choice **b** each leave out one of the people who have been to France before, and choice **c** is inaccurate.

58. a. The woman says, "I'm going to France next week for a wedding." She mentions that she loves the food in France, but that is not the specific reason for travel, so choice **b** is incorrect. She has been to France to study before, but that is not the purpose of her trip this time, so choice **c** is incorrect. It is the man who enjoys the art galleries in France, so choice **d** is inaccurate.

59. b. The woman says, "I hate to wake up early after sleeping in." It is the man who likes to stay in and read, so choice **b** is incorrect. The woman says two days is "lots of time to go boating," so choice **c** is incorrect. Answer choice **d** is the opposite of what the woman says; she loves weekends.

60. c. The woman says, "That gives me lots of time to go boating." It is the man who likes to read, so choice **a** is incorrect. The woman does not mention shopping or concerts, so choice **b** and choice **d** are incorrect.

61. a. The man says, "If we didn't have to come back on Monday we'd have to come back to work on Tuesday" and "At least we get two days off on the weekend." The man mentions he likes to read on weekends, not Mondays, so choice **b** is incorrect. He does not mention productivity or making money, so choice **c** and choice **d** are not correct.

62. c. The man says, "I'm going to take a business degree so that I can get a better job." He does not mention his English or a visa, so choice **a** and choice **b** are incorrect. While he may want to impress his employer, the man does not mention this directly and therefore choice **d** is incorrect.

63. a. The woman says, "but it was hard for him to take four years off. He has big student loans." She does not mention any problems with homework and instructors, so choice **b** and choice **d** are incorrect. It is the man taking night school—the woman's cousin attended school during days—so answer choice **c** is incorrect.

64. a. The man says, "I'm going to night school so that won't happen" when the woman mentions her cousin taking time off for school and having big loans. He does not mention study time, instructors, or having less homework, so choice **b**, choice **c**, and choice **d** are incorrect.

65. b. The woman says, "I will go door to door to talk to voters about the next general election." She does not mention fliers or raising money, so choice **a** and choice **c** are incorrect. She mentions specifically speaking to people in person (not on the telephone), so choice **d** is incorrect.

66. a. The man says, "I don't vote because I'm not a citizen yet." He does not talk about his beliefs regarding voting, so choice **b** is wrong. He does not mention that he has not spoken to a party representative, so choice **c** is incorrect. The man does not mention issues, so choice **d** is incorrect.

67. b. The woman says, "I think more voters would vote if they could talk to a party representative about it." She does not mention running for office, meeting new people, or specific issues, so choice **a**, choice **c**, and choice **d** are incorrect.

68. d. The woman says, "I still have to read the manual for it." She does not mention her monitor being turned off or her mouse being unplugged, so choice **a** and choice **b** are incorrect. Neither she nor the man mentions technical support, so choice **c** is incorrect.

69. a. The man says, "I'll stop by your office after lunch to help you." He does not mention buying her a computer, technical support, or viruses, so choice **b**, choice **c**, and choice **d** are incorrect.

70. b. The man says, "Are you sure you don't have your monitor set on a timer so it turns off after a while?" suggesting that the issue is simply a small problem stemming from unfamiliarity. The man does not mention a virus, so choice **a** is incorrect. The man does not mention plugging the computer in or files, so choice **d** and choice **c** are not correct.

71. d. The speaker says, "we hope we will also see improved productivity and cooperation after this workshop." Although the speaker mentions fun as an outcome, this is a work-related event, so choice **a** is incorrect. There will be no customers at the event—it is a sales meeting—so choice **b** is incorrect. There is no mention of a marketing campaign, so choice **c** is incorrect.

72. c. The speaker says, "employees across all departments." Volunteers, executives, and new employees are not specifically mentioned, so choice **a**, choice **b**, and choice **d** are incorrect.

73. c. The speaker says, "Every employee will be grouped into a team, consisting of employees across all departments. Each team will have a mentor." Since the speaker says specifically that employees will be paired with people from different departments, choice **a** is incorrect. The speaker says specifically that each group will have one mentor, so choice **b** is incorrect. The speaker does not mention executives, so choice **d** is incorrect.

74. c. The speaker says, "Here at this year's 'Reaching the Stars' business conference." Classrooms, business meetings, and libraries are not mentioned by the speaker, so choice **a**, choice **b**, and choice **d** are not correct.

75. a. The speaker says, "Mr. Smith is a motivational speaker, an author, and a global expert on creativity in the workplace." He does not mention personal training or sales executives so choice **b** and choice **c** are incorrect. Although the speaker mentions that Mr. Smith has traveled to Japan, he does not say that Mr. Smith is from Japan, so choice **d** is incorrect.

76. c. The speaker says, "We all know that creative thinking is important in creating new ideas, in marketing and in every area of business." Although choice **a**, choice **b**, and choice **d** may be true statements about creativity generally, they are not mentioned by the speaker.

77. a. The speaker says, "our conference helps sales and marketing professionals develop their skills. Through workshops, discussions, and lectures we help professionals learn the latest news in the world of sales and marketing. Of course, we also provide opportunities for networking." The speaker does not mention making money or fun, so choice **b** is incorrect. There is no traveling at the conference and lecturing is something that happens at the conference (it is not a goal), so choice **c** is incorrect. Promoting and selling are not mentioned as goals, so choice **d** is incorrect.

78. c. The speaker says, "fill out your registration sheet, checking off the events you will participate in." The speaker does not mention volunteering, donating, or next year's conference, so choice **a**, choice **b**, and choice **d** are incorrect.

79. b. The speaker says, "Through workshops, discussions, and lectures we help professionals learn." Since more than lectures are used, choice **a** is incorrect. Team events and sales pitches are not mentioned, so choice **c** and choice **d** are incorrect.

80. a. The speaker says, "I am your new instructor for this class, 'History 101.' Dr. Stevens, your former instructor, has asked me to take over this class." Although Dr. Stevens may be ill or retired this is not mentioned, so choice **b** and choice **c** are incorrect. Since the instructor is lecturing and not leading a workshop activity, choice **d** is incorrect.

81. b. The speaker says, "if you have any questions, please see me after class." Since the speaker identifies himself as an instructor at a university, choice **a**, choice **c**, and choice **d** are not correct, as these are not generally places where university classes take place.

82. c. The speaker says, "The only significant change is that your final term papers will be due on April 8 instead of March 31." He notes specifically that no new topics will be covered, so choice **b** is not correct. He does not announce any new tests or term papers, so choice **a** and choice **d** are not correct.

83. a. The speaker announces what will be happening and asks passengers to do specific things before the flight. No delay is mentioned, so choice **b** is incorrect. The speaker says that "The flight safety demonstration will begin shortly," so no safety instructions have been given yet and therefore choice **c** is incorrect.

84. b. The speaker says, "Please wait until we have landed in London to use your mobile devices." The speaker specifically asks passengers to put away their mobile devices now and not use them while the plane is in flight, so choice **a**, choice **c**, and choice **d** are incorrect.

85. c. The speaker says, "This is a nonsmoking flight and we will be offering a film as well as a lunch." The food offered is lunch, so choice **a** is incorrect. Music is not mentioned, so choice **b** is not correct.

86. b. The speaker says, "Hello, class, I am your guest lecturer today," suggesting a school environment. Since this is a lecture, it is unlikely to be taking place in a school cafeteria, so choice **a** is incorrect. Since this is not a business environment, choice **c** and choice **d** are also incorrect.

87. a. The speaker says, "I will be speaking about the Romantic Era. The Romantic Era, or the Age of Romanticism, began in the late 1700s in Western Europe." Although he mentions art and science, he does so only in explaining the period in history, so choice **b** and choice **c** are not correct. He does not mention conflict, so choice **d** is incorrect.

88. a. The speaker says, "Romanticism was a reaction to the Age of Enlightenment, which emphasized science and reason." He does not mention pollution, so choice **b** is not correct. He mentions artists and foreign countries as something that interested the Romantics, but Romanticism was not a reaction to these, so choice **c** and choice **d** are not correct.

89. d. The speaker says, "Train 7707 with service to Boston has been delayed due to bad weather." No other reason for the delay is mentioned, so choice **a**, choice **b**, and choice **c** are incorrect.

90. a. The speaker says, "We ask that all passengers remain in the train terminal and await further instructions" and "If you wish to get a refund for your ticket, please go to the refund desk near the clock." Although passengers may be able to take a car or plane, these are not options suggested by the speaker, so choice **c** and choice **d** are incorrect. The speaker does not mention the possibility of exchanging tickets, so choice **b** is incorrect.

91. b. The speaker says, "We will announce any changes or updates over the intercom system as information becomes available." The train is delayed, so choice **d** is not possible. The speaker does not mention taxis, so choice **a** is not possible. Although the speaker apologizes, no promise of more apologies is offered, so choice **c** is not correct.

92. d. The speaker says, "we'd like to thank callers for reporting that to our studios" and "Our CRKC Radio Boston helicopter crew reports that there is heavy traffic through the downtown area." The Internet and satellites are not mentioned, so choice **b** and choice **c** are incorrect.

93. c. The speaker says, "There is a stalled car on Windmill Road," "heavy traffic through the downtown area, where congestion seems to be a problem," and "Construction work is slowing traffic in the East End." The speaker does not mention malfunctioning traffic lights, pedestrians, or rush hour, so choice **a**, choice **b**, and choice **d** are not correct.

94. b. The speaker says, "Stay safe on the roads, listeners, and call in your traffic reports as you see them." Although choice **a** and choice **c** are implied (and good advice), the speaker does not mention them directly. The speaker does not tell listeners to stay home, so choice **d** is not correct.

95. b. The speaker says, "I have worked as an attorney in this neighborhood for 20 years." Although the speaker is giving a public address, he does not do this for a living so choice **a** is incorrect. He does not mention working as an executive, so choice **c** is not correct. If he is running for local office, he is not a congressperson, so choice **d** is not correct.

96. b. The speaker says "I am asking for your vote today." He does not mention money or changes to the legal system, so choice **a** and choice **d** are not correct. Although he thinks that education is important, he also implies that his listeners already know that education is important and therefore he does not have to convince them of this. Therefore, choice **c** is not correct.

97. c. The speaker says, "If you vote for me, I will work very hard to improve our schools, our hospitals, and the safety of our streets." He does not mention taxes, funding for politics, or changing laws, so choice **a**, choice **b**, and choice **d** are not correct.

98. a. The speaker says, "here is your local weather." Although she is announcing a worrying storm system, she does not mention that it is an emergency, so choice **b** is not correct. Although the speaker offers suggestions as to what viewers can do to prepare, the focus is on weather and not advice, so choice **c** is not correct. The speaker does not mention specific cancellations and only says that things may be cancelled at some point, so choice **d** is incorrect.

99. c. The speaker says, "It's our first major snowstorm of the season, so get ready, New York." Although she mentions high winds, she mentions that weather system for New York, so choice **d** is not correct.

100. a. The speaker says, "get ready, New York" and then offers specific suggestions on getting ready. She suggests things to do now, so choice **b** is not correct. The speaker does not ask viewers to call in, so choice **c** is not correct. The speaker says, "Once the snow starts, avoid driving if possible," so choice **d** is not correct.

101. c. At a conference one usually sits in a seat. Although one can sit in a train or airplane, these are modes of transportation to a destination, not places where one sits at a conference, so choice **a** and **b** are incorrect. Although it is possible to sit in on a lecture, the statement clearly refers to a specific seating arrangement—a chair or a seat—rather than a specific event, so choice **d** is not correct.

102. a. The sentence is in imperative form—the statement is asking people to turn devices off now. Choice **b** is incorrect because it is in the past tense. Choice **c** and choice **d** are not correct because they do not fit in an imperative sentence.

103. b. The sense of the sentence is that the subject, *he*, has already seen the movie. Choice **a** and choice **c** are incorrect because the verb is in the present tense.

104. c. *Quickly* is the appropriate adverb to modify the verb *fall*. Although choice **a** and choice **d** are also adverbs, they do not reasonably describe how confetti might fall, so these answers are not correct.

105. a. *Eat* describes accurately what panda bears do. Choice **c** and **d** are incorrect because the verb is in the past tense.

106. b. The sentence describes a cause and effect—because the professor was late, therefore he had to stay late. Choice **a** is incorrect because it does not establish a cause and effect. Choice **c** and choice **d** are incorrect because they do not grammatically fit into the sentence.

107. b. The sentence is missing an adjective and the adjective *sunny* best fits into the sense and logic of the sentence. Although choice **a** and choice **b** are also adjectives that might describe weather, they are not correct because they do not fit into the logic of the sentence. That is, no one would go swimming on a day that was warm and either rainy or stormy. The adjective *saturated* does not fit the logic of the sentence, so choice **d** is not correct.

108. c. The form *when + gerund* (a verb ending in *-ing*) can be used to express the present tense in this sentence. Choice **b** is not correct because the phrase does not make sense. Choice **a** and choice **d** are not correct verb tenses for the sentence.

109. d. *Silent* is the most appropriate adjective for the sentence. It is unlikely that attendees would fall asleep or become numb if they were anticipating a speaker, so choice **b** and choice **c** are not correct. Answer choice **a** is not correct because it does not fit grammatically into the sentence (one does not *fall awake*).

110. d. The present tense is the right verb tense for an imperative sentence. Choice **a** and choice **c** are in the past tense and so do not fit an imperative sentence in which a speaker is trying to explain what to do now (in the present tense) and in the future. The gerund (*-ing*) verb form is also not correct for an imperative sentence, so choice **b** is incorrect.

111. b. *Review* means to look at something closely, and it would make sense to review a report before an important call. *Reveal* means to make something known, to *revive* something is to bring it back to life, and to *revoke* means to cancel. These verbs would not make sense in the context of the sentence, making choice **a**, choice **c**, and choice **d** incorrect.

112. d. *Although* is a subordinate conjunction that means *in spite of the fact that*, which fits in with the meaning of the sentence. *But* is a connecting adverb that shows a conflict between two clauses of a sentence, but there are no conflicts between the two parts of this sentence, so choice **a** is not the correct answer. The word *neither* is used in a pair (with the word *nor*, which does not appear in this sentence,) so choice **c** is incorrect.

113. b. *Run* is the future simple tense with the verb *decided to*. Choice **d** is the incorrect verb (*rue* means *to regret*). Choice **c** is incorrect because it would imply that the speaker has already run the marathon. The gerund (*-ing*) verb form does not fit with the future simple tense, so choice **a** is not correct.

114. b. *Rapidly* is the adverb that best fits the meaning of the sentence. One stirs batter rapidly. Although choice **a**, choice **c**, and choice **d** are also adverbs, they are not usually used to describe how someone might mix.

115. d. *Running* creates a past progressive verb tense with the word *was* and the past progressive tense is the appropriate tense in this sentence, as this is the tense we use to describe what was happening at a specific point in the past. Choice **a** and choice **b** are not the correct tenses for the past progressive (which is formed with the *-ing* form of a verb). Choice **c** is the wrong idiom—one *runs*, not *jogs*, for office.

116. b. *Report* is the noun most appropriate for the sentence. One prepares a report for a meeting. Marathons have nothing to do with meetings, so choice **c** is incorrect. Although meetings are related to a job or a career, one does not prepare these things for a meeting, so choice **a** and choice **d** are not correct.

117. a. *Strong* is the adjective that best describes the noun *resume* in this sentence. Although resumes can be *posted*, *sent*, and even *blue*, resumes with these characteristics are not more likely to result in a good job, so choice **b**, choice **c**, and choice **d** are not correct.

118. b. The future simple tense makes the most sense for this sentence, and the future simple is made by using a verb and the *-ing* (gerund) form of a verb. The future simple is correct because it describes an action that started previously or has been going on and which was decided previously. In this case, the man decided to run at some point in the past and has been running (ongoing). *Exercises* is the wrong form of the verb, so choice **d** is not correct. Choice **c** is the incorrect verb. Choice **a** is in the present tense, which does not create a future simple tense in this sentence.

119. b. This is the most appropriate adjective to describe the accountant's mood. If files are lost, it is natural for the accountant to react badly. Although choices **a**, **c**, and **d** are also adjectives to describe someone, they are not usually used to describe someone's reaction to a bad situation.

120. c. This is an imperative sentence—the speaker is making a request—and the present tense is the correct tense for an imperative sentence. Choice **b** is the wrong verb. Choice **d** is in the past tense, which is not correct. Choice **a** is a gerund form, which is not used in an imperative sentence.

121. d. *Carefully* is the correct adverb to modify *open*. Choices **a** and **b** are verbs, and therefore incorrect. Choice **c** is a noun or a verb, and therefore not an adverb, which can modify a verb.

122. b. *Files* is the most appropriate noun to describe what might be lost on a computer. Notebooks are not usually on computers, so choice **a** is not correct. Printers are attached to computers, not on them, so choice **c** is not correct. The Internet is not located on any one computer and therefore cannot be lost, so choice **d** is not correct.

123. b. The sentence describes what will occur in the future. *Going* is in the present (gerund or *-ing*) tense, so choice **a** is not correct. *Go* is the present or imperative case, so choice **c** is not correct. Choice **d** is not the correct verb.

124. b. The sentence describes something that was going on in the past over a longer period of time. For this, we use a past tense. Choice **a**, choice **c**, and choice **d** are not correct because the verb is in the present tense.

125. a. *Delicious* is the best adjective to describe the noun *pizza*. Since the speaker is saying that pizza is his or her favorite food, it is unlikely that he or she would use negative adjectives to describe the food, and choice **b**, choice **c**, and choice **d** are all negative adjectives.

126. a. *It's* is a contraction of *it is*, and *it is* fits perfectly well in this sentence. *Its* is a possessive pronoun, so choice **b** and choice **d** are not correct. *It* does not provide the sentence with a needed verb, so choice **c** is not correct.

127. b. *Than* is a conjunction that is used with comparisons. In this case, it is used to describe and compare two possible scenarios (a late movie and an early movie). *Then* is an adverb that is used to describe time, so choice **a** is not correct. Choice **c** and choice **d** are not correct because these words are either used in questions (*When was the movie?*) or are used to describe time and place (*This is where the movie is shown*).

128. b. *Your* is a possessive pronoun, used to describe ownership of an object in many cases (*your car*). *You're* is a contraction that means *you are*, so choice **a** is not correct. *You* and *us* are not possessives that would modify the noun *car* so choice **c** and choice **d** are not correct.

129. d. In this case *there* is used as a pronoun, which is what is missing from the sentence. Choice **a** and choice **c** are not correct, because *their* and *theirs* are possessive pronouns, used to modify a noun (*their car or the car is theirs*).

130. a. *Affect* is the verb that is needed in the sentence. Choice **c** is not correct because *effect* is a noun. Choice **b** and choice **d** are incorrect verb tenses.

131. a. *Doesn't* is a contraction that means *does not*, which fits in the sentence. Don't is a contraction for *do not* which does not make sense in the context of the sentence, so choice **b** is not correct. Choice **c** and choice **d** do not make sense in the context of the sentence.

132. a. The term *less* is used in cases in which we speak of something that cannot be counted. *Fewer* is used with nouns that can be counted, so choice **b** is not correct. *Lesser* describes a degree of something, not an amount, so choice **c** is not correct. *Few* is a qualifier used with plural nouns, so choice **d** is not correct.

133. b. *Ad* is a noun, a contraction of *advertisement*, a word that makes sense in the context of the sentence. *Add* is a verb, so choice **a** is incorrect. Commercials run on television, not in newspapers, so choice **d** is not correct. One cannot run an aesthetic in a newspaper, so choice **c** is incorrect.

134. c. The speaker is offering advice in this sentence, which calls for *should* and the present tense of a verb. Choice **b** is the past tense and therefore incorrect. Choice **a** and choice **d** are the incorrect tenses of the verb to use with an imperative sentence.

135. d. An apostrophe and an *s* added to singular nouns indicate possession, and in the sentence, the toys belong to the cat. *Cats* is a plural noun, so choice **a** is incorrect. *Cot* refers to a small bed, which makes choice **b** incorrect. *Cat* is a singular noun, so choice **c** is not correct.

136. c. The other items in the list (*working* and *learning*) are also in the *-ing* form, and in lists we make verb tenses parallel. Choice **a**, choice **b**, and choice **d** are not the same tense as *working* and *learning* and would therefore not be correct.

137. d. The sentence calls for the future continuous tense, since the person being addressed will be doing this action in the future. For the future continuous tense, the gerund (*-ing*) tense of the verb is used. *Enter* is in the present tense, so choice **a** is not correct. *Has entered* and *entered* refer to the past, so choice **b** and choice **c** are not correct.

138. c. This sentence is in the present perfect continuous, which is created with two auxiliary verbs (*has* and *been*). The sentence is describing something that is ongoing and current, which is why the present perfect continuous is used. Choice **a** and choice **b** use only one auxiliary verb, so these answers are not correct. *Be* is the present tense with no auxiliary verbs, so choice **d** is not correct.

139. a. *Loose* is the best adjective to fit the sentence and describe a suit. *Lose* is a verb meaning *to misplace*, so choice **b** is not correct. *Looses* and *loses* are both verbs, so choice **c** and choice **d** are not correct.

140. a. *A lot* is an adverb that means *a great deal*, which fits in the context of the sentence. *Lots* and *lot* are nouns referring to land and can also be used to describe quantities, although only when used with *of*. Therefore, choice **b** and choice **c** are not correct. *Alot* is a word that does not exist in the English language (although *a lot* is often misspelled this way), so choice **d** is not correct.

141. a. The president is referring to something the employees currently know; therefore, the present tense is appropriate. The past tense is not correct, so choice **c** is incorrect. *Now* is not a verb tense of the verb *to know*, so choice **d** is incorrect.

142. d. In a request or imperative sentence, the present tense of a verb is used, and in this sentence, the president is making a request or offering advice. *Chosen* is past tense, so choice **a** is not correct. The gerund (*-ing*) case is not used when giving advice or making a request, so choice **b** is not correct. *Chase* is the past form of another verb (not *to choose*), so choice **c** is not correct.

143. a. In this context *for rent* means *available to rent*, which fits with the sense of the statement. *Rents* and *rent* are verbs, so choice **c** and choice **d** are not correct. *Rental* is a noun, so choice **b** is not correct.

144. b. The idiom *feel free to* indicates permission to do something, which is in keeping with the context of this sentence. Both *gratis* and *no charge* mean *at no cost* and do not make sense in this sentence, so choice **a** and choice **c** are incorrect. *Able* is a verb, so choice **d** is incorrect.

145. a. This clause means *are not widely hunted* and *extensively* is an adverb that indicates this meaning. Although *badly*, *quickly*, and *largely* are also adverbs, they do not fit the context of this sentence because they would not be used to describe how kangaroos are hunted. Therefore, choice **b**, choice **c**, and choice **d** are not correct.

146. b. *Can* is an auxiliary verb and the main verb used with *can* is always the bare infinitive. *Life* is a noun, so **a** is incorrect. *Lifes* is not a word in the English language, so **c** is incorrect. *Lives* is not the bare infinitive, so **d** is incorrect.

147. c. *Because* is a conjunction, generally used at the beginning of a clause, before a subject and verb. *Because of* is a preposition, and is used before a noun or a pronoun; therefore, choice **a** is incorrect. *Although* and *even though* would be used if the two parts of the sentence were in contrast or conflict; this is not the case, so choice **b** and choice **d** are not correct.

148. b. *Prefer* is used with *to* in order to compare two things. *With* does not suggest a comparison or preference, so choice **a** is incorrect. *Then* is an adverb and *than* is a conjunction, so choice **c** and choice **d** are incorrect.

149. a. The sentence uses second conditional tense to discuss an unlikely situation. In the second conditional tense, *if* is used along with two verbs that have a direct relationship—in this case, if I *had* more time, I *could* be organized. The present form must be used with second conditional, and *have* and *has* are past tense while *having* is the gerund tense, so choice **b**, choice **c**, and choice **d** are all incorrect.

150. b. In this context *can* means one is able to do something. The speaker is saying anyone *can* get organized, meaning everyone is able to learn the skill of getting organized. *Able* would only work in this sentence if the speaker added a few words, such as *organization is a skill you are able to learn*, and even if this were the case, the phrasing would be awkward, so choice **a** is incorrect. The speaker is focusing on the audience's ability to learn and on the possibility of learning, so *will* and *must* do not fit the logical meaning of the sentence. Therefore, choice **c** and choice **d** are incorrect.

151. a. The speaker is saying that one should have no more than three containers. *Least* would indicate that the audience needs three or more containers, which is not the case, according to the speaker, so choice **b** is incorrect. *Less* would only be used if the sentence was comparing the number of containers to something else, and this is not the case, so choice **d** is incorrect.

152. d. The statement is in the passive voice and two verbs are needed to explain what is happening to the subject. *Put, placing,* and *place* do not include two verbs to create the passive voice, and therefore choice **a**, choice **b**, and choice **c** are incorrect.

153. d. The prices are quite low, the food is casual (soup and sandwiches), and only a lunch menu is listed. The simple food and low prices suggest it is not a formal restaurant, so choice **a** is incorrect. Servers are mentioned, so it is clearly an eating establishment and not a catering company, making choice **b** incorrect. No dinner options are mentioned, so choice **c** is not correct.

154. a. The text reads: "we have a daily lunch special," "we make our pies from scratch, four different flavors each day," and "ask your server about the soup of the day." Dinner is not mentioned at all, so choice **b** is incorrect. The drinks are coffee, soda, tea, and hot chocolate every day, so choice **c** is incorrect. Breakfast items are not mentioned, so choice **d** is incorrect.

155. c. The menu claims sandwiches are "served on either whole wheat or white home-style bread." Buns, wraps, multigrain bread, sourdough bread, and gluten-free bread are not mentioned, so choice **a**, choice **b**, and choice **d** are not correct.

156. a. The menu claims, "we make our pies from scratch, four different flavors each day." The pie slices are only $4 apiece, so choice **b** is incorrect. The ice cream is served in a cone or dish, so choice **c** is incorrect. While it may be true that the pie is served hot, there is no mention of this on the menu, so choice **d** is incorrect.

157. b. The text states that "There are many ways to get started in real estate": "You can act as a scout, gathering information for other investors"; "you can also buy homes to rent or lease"; "Another option is to buy homes, renovate them, and resell them at a profit."

158. a. The text claims, "Anyone can get started in real estate investing." Although the text mentions that professional investors and mortgage lenders are resources for investors, the text clearly states that property investment is not just for these groups, so choice **b** and choice **d** are incorrect. The text does not mention real estate agents at all, so choice **c** is incorrect.

159. b. The author of the text writes, "If you want to get started today, you may want to read more about real estate investing." Although saving money, buying property, and getting financing are common-sense things that someone might do when buying real estate, they are not mentioned in the article, so choice **a**, choice **c**, and choice **d** are not correct.

160. c. The author of the text writes, "There are many ways to get started in real estate. You can act as a scout, gathering information for other investors." The article does not mention saving money or researching loans, so choice **a** and choice **b** are not correct. Although the article suggests talking to other investors, it suggests that investors do this before investing. The article does not suggest that talking to investors makes investing a smaller risk. Therefore, choice **d** is not correct.

161. b. Bob writes in his e-mail, "I just wanted to check to see whether you are still on board for David's party next week." Allen is the one receiving the e-mail, so choice **a** is incorrect. Bob is the one sending the e-mail, so choice **c** is incorrect. Betty is David's wife, so choice **d** is incorrect.

162. c. Bob writes in his e-mail, "we thought it would be fun to surprise him for his birthday on Friday." There is no mention of Betty and David having children, so choice **a** is not correct. Bob writes that David and Betty are married, not that they are newly married, so choice **b** is not correct. No mention is made of David's job, so choice **d** is not correct.

163. d. Bob writes in his e-mail, "we'll have cake and refreshments. I'll take care of those," and "I'll take care of all the organizational details." Bob is asking others to sign the card, so choice **a** is not correct. Everyone will be yelling "surprise," according to the e-mail, so choice **b** is not correct. David will visit Betty to pick her up from work, so there is no need to get David to visit Betty. Therefore, choice **c** is not correct.

164. b. Bob tells Allen, "All I need you to do is NOT tell David about the party. Also, I have a card for David here in my office. If you could sign it, that would be great." Bob writes that he will take care of the organization of the party, which includes getting supplies, so choice **a** is not correct. Bob also mentions that he will take care of the cake, so choice **c** is not correct. In his e-mail, Bob specifically asks Allen not to get a gift ("As I told you at lunch, we won't be exchanging presents"), so choice **d** is not correct.

165. a. The author of the text writes, "practice seems to be a key way of reducing speaker stress." The article does not mention Internet groups or reading books about public speaking, so choice **b** and choice **c** are incorrect. Although the author talks about what public speakers have suggested, in the article there is no suggestion that speakers talk to other speakers about tips. Therefore, choice **d** is not correct.

166. c. The author writes, "Public speaking is an important skill to develop." The article does not mention the disadvantages of fear, so choice **a** and choice **b** are not correct. The author does not mention whether public speaking will make a speaker stronger, so choice **d** is not correct.

167. b. The author writes, "There are local groups known as Toastmasters that help people to develop their public speaking skills." The author does not mention books or online chat groups, so choice **a** and choice **c** are not correct. Although many speakers use PowerPoint programs, this presentation tool is not mentioned in the text. Therefore, choice **d** is not correct.

168. c. The author writes that many speakers "strongly advocate writing down and memorizing key points or entire speeches so that you will never be at a loss for what to say next." Although getting comfortable with public speaking is the main point of this text, the author does not suggest this will help speakers remember their presentations, so choice **a** is not correct. The author does not suggest developing memory skills, so choice **b** is not correct. The author suggests that speakers can picture the audience naked in order to feel less intimidated. This is not suggested as a memory technique, so choice **d** is not correct.

169. a. The author of the text writes, "No matter who you are, your skills are in demand somewhere." The text does not state that only adults can volunteer, so choice **b** is incorrect. The author specifically states that volunteers only need to have "some time" to volunteer, so choice **c** is not correct. The author does not state whether having or not having a job is a requisite, so choice **d** is incorrect.

170. c. The author of the text writes, "Volunteerism is a great way to build your resume and "improve your communication skills" as well as "Volunteering time often means more experience and more letters of recommendation for a resume." The article does not mention raises or budgeting time, so choice **a** and choice **b** are not correct. While some groups hire their volunteers, the article does not discuss this, so choice **d** is incorrect.

171. b. The author of the text writes, "There are groups that match volunteers with organizations that need help. If there is a specific skill that you would like to develop or share, this is often a good way to find a group in need of your services." The text does not mention looking in the phone book, so choice **a** is not correct. The text does not mention asking friends or looking in a newspaper, so choice **c** and choice **d** are incorrect.

172. c. The author of the text writes, "No matter who you are, your skills are in demand." While compassion may be a good skill to have when volunteering, it is not mentioned in the text, so choice **d** is not correct. While listening skills and speaking skills may be important in some volunteer positions, the text stresses that all types of skills may be important to groups, so choice **a** and choice **b** are incorrect.

173. c. The text states, "This product contains enough medication to seriously harm a child." Although the bottle is described as "childproof," this is not the reason why users need to keep the medicine away from children, so choice **b** is incorrect. The label does not specifically state how effective or ineffective the medicine would be for children, so choice **a** and choice **d** are not correct.

174. a. The label reads, "close the childproof cap of the bottle after using the product." The label states, "Do not use this product if the security cap is broken," which means that the seal can be broken. Therefore, choice **b** is incorrect. The bottle can clearly be opened (so that people can take their medicine), so choice **c** is incorrect. The label does not mention the taste of the medicine, so choice **d** is not correct.

175. d. The label reads, "Never take more than four pills in any 24-hour period." The label does not mention liquids, syringes, or creams, so choice **a**, choice **b**, and choice **c** are incorrect.

176. b. the label states, "In the event of accidental overdose, do not induce vomiting." The label does not mention a cream or lying down, so choice **a** and choice **d** are not correct. The label suggests eating something if the medicine causes stomach upset (not in case of accidental overdose), so choice **c** is not correct.

177. c. The text reads, "The public library is a resource available to everyone," and "if it's been a while since you have been at your local library, maybe it's time to find that library card." Although the text mentions volunteering and taking classes at the library, the overall text suggests that there are many things to explore at the library, and the text does not focus on these two things. Therefore, choice **a** and choice **d** are not correct. Although the text mentions what is available in the library besides reading material, the text does advise people to read, so choice **b** is incorrect.

178. a. The text reads, "The library is no longer a place just to find books. Today, it's a place to find information of all types. It's also a place to meet people and pursue any interest." The text does not mention being quiet or funding, so choice **b** and choice **c** are incorrect. Although the text mentions visiting the website, this is not the main argument of the text, so choice **d** is not correct.

179. b. The text reads, "If it's been a while since you have been at your local library, maybe it's time to find that library card. Log on to your local library's website." The text does not mention reading a book or buying books, so choice **a** and choice **c** are not correct. The text mentions that library tours are available online (not through a librarian) so choice **d** is not correct.

180. d. The text explains that, "The public library is a resource available to everyone." The text does not mention students or volunteers specifically, so choice **a** and choice **c** are not correct. The text clearly states that "you don't have to be a bookworm to enjoy" the library, so choice **b** is not correct.

181. d. Allen Doe thanks Albert for his resume. Allen points out that he has very few new career opportunities and does not mention advertising them, so choice **a** is not correct. Allen Doe's letter is not a form rejection letter, since he does offer a type of position and speaks specifically about Albert's resume, so choice **b** is incorrect. Allen does not mention holding interviews for the open positions yet, so choice **c** is incorrect.

182. b. Allen writes, "Unfortunately, the only vacancies we currently have are for cultural assistants to help us develop school programs and brochures. This is, however, and entry-level position." He does not mention a lack of applicants, so choice **a** is incorrect. Allen specifically mentions that the entry-level positions are open, not filled, so choice **c** is incorrect. He does not mention money problems, so choice **d** is not correct.

183. a. Allen expresses regret that the only positions available are "entry-level" and later praises Albert for his strong resume. Although Albert lives in New York City and the job he has applied for is in Massachusetts, from Allen's reply it appears that Albert applied for the job, suggesting that a job in another state is not a problem for him. Therefore, choice **b** is incorrect. No mention is made of competition for the jobs or starting dates, so choice **c** and choice **d** are incorrect.

184. b. Allen writes that the entry-level job requires the applicant to "help us develop school programs and brochures." No mention is made of reading books about culture, so choice **a** is incorrect. Albert completed office tasks and research as part of his previous jobs (listed on his resume). They are not the tasks that Allen says would be required of him, so choice **c** and choice **d** are not correct.

185. d. Albert mentions research as one of his duties at both of the jobs he has held so far. According to his resume, Albert "Assisted professors at the Stanford University Culture Studies Department by compiling research and conducting primary research at the library," and "Compiled research about members' cultures." Although Albert may have answered phones as part of the "office tasks" he mentions doing as a research assistant, phone work does not seem to have been the focus of his work, so choice **a** is incorrect. He does not mention presentations or speeches, so choice **b** and choice **c** are incorrect.

186. c. Delia mentions getting a security system and is quoted as saying, "I wouldn't be surprised if I were robbed one day." She complains about rude and frightening children, not too many children, so choice **a** is incorrect. It is Mosand who complains about bias and stereotypes, so choice **b** and choice **d** are not correct.

187. b. Mosand signs her letter to the editor "Mosand Jane, age 14." Mosand does not state that she lives in the same neighborhood or her own worries about crime, so choice **a** and choice **c** are incorrect. We do not know from the letter how Mosand dresses, so choice **d** is not correct.

188. d. The article states, "Recently, Delia added a security system to her home, noting that she is worried about robberies." She does not mention a new purse, so choice **a** is incorrect. The article specifically states that Delia has lived in the same place for 40 years, so choice **b** is incorrect. The newspaper story is written by choice **a**, Priors, so choice **c** is incorrect.

189. c. *One-sided* means that only one opinion is presented, and the only opinion presented in the article is the opinion of Delia Rodriguez. Mosand expresses no opinions concerning the way young people dress, so choice **a** is incorrect. Delia's lack of communication with young people and her security system are not relevant to the reporter's one-sided story, so choice **b** and choice **d** are incorrect.

190. d. Mosand writes, "She should get to know the younger people in her neighborhood—she might find out that some younger people are really nice." She does not mention books or volunteering, so choice **a** and choice **b** are incorrect. Since Delia did not write the article, Mosand is not offering her advice on how to write differently. Therefore, choice **c** is incorrect.

191. d. Steve writes, "I am very upset about the inaccuracies in your latest flyer. When I visited your store, I found that many of the items I wanted had different prices than the prices advertised in your flyer." There is no mention of items out of stock or different policies, so choice **a** and choice **c** are incorrect. Steve specifically mentions that some of the items he wanted were in the store and on sale, just at the wrong prices, so choice **b** is not correct.

192. b. Steve writes, "I spoke to your manager about it." He does not mention the store owner or other customers, so choice **a** and choice **c** are not correct. Steve mentions switching stores only after he was unhappy with the manager's response, so choice **d** is not correct.

193. a. Steve writes, "I will be shopping at Savings Grocery Store from now on." He does not mention telling others or writing to the newspaper, so choice **b** and choice **c** are incorrect. He mentions that he spoke to the manager and was unsatisfied with the response, so choice **d** is incorrect.

194. b. Steve writes, "When I spoke to your manager about it, I was treated very rudely." Steve does not mention that the manager was rushed or lacked knowledge, so choice **a** and choice **d** are incorrect. Since Steve spoke with the manager, the manager was clearly available, so choice **c** is not correct.

195. b. The flyer indicates, "All prices in effect February 17–26." The other months are not mentioned, so choice **a**, choice **c**, and choice **d** are not correct.

196. b. Peggy writes, "I would like to schedule an interview with you." Peggy is researching low-cost travel for students, not airplanes, so choice **a** is not correct. Peggy already has a job, so choice **c** is not correct. Peggy does not mention wanting to take a trip, so choice **d** is not correct.

197. d. Peggy writes, "I am a reporter with the Daily News." She mentions that she is a reporter, not a volunteer or airline attendant, so choice **a** and choice **c** are not correct. The person she is writing to is the businessperson, so choice **b** is not correct.

198. d. Peggy writes, "I am writing about budget travel for students." Although the airline travels to Sydney, Peggy does not mention special interest in this city or in the airline industry, so choice **a** and choice **c** are not correct. The airline does not even fly to Toronto, so choice **b** is not correct.

199. c. Peggy writes, "I am especially interested in your student discount and possible reward program." Since her article is not about airline safety, destinations, or the airline industry, she is unlikely to ask about these topics. Therefore, choice **a**, choice **b**, and choice **d** are not correct.

200. c. Peggy says she is writing about "budget travel for students." Businesspeople, the elderly, and children would not get much useful information from an article targeted at students, so choice **a**, choice **b**, and choice **d** are not correct.

201. **To hear this passage, listen to Track 121.** This passage is about buying a house. Some of the more difficult words to pronounce are:

    challenge—CHAL-inj
    services—SUR-viss-es
    estate—eh-STEYT
    agent —AY-(juh)nt
    suits—SOOTS
    budget—BUHJ-it
    guide—GAHYD
    process—PROSS-es
    mortgage—MAWR-gij
    loan—LOHN
    workshops—WURK-shops
    homebuyers—HOHM-bahy-ers
    seminars—SEM-(uh)-nahrs

202. **To hear this passage, listen to Track 122.** This passage is an advertisement for a spa service. Some of the more difficult words to pronounce are:

> spa—SPAH
> technology—tek-NOL-(uh)-jee
> makeup—MEYK-uhp
> application—ap-li-KEY-(shuhn)
> massage—muh-SAHJ
> relaxation—ree-lak-SEY-shuhn
> ease—EEZ
> waxing—WAK-sing
> appointment—uh-POINT-muhnt
> occasion—uh-KEY-zhuhn
> facilities—fuh-SIL-i-tees

203. Sample response: The woman, man, and two boys are fishing outdoors. The boys are holding the fishing rods. Everyone is looking at the camera and smiling. The weather is bright and the adults are wearing sunglasses.
To hear this sample response, listen to Track 123.

204. Notice that the question is asking you two things—how well you use computers and how much you understand computers. You can respond by explaining how long you have used computers, to show how often you work with them. A sample response might be: "I have worked with computers three years and have studied them in school. I am familiar with them and use them every day."
To hear this sample response, listen to Track 124.

205. This question asks for your opinion, specifically the type of computer you like best. A sample response might be: "I prefer laptop computers with a Windows system. I like to be able to travel with my computer."
To hear this sample response, listen to Track 125.

206. This question is asking you about how you use your computer usually. A sample response might be: "I most often use my computer for word processing and e-mail at work. I surf the Internet each day, so the Internet is important to me. Once a week, I create a presentation using PowerPoint. A few times a month, I use a spreadsheet to calculate sales."
To hear this sample response, listen to Track 126.

207. The speaker is asking about options with no meat. A sample response is: "We have a vegetarian stir-fry made with grilled vegetables and tofu. If you enjoy seafood, we offer a salmon dinner with vegetables or seafood pasta."
To hear this sample response, listen to Track 127.

208. The speaker wants a general idea of prices in the restaurant. It is not necessary to give the price for many items. A sample response might be: "Our prices range from $9 for a child's dinner to $30 for a steak dinner."
To hear this sample response, listen to Track 128.

209. The speaker wants to know what her son can order. It is good to give a little bit of detail. A sample response might be: "Our child menu items are $9. We offer fish and chips, hamburger and French fries, or sandwiches for children under twelve. Your son will also receive an ice cream with his choice of dinner."
To hear this sample response, listen to Track 129.

210. Stacey is asking for details of how to apply for a job, even though she already knows she should upload her resume to the website. You will want to encourage her to apply, provide her with good steps to follow, and offer extra help. A sample response might be: "Hello, Stacey, my name is Anna and I work for Wilson Recruiters. You are correct—you can apply for any position by uploading your resume to our website. Once we have your resume, we pair you with companies who ask us to find them good employees. We sometimes call to ask for additional information about your experience and education, so that we can better help you find a job. You can also choose to come in to the offices to drop off your resume in person. That way, we can discuss your work search further. If I can be of any assistance, please feel free to call."
To hear this sample response, listen to Track 131.

211. A sample response might be: "I think that both natural medicine and modern medicine have their place, because they are not two different things. Many modern medicines are based on old practices. Modern scientists are always finding new herbs and plants that cure diseases, and plants have been used for a long time to make us healthy. Not all plants and natural cures are healthy, either, while many modern medicines have side effects. I think that trying to stay healthy with good diet and exercise is important, even though diet and exercise are not very modern ideas. However, if someone gets sick it is very useful to be able to run accurate tests with modern scanners and equipment to find the cause of the problem. I would not want to choose between natural and modern medicine, because both are important and both work together to keep us healthy."
To hear this sample response, listen to Track 132.

212. Sample answer: While hiking, the couple decided to check their map.

213. Sample answer: On summer days, playing in a field can be fun for a child.

214. Sample answer: Lunchtime in cities is often a time of crowds, as everyone leaves work for a meal.

215. Sample answer: On hot summer days, barbecue food is often served at outdoor parties.

216. Sample answer: When some people really want to celebrate, they head outdoors.

217. Sample answer:

Hi Bob,
I'd be happy to help, and I think a party for Anne sounds like a great idea. I could order a cake from the bakery and I could get the baker to write "Welcome, Anne" on it. I would also be happy to ask everyone in accounting to put in a few dollars so that we could buy Anne a small gift. What do you think?
Cheers,
Sarah

218. Sample answer:

Dear Mr. Jones,
Thank you for following up with me about my stolen bank card. I am happy to report that Anderson was helpful in getting me a new bank card and I have had no problems since. My recent experience did make me realize, however, that it would be very useful if RRR Banking made it possible to report stolen bank cards over the telephone. I would have been able to report my stolen card earlier if I had not had to visit the bank in person.
Sincerely,
Andy Washington

219. The opinion essay should be well organized. Clear details and supporting statements should back up the opinion. Words should be spelled correctly and the grammar of each sentence should be correct. A sample response is:

Learning a language is best done by practice. Children learn to speak their native language by being spoken to and by being encouraged to speak. Adults can use the same methods. Any skill takes practice, and this includes language. No one would learn to drive a car without practice behind the wheel, and no one would learn to swim without spending time in a swimming pool. It is almost impossible to learn to speak without actually speaking. Just reading about a language does not allow us to make mistakes. Just reading does not let us try to pronounce words correctly. We all need practice.

Luckily, there are many ways to practice a language. There are audiotapes and programs that let students practice in their own homes, and there are classes where students can learn with a teacher. Library and community programs sometimes pair native speakers with students trying to learn a new language. This lets students practice their language skills without a lot of stress.

I think speaking and practicing are the best ways to learn, but I don't think that one method of practice is better than another. Different students learn differently. Some students are very competitive and learn well in a classroom with others. Students who are shy might prefer audiotapes at home. Many people have learned languages using different methods. The one common factor in all techniques, however, is practice. Students should find a way to practice their language skills in a way that feels comfortable and should practice as much as possible.

When small children learn a language, for example, parents do not worry exactly how their children learn to speak. Parents try lots of methods. They read to their children, talk to them, encourage children to speak, show them books and letters, and play word games. With all this practice, most children learn to speak very effectively. Clearly, parents focus on practice rather than specific learning processes. Adult students might wish to do the same.

4 ▶ LISTENING COMPREHENSION REVIEW

Listening is an important part of the English language. Whether you are in business and need to understand instructions being explained by an employer, or whether you need to listen and participate in a seminar, you need to be able to accurately understand English speech. To do this, you need to have an adequate vocabulary and you need to understand grammar and syntax as well as the context of what you are hearing.

The listening section of the TOEIC test examines your ability to understand spoken English. This section of the test consists of 100 questions and will take about 45 minutes to complete. There are four parts to the listening section. Part One will require you to look at a photograph and listen to statements made about the picture. Part Two will require you to listen to a statement and make a selection from written answers in your exam booklet. Parts Three and Four will ask you to listen to short conversations. You will be required to answer questions about the conversations you hear. During the listening portion of the TOEIC test, you will be listening to speech played by your examiner via a CD. You will need to listen carefully and answer the questions in your booklet.

Part One: Photographs

In this section of the TOEIC test, you will be shown a photograph or picture in your test booklet. Then, your test examiner will play four sentences spoken out loud. Once you have listened to the short statements, you will need to select the spoken statement that best describes the photograph in your test booklet. For example, you might see the following photo in your test booklet.

You might then hear these statements about the picture:

a. This man is typing on a laptop computer.
b. This man is listening to music.
c. This man is late for a meeting.
d. What is the weather like today?

You will not see these statements printed in your test booklet. Instead, you will simply fill in the letter on your answer sheet that corresponds to the correct statement. In this case, choice **a** will correspond to the spoken statement, "This man is typing on a laptop computer," choice **b** will correspond to the spoken statement "This man is listening to music," and so forth. To succeed on this portion of the test, you must select the letter that corresponds with the spoken statement that best describes the picture. In the preceding example, for instance, you would select choice **a** in

your test booklet, since it corresponds with the spoken statement "This man is typing on a laptop computer," because this is what the picture shows. Although the man might be going to a meeting or might be listening to music while working on his computer, there is no way to ascertain this from the photo, so choices **b** and **c** are not correct; choice **d** is an irrelevant question, so this option is also not correct.

Let's consider another example. In your booklet, you might see the following photograph.

Your examiner would then play a CD and you might hear these four statements:

a. Where is my doll?
b. Children love to play.
c. The weather is good for a picnic today.
d. Let's go outside.

In this case, you would mark choice **b** in your test booklet, since the spoken statement "Children love to play" best describes the photo. Although the child might play with a doll, too, there is nothing about the photo that suggests the child prefers a doll, so choice **a** is not correct. Although the weather might be nice enough to go outdoors, there is nothing in the photo to suggest that someone wants to go outside. In fact, the child is already outdoors. Therefore, choices **c** and **d** are not correct.

You will notice that this second example is a little bit more complex than the first example. In the first example provided, the correct spoken statement ("This man is typing on a laptop computer") simply describes what is taking place in the picture. In this second example, the statement does not describe what is happening in the picture. Instead, the correct statement is a general statement that can be made based on what is taking place in the picture.

This is an important thing to consider when preparing for the photograph questions on the TOEIC test. While some correct answers will simply describe what is occurring in the photo, some questions will expect you to think about the picture a little bit more. In other questions, you may hear a statement about only one detail in the picture, as in the following example.

You may hear:

a. This man is studying.
b. This man is checking his watch.
c. This man will attend a meeting.
d. This man is wearing a jacket.

In this example, choice **d** is correct. Although the main subject or action in the photo is the man playing an instrument, of the spoken sentences only choice **d** is correct, because the man is wearing a jacket as he plays the instrument.

It is helpful to listen to all the options and statements before deciding which is correct. This allows you to evaluate each sentence. Some possible answers may be close to being correct but may not necessarily be the best answer. Listening to and considering all answer choices is the only way to find the best possible answer.

Preparing for the Photograph Section of the TOEIC Listening Test

There are many things you can do to get ready for the photograph portion of the TOEIC test. There are practice questions at the end of this chapter and in the appendix that can help you prepare. You can also select a number of photos from a book or from magazines and ask a friend to state four sentences about each one. Explain to your friend that only one statement should be an accurate statement about a photo. Three other statements should not accurately describe what is in the picture. Have your friend state each sentence only once and then choose which statement is correct. This is a good exercise when preparing for the TOEIC test, because it represents very closely what will happen during the exam.

When practicing, consider the best ways to approach this type of question. Practice looking at the photo first, and then listening to the statements. Then, practice listening to the statements first and looking at the photo only after hearing the statements. Next, practice looking at the photo while listening to the statements. Which strategy seems to help you the most in choosing the right answer? If you notice that one strategy is especially useful, you might want to practice this specific strategy more and use the same strategy during your TOEIC test. If you find that it does not seem to matter when you look at the pictures, do what feels most comfortable.

There are some specific challenges with the photographs section of the test that you will want to prepare yourself for:

- Each sentence will only be spoken once.
- There will be no written text in your test booklet to assist you.

- You will need to be able to analyze a photograph.
- Some answers may be close to the correct statement but may not be correct.
- You will have a limited amount of time to answer each question.
- The statements spoken out loud might not specifically describe what is taking place in the picture.

You can achieve success on this part of the test by listening carefully to the spoken portion of each answer. Note which answer corresponds to each letter in your test booklet. Once you know which answer is correct, mark it in your test booklet and prepare to focus on the next question. Do not fall behind or second-guess your answers. Once the examiner has moved on to the next question, do not go back over the previous questions. This could confuse you and will take away the limited time you have for each question. It may be helpful to mentally (not out loud) state in your own words the subject of each picture before the examiner plays the audio portion of each question. This will help you think in English about the picture and will alert you to any similarities in theme and words between your own statement and the answers read aloud by the examiner.

You can also succeed in this portion of the test by examining each picture carefully and identifying all the people, locations, items, and actions in a picture. For example, when looking at a picture, try to quickly identify the number of people, their genders, and any obvious occupations they have. Try to state the general location of each picture (examples may be a factory, a field, a park, or a lake). Then, try to note any significant items in the picture—are there machines, computers, toys, or musical instruments? The TOEIC test will not ask you to identify specialized items (such as a *cello* or a *welder*), but you might be expected to identify a *machine*, *computer*, or *musical instrument* generally. You may also be expected to describe what is happening in a picture or what actions are taking place. The ability to quickly identify the people, ac-

tions, locations, and items in each picture will help you master the photo comprehension and analysis skills you will need for this part of the TOEIC test.

Review: Tips for Success

- Where possible, examine the picture carefully before the examiner plays the spoken statements about it.
- Practice with a friend, if possible, and with pictures from books or magazines.
- Glance at the photo when listening to the answers, but focus on the spoken statements being made.
- Listen to all statements before deciding which statement is correct.
- Be careful to select a statement that describes what is shown in the photograph.
- When looking at a photo in practice or on the test, try to identify people, actions, locations, and items in the photo.

Part Two: Question Response

In this section of the TOEIC test, your examiner will play an audio selection for you using a CD. You will hear one statement or one question as well as three responses for each question. Each statement will be made only once, and you will need to select the letter corresponding to the most appropriate statement or answer in your test booklet.

For example, you may hear the following:

What time is the meeting today?
   a. It is cold outside.
   b. It is at three o'clock.
   c. Please wear a suit to the event.

These responses will not be printed in the test booklet. In your booklet, you will see the following:

11. Mark your answer on your answer sheet.

In this example, you would mark choice **b** on your answer sheet, since choice **b** corresponds to the statement "It is at three o'clock," which is the most appropriate answer to the question asked. Since the question does not ask about the weather, choice **a** is not correct. Although suits may be required at the meeting, choice **c** does not answer the question, so choice **b** is incorrect as well.

It is important to remember that in the question response section of the test, there may be two types of statements and responses:

1. a statement followed by a response
2. a question followed by an answer

Let's consider the first type of question—a statement followed by a response. You might hear something like the following:

> The meeting has been moved to the office next door.
> a. Where can we buy report covers?
> b. Where will the vice president go?
> c. We should make sure everyone attending has heard about the change.

In this case, the correct answer is choice **c**, "We should make sure everyone attending has heard about the change." Neither report covers nor mention of the vice-president are relevant to the statement, so choices **a** and **b** are not correct. After being told of a location change, it is appropriate to make sure everyone has heard about the change, so choice **c** is correct.

The second type of question might include a query. For example, you might hear something such as:

> How formal is this luncheon?
> a. It is important to present professionally.
> b. We are expected to dress business casual.
> c. Where will the meeting take place?

In this case, the correct answer is choice **b**, "We are expected to dress business casual." This is the most ap-propriate response to a query about clothing. "It is important to present professionally" is a general statement that does not answer the question, so choice **a** is not correct. "Where will the meeting take place?" is a question and not a response regarding the luncheon, so choice **c** is not correct.

The main challenge of this section is that you will not have any visual or text clues in your test booklet. You will hear both the question or the statement and possible responses once, and you will need to listen carefully to ensure that you can select the best response.

Preparing for the Question Response Section of the TOEIC Listening Test

There are several ways you can prepare for the question response section of the TOEIC Listening Test. One excellent idea is to try the sample questions at the end of this chapter and in the appendix. You might also want to listen to spoken conversations more often. Listen to talk radio programs to get familiar with listening to statements made once. If possible, consider studying with a friend. Have a friend ask a question and give three possible responses. Make sure your friend understands that only one answer should be correct.

In the question response section, questions focus on understanding what the statement or question is asking. Look for specific keywords. If a question is "What time. . . ?," for example, you are looking for an answer with a time included. When listening to the responses, listen carefully to each one and keep note of which response is linked to which letter.

There are some specific challenges with the question response section of the test that you will want to prepare yourself for:

■ You will hear each statement or question and response only once.
■ You will need to remember which response corresponds to which letter—choice **a**, **b**, or **c**.

- You will have no visual or text clues in your test booklet at all—you will need to rely on your listening and memory skills.

Although this portion of the test will present no text clues in your test booklet, you can still succeed if you focus on the audio portion of the test carefully. Concentrate on the audio being played for each question and try to determine the basic idea or theme of each question. Focus on the overall meaning rather than each word individually—this will help you with listening comprehension, which is the skill being tested in this portion of the test.

Review: Tips for Success
- Practice with a friend if possible.
- Look for key words in the question or statement.
- Keep track of which response corresponds to each letter—choice **a**, **b**, or **c**.

Part Three: Conversations

In this portion of the TOEIC Listening Test, your examiner will have you listen to some short conversations taking place between two people. After each short conversation, you will be asked three questions about the conversation you have just heard. Each question will be asked verbally and will also be printed in your test booklet. Each question will have four possible responses, printed in your test booklet. You will need to select the best answer to each question, based on what you have heard.

For example, you may hear a conversation such as this:

(Man) I'm really looking forward to next week's sales meeting. I am completely prepared.
(Woman) Really? I still need to prepare my sales report. I had a hard time finding customers to interview.

(Man) I could help you. I was able to find lots of customers by conducting online questionnaires and polls.
(Woman) I tried to interview customers in person in stores and it really didn't work well.

You will then hear a question such as:

What seems to be the best way of interviewing customers, according to this conversation?

In your test booklet, you will see:

What seems to be the best way of interviewing customers, according to this conversation?
- **a.** By scheduling interviews
- **b.** In person
- **c.** Online
- **d.** Mailed polls

In this case, you would mark choice **c** on your answer sheet, since choice **c** is the correct answer. The man states, "I was able to find lots of customers by conducting online questionnaires and polls," suggesting online methods seem to work best. The woman clearly states, "I tried to interview customers in person in stores and it really didn't work well," so choice **b** is not correct. Scheduled interviews and mailed polls are not mentioned in the conversation, so choices **a** and **d** are incorrect.

You will hear each question in this portion of the test, so that you can listen to it. It will also be printed in your test booklet, so that you can examine it more closely. This may be helpful. When taking this portion of the test, keep track of which speaker makes which comments. This may be important, as in the following example:

You might hear:

(Woman) I think they should add a new walking trail near our place of business.

(Man) Actually, I was hoping that they would build a new parking garage nearby. I have trouble finding a spot for my car each day when I come to work.

(Woman) But if they built a walking or hiking trail, more people could come to work by riding bikes or by walking. It would be better for us and the environment.

(Man) Well, I live too far away to bike or walk. Anyway, I certainly wouldn't want to be using a trail in bad weather.

You may then hear a question such as:

What does the man think of the idea of a hiking trail near his place of work?

In your test booklet, you would see:

What does the man think of the idea of a hiking trail near his place of work?

    a. He loves the idea.

    b. He thinks it will help people stay fit and save the environment.

    c. He does not care for the idea.

    d. He is indifferent about the idea.

In this case, the correct answer is choice **c.** The man clearly does not care for having a walking trail nearby—he would rather have more parking spaces. It is the woman who likes the idea and thinks it would be a way to encourage fitness and less pollution, so choices **a** and **b** are not correct. The man has a definite opinion, so choice **d** is incorrect.

In this question, it is important to remember which speaker states which opinion in order to answer the question. When listening to the test, keep track of what each speaker says. Attributing the right ideas to the wrong speaker is still incorrect.

It may be helpful to think of each person as having a specific role. In the above example, for instance, you may think of the woman as a walker who wants a walking trail and the man as a driver who wants a parking lot. This will make it easier for you to remember which speaker holds which opinions.

Preparing for the Conversations Section of the TOEIC Listening Test

There are many ways to prepare for the conversations section of the TOEIC Listening Test. One great option is to review the sample questions at the end of this chapter and those in the appendix. Knowing what to expect is important, and trying sample questions helps you feel more confident about taking the short talks section of the test.

You can also enhance your confidence with spoken English in general. Listen to the spoken word as much as possible and take part in conversations yourself. If you are very comfortable with listening to spoken English, you will retain information more accurately when you hear it. Consider listening to audio books about subjects that interest you and discuss these books with colleagues or friends. This is a good way to build listening comprehension, which is the skill being tested in the conversations section of the TOEIC Listening Test. As well, you can ask two friends to have a short conversation and ask you basic comprehension questions about their conversation. This is a great way to build the exact skills you will need on the conversations section of the TOEIC Listening Test.

There are some specific challenges with the conversations section of the test for which you will want to prepare yourself:

- You will be listening to a longer stretch of dialogue and you will need to keep up with the conversation.
- You will hear each conversation only once.
- You will need to remember which speaker says what about each subject.
- You will need to understand and remember the conversation well enough to answer three questions about it.

There are many effective ways to overcome these challenges successfully. Plenty of practice will help you retain spoken information more effectively and will improve your listening comprehension skills. When taking the conversations section of the TOEIC Listening Test, listen carefully to the conversation. Your test booklets will have questions and answers printed for you, and this can help you jog your memory about the conversation you have just heard and can help provide you with important visual cues that can help you answer questions successfully.

Review: Tips for Success

- Practice with a friend if possible.
- Listen to plenty of spoken English before your test to become familiar with the spoken language.
- Listen to audio books or radio programs and discuss what you hear with friends and colleagues—this will help you improve understanding and memory.
- When taking the test and listening to a short talk, assign each speaker a role, so that you can keep speakers distinct.
- Use the visual cues in your test booklet to help you.

Part Four: Short Talks

This portion of the TOEIC Listening Test assesses your listening skills, memory, and reading comprehension. In this section of the TOEIC Listening Test, you will hear a short talk by a single speaker. After your examiner has played the audio portion of the test, you will need to answer three questions based on each short talk. You will need to mark the correct answer on your answer sheet. Each short talk will be played only once and will not be printed in your test booklet.

For example, your examiner may play an audio selection such as this one during the test.

Hello, my name is Helen Paige and I am returning your call about our services. Here, at Smith Telephone Company, we offer several options that I think might suit your needs. One of our most popular phone packages includes fast Internet access, a land telephone line with an answering service, 10 hours of free long distance, and a basic cell phone package for just $100 a month. Another of our packages includes only a home phone service with five calling features, such as an answering service or conference calling, as well as 20 hours of free national long distance per month for just $40 a month. We offer free installation and competitive long distance rates to countries overseas. If you need a fax service, we can offer a dedicated fax line at your home for just $5 a month.

Then, your examiner would play the first question based on this short talk.

What is the main purpose of this talk?

In your test booklet, you would see the following:

What is the main purpose of this talk?
a. The speaker wants to describe how her company works.
b. The speaker is asking questions.
c. The speaker is returning a telephone call.
d. The speaker wants to apologize for a service interruption.

You will have to select the best answer, based on what you have heard. In this case, the correct answer is choice **c**, since the speaker says, "I am returning your call about our services." Although the speaker is describing the services her company offers, she is not describing how the company works, so choice **a** is incorrect. The speaker asks no questions, so choice **b** is not correct. The speaker does not mention a service interruption, so choice **d** is incorrect.

When answering this sort of short talk question, you will want to consider what the speaker is saying, but you will also want to consider in what context the short talk may be taking place. Where the short talk takes place can offer good clues that can help you answer questions. As well, some questions will ask specific questions about the context of a short talk. For example, you might hear something similar to the following short talk.

Attention passengers of Flight 345 to Boston. We are sorry to announce that your flight has been delayed due to poor visibility. As a snowstorm moves into our area, visibility on the tarmac has become poor and flight conditions have become dangerous. Currently, we are monitoring weather conditions carefully and we hope that we can have the flight on its way soon. In the event that the flight has to be delayed for some hours, we will be offering hospitality suites at the nearby airport hotel for travelers. Those travelers who wish to reschedule or rebook their flights are asked to proceed to the customer service desk. We will keep you updated as news about the weather conditions becomes available. Thank you for your continued patience.

Your examiner would then play a question such as this one for you to listen to:

Where would this speech most likely take place?
a. An airport
b. A train station
c. A bus station
d. A cruise ship

In this case, the correct answer is choice **a**. The speaker refers to "Flight 345 to Boston." Flights leave from airports. If this announcement were made in a train station, the speaker would refer to a train. If this announcement were made at a bus station, the

speaker might refer to a bus or bus number. If this announcement were made aboard a cruise ship, the speaker might refer to a port of call. For these reasons, choice **a** is the only possible correct answer.

Questions in the short talks section of the TOEIC Listening Test may come from a variety of sources. They might be seminars or business talks, announcements made in public places, announcements about changes, greetings in retail areas, and telephone messages. Some of the questions may ask you about the purpose of these talks as well as the context in which these talks take place.

Preparing for the Short Talks Section of the TOEIC Listening Test

When preparing for this section of the test, start by practicing with the test question samples at the end of this chapter and those at the end of this guide. You may also want to notice more carefully the short talks that take place around you. When an announcement is made somewhere in public, use this as an opportunity to practice. For example, if you are flying and the flight attendants go through a safety demonstration, listen carefully. If you are in a store and hear an announcement about the store's specials, listen. Each time you hear such a short speech, take the opportunity to compose in your mind a few basic statements about the announcement. What can you remember about the announcement when it is over? Listening to these announcements and thinking about them will hone your memory and comprehension skills and will also familiarize you with some of the types of short talks that may appear in your TOEIC Listening Test.

There are some specific challenges with the short talks section of the test that you will want to prepare yourself for.

- These talks tend to be longer than the spoken selections earlier in the test.
- These short talks tend to be from a variety of contexts.

- You may be asked about the context or reason for the talk, or you may be asked general comprehension questions about what is said.

When taking the short talks section of the test, consider the purpose and possible location of the short talks as you listen. If possible, review the test questions for the short talk before you listen to the audio segment. These questions can help you understand what you need to listen for. Finally, use the written cues in your test book. Your test booklet will have the printed version of each question as well as the possible answers. These cues can help you recall what you have listened to and can help you decide on the right answer.

Review: Tips for Success

- Practice with the sample questions in this book and by listening to announcements you hear in public.
- Use the text cues in your test booklet to help you.

Tips for the TOEIC Listening Test

The listening portion of the TOEIC test mostly examines your listening comprehension and your mastery of the spoken English language. However, you will also need to be able to analyze a photo, work quickly, and have a strong vocabulary and memory to succeed in this part of the test.

Many audio cues can help you when you take the TOEIC test:

- words that sound the same but have different meanings in different contexts
- words indicating time
- words indicating negation
- relationship clues

One thing you will need to consider when taking the test is that words you hear may sound the same but have different meanings. For example:

ad	advertisement
add	to perform addition
aid	to help
aide	a professional who acts as an assistant
err	to make an error
heir	a person who will inherit money or an estate
allowed	permitted
aloud	not silent, spoken out
ascent	a climb
assent	to concur or agree
caller	a person making a call (by shouting or on the telephone)
collar	an item worn around an animal's neck or a part of a shirt or jacket
cent	one penny
scent	an odor or aroma
sent	dispatched
sense	detection or one of the faculties (sense of smell or "I sense that we are not alone")
flour	an ingredient in cooking
flower	the bloom of a plant

You may wish to create your own list of homonyms and get to know some words that sound the same but have different meanings in different contexts. Create sentences using two homonyms, such as *The heir will err if he argues with his father*. This will help you see how the words have different meanings, depending on how they are used.

Since understanding time is an important part of listening comprehension, you will want to stay alert for words that indicate when things occur. When practicing for the TOEIC listening test, become familiar with these words:

before

when

already

as

after

once

then

next

following

while

prior

during

no later than

until

preceding

afterward

as soon as

and

When you see these words or hear them on the TOEIC test, take note. These words mark time and can help you understand what you are hearing. For example, imagine that you hear the following sentence during the TOEIC test: *When the accountant came home, he realized he had a meeting the following day.* To answer any questions based on this sentence successfully, you need to understand that the accountant arrived home first, then realized that he had a meeting the next day. Understanding the words on the list of time markers can help you understand sentences like this more effectively.

You may also want to be alert for words of negation on the TOEIC test. These include words such as:

not

nor

never

rarely

seldom

scarcely

no

nowhere

neither

barely

nothing

impossible

hardly

These words change the meaning of words around them. If you hear the phrase *I seldom drive a car*, the speaker is saying that he or she does not usually drive a car. However, if double negatives are used, such as *It's impossible to not like this movie*, the meaning is not negative. In the previous example, the speaker is saying that he does like this movie.

When taking the TOEIC test, many questions will be about relationships between things, ideas, or people. For example, in the photograph section of the test, you may see a photo such as this one in your test booklet.

You may be asked a question such as:

What is the girl with the barrette in her hair doing?
- **a.** She is showing that she is taller than the other girl.
- **b.** She is playing a game.
- **c.** She is asking a question.
- **d.** She is having fun.

In this case, the correct answer would be choice **a**, the girl is measuring height and showing, therefore, that she is taller. To answer this question correctly, however, you need to understand the relative relationship between the girls and you must have the vocabulary for comparisons (in this case, the word *taller* to describe the relationship).

LISTENING COMPREHENSION REVIEW

You may have to discuss the relationship between speakers in the conversations portion of the test. Knowing how to explain relationships or connections accurately is important. In the conversations section of the test, for example, you might hear a conversation such as:

> *(Man)* The president seems really upset today.
> *(Woman)* Yes, he has seemed grumpy ever since I joined the company, and that was three years ago.
> *(Man)* That's nothing. I have been in our HR department for six years and I have never seen him in a good mood.
> *(Woman)* At least our vice-president is really friendly.

You may then see the following question in your test booklet:

1. Who are the man and woman complaining about?
  a. The vice-president
  b. A coworker
  c. The president
  d. The accountant

In this case, the correct answer is choice **c.** To understand this answer, you must understand that the two speakers are coworkers in the same company, with the same president. They are complaining about an employer and stating that their vice-president is far less grumpy.

The best overall way to study for the listening portion of the TOEIC test is to listen to as much English as you can and to speak as much as possible with English speakers. This way, you will build your listening comprehension skills. Consider starting small conversations with colleagues or friends. Some libraries and community centers also have volunteers who work with students who are learning to speak English. These services are a great way to practice your listening skills. You can even bring this guide to your volunteer or tutor and ask him or her to test you on the specific question styles found on the TOEIC.

You will want to practice as much as possible, even when you are not with a volunteer or tutor. You can practice on your own by completing the practice questions in this book. For the photograph section of this test, practice by looking at photos and making short statements about the people, actions, items, and places in the photos. For the short talks section, practice by listening to announcements in public places. You can practice for all parts of the test by building your listening skills. You can do this by getting audio books from your local library, listening to podcasts online, and listening to news on the radio. The more you listen, the better your listening comprehension will be. If you are having trouble understanding the spoken word in audio books or on the news, look for simpler books or programs that you can understand more clearly.

Practice

Look at each photograph. Select the one statement that offers the best description of the photograph.

1.

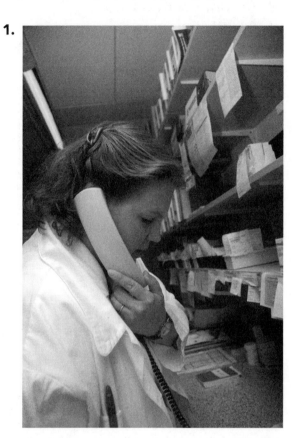

Now, listen to Track 133.

2.

Now, listen to Track 134.

3.

Now, listen to Track 135.

4.

Now, listen to Track 136.

5.

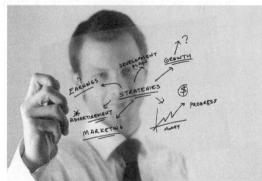

Now, listen to Track 137.

6.

Now, listen to Track 138.

7.

Now, listen to Track 139.

For these questions, you will hear a statement or question and three possible responses. You will select the best response, based on what you have heard.

8. Now, listen to Track 140.
Select the best response.

9. Now, listen to Track 141.
Select the best response.

10. Now, listen to Track 142.
Select the best response.

11. Now, listen to Track 143.
Select the best response.

12. Now, listen to Track 144.
Select the best response.

13. Now, listen to Track 145.
Select the best response.

*In the following questions, you will listen to short conversations between two people. After each conversation, you will be asked three questions about the conversations you have just heard. Choose **a**, **b**, **c**, or **d** for each question.*

Now, listen to Track 146.

14. **Now, listen to Track 147.**

How much do the speakers know about Caribbean food?

a. Both have researched it well.

b. Both have tried authentic food in the Caribbean.

c. Neither has tried it.

d. The woman has eaten Caribbean food.

15. **Now, listen to Track 148.**

What specific diet does the woman follow?

a. low-fat

b. diabetic

c. no sugar

d. vegetarian

16. **Now, listen to Track 149.**

Overall, how open are both speakers to trying new foods?

a. Both seem open to trying new things.

b. Both dislike trying new things.

c. The woman is open to trying new food, but the man is not.

d. The man is willing to try new food, but the woman is not.

Now, listen to Track 150.

17. **Now, listen to Track 151.**

What does the woman like to read?

a. romance novels

b. horror novels

c. biographies

d. uplifting nonfiction

18. **Now, listen to Track 152.**

What does the man like about the book he has just read?

a. It doesn't gloss over difficulties the main character experienced.

b. It is about French cooking and about buying a house in France.

c. It's set in France.

d. It's nonfiction and offers good practical suggestions.

19. **Now, listen to Track 153.**

What is the book the man read about?

a. a British man who sets up a new life in a foreign country

b. a romance a man has with a French woman

c. how to buy a house abroad

d. practical tips for starting over

In the following questions on the test, you will listen to a short talk by one speaker. After each short talk, you will have three questions to answer, based on what you have heard. On these practice questions, read each short talk. Then, select the best answer for each question.

Now, listen to Track 154.

20. **Now, listen to Track 155.**

What sort of novels does Emma Hardy write?

a. romance

b. horror

c. nonfiction

d. mystery

21. **Now, listen to Track 156.**

Where does this short talk take place?

a. at a bookstore

b. at a conference

c. at a book club

d. at a seminar

22. Now, listen to Track 157.

How would you best characterize this talk?

a. making an announcement

b. introducing someone who will speak

c. announcing a change

d. summarizing facts

Now, listen to Track 158.

23. Now, listen to Track 159.

Where is this announcement taking place?

a. a train station

b. a safety seminar

c. a ferry terminal

d. a cruise ship

24. Now, listen to Track 160.

What should passengers do in an emergency?

a. leave by an emergency exit, which is clearly marked

b. put on a life preserver

c. put on a life jacket

d. put on a life jacket and move to the closest emergency exit

25. Now, listen to Track 161.

What safety devices are provided?

a. life preservers and life jackets

b. whistles to signal for help

c. emergency exits

d. life rafts

Answers

1. d. The pharmacist is speaking on the phone. There is no way to tell from the picture whether the person has a medical condition, so choice **a** is incorrect. The picture shows the woman in a pharmacy, not a clothing store, so choice **b** is not correct. This woman looks like a pharmacist, and there is no way to tell from the picture whether she is a laboratory assistant, so choice **c** is incorrect.

2. a. The woman is pointing to something on the computer screen. Although the woman is smiling, she is not laughing and there is no way to tell whether a joke has been told, so choice **b** is incorrect. Although the man and woman might be studying or preparing a report, there is no way to determine this from the photo, so choices **c** and **d** are not correct.

3. b. The photo shows a group of people looking at documents. Although they may be preparing for a presentation, there is no way to determine this from the photograph, so choice **a** is incorrect. The group is looking at papers, not a newspaper or newsprint, so choice **c** is incorrect. A few people in the group are smiling and do not look worried, so choice **d** is incorrect.

4. a. The photo shows people waiting before a projector screen with the words "Company Seminar" on it. Since the group is waiting, this suggests that the seminar room has not been changed and the seminar will go ahead, which makes choices **b** and **c** incorrect. Choice **d** contains an irrelevant question, so choice **d** is incorrect.

5. c. The man is creating a map with possible strategies. He does not look worried, so choice **a** is not correct. Choice **b** contains an irrelevant question, so choice **b** is incorrect. There is no way to tell from the photograph whether the man is late for anything, so choice **d** is not correct.

6. d. These people are rushing. Although they may be late for a meeting or may be late because of specific reasons, there is no way to tell from the photograph whether the businesspeople are late for anything or why they might be late if they are in fact behind. Therefore, choices **a**, **b**, and **c** are incorrect.

7. a. The photo shows vegetables for sale at a market. The vegetables do not look spoiled, so choice **b** is not correct. While the statement "Vegetables help lower the risk of heart disease" is factually true, there is nothing in the photograph to suggest any information about heart health, so choice **c** is not correct. While the photo shows spicy peppers, the question "Is spicy food bad for you?" is not relevant to photograph, so choice **d** is incorrect.

8. c. This answer indicates a change to the trains. Choice **a** explains that there is no change in the washrooms, but the speaker of the question is asking specifically about train schedules, so choice **a** is not correct. Choice **b** is making a statement about flights out of an airport, which does not have anything to do with trains. Therefore, choice **b** is incorrect.

9. a. The statement elaborates on the first statement made. The speaker saying "Yes, I think white and blue go together well" is agreeing with the idea that the shirt and tie look good together. Choice **b** is an irrelevant statement and is not correct. Time is not relevant to the discussion about clothes, so choice **c** is not correct.

10. b. This answer offers a suggestion, which is what the question is asking for. Although choice **c** is also a suggestion, it is a suggestion about films, which are not relevant to the business discussion. Choice **a** contains an irrelevant question, so choice **a** is not the correct answer.

11. a. The statement disagrees with the original statement made and gives a reason. The first speaker says that the ride is too scary, but the speaker responding with choice **a** is disagreeing. Accountants are not relevant to amusement park rides, so choice **b** is not correct. While it may be a nice day, this does not have anything to do with a scary ride, so choice **c** is not correct.

12. a. "Tucson" is a place where a seminar may be held, which is what the question is asking. Both "three o'clock" and "next week" are answers about when a seminar may be held, so choice **b** and choice **c** are not correct.

13. b. The statement "Sure, I love pizza" indicates that the speaker is willing to go along with the suggestion to have lunch at an Italian restaurant. There is nothing complicated about the suggestion for lunch, so choice **a** is not correct. Although the idea of lunch includes buying lunch, the answer "Let's go ahead and buy it" is not the correct answer for a suggestion for lunch. Therefore, choice **c** is not correct.

14. c. The woman says "I don't really know much about Caribbean cuisine" and the man says "I've never tried it either." Both seem to know a little bit, but the man only says that it is spicy and offers vegetarian and meat dishes, suggesting they have done no extensive research. Therefore, choice **a** is not correct. Neither has tried the food, so choices **b** and **d** are not correct.

15. d. The woman says "I've been a vegetarian for five years." She does not mention a low-fat, no sugar, or diabetic diet, so choices **a**, **b**, and **c** are not correct.

16. a. The man says "I'd love to try that new Caribbean place" and the woman says, "I love to try new foods." Since both show an interest in trying a new cuisine, choices **b**, **c**, and **d** are not correct.

17. d. The woman says, "I like to read true stories that are uplifting and not about hardship." Although she likes the romantic aspect of the book the man has read, she does not say she likes romantic novels, so choice **a** is not correct. She does not mention horror novels or biographies at all, so choice **b** and choice **c** are not correct.

18. a. The man says, "what I really love about the book is that it does not focus too much on the romantic. It really shows the man's struggle to make a new life for himself." Although the book is about cooking and buying a house in France, the man does not say this is the best part of the book for him, so choices **b** and **c** are not correct. The man does not say the book mentions any practical suggestions, so choice **d** is not correct.

19. a. The man says, "It was the true story of a British man who lives in France for a year and starts a new life there." The man does not mention any romance the character has, so choice **b** is not correct. The book does not seem to contain any practical advice or tips, according to the man, so choices **c** and **d** are not correct.

20. b. The speaker says that Emma Hardy has "earned a reputation as one of the best horror writers in our community." Since the question asks specifically what sort of fiction Emma Hardy writes and she clearly does not write nonfiction, so choice **c** is not correct. Since the author does not seem to write romance or mystery, choices **a** and **d** are also incorrect.

21. c. The speaker says, "We are pleased to welcome author Emma Hardy here today to speak to our book club." While the book club may meet at a bookstore, we are not given this information from the short talk, so choice **a** is incorrect. Since this is clearly not a business conference or seminar, choices **b** and **d** are not correct.

22. b. The speaker describes the book club as welcoming the author. Although the speaker is announcing that Emma Hardy is about to speak, her main purpose is to introduce the author, so choice **a** is not correct. There is no change to the reading mentioned, so choice **c** is incorrect. While the speaker does summarize Emma Hardy's career, this is done only to introduce the author, so choice **d** is incorrect.

23. c. The speaker welcomes listeners to "the Halifax ferry." No mention of a train is made, so choice **a** is incorrect. While the announcement focuses on safety, this is clearly not a safety seminar as it relates only to ferry safety, so choice **b** is not correct. While a ferry is a type of boat, it is not a cruise ship, so choice **d** is incorrect.

24. d. The speaker says, "In the unlikely event of an accident, please remove life jackets from their storage places and put them on before proceeding to the nearest emergency exit." Choice **a** and choice **c** are not complete and are therefore incorrect. No mention is made of using a life preserver—the announcer only tells people where they are—so choice **b** is incorrect.

25. a. The speaker says, "life jackets are located in the bins above each seat" and "Life preservers are located near the life jackets." No mention is made of whistles or life rafts, so choices **b** and **d** are not correct. Although the speaker mentions emergency exits, these are ways of leaving the ferry; they are not life-saving devices. Therefore, choice **c** is incorrect.

5 ▶ READING COMPREHENSION REVIEW

The reading section of the TOEIC includes three separate parts:

- incomplete sentences
- text completion
- reading comprehension

Incomplete sentences consist of a single sentence with one blank. You will need to pick the correct word to complete the sentence. There are 40 of these questions.

Text completion consists of a short passage with three or four blanks. You will need to pick the correct word using the context or meaning of the paragraph. There are 12 of these questions.

Reading comprehension consists of a variety of single and double passages with reading comprehension questions following them. Sometimes, you will read a single passage. There are 28 questions that relate to single passages. In other cases, you will read two passages. There are 20 questions that relate to double passages.

You will have about 75 minutes to complete the entire reading section.

Types of Reading Materials

The TOEIC reading comprehension section has a large variety of reading passages. These may include, but are not limited to:

- newspaper articles
- letters
- e-mails
- advertisements
- coupons
- menus

The passages are similar to those that you would encounter in everyday life and the business world. When you read these passages, think about what they are mostly about. Don't try to remember all the information in a passage. You can go back and reread it after you have read the questions that are asked about it. Try to figure out what the reason was for the passage as well.

For example:

- newspapers are used to let people know what is going on
- letters and e-mails are used to communicate
- advertisements are used to let people know about a product, a store or restaurant, or a service
- coupons are used to provide a price break on products and services
- menus are used to let people know what a restaurant serves

Kinds of Questions

The next part of this chapter shows you the kinds of questions you will see on the TOEIC and how you can best prepare to answer them.

Incomplete Sentences

To answer an incomplete sentence question you will have to pick the correct choice by using your knowledge of verb forms, parts of speech, usage, and the context of the sentence.

Most of the questions will call for choosing a correct verb form. A good way to prepare for this kind of question is to review verb forms so you are familiar with the present, past, and future forms of verbs. Pay special attention to irregular verbs that do not follow the rules that regular verbs do. Review auxiliary or helping verbs. Remember to always check for the correct tense of the verb. Remember to check to see if the subject and verb agree.

Verb Form Questions

Here is an example of an incomplete sentence question that requires a correct verb form to complete it.

> **Example**
> The office _____ food at the company picnic next week.
> **a.** was providing
> **b.** will provide
> **c.** had provided
> **d.** were providing

The correct answer is choice **b.** The picnic is taking place next week, so the correct verb form needs to be in a future tense. This is the only future tense of the four possibilities.

Sometimes you need to choose the correct auxiliary or helping verb.

Example

The institute _____ founded two years ago on the principle of providing service to others.

a. is

b. been

c. was

d. were

The correct helping verb is **c**. It is in the past tense, since the action took place in the past. It is in a singular form, since *institute* is a singular noun; choice **a** is a singular form, but it is in the present tense, which is incorrect; choice **b** is an incorrect form of a helping verb and choice **d** is in a past tense, but is plural.

> When choosing the correct verb form, make sure to ask yourself:
>
> - Does the action take place in the present, future, or past? Then choose a verb that is in the same tense as when the action takes place.
> - Is the subject singular or plural? Then choose a verb that agrees with the singular or plural subject.
> - Is the helping verb in the correct tense? Does it agree with the subject?

Coordinating Conjunction Questions

Not all sentences are completed with verbs. Sometimes you will need to choose the correct coordinating conjunction to complete the sentence. To prepare for this kind of question, review the meanings of coordinating conjunctions.

Example

It was a bad year in terms of production, _____ our profits were still high.

a. for example

b. as a result

c. therefore

d. but

The correct answer is choice **d**. This conjunction expresses a contrast of one piece of information to another. Choice **a** is not correct because it suggests a continuation of choices thought. Choices **b** and **c** suggest a cause and effect relationship, but none exists.

> Use the context or meaning of the sentence and the meaning of the coordinating conjunction to choose the correct one. Substitute each conjunction for the blank and read the sentence. Ask yourself:
>
> - *Does this make sense?*
> - *Does this choice keep the meaning of the sentence the same or change its meaning?*

Adjective Questions

Sometimes you will need to pick the correct comparative form of an adjective. To prepare for this kind of question, review the comparative and superlative forms of adjectives. Remember that most comparative forms of adjectives are formed by adding *-er* to the end of the adjective, such as *nicer*, *prettier*, and *older*. Most superlative forms of adjectives are formed by adding *-est* to the end of the adjective, such as *nicest*, *prettiest*, and *oldest*.

The comparative form of longer adjectives is formed by adding *more* in front of the adjective, such as *more beautiful* and *more interesting*. The superlative form of these adjectives is formed by adding *most* in front of the adjective, such as *most beautiful* and *most interesting*.

Example

The position of director will go to the _____ candidate of the four who have applied.

a. goodest

b. better

c. best

d. good

The correct answer is choice **c**. This is the superlative form of the adjective *good*. The superlative form is called for here since the comparison is being made between more than two applicants. Choice **a** is an incorrect form of the superlative. There is no such word. Choice **b** is the comparative form and would be used when comparing two applicants, but not more. Choice **d** is not in a comparative form.

> When choosing a correct comparative form of an adjective, ask yourself:
>
> - *Are two things being compared?* If so, then use the comparative form of the adjective.
> - *Are more than two things being compared?* If so, use the superlative form of the adjective.

Context Questions

Often the best way to figure out which choice is correct is through the context, or meaning, of the sentence. To find out which answer choice is correct, substitute each one for the blank and ask yourself which one makes the most sense.

> **Example**
> Frank Schwarz was named _____ officer of the bank last week.
> **a.** latest
> **b.** only
> **c.** fine
> **d.** chief

The correct answer is choice **d**. If you substitute each word for the blank you will see that this is the one that makes the most sense. The phrase should read *chief officer*. There wouldn't be *latest officer* nor would there be *only officer*. *Fine* doesn't fit in with the context of the sentence, either.

> Always substitute each choice for the blank and make sure the word you choose makes sense in the context of the sentence.

Text Completion

Text completion includes a short passage, often a short letter or e-mail, with three or four blanks. Unlike the sentence completion, the blanks do not call for you to pick out the correct form of verbs. What you must do is pick out the word or phrase that makes the most sense. In order to do this, you need to understand the context of the paragraph as well as the meaning of the answer choices.

> The first thing to do when you see the text is to read through it completely and get an idea of what it is about. Then look at each blank and substitute each answer choice for the blank. Choose the one that makes the most sense.

> **Example**
> Dear Mr. Arnold:
> I am writing to thank you for your input at our last board meeting. You made some (1) _____ points about our upcoming fundraiser and I appreciate it. (2)_____, I thought perhaps you might be willing to join the committee that is working on organizing the race. With your background and (3) _____ you would be the ideal addition to this group. I look forward to hearing from you and I certainly do hope you will decide to join us. Meetings are each Tuesday from 5:30 to 7 P.M. You can reach me at 876-9021.
>
> Best wishes,
> Janet Hodges
> President
> Caring Kids, Inc.

1. **a.** careless
   b. funny
   c. important
   d. defeating

2. **a.** Because
   b. However
   c. Although
   d. As a result

3. **a.** future
   b. friends
   c. abilities
   d. hardships

For question 1, choice **c** is the correct answer. If you substitute *important* for the blank it makes sense. The other choices do not. Certainly the author of the letter wouldn't call Mr. Arnold's points *careless*. That would be an insult and that is not the purpose of the letter. Nor would she call them *funny* or *defeating*, since both would change the meaning to something negative, not positive.

For question 2, choice **d** is the correct answer. This conjunction makes sense when it is substituted for the blank. It suggests a cause and effect relationship, which exists here. The others do not make sense.

For question 3, choice **c** is the correct answer. This is the logical choice since it makes the most sense. It is unlikely that the author of the letter would mention Mr. Arnold's *future* or *friends*. Certainly she wouldn't mention his *hardships*.

Context Clues

Besides using the context of the e-mail, knowledge of what each word means is equally important. That is why it is important to increase your vocabulary. Reading helps you increase your vocabulary. So does figuring out the meaning from context clues.

Question 3 in the preceding example is a good example of using context clues to figure out which word should be used. As was stated in the feedback, the phrase *your background* is a context clue that the correct choice would mean something similar to *background*. That word is *abilities*. Look for context clues in sentences that surround the word in question.

Word Structure

There is another way you can figure out the meaning of a word. You can break it down into its parts.

For instance, *careless*, which is choice **a** in question 1, is made up of a stem, *care*, and a suffix, *-less*. If you know the meaning of *care* and know that the suffix *-less* means *without*, you can figure out that *careless* means *not caring*.

Here are a list of some common prefixes and suffixes. If you do not already know what each means, take a few minutes to become familiar with them.

COMMON PREFIXES		
PREFIX	**MEANING**	**EXAMPLE**
anti-	against	*antigravity*
co-	together	*cooperate*
dis-	not, opposite of	*dislike*
in-	into, within	*inside*
mis-	bad, wrong	*misguided*
non-	not	*nonbinding*
pre-	before, in front of	*preschool*
re-	again	*reopen*
sub-	under, below	*subway*
un-	not	*untie*

COMMON SUFFIXES		
SUFFIX	**MEANING**	**EXAMPLE**
-able	capable of, given to	envi*able*
-er	person or thing that performs an action	play*er*
-ful	full of	hope*ful*
-ion	action, process	content*ion*
-ly	in a certain way	slow*ly*
-less	without or not	effort*less*
-like	similar	child*like*
-ness	being that thing or way	happi*ness*
-ship	quality or state	steward*ship*
-ward	progress in a direction	down*ward*

Figure out the meaning of the word *hardships* from its parts.

Reading Comprehension

In this part of the test, you will be asked to read passages and then to answer questions. Sometimes two related passages are grouped together.

The kinds of questions that are asked vary. Some are easier than others. Some of the answers are found in the text. Other answers you have to figure out from the clues that are in the passages and from your own personal knowledge and experiences.

Here is a list of the kinds of questions that you will find in this section of the TOEIC. Each one requires a different skill to find an answer.

Main Idea Questions

To answer this kind of question, read through the entire passage. Figure out what it is mostly about. Distinguish between details that the passage includes and what it mostly talks about.

Purpose Questions

To answer this kind of question, figure out why the author wrote the passage. Determine what the passage is trying to tell you.

Detail Questions

Some questions will ask you about details in the passage. The best way to answer this kind of question is to look back in the text for the topic that is being asked about. You can use keywords. If a question is about how old an antique is, skim through the passage and locate where the keywords *old* and *antique* are located. Then you will find your answer.

Synonym Questions

Synonym questions ask you to find a word that is closest in meaning to a word in the passage. You can use context clues to figure out the meaning of the word. Then decide which word is closest in meaning. Another way to approach this question is to substitute each of the answer choices for the word and see which one makes the most sense.

Inference Questions

Inference questions will ask you to draw a conclusion based on the information in the passage and your own knowledge. You will need to look for evidence or clues and then decide the most likely answer based on what you know. These are usually the hardest questions to answer. You must make your most informed guess here.

Comparison Questions

Comparison questions are asked about two passages that are linked together. They may ask you to figure out what information is in one passage and not the other or how the passages compare. You need to read both passages carefully to determine the answers to these questions. You need to compare the two passages and what information they contain.

Example

When researching what to do for your next vacation, you may want to consider resorts that include food as well as room and amenities. The advantage of booking an all-inclusive resort is obvious: You will know just how much the trip will cost you up front and not after it is all over. The obvious disadvantage is that you will not be able to pick and choose where you dine, so sampling local fare will be limited. Since you have already paid for your meals, you will feel obliged to eat them.

Some of these resorts also include activities, such as the use of a golf course and tennis courts. Fewer include such activities as horseback riding, scuba diving, or deep sea fishing. These are items you will want to check out when making your plans.

Another amenity, that may or may not be included in the resort charge, is children's activities. Many resorts offer children's clubs, but some ask an additional charge for their use.

1. What is this article mainly about?
   a. considering staying at an all-inclusive resort
   b. the many amenities that resorts offer
   c. which resorts have programs for children
   d. why staying at an all-inclusive resort is a bad idea

This is a main idea question. To answer it you need to read through the entire article and decide what it talks about most. In this case, choice **a** is the correct answer. While the many amenities that resorts offer are mentioned in the article, this is not what it is mostly about. While children's activities are mentioned as offered by resorts, this is not what the article is mostly about. Choice **d** is incorrect as well. One disadvantage was mentioned, but, again, that was not the main idea of the article.

> When answering a main idea question, read through the article and find out what it talks about most. Rule out answer choices that are details in the passage. Look for the general topic of the passage.

2. Which activity will an all-inclusive resort most likely include?
   a. playing tennis
   b. children's activities
   c. scuba diving
   d. horseback riding

This is a detail question and it requires you to look back at the article to find the answer. If you read the article carefully you will see that tennis is among those activities most likely to be included. The article says that sometimes children's activities are included and sometimes they are not, so you can rule out this choice. The article also states that scuba diving and horseback riding are usually extra, so they can be eliminated also.

> The easiest way to find the information you need to answer a detail question is to skim the article and look for the key words. In this case you would skim for the following words: *tennis*, *children*, *scuba*, and *horseback*. Reread those parts of the passage and find your answer.

3. The word *sampling* in paragraph 1 sentence 3 of the article is closest in meaning to
   a. noticing
   b. thinking
   c. eating
   d. wanting

To figure out which choice is correct in this synonym question, look for context clues in the sentence containing the word and in the sentences before and after it. The sentence that *sampling* is in states, "The obvious disadvantage is that you will not be able to pick and choose where you dine, so sampling local fare will be limited." The mention of "where you dine" is a context clue. It suggests that *sampling* is the same as *eating*. If you substitute *eating* for *sampling*, the sentence still makes sense. If you substitute the other choices, they do not make sense.

> When looking for a synonym, check the sentence it is in and those around it for context clues. Choose the word you think is suggested by the clues. Then substitute the word and see whether the sentence still makes sense.

4. Why do you suppose that deep sea fishing is not included as a covered activity?
   a. It is more dangerous than covered activities.
   b. It isn't a group activity.
   c. It doesn't take place on the resort grounds.
   d. It is probably fairly expensive to do.

To answer this inference question, you need to find clues in the passage and then use your own experiences to come up with the answer. Sometimes it is useful to eliminate the wrong answers first. Choice **a** says that deep sea diving is more dangerous than covered activities. From what you know, does this statement make sense to you? Golf and tennis are covered activities. Are you less likely to get hurt while playing golf or tennis than going deep sea fishing? If you answered no, then you might want to eliminate choice **a**.

Choice **b** says it isn't a group activity. But is that true? Don't you go deep sea fishing with other people? This could mean that choice **b** is not the correct answer. Choice **c** might be considered, but the golf course might not be on the resort grounds either, so this makes this option incorrect.

The article says that most resorts do not cover such items as horseback riding, scuba diving, or deep sea fishing. This is a clue to the correct answer. What do all these have in common, you might ask yourself. They are all fairly expensive. Therefore, choice **d** is the most likely answer to the question.

> When looking for the answer to an inference question, look for clues in the text and use your own knowledge and experience to find the best answer. You probably can't be certain you are correct, but choose the answer that makes the most sense to you.

Next read the advertisement and then choose the answers to the questions that follow it.

Used Computer Equipment Sale

Up to 50% off: Week of July 7 to 14 only

All types of computers including Dell, Gateway, Apple, and others

Excellent condition at a fraction of usual cost

Call or visit today!

Computer Ace
234 Broadway
919-3456

Let us resolve your computer problems and needs! And don't forget—our special on upgrades runs through July 30

5. What is the purpose of the advertisement?
   a. to tell where the computer store is located
   b. to announce a sale of computer equipment
   c. to show that the store has a lot of computer equipment
   d. to explain how an upgrade is done

Choice **b** is the correct answer. This is the main purpose of the advertisement. Choice **c** is possible, but that is not the main reason for the advertisement. The advertisement does have the location of the store, but that is not the purpose for it. Choice **d** is not correct either. The advertisement does not explain how an upgrade is done.

6. Why does the advertisement mention Dell, Gateway, and Apple?
   a. to explain which computer company is best
   b. to suggest that brand name computers are commonplace
   c. to show that the store has popular brands
   d. to show that their computer equipment is expensive

To answer this inference question you need to use clues in the advertisement and your own experiences and knowledge. Choice **a** doesn't seem likely. There is no mention of which computer company is best. Choice **b** is also unlikely. That doesn't seem to be the reason for mentioning these computer companies. Choice **d** is not the best answer. Why would a computer store want to advertise that its equipment is expensive? Choice **c** seems to be the best answer. Logically, this is why the advertisement mentions brand names.

7. The word *fraction* in line 4 of the advertisement is closest in meaning to
   a. none
   b. most
   c. small part
   d. whole part

Choice **c** is the correct answer. This is the meaning of *fraction*. If you didn't know the meaning of the word, you could figure it out from the context of the sentence. Just substitute the other words and you will see that they don't make sense. Only choice **c** makes sense.

8. What happens at the end of July?
   a. The 50% sale is over.
   b. The store is going out of business.
   c. The special on upgrades is over.
   d. There will be no more computers left.

To answer this question, you need to look the advertisement over carefully. Look for the phrase *end of July* in the advertisement and see what it is linked to. Choice **c** is the correct answer. The others are not correct. Don't be fooled by choice **a**. That sale is only on from July 7 to 14.

Coupon
Buy One Get One Free
Amy's Tortilla Shop
Good for any taco or burrito
Offer runs through Friday, March 10
One coupon to a customer

Full line of Mexican fare served daily
Corner of Main and Broadway
230-8645
We deliver
Join Amy's Club and receive one taco free for five tacos purchased.

9. What is the main purpose of the coupon?
   a. to announce the start of Amy's Club
   b. to list the different kinds of tacos that the restaurant serves
   c. to tell how to telephone the restaurant
   d. to increase business by bringing more people in

Choice **d** is the correct answer. This is the main purpose of the coupon. Amy's Club is mentioned and the restaurant's phone number is mentioned, but neither one is the main purpose. While the coupon is for tacos, the different kinds are not listed, so choice **b** is also incorrect.

10. The word *fare* in line 7 of the coupon is closest in meaning to:

   a. sweets
   b. food
   c. pastries
   d. jewelry

The best answer is choice **b.** This word is closest in meaning to *fare.* Choice **a** is a kind of food, but it is too specific and that is the same problem with choice **c.** Choice **d** is incorrect. There is nothing in the coupon about Mexican jewelry.

11. What limitation does the coupon have?

   a. A customer cannot use the coupon on Fridays.
   b. A customer needs to buy two tacos to get one free burrito.
   c. A customer can only use one coupon at a time.
   d. A customer needs to be a member of Amy's Club to use the coupon.

The correct answer is choice **c.** If you read the coupon carefully, you will see that it says, "One to a customer," which means a customer can only use one coupon at a time. Choice **a** is not correct. The only mention of Friday is that of Friday, March 10, when the coupon offer runs out. Choice **b** is not what the coupon says. It is a *buy one get one free* offer, which means if you buy a taco or a burrito, you can get a second one free. There is no mention that choice **d** is correct either, even though Amy's Club was mentioned.

12. What is the benefit of being a member of Amy's Club?

   a. You get a free taco after you buy five.
   b. You get a free taco if you buy one.
   c. You get three coupons for free tacos.
   d. Your coupon will still be good after March 10.

The correct answer is choice **a.** The coupon says that if you become a member of Amy's Club, you will get a free taco after you buy five tacos. It does not say that you will get a free taco if you buy one. That is what the coupon offers. Choice **c** is not mentioned nor is choice **d** so they are both incorrect.

Hi Gary,

   I wanted to give you a heads-up on your next project and to say that I feel it will be a boon to our company. We need to be proactive when it comes to our goals, and I think this project is going to be a great success. I know that it requires you to move here temporarily, but that cannot be avoided.

   By the way, when you get to Mississippi you should take some time off to visit the wonderful car museum that is just down the street from our offices. I know you are a history buff and thought you might like to visit it. They have cars dating from the late 1800s, including a Stanley Steamer. Do you know that some of them could go as fast at 127 miles an hour? Of course they stopped making them, because the steam engines could blow up!

   Anyway, I look forward to seeing you again. I've enclosed a museum handout so you will know when they are open.

See you soon,
Harold

Come See Our "Horseless Carriages"
Largest collection in the state
Stanley Steamers to Model T Fords and more
Open Tuesday through Sunday
9 A.M. to 4 P.M. weekdays and Saturday
12 P.M. to 5 P.M. on Sunday
Admission: $8 adults; $6 senior citizens and students; $4 children between 12 and 6 years; under 6 free
High Ridge Antique Car Museum
707 Maple Drive
Jackson, Mississippi
601-6523

13. What is the main purpose for the letter?

    a. to tell Gary where the car museum is located

    b. to tell Gary what his next project will be

    c. to tell Gary that his project is approved

    d. to tell Gary that the car museum has a Stanley Steamer

Choice **c** is the most likely answer. This is why the letter was written. Harold does tell Gary where the car museum is located and that it has a Stanley Steamer, but neither one is the main purpose for the letter. Choice **b** is not correct since Harold does not tell Gary what his next project will be, only that it was approved.

14. Why does Harold tell Gary about the car museum?

    a. Gary likes history.

    b. Gary has an antique car.

    c. It is close to the office.

    d. Gary wants to buy an old car.

If you read the letter carefully, you will see that Harold says that he knows Gary is a history buff. This means he likes history, so the correct answer is choice **a.** We don't know whether he has an antique car or wants to buy an old car. These weren't mentioned, so they cannot be correct. Choice **c** is true, but not the reason that Harold tells Gary about the car museum.

15. Which day of the week is the museum open the shortest time?

    a. Saturday

    b. Sunday

    c. Monday

    d. Tuesday

Choice **b** is the correct answer. If you look carefully at the museum handout you will see that the museum is open only Tuesday through Sunday and that the hours are shortest on Sunday. Since the museum is closed on Mondays, Sunday is the correct answer.

16. Who pays the least amount for admission to the car museum?

    a. Students

    b. Children between six and twelve

    c. Senior citizens

    d. Adults

Choice **b** is the correct answer. To answer this question, simply look back and find the information in the museum handout. Find the section that talks about admission and you can see that children between six and twelve pay the least of those listed.

17. What information is found in the letter but not the handout?

    a. how much a ticket to the car museum costs

    b. the number of cars in the museum

    c. the location of the car museum

    d. how fast a Stanley Steamer could go

This is a comparison question. Choice **d** is the correct answer. This piece of information is only found in the letter, not the handout. Choice **a** is only found in the handout. Choice **b** is not found in either one. Choice **c** is mentioned in both, so it is not correct.

When answering a comparison question, look through both passages and find the information that the question asks about.

11th Annual Fur Ball
Held at the Civic Center
February 17th, 6 P.M. to 12 A.M.
Tickets: $50; Couples $100
Cocktails, three-course dinner, and dancing to the music of Watercolor
All proceeds benefit homeless dogs & cats at the county animal shelter. Live auction at 8:00 of an 18 × 24 framed color photograph of Honey, a rescued Great Dane, signed by renowned animal photographer Josh Flint. Silent auction from 6:30

until 10:00. For a list of items available or to reserve tickets, go to www.bestfurball.com.
Black Tie Optional
Let's all get dressed up and help those kitties and puppies!

From: Jcastelli@yahoo.com
To: Lhunter24@aol.com
Re: Fur Ball

Hi Linda,

You will never guess how successful this year's Fur Ball was. Thanks to a large turnout, many generous bids for auction items, and great organizers, some $4500 was cleared. This will be a great assistance to the shelter, which, as you know, has been suffering cutbacks lately due to less city funding.

I want to thank you personally for donating the photograph of Honey. This was a great draw and it brought in $550. It was a fine thing for you to do and we will be pleased to place your name on our Wall of Contributors for this past year.

Please drop by and say hello to all our residents as well as to me. We would all love to show you around.

Best wishes,

Joseph

18. What is the reason for the Fur Ball?
   a. to raise funds so that homeless dogs and cats can be vaccinated
   b. to get people who support the shelter together
   c. to raise funds for Honey, the rescued Great Dane
   d. to raise funds for an animal shelter

Choice **d** is the best answer. This is why the Fur Ball was to be held. Choice **a** is a possibility and perhaps some of the money will be used for that, but it is not the overall reason for the ball, so it is not the correct answer. People who support the shelter will be getting together, but that is not the real reason why the Fur Ball is taking place, so choice **c** is not correct either.

19. How can you find out what items will make up the silent auction?
   a. go online to the Fur Ball website
   b. buy a ticket since the items are printed on it
   c. check newspaper advertisements
   d. go to the Fur Ball

Choice **a** is the correct answer. This is what the advertisement advises people. None of the other choices is mentioned. Perhaps the items might be on a ticket, but perhaps not. Certainly you would find out what items were going to be auctioned off, but that is not what the advertisement says.

20. What is the e-mail mostly about?
   a. why the shelter is suffering
   b. the success of the Fur Ball
   c. how much the sale of Honey's photo brought in
   d. why the Fur Ball took place

Choice **b** is the correct answer. This is what the e-mail is mostly about. Although choices **a** and **c** are mentioned, they are details, not the main idea. Choice **d** is suggested, but it is not correct either.

21. What does Joseph probably do?
   a. He probably organized the Fur Ball.
   b. He is probably the director of the shelter.
   c. He is most likely a photographer.
   d. It is likely he is a dog trainer.

You need to use the clues in the e-mail to figure this answer out. The way Joseph talks about the shelter and his invitation to come and visit the animals and him suggest that he may work at the shelter, so choice **b** is the most reasonable. Choice **a** is unlikely. Generally events like fundraisers are organized by interested volunteers and, in fact, he thanks the organizers. Choice **c** is not at all likely. There is no mention of him being a photographer. Choice **d** may be true, but there is no evidence that it is.

22. What do you learn about the photo of Honey in the advertisement that you do not learn in the e-mail?
   a. that the photo was donated
   b. that shelter has had cutbacks
   c. who took the photo
   d. the amount the photo raised

Choice **c** is the correct answer. This bit of information was in the advertisement, but not in the e-mail. Choice **a** is only in the e-mail, as are choices **b** and **d**.

Tips for Taking the TOEIC Reading Test

To Prepare for the Reading Test

- Learn the meanings of suffixes and prefixes.
- Learn and recognize the parts of speech.
- Recognize correct verb usage.
- Review coordinating conjunctions.
- Review comparative and superlative forms of adjectives.
- Understand the kinds of passages that will be on the TOEIC.
- Understand the types of questions asked on the test.

To Complete Sentences and Paragraphs

- Substitute words for blanks to see which make the most sense.

- Choose the correct verb by looking for verb-subject agreement and appropriate tense.
- Use context to figure out which word belongs .

To Analyze Reading Passages

- Scan the reading passages for main ideas.
- Figure out why an author wrote a passage.
- Figure out what kind of question is being asked.
- Use key words to find answers to questions in passages.
- Use context clues to find synonyms of words.
- Locate clues in passages and use your own experiences to help you figure out the answers to inference questions.
- Eliminate wrong answers.

Practice

A word or phrase is missing in each of the sentences below. Four answer choices are given below each sentence. Select the best answer—a, b, c, or d—to complete the sentence.

1. When our company _____ started, it only had two employees, but now we have two hundred.
   a. was
   b. were
   c. is
   d. are

2. Our company _____ guidelines for training new employees and they are almost completed.
   a. to develop
   b. were developed
   c. will be developing
   d. is developing

3. She picked out the _____ printer they had since that was what her supervisor wanted.
a. most fastest
b. fastest
c. more fast
d. faster

4. The next opportunity for us to meet to discuss the development of new products _____ at the end of the month.
a. were
b. was being
c. will be
d. is being

5. The vice president of Human Resources wants to have _____ employee read through the company's new manual.
a. few
b. none
c. some
d. every

6. If we _____ our plans to the engineering department this afternoon, we will probably get a review of them by late tomorrow.
a. were submitting
b. is submitting
c. submit
d. was submitting

7. The college _____ holding a seminar today on new communication procedures that can be instituted by small businesses.
a. is
b. are
c. were
d. have

8. Management said that the officers cannot be present for the meeting _____ time constraints.
a. for example
b. until
c. because of
d. meanwhile

Read the text that follows. A word or phrase is missing in some of the sentences. Four answer choices are given below each of the sentences. Select the best answer—a, b, c, or d—to complete the text.

From: Van Nelson, Personnel Supervisor
To: Sally Andrews
Re: ID number
Dear Ms. Andrews,
I am sorry it has taken so long for you to get your company identification number. (9)_____we installed a new computer system that did not work properly, the entire process was slowed down. Now that you have it, you will be able to log onto our company's website and take the (10) _____ programs that I mentioned to you.

Make sure to complete each one, so you will be ready to start work on the fifteenth of this month. I know that your supervisor has many projects lined up for a person with your special (11) _____ and experiences, so it will be exciting to see how you tackle them.

Again, I am extremely happy that you will be joining our (12) _____. If you need any additional information please call on me.

9. a. Because
b. Although
c. However
d. Yet

10. a training
   b. careless
   c. expensive
   d. fortunate

11. a. appearances
   b. realities
   c. impulses
   d. talents

12. a. surveillance
   b. corporation
   c. coffers
   d. fraternity

In this part you will read a selection of texts, such as magazine and newspaper articles, letters, and advertisements. Each text is followed by several questions. Select the best answer—a, b, c, or d—for each question.

To: All Employees
From: HR
Re: Child Care

Great news! In response to all your requests, the company is planning to open child care facilities on the third floor. The location will be in the former Royalties Division space. Royalties is moving to a new, larger space on the fourth floor.

The target opening is set for the fifteenth of next month. All those who want to register a child must stop by HR and pick up the necessary forms. Have your doctor's office fill out the medical data form. The completed forms must be returned to HR before a child can attend. You will also need to fill out the information form so there will be a record of any emergency numbers that may be needed.

The facility will be open Monday through Friday, 7:30 A.M. to 5:30 P.M., and will be under the supervision of Celia Riverton, who has 22 years of child care experience.

If you have any questions, contact HR.

13. What is this e-mail mostly about?
   a. what forms parents need to fill out
   b. the age range of children who can go to the day care facility
   c. the opening of a day care facility
   d. when the day care facility will be opened

14. Why is the Royalties Division moving to the fourth floor?
   a. It is being shut down.
   b. It needs more space.
   c. The day care needs more space.
   d. The day care is opening.

15. Why might emergency numbers be needed?
   a. to contact a relative if something happens to a child
   b. to contact Human Resources when a child is sick
   c. to contact the employee's relatives in case of injury
   d. to contact the child's doctor

16. How much experience does Celia Riverton have?
   a. 3 years
   b. 4 years
   c. 15 years
   d. 22 years

Oceanic Restaurant

Overlooking the Picturesque Ocean Indoor— Outdoor seating

Soups and Chowders		Salads	
Lobster Bisque	$6	Tossed Salad	$4
New England Clam		Caesar Salad	$5
Chowder	$4	Greek Salad	$5
Onion Soup topped			
with cheese	$5		

Entrees		Desserts	
Grilled Swordfish	$17	Key Lime Pie	$4
with rice and		Chocolate Mousse	$5
asparagus		Parfait	$6
Fried Flounder	$14		
with French fries			
and cole slaw			
Fried Oysters	$15		
with French fries			
and green beans			
Broiled Scallops	$15		
with baked potato		Children's Menu	
and spinach		Available	

17. Which vegetable is served with the scallops?
  a. French fries
  b. Spinach
  c. Tossed salad
  d. Lobster bisque

18. What seems to be true about the fried seafood dishes?
  a. They both cost $14.
  b. They both come with French fries.
  c. They both come with green beans.
  d. They both come with salads.

19. What can you infer about the restaurant?
  a. It gives senior citizens a break in price.
  b. It only serves seafood entrees.
  c. It is more expensive to sit outdoors.
  d. Children are not allowed.

20. The word *picturesque* in line 2 is closest in meaning to
  a. rugged
  b. partial
  c. ugly
  d. lovely

From: fdaniels@Media.com
To: All Board Members
Re: Retreat

Hello, Everyone:

As president of the board, I am certain that our upcoming retreat will be a great time for us to assess our goals and to get to know each other better. I have heard on great authority that the 5 Circle Dude Ranch is a perfect spot for our retreat since the atmosphere is so unlike what we are used to.

I want to remind you to pack clothes that are suitable for riding horses and herding cattle. We will be sleeping in sleeping bags outside as well. That will be something new for me and for you, too, I suppose.

I understand that the experience is a very grounding one. Since we are for the most part living in our heads, this will indeed be a change. I am sure it will allow us to focus more on our ultimate goals rather than our individual concerns.

We are leaving promptly at 8 A.M. Thursday and will return Sunday evening. See you there! I'm attaching their ad. You might want to visit their website.

By the way, I'm bringing my cowboy hat.

Frank

5 Circle Dude Ranch
Ride like the cowboys do out on the range
Herd cattle
Sleep outside under the stars
Eat lunch and dinner from a chuck wagon
Find the inner you
You will never forget your time at our ranch
It's an experience of a lifetime
Visit us online at 5circleduderanch.com
Wyoming's Favorite Dude Ranch

21. Why does the board president say he is bringing his cowboy hat?
  a. to suggest he's gone to a dude ranch before
  b. to remind board members to bring their cowboy hats
  c. to let board members know they are expected to buy cowboy hats
  d. to show he is into the dude ranch experience

22. What does the president of the board hope will be accomplished at the retreat?
  a. board members will have more focus on the board's goals
  b. board members will learn how to herd cattle
  c. board members will learn to cook on an open fire
  d. board members will solve their personal concerns

23. What is the main purpose of the advertisement?
  a. to explain what the life of most cowboys is like
  b. to detail exactly what happens when staying at the ranch
  c. to suggest that the activities that the ranch offers are dangerous
  d. to attract people by portraying a stay at the ranch as special

24. Who is the dude ranch probably hoping to attract?
  a. people who love luxury vacations
  b. people who want a new experience
  c. people who rarely travel
  d. art students

25. What information is found in the advertisement but not in the e-mail?
  a. that they will sleep outside
  b. the location of the dude ranch
  c. that they will be riding horses
  d. that they will herd cattle

Answers

1. a. This is the correct helping verb. It is in the past tense, since the action took place in the past. Choice **b** is in the past tense, but it is a plural form when a singular form is needed. Choices **c** and **d** are both incorrect because they are in the present tense.

2. d. If you checked for tense, you would see a present tense is needed here, so choice **c** can be eliminated. Choice **b** can be eliminated as well, since it has a plural helping verb when a singular is needed. Choice **a** is an infinitive form of the verb, which is incorrect here.

3. b. This is the correct adjective. This is the superlative form, which is needed since the comparison is with three or more items. Choice **a** is an incorrect form of a superlative form. Both *most* and *fastest* are superlative forms, so they shouldn't be together. Choice **c** is an incorrect form of a comparative adjective. Choice **d** is the correct comparative form, but not the correct answer, since the superlative form is called for.

4. c. This verb is in a future tense, since the action is going to take place in the future. Choices **a** and **b** are incorrect. Choice **a** is a past tense while choice **b** is an incorrect verb form, as is choice **d**.

5. d. If you substitute each answer choice for the blank, you will find that the only choice that fits the context of the sentence is choice **d**. Choices **a** and **c** call for a plural form of *employee*. Choice **b** doesn't make sense.

6. c. This is the correct verb form. It is in a plural form and in the present tense since the action is in the present. Choice **a** is in an incorrect past tense, although it is a plural form. Choice **b** is in a singular tense, and choice **d** is incorrectly in a past tense.

7. a. This is the correct helping verb. You should realize this because the action is in the present. We can tell that from the statement that the seminar is today. Choice **b** is in a plural form and the subject is singular, so that cannot be correct. Choices **c** and **d** are past tenses so they are wrong.

8. c. This is the correct coordinating conjunction since it suggests a cause and effect relationship. It is also the only choice that makes sense in the sentence.

9. a. This is the connecting conjunction that makes sense. *Because* suggests a cause and effect relationship, which exists here. Because the new computer system didn't work properly, Ms. Andrews didn't get her ID number. If you substitute the other choices for the blank, they either do not make sense or they change the meaning.

10. a. Training programs make sense in the context of the e-mail. A person asking someone to take the company's programs would not call them *careless*. It is unlikely the writer would describe them as *expensive*, although their development may well have been that to the company. You might consider this choice, but compared to choice **a**, it is not as appropriate. Programs would not be called *fortunate*, so that choice is incorrect as well.

11. d. This word fits in with the rest of the phrase *and experiences*. If you substitute choice **a** for the blank, it doesn't make much sense in terms of the context of the e-mail. Choices **b** and **c** are equally unlikely.

12. b. This is the only word that fits into the context of the e-mail. Choices **a** and **d** don't make sense. Choice **c** would change the meaning of the e-mail, so it is incorrect.

13. c. This is what the e-mail is mostly about. The e-mail does talk about the forms that need to be filled out and when the day care facility will be opened, but these are details, not the main idea. Choice **b** is not mentioned in the e-mail.

14. b. Choice **a** is clearly wrong, since there is no mention of the Royalties Division being shut down. But choices **b**, **c**, and **d** should all be considered. Choice **c** isn't quite correct. The day care needs space, not more space, since it is just opening. Choice **d** could be correct, but the real reason that the Royalties Division is moving is that it needs more space. That is why the e-mail says it is moving to larger space. The fact that the day care is opening is really not related to the move, although it might have been.

15. a. This is probably why the emergency numbers are needed. Choice **b** doesn't make sense, since Human Resources has the emergency numbers. Choice **c** is incorrect because the emergency numbers aren't for the employees, but for the children. Choice **d** must be wrong too, since the doctor's number would most likely be on the medical form.

16. d. You can find the answer right in the e-mail if you look back and read it carefully. The other numbers are all mentioned in the e-mail, but they are not the number of years of experience that Celia Riverton has.

17. b. This vegetable is served with the scallops. Choice **a** is incorrect. While a tossed salad might be ordered to go with the scallops, it doesn't come with it. Choice **d** is not a vegetable.

18. b. They both are served with French fries. Choice **a** is not correct. The oysters are $15. Choice **c** is not correct, either. The flounder comes with green beans. There is no mention of either one coming with salads, so choice **d** is incorrect also.

19. b. Looking through the menu you find nothing but seafood entrees. There is no indication that choice **a** is correct, nor is there any mention that it is more expensive to sit outdoors. Choice **d** is incorrect. The menu says that a children's menu is available.

20. d. This word is the closest in meaning to *picturesque*. Choice **a** does not mean anything similar to *picturesque*, nor do *partial* or *ugly*.

21. d. This seems to be the most likely choice. There is nothing in the e-mail to suggest he's gone to a dude ranch before. There is information that suggests he's never been to this dude ranch and that he has never slept under the stars before. This comment might remind other board members to bring their cowboy hats, if they have them, but this is not the reason for the comment. There is no reason to believe that choice **c** is correct either.

22. a. This is what the board president writes in the e-mail. Choices **b** and **c** may happen, but that is not his goal. Choice **d** is exactly what the board president says he doesn't want board members to do.

23. d. It is the closest to the main purpose of the advertisement. Choice **a** can be eliminated. This is not the purpose of the advertisement. Choice **c** is not correct, either. Whether the activities could be dangerous is not mentioned in the advertisement. Choice **b** could be the correct answer. The advertisement does let people know what happens when staying at the ranch, but not everything that will happen. Choice **d** is a best answer. The main purpose is to attract people and portray the experience of staying at the ranch as special.

24. b. Choice **a** is unlikely because people who love luxury vacations may not want to sleep outdoors under the stars or eat out of a chuck wagon. Choice **c** seems unlikely as well, since this type of vacation seems to be more suitable to someone who has done a lot of traveling. There is no reason to believe that choice **d** is correct.

25. b. If you check back, you will see that choices **a**, **c**, and **d** are mentioned in both the advertisement and e-mail. The location of the dude ranch is found only in the advertisement, however.

6 ▶ SPEAKING REVIEW

The TOEIC Speaking Test consists of only 11 questions, and lasts about 20 minutes. This is the portion of the test in which you will show how well you are able to speak and share your ideas in English. Basically, you will be asked to respond orally to certain photographs and questions. Your responses will be recorded and scored. Do not worry if your spoken English is not perfect—this test was designed to assess the speaking abilities of a wide range of people. This chapter explains exactly what types of questions you will be asked, as well as how to approach each in order to earn the best possible score.

The TOEIC Speaking Test is designed to measure your ability to:

- speak English in a way that can be understood by proficient English speakers
- choose appropriate language for interacting with others in a variety of common situations
- create connected dialogue needed to communicate in daily life and at work

These three tasks build on each other. People who are able to successfully complete the third are likely to be able to complete the first and second as well. Think about it; if someone can create connected dialogue to communicate, they can most likely speak in a way that can be understood by others. The activities on the test build on each other in the same way. The first tasks you will complete measure the ability to speak clearly. As you progress through the activities, a greater proficiency with English will be required.

There are several types of questions on the TOEIC Speaking Test. The first will test pronunciation, intonation, and stress as you speak in English. Basically, this measures the way the speech sounds. *Pronunciation* refers to the ability to say each word correctly. *Intonation* and *stress* refer to the ability to use emphasis and pauses correctly, and to change the pitch of one's voice to show meaning. Each question following this will require the same skills, as well as a few more. By the end of the test, the questions measure the following skills:

> pronunciation
> intonation
> stress
> grammar
> vocabulary
> cohesion
> relevance of content
> completeness of content

The activities on the test are designed to determine the test takers' ability to communicate in English. The questions in the later part of the test will distinguish between moderately high-level speakers and those who are very high-level English speakers. These questions measure not only the ability to speak the words, but also the ability to use the language. These questions ask test takers to show how well they can choose appropriate words, and put these words together to express ideas. The following list shows the types of questions that are included on the test. It also shows how many of each type of question you will be given. Each type of question is discussed in detail later in this chapter.

- read a text aloud—2 questions
- describe a picture—1 question
- respond to questions—3 questions
- respond to questions using information provided—3 questions
- propose a solution—1 question
- express an opinion—1 question

The test does not require any previous knowledge of business, current events, or any other topic. You will only be tested on your ability to communicate in English. You will either be asked for your opinion, or will be given any information needed to answer the questions. Your responses will be assigned a score from zero through three, or zero through five, with three points or five points being the highest. The scores for each question will be totaled, and converted to a scaled score. Those earning the highest scores are able to create dialogue that makes sense and is appropriate for a work environment. They express their opinions, answer questions, and give information in a way that is highly understandable. Their use of grammar and vocabulary is accurate, and their pronunciation, stress, and intonation are consistently very easy to understand.

Taking the TOEIC Speaking Test is a great way to show your current level of English proficiency. It's also a great way to monitor your progress with the language. After taking the test, you can set your own goals for improving your speaking skills, and even get your employer involved in helping you further your ability to communicate in English. One of the best ways to ensure that you do your best on this test is to understand exactly what types of questions will be asked.

Read a Text Aloud

Two questions on the TOEIC Speaking Test will ask you to read a text aloud. As mentioned earlier, these questions evaluate **pronunciation**, **intonation**, and **stress** as you speak. You will be given two passages, each containing about 100 words. For each passage, the directions and the paragraphs will appear on the computer screen. The directions will be read aloud by a narrator. They will be similar to the directions below.

In this part of the test, you will read aloud the text on the screen. You will have 45 seconds to prepare. Then you will have 45 seconds to read the text aloud.

You will then be given 45 seconds to read the first passage to yourself. Then, the narrator will say, "Begin reading aloud now." You will read the passage aloud. As you read, your response will be recorded. You will receive two scores; one for pronunciation and one for intonation and stress. The highest score for each is three points. To receive the highest score for pronunciation, your speech must be highly intelligible, or easily understood. It does not have to be perfect. Minor lapses or influences of your native language will be acceptable. To receive the highest score for intonation and stress, you must emphasize words and phrases appropriately, use pauses effectively, and allow the pitch of your voice to rise and fall correctly.

The key to doing well on the Read a Text Aloud questions will be the 45-second preparation time. Use this time wisely. Read the passage quickly and carefully. As you review the passage, keep the following tips in mind to score well on each of the criteria.

Pronunciation

Look for any words you are unsure of, and do your best to figure out what they are. Here are a few ways to do this.

- Sound out the word. Focus on the first and last letter sounds, then try different vowel sounds in the middle of the word.
- Look at the rest of the sentence. Think about how that word would make sense.
- Look at the rest of the passage. Think about what words are related to the topic and would make sense in the paragraph.

If you get stuck, don't spend too long figuring out a single word. You only have 45 seconds. Be sure to give yourself time to read the entire passage at least once, in case there are other words you need to figure out. You can always come back to that tricky word after you've read the entire passage.

Intonation and Stress

As you read, think about how the sentences would sound if someone were speaking them. Is the message serious and sad? Is the message exciting? Make your voice reflect the feeling and tone of the passage. Also, pay attention to punctuation. Show enthusiasm when reading sentences that end with an exclamation point. Make your voice rise a little bit as you read the end of a question. Pause briefly when you see a comma or semicolon. Stop when there's a period.

As you read, think about the overall message of the passage. This way, you know what words and ideas are most important, and you will be able to emphasize key words as you read aloud.

Read aloud the following. Think about how you could best use intonation to reflect the meaning and feelings of each.

1. I could not believe that Mr. Sanchez fired everyone in the entire department!
2. Do you know who asked for an agenda from Friday afternoon's meeting?
3. Marla will be ordering new laptops, a DVD player, and four office chairs for the conference room.

4. Beginning immediately, all employees will earn two extra vacations days per month!
5. We regret to inform you that Mary, Lou, and Robert are no longer with the company.
6. Why did he say that?

As you read the sentences, you probably figured that the speaker in sentence number one was likely angry or surprised. The tone of your voice should reflect such feelings as you read this sentence aloud. You might also emphasize the word *entire*, since that is a key word in the sentence. It is a very important detail, and you should use your voice to point it out.

Sentences two and six ended with question marks. Read those aloud, as if you are asking someone these questions. Did your voice sound a little big higher at the end of the sentence? It should have.

How would you feel if you were able to share the news of sentence number four with your coworkers? You'd probably be excited to tell them something good like this. Be sure the tone of your voice indicates that what you are saying is very exciting, and is great news! Key words you might emphasize are *two extra*.

Sentences three and five are statements. Read these as if you are telling someone this information. Be sure to pause after each comma. When reading sentence number five it should be clear that *three* people (Mary, Lou, and Robert) have left the company. Without pausing effectively, the listener might think only *two* people left (Mary Lou and Robert).

Describe a Picture

One question on the TOEIC Speaking Test asks you to describe a picture. This question not only measures **pronunciation**, **intonation**, and **stress**, but also **grammar**, **vocabulary**, and **cohesion**. You will see the directions and the picture on the computer screen. The narrator will read aloud the directions, which will be similar to those below.

In this part of the test, you will describe the picture on your screen in as much detail as you can. You will have 30 seconds to prepare your response. Then you will have 45 seconds to speak about the picture.

After listening to the directions, you will be given 30 seconds to study the picture. Then, the narrator will say, "Begin speaking now." Your response will be recorded as you describe the picture. Your answer will be given a score from zero through three, with three points being the highest. To receive the full three points, you will need to:

- describe the main features of the picture
- speak in a way that is easily understood
- use vocabulary and sentence structure that express your ideas clearly

The key to doing well on this question is to tell as much as possible about the picture. Begin by describing the most important facts or details. Then, tell about the smaller, less important parts. As you study the picture, ask yourself questions such as:

- **Who** or **what** is the main focus of the picture?
- **What** is going on?
- **Where** is the person or object?
- **When** is the event taking place?
- **How** are the people completing the actions?

Not all the questions will fit for each picture, but they are a starting point for what you should think about as you plan your response.

Imagine that you are describing the picture to someone who is unable to see it. Think about what would be the most important things to tell this person about the picture. Add as many details as time allows. Don't stop talking until time runs out.

Let's try an example. Study the picture below. As you look at it, ask yourself the questions listed above. Think about what you will say.

is *who* or *what* the sentence is about; the **verb** is the action, or what the subject *is* or *does*. Make sure the subject and verb agree, or match. A singular subject needs a singular verb; a plural subject needs a plural verb.

> His **secretary talks** on the phone quite a bit.
> The other **secretaries** do not **talk** on the phone as much.

In the first sentence, a singular subject, *secretary*, is used. It agrees with the singular verb *talks*. In the second sentence, the plural subject, *secretaries*, agrees with the verb *talk*.

Verb tenses must be consistent throughout the response. That means that all the verbs in the same response must be in the past, or all must be in the present, or all must be in the future. Look at the following incorrect example.

> The woman **is getting** on a plane. She **went** on a business trip. She **will hold** her suitcase.

The verb *is getting* tells that the action is happening right now, in the present. *Went* indicates that the action already happened in the past. *Will hold* tells about an action that will happen later, in the future. For this response to be correct, all of the verbs must be in the same tense.

> The woman **is getting** on a plane. She **is going** on a business trip. She **is holding** her suitcase.

Vocabulary

Vocabulary refers to the words you use. A few hints for scoring well on vocabulary are listed below. These are true throughout the test, not just on this question.

Discuss the main idea, or most important information first. Then add details. Be sure to tell *who*, *what*, *where*, *when*, and *how*. Here is one way to describe the picture.

> A man and woman are gardening. They are smiling and having a good time as they work together. The woman is watering plants in a pot on a deck. The couple is outside and the pot is on the edge of the deck.

The key to doing well on this question is to tell as much relevant information as possible. As you study the picture and plan your response, keep the following tips in mind to meet the scoring criteria.

Grammar

Be sure to speak in complete sentences. Each sentence should have a subject and a verb. The **subject**

- Use words when you are sure of their meaning. If you are not absolutely sure of a word's meaning, choose another word.

- Use a variety of words, rather than repeating the same vocabulary. Ask yourself, *What other word could I use that has the same meaning?* Think about the following sentences: *I **work** five days each week. I go to **work** at 9:00 A.M. I enjoy my **work**.* These sentences repeat the word work several times. By using a variety of words with similar meanings, you could say: *I **work** five days each week. I go to the **office** at 9:00 A.M. I enjoy my **job**.*

- Use exact, accurate words. For example, rather than saying *animal*, say *dog*. Better yet, say *German shepherd*. Choose vocabulary that is as precise as possible.

Cohesion

Cohesion means that your dialogue is logical and consistent, or that the speaking makes sense as a whole. To score well in this area, stick to the topic. Make sure you focus on the main idea, and that your sentences fit together in a way that makes sense. Again, this applies throughout the test, not just on the question in which you describe a picture.

Respond to Questions

Three questions on the TOEIC Speaking Test will ask you to respond to questions. These will test the same areas as the previous question, as well as **relevance of content** and **completeness of content**. You will be asked three short questions about the same topic. You will have 15 seconds to respond to each of the first two questions, and 30 seconds to respond to the third. You will see the directions on the screen and hear them read aloud by a narrator. The directions will be similar to these:

In this part of the test, you will answer three questions. For each question, begin responding immediately after you hear a beep. No preparation time is provided. You will have 15 seconds to respond to Questions 4 and 5, and 30 seconds to respond to Question 6.

Next, the introduction and Question 4 will appear on the screen. The introduction will explain the scenario about which the questions will be asked. These will then be read aloud by the narrator, and you will hear a beep. As soon as you hear the beep, begin answering the question. Your response will be recorded. Keep in mind that although you were given time to prepare your answers to the previous questions, this time it is different. You will need to answer immediately following the beep. Remember, you only have 15 seconds, so be careful not to waste time. State your answer right away. After the 15 seconds have passed, Question 5 will appear on the screen and be read aloud by the narrator. Again, you will hear a beep and have 15 seconds to record your response. After that, Question 6 will appear on the screen and be read aloud by the narrator. You will hear a beep, and this time you will have 30 seconds to respond. Your answer will be recorded.

You will receive a score of zero through three for each answer. To receive the highest score, your response should be complete, relevant, and socially appropriate. The response should be easily understood, use appropriate vocabulary, and demonstrate acceptable English structure.

Let's try an example. Consider the following scenario, then state an answer to each question. Remember, you have 15 seconds to answer the first two questions, and 30 seconds to answer the third.

Suppose you are selected by a representative of your company's health insurance provider to complete a health and wellness survey. You have agreed to answer questions regarding your own exercise habits.

Question 1: How often do you exercise?

Question 2: What types of exercise or physical activities do you generally choose?

Question 3: Explain your reasons for choosing the types and amount of exercise you do.

Be sure your responses directly answer the questions. Stay focused on the topic. You have a short amount of time, so get right to the point. In order to help yourself stay on track, restate the topic of the question in the response. Possible responses to the preceding questions might include the following:

Question 1: *I exercise at least five days each week. I exercise for about 45 minutes on Monday, Wednesday, and Friday, and about an hour each day on the weekend.*

Question 2: *The exercises and physical activities I generally choose are things I can do with my family. We ride bikes together after dinner, and enjoy hiking and swimming when we are off of work and school. On rainy days, we put on music and dance around the house.*

Question 3: *The reason I choose these activities is that they are fun and allow me to spend time with my family. I used to go to the gym, but found that I got bored easily and hurried to get home. Now, we are involved in enough different types of activities that no one gets bored. Also, it teaches my kids good habits. They are developing an active, healthy lifestyle, and a love for exercise.*

The key to doing well on these questions will be answering questions appropriately with no preparation time. As you state your responses, keep in mind that the answers will be scored on relevance and completeness of content.

Relevance of Content

Responses to the questions asked on the TOEIC Speaking Test should be relevant. That means that the answer you give should have a logical connection to the question that is asked. The types of questions you will be asked will not require any studying, or ask you to recall facts. You will be asked to give information about yourself or situations in general. The information does not have to be true. It just needs to be a reasonable, logical response that relates to the question. Make sure that whatever you say clearly relates to the topic.

Completeness of Content

Responses to the questions asked on this test should be complete. Make sure that you give enough information to fully answer the question. Do not simply say yes or no. Answer in complete sentences that give plenty of information to satisfy the question, without straying from the topic.

Respond to Questions Using Provided Information

The next three questions on the TOEIC Speaking Test will ask you to use given information to respond to questions. These will test the same areas as the previous question. You will be given information to read that will include about 100 words, then you will be asked three short questions about the information. You will have 15 seconds to respond to each of the first two questions, and 30 seconds to respond to the third. You will see the directions on the screen and hear them read aloud by a narrator. The directions will be similar to these:

In this part of the test, you will answer three questions based on information provided. You will have 30 seconds to read the information before the questions begin. For each question, begin responding immediately after you hear a beep. No additional preparation time is provided. You will have 15 seconds to respond to Questions 7 and 8, and 30 seconds to respond to Question 9.

Next, the information will appear on the screen. You will have 30 seconds to study it, then you will hear the beginning of a telephone call, which will include questions about the information. The information will remain on the screen while you are answering the questions. After the caller's first question, you will hear a beep and have 15 seconds to respond. You will then hear a second question, followed by a beep. You will have 15 seconds to respond to this question. Then, you will hear a third question, followed by a beep. You will have 30 seconds to respond to this question.

As with the questions on the previous section of the test, you will receive a score of zero through three for each answer. To receive the highest score, your response should be complete, relevant, and socially appropriate. The response should be easily understood, use appropriate vocabulary, and demonstrate acceptable English structure.

Let's try an example. Read the following brochure, then answer each question. Remember, you have 15 seconds to answer each of the first two questions, and 30 seconds to answer the third.

The Parkside Inn and Suites
Winter Getaway Vacation Packages

Prices Effective January 4 through February 28

Family Fun in the Flurries Getaway (based on four guests) includes:

- Standard room
- Ice skate rental
- Continental breakfast

$139/night

Cocoa and Snow Getaway (based on four guests) includes:

- Two-bedroom suite with courtyard view
- Ice skate rental
- Continental breakfast
- Ski lift tickets
- Hot cocoa and cookies each evening

$189/night

Let it Snow Getaway (based on two guests) includes:

- One-bedroom suite with fireplace
- View of the snow-topped mountains
- Four-course dinner in our finest restaurant
- Wine and cheese tasting

$209/night

You will have 30 seconds to review the brochure. Then you will hear the following phone call:

Hello, I'm calling about the Winter Getaway vacation packages that are advertised on your website. I'm interested in booking a vacation, and was hoping you could give me some information.

Question 1: Could you tell me when these packages are available?

Question 2: What is included in your least expensive package?

Question 3: What differences are there in the packages that are available?

Be sure your responses directly answer the questions and are based only on the information given. As with the previous set of questions, stay focused on the question that was asked. You have a short amount of time, so get right to the point. In order to help yourself stay on track, restate the topic of the question in the response, and locate the answers in the text. Possible responses to the preceding questions might include the following:

Question 1: *Our Winter Getaway vacation packages are available from January 4 through February 28.*

Question 2: *Our least expensive package is our Family Fun in the Flurries Getaway, which is for a family of four and includes a standard room, ice skate rental, and continental breakfast for $139 per night.*

Question 3: *Our Cocoa and Snow Getaway is also for a family of four, and includes a two-bedroom suite with a courtyard view, ski lift tickets, and hot cocoa and cookies each evening in addition to what is included in the previous package. This costs $189 per night. Our Let it Snow Getaway is for two guests and includes a one-bedroom suite with fireplace and a view of the mountains, a four-course dinner in our finest restaurant, and a wine and cheese tasting for $209 per night.*

The key to doing well on these questions will be answering questions appropriately using the information given in the text. Do not make up information, or create your own answers to respond to these questions. Only use the facts that you see on the computer screen. As you state your responses, keep in mind that the answers will be scored on relevance and completeness of content, as were the previous set of questions.

Propose a Solution

The next question on the TOEIC Speaking Test will ask you to offer a solution to a problem. This question will test the same areas as the previous questions: **pronunciation**, **intonation**, **stress**, **grammar**, **vocabulary**, **cohesion**, **relevance of content**, and **completeness of content**. You will see the directions on the screen and hear them read aloud by a narrator. The directions will be similar to these:

In this part of the test, you be presented with a problem and asked to propose a solution. You will have 30 seconds to prepare. Then you will have 60 seconds to speak.

You will be told your role, and what types of information to include in your response. Then, you will hear a telephone message, which will last between 30 and 45 seconds. The caller will explain a problem he

or she is having, related to your company. You will suppose that you are the person receiving the message, and respond with your plan to solve the caller's problem. After hearing the message, you will have 30 seconds to prepare your response. Then, you will hear a prompt telling you to "Begin speaking now." You will have one minute to give your response, which will be recorded.

You will receive a score of zero through five for your response. To receive the highest score, your response should:

- be complete, easily understood, make sense, and remain on topic
- demonstrate your ability to take on the given role, and show that you understand the relationship between the caller and the employee responding to the message
- show that you clearly understood the situation, and offer an appropriate, detailed way to solve the problem
- include speech that is clear, uses effective vocabulary, and is paced appropriately

Your response does not have to be perfect; however, any mistakes should not interfere with the meaning of your solution to the problem.

Let's try an example. Read the phone message below. Respond as if you work at the dry cleaner. In your response, be sure to:

- show that you recognize the problem
- propose a way of dealing with the problem

Hi, this is Karina Roberts. I'm calling about a blouse you recently cleaned for me. When I picked up my dry cleaning yesterday, I was in a hurry and did not check the clothes very closely. This morning, when I was getting dressed for work, I pulled out one of the blouses. There is a stain on the front of my blouse that was not there when I dropped it off to be cleaned. There is no way the blouse can be worn in this condition. So, I decided to wear the green dress that was supposed to be cleaned at the same time, but it is not here. You've been cleaning my clothes for quite some time, and there's never been a problem. But, this time, a blouse was returned with a stain, and a dress is missing. I'd like to get this solved and continue using your services. Please let me know what I should do about the clothes. My number is 555-9462. Again, this is Karina Roberts. Thank you.

Remember, you have 30 seconds to think about what to say. Be sure your response indicates that you understand the problem and tells how you plan to solve it. Ask yourself:

- What is the problem?
- If I had this problem myself, how would I want it to be solved?
- If I worked at this company, what solution could I offer?

You have 60 seconds to state your response. That may sound like a lot of time, but you need to be sure the solution is given before time runs out. Do not rush your speech, but get to the point quickly. If time allows, you can add extra details after you have given solutions. A possible response to this scenario could be:

Hello, Ms. Roberts; this is Chris from the dry cleaners. We apologize for any inconvenience caused by the stain on your blouse and the missing dress. Let me assure you that we will these problems will be taken care of, so that you remain a satisfied customer. Please bring the blouse back, and we will clean it again, free of charge. Also, please provide a description of the green dress. We will look through all our other orders to be sure it did not accidentally end up

with someone else's clothes. Some of our clothing is cleaned off-site, and I will personally call that location to see if they still have the dress. If we cannot remove the stain on the blouse or locate the dress. We will reimburse you double their value. We appreciate our loyal customers, and will make sure that you remain satisfied with our services. When you come in with the blouse, please ask for me, Chris. I look forward to talking with you.

The key to doing well on these questions will be restating the problem and offering a reasonable, logical, detailed solution that directly relates to the problem. You cannot simply state, *I'm sorry. We'll fix the problem.* You must give a detailed explanation of *how* you will fix the problem.

As you give your response, keep in mind that the answer will be scored on how well you play the role you are given, and how well you understand the relationship between your role and the person who left the original message. Be respectful, speak slowly and clearly, and explain exactly how you plan to resolve the situation.

Express an Opinion

The final question on the TOEIC Speaking Test will ask you to express your opinion about a given topic. This question will also test the same areas as the previous questions: **pronunciation**, **intonation**, **stress**, **grammar**, **vocabulary**, **cohesion**, **relevance of content**, and **completeness of content**. You will see the directions on the screen and hear them read aloud by a narrator. The directions will be similar to these:

In this part of the test, you will give your opinion about a specific topic. Be sure to say as much as you can in the time allowed. You will have 15 seconds to prepare. Then you will have 60 seconds to speak.

Once you hear these directions, you will have 15 seconds to think about your response. Then, you will hear a prompt telling you to "Begin speaking now." You will have one minute to give your opinion, which will be recorded.

You will receive a score of zero through five for your response. To receive the highest score, your response should:

- clearly state your choice or opinion
- include details, information, or examples to support the opinion
- offer support that is logical, relevant, and clearly related to the opinion
- use speech that is clear and well-paced
- demonstrate understanding of the structure of the language
- use effective vocabulary

Minor errors are acceptable, as long as they do not interfere with the meaning of the response. Try stating your opinion about the following prompt. Read the prompt and think about your answer for about 15 seconds. Then, begin talking. Remember, you will have 60 seconds to respond.

> Some people prefer not to take a job that requires them to travel for business. What is your opinion about not accepting a job that requires business travel? Give reasons for your opinion.

To prepare for this question, ask yourself:

- How do I feel about this topic?
- Why do I feel that way?
- If I wanted to convince someone to agree with me, what would I say?
- What reasons or examples could be used to convince someone that my opinion is valid?

After considering these questions, restate the topic of the prompt and give your opinion at the very beginning of your response. Then, go on to offer examples. A possible response to the example prompt is given below.

I think it is fine to not accept a job offer that requires travel for business. One reason I think this is acceptable is that there are plenty of other job opportunities that do not require travel, and would be better suited for someone who does not want to be away from home. Accepting a job that requires travel could cause the person to not be happy, and he or she might not stay at the job very long. In this case, accepting the job would be unfair to the employer as well, because the company would have to replace the unhappy employee, and possibly spend a lot of time and money training the replacement. Another reason I believe it is fine to not accept a job that requires travel is that some people have personal reasons for being unable to be away from home. Family obligations, medical conditions, or other commitments might cause the person to need to be in town. Not everyone wants or is able to travel. I think it is acceptable to only consider job offers that are a good match to the employee's needs.

Keep in mind that an *opinion* is just that. It is what you think. There is no right or wrong answer. The key to doing well is to clearly state your opinion. Then, include plenty of reasons that explain why you have that belief. Make sure your reasons and examples are clearly related to the opinion you state. If the topic is one that you have mixed feelings about, quickly choose a side for the sake of the test. Then, only include details that support that belief.

Tips for This Section of the Test

As you prepare for the TOEIC Speaking Test, keep the following tips in mind.

- Don't worry about the information you will be asked about on the test. You will not be tested on your knowledge of business. It is not necessary to know any specialized or technical vocabulary. The words you are expected to know are those that you encounter in your everyday life and work experiences.
- Becoming familiar with the format of the test will help you become more comfortable on test day. Review the questions in this book, and get used to the types of activities you will be asked to complete. On test day, you can focus on the questions rather than the format.
- Speak and listen to English as much as possible. Read, watch TV shows and movies, listen to CDs and audio books, and practice speaking the language with your friends, family, and coworkers.
- Say as much as possible during the test. Try to keep talking until the allotted time runs out.
- Keep the directions in mind as you answer each question. One way to do this is to restate the main idea or topic of the prompt as the beginning of your response.
- Speak clearly and slowly enough that the person scoring the test will easily be able to understand your response. Be sure to pronounce the words distinctly. Remember to articulate each sound, and focus on the beginning and ending sounds of words.
- Record yourself reading aloud and talking in order to become more comfortable with this process. Listen carefully to the recording and critique yourself. Ask your friends to listen and offer suggestions or advice.
- If you are not already comfortable using a standard English-language computer keyboard, practice typing on one. This device is known as a QWERTY computer keyboard, because these are the first six letters displayed on the top row of keys.
- Ask questions. If you come across a word in a book or in conversation that you are unsure of, ask someone. The more comfortable you are with English, the better prepared you will feel for the test.

Practice

Read aloud the text given. You will have 45 seconds to prepare. Then you will have 45 seconds to read the text aloud. Use a stopwatch or clock to time yourself.

1. One of the most difficult aspects of beginning a new job may have little to do with the job requirements themselves. New employees often report that relationships with coworkers and being unfamiliar with office procedures are the biggest hurdles to overcome in the workplace. Obviously, it is important to build a professional relationship with colleagues. But, such relationships often take time to nurture. Maintaining a polite attitude and offering a friendly smile are easy ways to set the right tone with coworkers. Learning office procedures is often a matter of time as well. Employee manuals, observation, and asking colleagues for assistance are likely the best sources of this information.

2. Have you been considering new furniture for your home or office? Well, now is a great time to take advantage of the closeout prices at Seat Yourself Furniture! Our entire stock is on sale from now until the end of the month. We have executive desks, swivel chairs, and file cabinets for the workplace. We have sectionals, ottomans, and recliners for the living room. Whether your style is comfortable or elegant, casual or professional, we have the pieces to suit your life. Buy individual pieces, or buy the entire room. Either way, everything is on sale!

3. As the holidays are approaching, we would like to inform all employees of changes to the work schedule during the next few weeks. Beginning November 15, all employees will have the option of a four-day work week through the end of the year. Employees taking advantage of this opportunity will be expected to report to work one hour earlier than their current eight-hour daily schedule, and stay one hour later each day, Monday through Thursday. This will allow them to continue working 40 hours per week, while being able to take Fridays off. Employees choosing to continue with their current schedules may do so.

Describe the picture in as much detail as you can. You will have 30 seconds to prepare your response. Then you will have 45 seconds to speak about the picture. Use a stopwatch or clock to time yourself.

6.

4.

5.

7.

Read the text provided and then answer three questions about that text. No preparation time is allowed. You will have 15 seconds to respond to the first two questions, and 30 seconds to respond to the third. Use a stopwatch or clock to time yourself.

Imagine that a travel agency is conducting a survey. You have agreed to answer several questions about your travel habits.

8. How often do you travel, either for work or for pleasure?

9. What is your preferred method of travel?

10. Describe the best vacation you have taken for pleasure.

Imagine that a marketing firm is conducting research about how you receive the news. You have agreed to answer several questions about your preferred method of staying aware of current events.

11. How do you learn of current events and news?

12. What is your preferred method of getting the news?

13. Explain what you feel are the advantages and disadvantages of television news.

In this section, you will answer three questions based on information provided. You will have 30 seconds to read the information before the questions begin. For each question, begin responding immediately after you hear a beep. No additional preparation time is provided. You will have 15 seconds to respond to the first two questions, and 30 seconds to respond to the third.

Tri-State Insurance Carriers Annual Conference

Date: March 24

Schedule of Events

8:00 A.M.	Registration and Breakfast*
9:00 A.M.	Changing Trends in Insurance
10:00 A.M.	Increasing Sales OR Tips for New Agents
11:00 A.M.	Helping Customers Choose a Policy
12:00–1:30 P.M.	Lunch (Enjoy lunch on your own. A list of nearby restaurants is available at the registration tables.)
1:30 P.M.	Home and Auto Policies OR Health Policies
3:00 P.M.	Updates on Continuing Education Requirements
4:00–5:00 P.M.	Questions and general discussion (ending time is approximate, depending on the number of questions and length of discussion)

Registration Fees:

Individual Agents—$45 each

Groups of three or more—$35 each

*registration fees include breakfast

Hello, I'm calling about the insurance conference on March 24. I'm a new insurance agent, and was hoping you could give me some information about the conference.

14. Could you tell me what time the conference begins and how long it will last?

15. Will breakfast and lunch be provided?

16. I'm new to the insurance business. What sessions will be available that might be helpful for new agents selling health policies?

Washington Heights College
Course Schedule, Spring Semester

January 14–April 30

Fees: $145/semester hour

Fees due by second class meeting

Writing for Business I—Monday and Wednesday
6:30–9:00 P.M.

Instructor: Dr. J. Diaz

Classroom: 104 C

Writing for Business I—Tuesday and Thursday
5:00–7:30 P.M.
Instructor: K. Franklin
Classroom: 212 B

Writing for Business II—Monday and Thursday
6:30–9:00 P.M.
Instructor: A. Wong
Classroom: Auditorium A

Advertising and Marketing—Tuesday and Friday
7:00–9:30 P.M.
Instructor: Dr. J. Diaz
Classroom: 225 G

Advertising and Marketing II—Monday,
Wednesday, and Friday 5:00–6:45 P.M.
Instructor: Dr. B. Moffett
Classroom: 117 C

Accounting—Tuesday 3:00–8:00 P.M.
Instructor: M. Lopez
Classroom: 330 B

Hello, I'm calling about the classes being offered during the upcoming semester. Would you be able to give me some information?

17. Could you tell me what the costs of the classes are, and when fees are due?

18. I have enjoyed classes taught by Dr. Diaz in the past. What courses will he be teaching?

19. I need to be finished with classes no later than 8:00 each evening. Could you give me information about the classes that end by that time?

In this section, you will be presented with a problem and asked to propose a solution. You will have 30 seconds to prepare. Then you will have 60 seconds to speak.

20. Respond as if you work at the gas station with the car wash. In your response, be sure to:
- show that you recognize the problem
- propose a way of dealing with the problem

Now, listen to Track 162.

21. Respond as if you work at the delivery service. In your response, be sure to:
- show that you recognize the problem
- propose a way of dealing with the problem

Now, listen to Track 163.

22. Respond as if you work at the florist shop. In your response, be sure to:
- show that you recognize the problem
- propose a way of dealing with the problem

Now, listen to Track 164.

In this part of the test, you will give your opinion about a specific topic. Be sure to say as much as you can in the time allowed. You will have 15 seconds to prepare. Then you will have 60 seconds to speak.

23. Some people prefer to hire people they know to work in their offices. What is your opinion about bosses hiring friends and family to work for them? Give reasons for your opinion.

24. When it comes time to hire managers or supervisors, some companies hire a person from outside the company; others promote from within. What is your opinion about whether these positions should be offered to new people or current employees? Give reasons for your opinion.

25. Some people prefer to take a job that does not pay well, but does offer benefits such as health insurance and a retirement fund. What is your opinion about taking a job with a low salary that has good benefits? Give reasons for your opinion.

Answers

1. **Now, listen to Track 165.** Here is a list of some of the tougher words in the passage and how they should be pronounced:
   aspects—AS-pekts
   colleagues—KOL-leegs
   nurture—NUR-chur

2. **Now, listen to Track 166.** Here is a list of some of the tougher words in the passage and how they should be pronounced:
   furniture—FUR-ni-chur
   advantage—ad-VAN-tij
   executive—ex-EK-u-tiv
   swivel—SWIV—el

3. **Now, listen to Track 167.** Here is a list of some of the tougher words in the passage and how they should be pronounced:
   approaching—uh-PROACH-ing
   schedule—SKEH-jool
   option—OP-shun

4. Sample response: The salesman and the happy couple are sitting at a desk in the car dealership showroom. There are new car brochures on the table. The salesman is handing the keys to the woman. There is a silver car behind the couple.
   Now, listen to Track 168.

5. Sample response: Several children wearing costumes are on the stage. They are looking at the audience. The children are dressed as bears and other woodland creatures.
   Now, listen to Track 169.

6. Sample response: A female hairstylist is cutting a woman's hair. They are in a salon. The hairstylist is holding scissors, and the customer is wearing a black cape. A row of chairs and a shelf with bottles are in the background.
   Now, listen to Track 170.

7. Sample response: A smiling man wearing a gray suit is presenting at a meeting. He is holding a marker and standing beside an easel with graphs on it. Several people are sitting at a table listening to him. There are cups and papers on the table.
   Now, listen to Track 171.

8. Sample response: I travel for business an average of about four days each month. I take one two-week trip for pleasure each year, as well as several weekend getaways.
   Now, listen to Track 172.

9. Sample response: I prefer to fly on business trips in order to get there and back as quickly as possible. My family and I enjoy driving on pleasure trips.
   Now, listen to Track 173.

10. Sample response: The best pleasure trip we have taken was a Caribbean cruise. The trip lasted seven days, and we visited several beautiful islands. We enjoyed the beaches and snorkeling while in the islands. On the ship, we enjoyed the amazing food and stage shows each evening.
    Now, listen to Track 174.

11. Sample response: I read the newspaper before work. During the day, I often use the Internet to get updates on important news and current events. In the evening, I watch the news on TV.
    Now, listen to Track 175.

12. Sample response: I especially enjoy the newspaper because I can read it at my own pace, and select which articles interest me most.
    Now, listen to Track 176.

13. Sample response: One advantage of TV news is that it is constantly being updated. World events can be reported as soon as they happen, and emergencies can be announced in a timely manner. The disadvantages are that you have to sit through commercials, and you have to watch stories you might not be interested in while waiting for the stories you do want to see.
    Now, listen to Track 177.

14. Sample response: Registration begins at 8:00 A.M. and the conference is scheduled to end around 5:00 P.M., depending on the length of the discussion and questions in the final session.

Now, listen to Track 178.

15. Sample response: Breakfast will be provided, and attendees will be on their own for lunch. A list of nearby restaurants will be available at the registration tables so you can choose a place to eat.

Now, listen to Track 179.

16. Sample response: In the morning, you will be able to choose a session offering tips for new agents. In the afternoon, you can choose a session specializing in health policies. General sessions for everyone will discuss changing trends in the business, helping customers choose a policy, and continuing education requirements. These should be helpful to everyone.

Now, listen to Track 180.

17. Sample response: Classes cost $145 per semester hour. Fees are due by the second meeting of the class.

Now, listen to Track 181.

18. Sample response: This semester Dr. Diaz will be teaching Writing for Business I on Monday and Wednesday evenings, and Accounting and Marketing on Tuesday and Friday evenings.

Now, listen to Track 182.

19. Sample response: Writing for Business I is offered on Tuesdays and Thursdays from 5:00 to 7:30 P.M. Advertising and Marketing II is offered on Monday, Wednesday, and Friday evenings from 5:00 to 6:45 P.M. Also, Accounting is offered on Tuesdays from 3:00 to 8:00 P.M. The other classes are in session until at least 9:00.

Now, listen to Track 183.

20. Sample response: Hello Amar, my name is Logan. I am calling from the gas station and want to apologize for the inconvenience with our car wash last night. I know that must have been frustrating for you. Please stop by the gas station at your convenience, and we will provide you with a new code for the car wash. I would be glad to personally oversee the wash process to be sure the code works properly, and that you are pleased with the outcome when your car is finished. Also, we would like to give you coupons for three free supreme car washes at our station. We appreciate your business, and want to be sure your experience with us leaves you happy. When you stop by, ask for me, Logan, or our manager Terrell. We're looking forward to serving you. Thanks.

Now, listen to Track 184.

21. Sample response: Hi, Jannelle. This is Adrienne with the delivery service. Let me apologize for the delay in getting your package picked up. Rest assured, we guarantee our work, and will get your package to Los Angeles in plenty of time. I will send a representative to your office right now to pick up the package. If you have to leave before he gets there, let us know. We will have someone pick up the package from your home, or from any other location that is convenient for you. I have upgraded the status of your order, and am sending the package overnight at our expense. It will be in your Los Angeles office by 10:00 tomorrow morning, which will be more than 24 hours before the meeting. We would also like to offer to upgrade your next delivery to priority shipping, at no extra charge. Thank you for your business.

Now, listen to Track 185.

22. Sample response: Hello, Mr. Jones, this is Aimee from the florist shop. I am so sorry about the oversight with your order. Our computer went down yesterday morning, and unfortunately several orders were lost. I understand your frustration and will make sure that you, your wife, and your secretary are happy with our services. We are delivering your orders right now, and have added a coffee mug filled with chocolate to your secretary's plant. Also, we added an extra dozen roses and some orchids to your wife's vase. Since you have been a valued customer for so long, we had both of these addresses on file. Also, we would like you to come in and select a potted plant for your own office as our way of thanking you for your loyal business.

Now, listen to Track 186.

23. Sample response: I think it is a nice idea for bosses to hire their friends and family. It is important to be able to get along with the people you work with. Hiring people you already get along with ensures that this will happen. This can make for a happier work environment for everyone. Also, bosses want employees who are honest and trustworthy. When hiring strangers, it's hard to know that the employee has these traits. By hiring people they already know, bosses can make sure that they have employees who can be trusted. Another advantage of hiring familiar people is that the boss already knows the person's skills. The boss can select friends or family members that he believes are capable, and a good match for the job.

Now, listen to Track 187.

24. **Sample response:** I think it is better that current employees be offered positions as managers and supervisors, as long as someone from within the company is qualified. Offering these positions to employees is a way to reward loyalty. It encourages other employees to work hard so that they might be considered for upper level positions in the future. Also, current employees are already familiar with the way the company runs. They can continue current projects with less disruption. They also already know the other employees. Everyone is used to working together, and everyone knows the expectations. Hiring from within can make for a seamless transition.

Now, listen to Track 188.

25. Sample response: I think taking a job with low pay and good benefits is fine, if the benefits are important to the employee. The rising costs of health care today make insurance a valuable part of an employment package. It could be very expensive to purchase private insurance. Paying for insurance out of one's higher salary still might not provide the employee with much money left over. A low-paying job with benefits could actually give the employee more money in his pocket. Saving for the future is also important. A low-paying job with retirement benefits may provide security for the employee. It may also provide more money in the long run, so he or she has enough money to live on later in life.

Now, listen to Track 189.

CHAPTER 7 ▶ WRITING REVIEW

The Writing portion of the TOEIC test consists of eight writing tasks. Test takers have one hour to complete these tasks. In this chapter we look in-depth at the kinds of questions you can expect to see on the writing portion of the test, how to approach them, and how they will be scored. There are only three types of questions to practice on this portion of the test, but the tasks are complex and require practice. Some items will require planning, organization, and editing. You can improve your writing score substantially by taking time to practice with these writing tasks. This section of the test will ask you to:

- write sentences based on pictures
- respond to written requests
- write a well planned and organized opinion essay

This part of the test is administered on a computer; you must enter your answers using a standard, English-language keyboard. This is also called a QWERTY keyboard. It is a good idea to practice typing on a QWERTY keyboard if you are not already used to it.

Writing Sentences Based on Pictures

The first five questions on the writing test ask you to write complex sentences. Responses to these questions should be one sentence long. You have eight minutes to complete the five questions. As in other TOEIC questions, you will look at a picture and describe it. Printed below the picture you will see a pair of words or phrases that you must incorporate into your sentence. It often stretches your grammar skills and vocabulary to express the complex relationships that piece together the three required components into a single sentence.

The pictures usually deal with situations that an adult professional might encounter in the course of a typical week. They often show scenes from business, transportation, travel, recreation, or community events. At least one of the words or phrases that you are given is usually a straightforward word, like a noun, verb, or adjective. As long as you know what this word means, you can usually use it fairly easily in a sentence that has some relevance to the picture. The other word is sometimes more complicated. It is often a preposition, a conjunction, or a continuative; it often calls for complex grammar and suggests complex relationships. You may change the forms of the words and the order of the words as necessary.

A question on this portion of the test will look like this:

after, pay for

An ideal response to the Write a Sentence Based on a Picture questions is grammatically perfect, is relevant to the picture, contains both of the words or phrases, and is exactly one sentence long. An answer that meets these criteria will receive a score of three on a scale of zero to three. To score a three on this part of the test, you must be comfortable with complex sentence structures. You should practice joining sentences with conjunctions, writing sentences with subordinate clauses, and expressing complex ideas like causality or conditionality. Often, when speaking a second language, people tend to simplify their grammar and avoid complex ideas and relationships. To prepare for this type of question, practice expressing complex ideas and using complex grammar.

A score-three response to the above question might read like this:

> After the woman finishes paying for her groceries, the checker can help the next person in line.

Or this:

> The woman will pay for the groceries after the checker finishes scanning all the items.

Use the following checklist to see if your answer can score a three:

Checklist for a Perfect Response
- ☐ The answer consists of ONE complete sentence.
- ☐ The answer contains NO grammatical errors.
- ☐ The answer is relevant to the picture.
- ☐ The answer uses BOTH key words (or phrases) correctly.

If you can't fit both words into a single sentence that is relevant to the picture, then try to do it in two sentences. You can still get a score of two if you write more than one sentence or have minor grammatical errors that don't interfere with the meaning of the sentence. As long as what you write is grammatically comprehensible, relevant to the picture, and contains both key words, you will usually score a two. There is an advantage to aiming for a two: unless you can make three-point sentences easily and quickly, you might aim for a two to begin with, so that you don't waste time on the test. Then, if you have time left over on the section, you can go back and refine your answer into a response that could score a three.

A score-two response to the above question might read like this:

> The woman is going to pay for her groceries at the supermarket. After that she will drive home.

Or this:

> After she finished shopping, the woman pay for her food.

The first example above would not receive three points because it includes two sentences rather than a single sentence. The second example does not use correct grammar. The word *paid* should be used rather than *pay*. To receive a score of three, it would need to state, *After she finished shopping, the woman paid for her food.*

You will score one point for a minimal response to this kind of question. A response with grammatical errors that make the sentence difficult to understand, a response that that is not related to the picture, or a response that leaves out one or both of the key words will usually score a one. A blank response, nonsense response, or response in a foreign language will score a zero.

A score-one response to the above question might read like this:

> She is paying for food in the store.

Or this:

> She to pay for the food and after went home.

Or this:

> The lady likes pineapple.

The first of the three preceding responses does not include the word *after*. The second is difficult to understand. It could read *She had to pay for the food, and went home after that.* The third does not use either of the key words.

Remember that you can move back and forward between the five questions in this section during the eight minutes you have to complete them. On the screen you will see the word NEXT and the word BACK; you can click on these to move between questions.

What to Study for Success on the Write a Sentence Based on a Picture Questions

- business-related vocabulary
- vocabulary related everyday life and activities
- conjunctions for combining sentences
- subordinate clauses
- conditional statements

Respond to a Written Request

There are two questions on the writing portion of the test that will ask you to respond to a written request. You will have 10 minutes to complete each question, so this part of the test will take a total of 20 minutes. The prompts for this section will be written as letters or e-mails, usually e-mails, that ask you to give information or instructions, or answer questions. Below

each letter or e-mail, you will find specific directions telling you exactly what to include in your response. These directions will vary, based on the task, but will generally tell you what the content of your response should be and how many details you must include. Read the specific directions for each task carefully to make sure you are giving the scorer exactly what he or she is looking for.

Respond to a Written Request Questions are scored on:

- organization
- logical and structural fluidity
- appropriateness to audience
- grammar and vocabulary
- quality and variety of sentences
- following directions

Time Management

A good answer to this type of question does not necessarily need to be long, probably four to eight sentences will suffice, but the response must be clear and organized. A big part of your score on these questions reflects the organization of your response. To write an organized response, you should consider the advantages of taking a minute or two for some quick prewriting. Before you begin to compose the response, figure out what the content of your response will be; that is, decide what two or three pieces of information, questions, or instructions you plan to give. As you draft, you can worry about how the response flows together. Once you know what you want to say, then it will be easier to focus on the conventions of writing. Thinking before you write will help you write a better, more organized response and manage your time.

Once you know what the content of your letter or e-mail will be, then compose the best draft containing the information that you can. You can always go back and add pleasantries or edit for word choice, if you have time. Strive for a first draft that uses good grammar, acknowledges your audience, and has logical and grammatical fluidity. Make sure that the composition is in the proper format for a letter or e-mail. But foremost, try to make your overall meaning clear, and be sure that you have answered all parts of the question.

If you have time to go back after composing, look for details. Consider using a different choice of words to make your meaning clearer. Consider adding or editing the words and phrases that join sentences together and make the ideas fluid (such as *furthermore, also, meanwhile, in addition*). You may also wish to add pleasantries and personality to your response, perhaps by thanking the sender for valuing your advice or input, or even wishing him or her a nice day. In the final minutes before your time expires for the question, add finishing touches and give the letter or e-mail a final edit. Remember that you will be composing this response on a keyboard, so it will be easy to go back and make minor changes to your work.

Tips for Managing Your Time on the Respond to a Written Request questions:

1. Think before you write. Decide on the content of your message before you begin writing, then you can focus on style and cohesion.
2. Write the best draft that you can. Focus on spelling, grammar, connection between ideas, and appropriateness for the audience.
3. Go back and edit if you have time. Use your remaining time to edit for word choice, add connecting words or phrases for fluidity, and add pleasantries and personality.

Scoring Criteria

Aside from following the directions and including everything that the prompt asks for, the most important criterion for scoring is the **organization and fluidity** of your response. The response should have a logical flow of ideas. Sentences and ideas should be connected with appropriate connecting words like *but, because, therefore, meanwhile, even though, also, in contrast,* and *furthermore*. These words help clarify the relationship between ideas and create cohesion in the composition as a whole. Familiarizing yourself with connecting words and practicing using them will help you write a fluid composition. Organizational logic can also be expressed simply by saying things in an order that makes sense. For example, if you had to write about the pros and cons of living in a certain city, you could create organization by breaking your response into two short paragraphs, the first listing the pros and the second listing the cons. This makes the information easier to read and helps the reader organize ideas in his own mind.

The response is scored, in part, on its **appropriateness to the audience.** You need to consider who will be reading the composition in the context of the given scenario. The tone should be appropriate to the situation, so if the subject is formal, you should use formal language, and if the subject is informal, you can be more casual. When you speak or write in different ways for different audiences it is called using the proper register. You would probably not begin an e-mail to your boss in which you were asked to report on sales figures with *Hey, man how's it going?* Likewise, you would not write back to a neighbor organizing a block party as if he were a royal ambassador. You can often gain points in this category by being polite and courteous, including appropriate titles, thanking the person for his or her time, or including commentary about the task that he or she is trying to carry out with this correspondence. For example, if the correspondence is with a customer, you should address the customer formally and remind him that you appreciate his business.

The scorer for this exam will also be looking at the **quality and variety of the sentences** you use. A string of short, choppy sentences, even if they are grammatically perfect, may indicate to your scorer that you are not able to express complex ideas or use complex grammatical structures. It is better to take a risk and use challenging sentence structures than to take the safe, simple, and easy route. For example, instead of writing, *I like living in Santa Rosa. The streets are clean. The climate is pleasant. The people are friendly*, you could combine these ideas into a single compound sentence such as:

> I like living in Santa Rosa because the streets are clean, the climate is pleasant, and the people are friendly.

The preceding sentence demonstrates a more complex understanding of and proficiency in English. You can still make a perfect score with a few minor grammatical errors that do not interfere with the meaning, so it is worth taking the risk on a more difficult sentence structure.

All these characteristics should combine to create a short composition that is **clear**, straightforward in meaning, and **addresses all parts of the prompt**. Be sure to read your directions carefully and include everything that they specify. Including everything required by the prompt in a clear way is the single most important thing you can do to score well on this part of the test. All other criteria are secondary to this crucial element of your response.

Sample Question and How to Approach It

STEP 1: Read the full question and directions. (Also, set a timer for practice questions.)

A Respond to a Written Request question might read something like this:

To: All Tenants of the Spring Falls Apartment Complex
From: Apartment Management
Re: Fall Maintenance
Sent: October 18, 2009, 5:45 P.M.

Hello, Spring Falls Tenants!

With the cold weather approaching, we need to make sure that all the building's systems and structures are in top condition for the winter season. So, two weeks from today, we have scheduled a full maintenance crew to come and make major or minor repairs to all our apartment units. Please send me a full list of any systems or structures in your unit that are in need of repair. Remember that even the most minor problems can build up, especially during the winter months, so please reply in the next three days with a full list of repairs that need to be made in your apartment. We take great pride in our building and want to ensure that it remains sound. Thank you for your prompt response.

Below this e-mail message, are the specific instructions:

Directions: Read the e-mail. Imagine that you live in Spring Falls Apartment Complex and write back to the apartment management with a list of repairs that your apartment needs. Please include at least THREE requests for repairs.

STEP 2: Determine what the response requires and write it down. This is your prewriting/planning, and it should be done quickly.

Here you might write:

Required: A list of 3 home repairs

1. leaking pipe or dripping faucet
2. cracked drywall
3. unlevel door

STEP 3: Compose the response. In the example here, when the word choice or grammar is tricky, the writer includes an asterisk (*) to remind himself to go back and check it. You might use another notation.

Here is a draft of the composition:

Dear Apartment Manager,

Thank you for being so thoughtful* about the maintenance of our complex. I have a few repairs that the maintenance crew is to* make to my apartment. I have a faucet in the master bathroom dripping.* I also have a door that is unlevel and does not close completely. I also have a small crack in the drywall above the entry. These are minor repairs, but they* will maybe get worse when you don't fix them immediately.*

Sincerely,
Fred Jones

STEP 4: Edit the composition with your remaining time and correct the places that you noted. Also add details and pleasantries and vary the sentence structure.

After editing, the response might read:

Dear Apartment Manager,

Thank you for being so diligent about the maintenance of our complex. There are a few repairs that the maintenance crew could make to my apartment, number 201. I have a faucet in the master bathroom that drips. While this is not a big problem for me, it does waste water. Also, the door to the bedroom does not close completely and needs to be leveled. There is a small crack in the drywall above the front door, as well. These are minor repairs and none of the problems interferes with my comfort, but they could get worse if they are not attended to

soon. I appreciate the notice and the excellent condition of our complex.

Thank you again,
Fred Jones

How the Response Is Scored

A perfect response on this kind of question will score a four on a scale of zero to four. It will:

- address all the tasks required by the prompt
- have organizational logic and fluidity
- have an appropriate tone and register
- have high quality, varied sentences
- will contain only minor, if any, grammatical errors

The final version of the above response would probably score a four.

A response will score a three if it is mostly successful, but doesn't completely address one of the tasks required by the prompt. A score-three response typically shows some logical coherence and some awareness of the audience. It may have a few notable grammar errors and may contain a sentence in which grammar errors interfere with meaning. The unedited version of the preceding response above might score a three.

A typical score-two response is unsuccessful or incomplete in addressing two or more of the required tasks. It may lack connections between ideas, or the connections may be difficult to understand. This level of response often doesn't show awareness of the audience and may have severe grammatical errors in more than one sentence.

A score-one response is relevant to the topic in some way, but doesn't clearly address the tasks required in the prompt. It has frequent and serious grammar errors that make it difficult to understand.

A score-zero response is usually a nonsense answer, is written in another language, or shows no understanding of the topic.

Write an Opinion Essay

The final question on the writing portion of the TOEIC test asks you to write a well-organized opinion essay that contains support for the opinion expressed. You have 30 minutes to plan and write this essay. The prompts for this section are open-ended and allow for a wide variety of responses. A good response will consist of several paragraphs, probably three to five, and will provide evidence that your opinion is solid and well-grounded.

The Format of a Standard Opinion Essay

The format of an opinion essay is very stylized and standardized. In the United States and many parts of the world, children begin writing this type of essay in middle school and continue with the same format through college. A very talented writer can stray from the standard format and still write a successful opinion essay, but for most people it is a good idea to stick to the following template. It will serve as a good guide to help you think deeply about the topic, examine the source of your own opinions, and organize your writing. The standard format divides the essay into the following three parts: a one-paragraph introduction, a one- to four-paragraph body, and a single-paragraph conclusion. Understanding and practicing with this essay format will help you succeed on the Opinion Essay question of the writing exam.

Introduction

The introduction is the first paragraph of a typical opinion essay. In it you clearly express and briefly explain your opinion, without going into much detail about why you hold that opinion or its implications. The introduction should be between three and six sentences long and should contain a thesis statement. The thesis statement is a single sentence that gives the idea of the essay. Ideally, every sentence in the entire composition should somehow relate to this one thesis statement sentence. A thesis statement might simply read, *Talking about personal problems in the office is dangerous,* or it may be more complex, as in *Talking about personal problems in the workplace is usually not a good idea, but there are a few instances where it seems inevitable.*

Other sentences in the introduction might vaguely indicate what kind of evidence you will use, without going into detail. For example, you might say, *A variety of life experiences has led me to believe that talking about personal problems in the office can have harmful effects,* without telling exactly what those life experiences are. Then your reader will know that you plan to go into detail about those experiences later in the essay. Other sentences in the introduction might also explain the idea a little better than you can in a single sentence. For example, *Talking about personal problems in the office can lower the morale of coworkers. Sometimes bad attitudes are contagious.* This gives some indication of what drives your idea, but still leaves room to explore the idea in detail in the body paragraphs of your composition.

Body

The body is the part of an opinion essay in which you lay out the reasons and evidence for your thesis in great detail. The body organizes your evidence. For the TOEIC essay, the body should be between one and four paragraphs long, with each paragraph dedicated to either a single piece of evidence, explored and explained in detail, or to a group of related pieces of evidence that all point to the same idea. All the evidence contained in the body should support the idea that you put forward in the thesis. It is often appropriate to explain how the particular evidence connects to the overall idea of the essay. Each body paragraph should contain a minimum of three sentences.

Conclusion

This is the place to tie everything together. You can editorialize a little, or explore implications in the conclusion as well, but mostly it is a place to bring your examples back into focus by connecting them together and connecting them back to the thesis statement, or overall idea of the essay.

Managing Your Time

Even a timed essay will turn out better if you take the time to go through the whole writing process: first, prewriting/planning; then drafting; and then editing/revising. Of course, for a 30-minute essay, you will have to abbreviate the process somewhat, taking only a few minutes for planning and a few for editing. Most of your time should be spent drafting a solid essay that strives for clarity, sentence variety, and good grammar.

STEP 1: Prewriting/Planning

Even though you have a short time to complete the essay, taking a few minutes to prewrite will pay off. Planning before you write will make for a clearer, more organized essay that is easier to draft. Don't spend too much time outlining your essay, but before you begin drafting, it is a good idea to figure out, in writing, what the content of each paragraph will be. This way you can do most of your thinking beforehand and just focus on writing. It will also force you to create the structure of the essay before you begin drafting it, so that the essay will have a strong organizational logic. A brief outline is a good way to plan for an opinion essay, it could be this simple:

I. Introduction: Write a one-sentence long, clear thesis that puts the idea of the essay forth.

II. Body Paragraph 1 (or B1): Decide on the evidence that will serve as the focus of this paragraph, and jot it down.

III. Body Paragraph 2 (or B2): Decide on the evidence that will serve as the focus of this paragraph, and jot it down.
Add additional body paragraphs as necessary.

IV. Conclusion (optional): Jot down any further ideas or implications that you might want to explore in the conclusion. You may have more ideas for the conclusion after you have finished writing, so you can skip this part of the prewriting, if nothing comes immediately to mind. As you outline, you should make certain that your response clearly addresses the topic and task given in the prompt and that the evidence, explanations, or examples you choose to use in the essay directly support your opinion. Referring back to this little outline will keep your writing flowing and on track during the drafting process. It will allow you to focus on writing a high-quality draft without having to search for ideas and words at the same time. It will take one or two minutes, but will probably save you time in the long run.

An outline for an essay asking what you think the best quality in a boss/employer is might look like this:

Intro–Idea: *Best quality in a boss = being understanding about family, home, kids, outside obligations*

Key words for thesis: *accommodating, understanding, flexible, obligations/needs*

Thesis: *The best kind of boss is one who is understanding, flexible, and accommodating about an employee's obligations outside the office, one who understands that happiness and success at work are impossible without a harmonious balance of work life and home life.*

B1: *Friend Kristi taking a lower-paying job after the birth of her first child because in the new job she had more flexibility to work from home.*

B2: *Old boss Susan, who insisted that I stay late for student tutorials 4 days a week even after I told her that my husband was going to have to drop out of school so that we would have care for our baby in the evenings.*

Conclusion: *It's interesting that both of these have to do with babies. I might comment on that in my conclusion as a very dramatic factor that can really highlight the importance of this quality in a boss.*

STEP 2: Drafting

With your ideas laid out for you in the outline, the drafting should move quickly. You should spend the majority of the 30 minutes allowed for this question on the drafting process, probably at least 20 minutes. As you draft, it is important to strive for clear language and clear ideas. Use of transitional phrases and connecting words is important to the fluidity, coherence, and unity of your essay. You should study and understand the meanings of transitional words and phrases such as:

- however
- therefore
- whereas
- in contrast
- nonetheless
- in addition

These words will keep your writing moving.

As in the Respond to a Written Request questions, you should try to use a variety of sentence structures. Really show off what you can do grammatically. You should also try to use lively, appropriate, and correct vocabulary, including idioms. But don't waste time laboring over a particular word or sentence during this phase of writing. Fill in with a less perfect word or less perfect structure and save a little time at the end to edit and clarify. As on the previous question type, you can make a perfect score with a few minor grammatical errors that do not interfere with the meaning, so it is fine to take some risks.

The draft should develop, expand, and explain the ideas in the outline. Go into detail about the examples or evidence that you give, and connect the examples explicitly to the thesis statement. In drafting, try to keep your work moving forward, and avoid digressions, redundancy, and unnecessary details. You should usually save editorializing and exploring implications for your conclusion. Keep your tone formal and consistent.

A draft of the outlined essay might read like this:

The best kind of boss is one who is understanding, flexible, and accommodating about an employee's obligations outside the office. A good boss understands that happiness and success at work are impossible without a harmonious balance of work life and home life. Such factors as needing to care for a sick child, needing to support a spouse's endeavors, or simply needing to pursue one's own passions and interests outside the office *alter*one's quality of work and happiness at work when not attended to. A good boss understands and responds to these needs.

Imagine this situation: a high-powered businesswoman in her late thirties quits her job and takes a job at half the pay after the birth of her first child. This is exactly what happened with my sister-in-law. Her first son was low birth weight and got sick often as an infant. Her old employer did not accommodate her needs, and she was stressed, unhappy and her performance at work began to slip. Even as the main breadwinner in the household, my sister-in-law quit her job and began consulting part-time job,*mostly from home.* In her new job, her boss allows her to work from home whenever possible, gives her ample sick and family leave, and generally supports her role as a mother. She says this is the best boss she has ever had, and that she will never leave this job.

I quit a job in a similar situation. I was working as a teacher and my principal at the time asked me to stay after school four days a week until 6:30 for student tutorials. I explained that my husband was taking classes in the evening to finish his college degree and that we could not afford child care for our infant four days a week. Many other teachers in my department offered to handle the tutorials for me. Even with all of this my boss demanded that I stay late. My husband had to drop out of college that semester. My resignation from the job soon followed, and I went back to work for my old boss who always said, "You can't be happy here unless your family is happy. Go take care of them first and come back here ready to go!" I took a pay cut and committed to a longer commute to work for that boss.

It is worth noting that both of these examples involve babies. This is appropriate because babies create an extreme home situation that can bring our priorities into focus. Other extreme home situations might include having a sick spouse or parent, a divorce, or even a feeling of urgent need to keep up with one's passions or interests. A good boss understands that employees are most importantly human beings, and that if they are denied their lives outside the office, they won't work well and they won't stay long.

STEP 3: Editing/Revising

It is always a good idea to save a few minutes at the end of the time allotted to read back through your essay. Even the most seasoned writers make mistakes and typos when drafting, especially in a timed writing exercise. A few minor errors are acceptable on the essay, but it is worth the effort to read back through your work at least once to look for glaring mistakes, and maybe once again dwell on details like word choice or spice up your sentences. As you edit, also consider the coherence of the piece as a whole, and look for any leaps in logic or missing connections. These can often be corrected by simply inserting a sentence or transitional phrase, or by rewording. The essay will be composed on a computer, so making changes will be easy.

You will notice that in this sample, the changes are few and minor. That is because most of the focus in this example went into drafting, and the draft took up the majority of the allotted time. Even so, a minor edit improves it drastically. The editing for this essay took five minutes. Here is the final version of the timed opinion essay:

The best kind of boss is one who is understanding, flexible, and accommodating about an employee's obligations outside the office. A good boss understands that happiness and success at work are impossible without a harmonious balance of work life and home life. Factors such as needing to care for a sick child, needing to support a spouse's endeavors, or simply needing to pursue one's own passions and interests outside the office, if not attended to, can seriously interfere with one's quality of work and happiness at work. A good boss understands and responds to these needs.

My sister-in-law was a high-powered businesswoman in her late thirties when she quit her job and took a job at half the pay. This might be hard to imagine until we consider why. Her first son was born prematurely and got sick often as an infant. Her old employer did not accommodate her needs, and she was stressed and unhappy. Her performance at work began to slip. Even as the main breadwinner in the household, my sister-in-law was happy to quit the job and take the pay cut to begin a part-time consulting job that allowed her to work from home. In her new job, her boss allows her to work from home whenever possible, gives her ample sick and family leave, and generally supports her role as a mother. She says this is the best boss she has ever had, and that she will never leave this job.

I quit a job in a similar situation. When I was working as a public school teacher, my principal asked me to stay after school four days a week for student tutorials leading up to a major standardized test. I explained that my husband was taking classes in the evening to finish his college degree and that we could not afford child care for our infant four days a week. Many other teachers in my department offered to handle the tutorials for me. Even with the support from my department, my boss demanded that I stay late. My husband had to drop out of college that semester. My resignation from the job soon followed, and I went back to work for my old boss, who always said, "You can't be happy here unless your family is happy. Go take care of them first and come back here ready to go!" I took a pay cut and committed to a longer commute to work for that boss.

It is worth noting that both of these examples involve babies. This is appropriate because babies create an extreme home situation that can bring our priorities into focus. Other extreme home situations might include having a sick spouse or parent, a divorce, or even a feeling of urgent need to keep up with one's passions or interests. A good boss understands that employees are foremost human beings, and that if they are denied their lives outside the office, they won't work well and they won't stay long.

Your essay will be scored on:

- how well it addresses the topic and task
- the quality and relevance of explanations, examples, and details
- its organization, flow, and progression
- its unity and coherence
- sentence variety and vocabulary
- grammatical complexity and correctness

How the Essay Is Scored

The essay is scored on a scale of zero to five. The scorers grade the essay using a rubric that describes a typical response at each level. The rubric describes a score-five response as one that, first and foremost, addresses the task and topic effectively. This means that the essay must accomplish everything required by the prompt; it must clearly express and defend an opinion. An essay that receives the highest score will also be well-organized; will be thoroughly developed; and will have strong evidence, examples, explanations, and/or details. It will be fluid, unified, and coherent. It can have a few, minor grammatical or lexical errors that do not obscure meaning, and still score a five. It will have solid word choice and a diversity of syntax and structure.

An essay that scores a four must address the topic well, but some of its points may not be fully developed. A score-four essay is generally well-organized, with sufficient details, explanations, or examples to defend the point. A little redundancy, digression, or vagueness is typical of a four, but the score-four essay is unified and shows good coherence and progression. Like score-five essays, this level of essay demonstrates a good range of vocabulary and a variety of sentence structures, but may have occasional notable errors in structure or word form that do not interfere with meaning.

A score-three essay is mostly successful, but may fall short in a few areas. It typically addresses the topic and task with moderately appropriate and

somewhat developed details, evidence, or examples. Although the connections between the evidence and ideas might be vague or partial. The connections between ideas may be occasionally obscured in a score-three essay, it does show some unity and coherence. Some grammar errors and imprecise word choices in a three essay may make it unclear in places and interfere with meaning. The grammar and vocabulary may be accurate, but limited in range and complexity.

An essay will score a two if it does not provide sufficient evidence or examples to support the opinion, or if the opinion is unclear. The organization of a score-two essay is often weak and the connections between ideas are sometimes unclear. A score-two essay may contain inappropriate word choices or word forms, and notable errors in sentence structure.

A score-one essay is seriously flawed. It might be very disorganized or underdeveloped, or have uncertain relevance to the prompt. It often contains little or irrelevant evidence or has serious errors in sentence structure and usage.

A score-zero response rejects the topic, is incoherent, is in another language, is nonsense, or is blank.

Understanding Your Overall Writing Score

It is impossible to fail the TOEIC writing section, because your overall writing score is not a pass/fail score. The score indicates a writing proficiency level, and different levels of proficiency are required for different jobs, tasks, and placements. The score report that you receive will explain the strengths and weaknesses typical of someone writing at that level. The overall writing score is arrived at by calculating the eight item scores on the test into an overall scale score that ranges from zero to 200. The scale score is then correlated with one of nine proficiency levels. Proficiency Level Descriptors then describe what someone at that level can usually do successfully in English writing. The proficiency level descriptors generally synthesize the scoring criteria for all the questions. For example, someone with a scale score of 200 will be placed at proficiency level 9, and the Proficiency Level Descriptor for this level might read:

Proficiency Level 9

Typically someone scoring at level 9 is a clear, coherent writer who can usually communicate information effectively and use reasons, examples, and explanations to support an opinion. The writing at this level is well-organized and well-developed, and the writer's English is natural, grammatically correct, appropriate in word choice, and varied in syntax and structure. A writer at this level can give information, ask questions, make requests, support his or her opinions, and describe or explain a situation.

Someone with a scale score of 73 is placed at proficiency level 4, and the Proficiency Level Descriptor for this level might read:

Proficiency Level 4

Typically, people writing at this level have some ability to express an opinion and give information, but their communication may be limited in some ways. When explaining an opinion, they may not offer enough or appropriate evidence, their organization may be inadequate, they may not develop ideas fully, or they may have serious grammatical and vocabulary mistakes. When giving straightforward information, they may leave out required information, they may omit the logical connections between sentences and ideas, or they may make serious errors in grammar and vocabulary. Writers at this level can produce grammatically correct sentences, but are typically inconsistent.

The scale scores correspond to proficiency levels as follows:

Proficiency Level 9—Scale Score 200
Proficiency Level 8—Scale Score 170–195
Proficiency Level 7—Scale Score 140–165
Proficiency Level 6—Scale Score 110–135
Proficiency Level 5—Scale Score 90–105
Proficiency Level 4—Scale Score 70–85
Proficiency Level 3—Scale Score 50–65
Proficiency Level 2—Scale Score 45
Proficiency Level 1—Scale Score 0–35

The score report will also allow you to look at your scores on each item to determine your own specific strengths and weaknesses in the context of those tasks. You can use your score report as a tool for understanding your own development with your English skills.

Practice

For the this set of questions, you will write ONE sentence that is based on a picture. With each picture you will be given TWO words or phrases that you must use in your sentence. You can change the forms of the words, and you can use the words in any order. Your sentence will be scored on

- *the appropriate use of grammar*
- *the relevance of the sentence to the picture*

1.

needs to, before

_____

_____

2.

fresh, because

_____

_____

3.

so, report

_____

_____

4.

find, where

_____

_____

5.

finished, more easily

_____

_____

6.

exercise, while others

_____

_____

9.

which, know

_____

_____

7.

explain, how

_____

_____

10.

enjoying, with

_____

_____

8.

results, later

_____

_____

11.

useful, when

_____

_____

12.

ready, hope

_____

_____

13.

about to, suitcase

_____

_____

14.

so, buy

_____

_____

15.

finished, because

_____

_____

16.

as soon as, delicious

_____

_____

For these questions, you will show how well you can write a response to an e-mail. Use a clock or stopwatch, and allow ten minutes to read and answer each e-mail. Read the e-mail.

To: All Staff
From: Una Harvey, Training and Staffing
Re: Training and Professional Development
    Calendar
Sent: November 8, 2009

Hello, Staff,

We are trying to put together our training and professional development calendar for the coming year, and we would like your input. Please write back to me and let me know which of your professional skills you would like to improve on in the coming year. I hope to incorporate some of your ideas into a training and professional development calendar that responds to your needs and will help you do your job better.

Thanks,
Una Harvey
Training and Staffing

Reply to the request as if you were an employee with this company. Respond with at least TWO ideas about how you could improve your skills.

17. _____

_____

_____

_____

_____

_____

To: All Staff
From: Tina Mitchell, Administrative Assistant
Re: Bulletin Board
Sent: February 22

Hi, Everyone!

I have a great idea for a bulletin board in the break room. I want to post some success stories from the year on the wall, to remind us of what a great team we have! I would like everyone to send in two or three success stories from this year. They don't need to be long, just a sentence or two to tell about something good that has happened in the last year.

Thanks,
Tina

Read the e-mail. Imagine that you received this e-mail at your current or most recent job and respond to the request with at least TWO short statements about good things that have happened at your job this year.

18. _____

_____

_____

_____

_____

_____

To: New Client
From: Endway Realty
Re: Basic Information about Home
Sent: August 12, 2007

Hello,

Thank you for contacting us to help with your upcoming move. We hope we will be able to help you find a home that meets all your needs. Based on the information you provide us now, we will assign a Realtor to your job who has specialized knowledge of the areas of the city and types of homes that best meet your needs. First we need some basic information from you about what you are looking for in a home. Please let us know what kind of home and what kind of neighborhood you are looking for.

Read the e-mail. Imagine that you have contacted a home locator to help you find a home in a new city. Please respond to the e-mail with at least THREE qualities you are looking for in a home.

19. _____

_____

_____

_____

_____

_____

To: Department Staff
From: Department Supervisor
Re: Reports Due Monday
Sent: March 18, 2008

Dear Staff,

As you know, your quarterly reports are due Monday. I will be out of town from Wednesday to Friday, so if you have any questions about the formatting or content of your reports, please e-mail them to me before 5:00 tomorrow. I will be happy to answer any questions you might have, and I look forward to seeing your work.

Thanks,
Department Supervisor

Read the e-mail. Imagine that you have received this e-mail from your department supervisor. Please respond to the e-mail with at least TWO questions about his expectations for the report.

20. _____

_____

_____

_____

_____

_____

To: Administrator at Kline and Associates
From: Janet Langly
Re: Directions to Meeting
Sent: June 5, 2008
Dear Administrator at Kline and Associates,
I have a meeting at your office tomorrow and need driving directions. Your boss said I should contact you for them. I will be stopping by the central post office on my way to the office, so it would be perfect if you could give me directions from there.
Thanks,
Janet Langly

Read the e-mail. Imagine that someone has e-mailed you to ask for directions about how to get from the central post office in your town to your place of business. Please write back with driving directions. Please include at least THREE details about the drive.

21. _____

_____

_____

_____

_____

To: Recent Hire
From: Human Resources at Ethercorp
Re: Welcome!
Sent: March 2, 2008

Hello, and welcome to the Ethercorp staff! We are pleased that you have accepted the job offer. I am sure you have many questions about your new job, from details about our benefits package, to advice about where to send your children to school in Madison. Please feel free to contact our Human Resources department with any questions that arise for you in the next few weeks. We look forward to having you on our team.

Read the e-mail. Imagine that you have just been hired by Ethercorp, and have received this message from the human resources department. Please write back to the department with at least TWO questions about your new job.

22. _____

_____

_____

_____

_____

_____

To: you@youremailaddress.com
From: Marcia Todd
Re: Advice on Interview
Sent: May 19, 2009

Hi!

I have very good news! I just got a job interview with a small software company in Austin! I am a little nervous because I have never been on a real job interview before. Do you have any advice for me? I would really appreciate any advice you can offer about interviewing for a job.

Talk to you later,
Marcia

Read the e-mail. Imagine that you have just received this e-mail from a younger friend. Give her at least THREE pieces of advice about what to do and say when interviewing for a job.

23. _____

_____

_____

_____

_____

_____

_____

For this set of questions, you will write an essay in response to a question that asks you to state, explain, and support your opinion. Generally, an effective essay will contain at least 300 words. Read each question below. Then, allow yourself 30 minutes to plan, write, and revise each essay.

24. Many people like to do all their work in the office and focus on home life when they are at home. Others are happy working from home, and don't mind, or even prefer, to bring some work home with them. Do you think that bringing work home is a good idea? Why or why not?

25. Modern life can be stressful. Even the best jobs often require long hours and strict deadlines. Balancing work and family can also be difficult. There are many ways people manage stress, both healthy and unhealthy. What do you think is the best way to manage stress?

Answers

1. Sample response: The man needs to get all the new inventory on the shelves before the end of the day.

2. Sample response: The women like to eat at this restaurant because it uses fresh ingredients and has excellent service.

3. Sample response: The coworkers are looking over the report together so that they can plan their presentation.

4. Sample response: She is putting her airline ticket in the briefcase pocket, where it will be easy to find.

5. Sample response: When the men are finished making the new road, people will be able to travel more easily between the two towns.

6. Sample response: Some of the people at the park jog for exercise, while others walk.

7. Sample response: She is explaining how the sales figures have increased, using a graph on her laptop.

8. Sample response: The scientists are reading the results of their experiments and writing them down for later analysis.

9. Sample response: The young man doesn't know which box he should put the letter into.

10. Sample response: The construction workers have been working hard this morning, and now they are enjoying their break with a cup of coffee.

11. Sample response: Big machines can be useful when the harvest has to be done quickly.

12. Sample response: He hopes that the paint will dry quickly, so that the apartment will be ready for the new tenants.

13. Sample response: The receptionist is about to call the bellman to take the lady's suitcase to her hotel room.

14. Sample response: She is withdrawing cash at an ATM so she can buy a birthday present for her husband.

15. Sample response: His coworkers applauded when John finished his presentation, because it was very inspiring.

16. Sample response: As soon as she finishes preparing the vegetables for the salad, she will be ready to serve a delicious meal.

17. Sample response:

Dear Ms. Harvey,

Thank you for valuing my ideas and for working to make a good professional development schedule. One of my personal goals for the coming year is to learn more about how to use slide show software. I think that using slide shows would improve my presentations of the departmental reports. I would also like to explore new ways to improve communication and morale among the workers in my department. So, any professional development opportunities that involve management training would be fantastic for me. Again, I appreciate for your hard work in making a training calendar that responds to our needs.

Sincerely,
Jane Longman

18. Sample response:

Hi, Tina,

What a wonderful idea! I think that will be a great thing for us to look at when we are getting our coffee! I have several success stories from the year, but I am just writing the first ones that come to mind. This year my sales team met all our goals. We had our best year for sales ever! I am proud of everyone's hard work. We also added two new clients this year. My department has had to work very hard to meet the demands of the new workload that this created, with everyone taking on extra duties. And now that work is going to pay off, because it looks like we will be able to hire two new staff to help with the additional work. Thanks for taking the time to make our break room inspiring.

Best,
Sam

19. Sample response:

Dear Endway Realty Representative,

Thanks for responding so quickly to my inquiry. I will be moving to Dallas in November, and am hoping to find a short lease on a downtown apartment. I want to get settled into the new city and new job before I commit to anything more permanent than a six- or nine-month lease on a one- or two-bedroom apartment. I don't like to drive, so I am looking for a location that is near a public transit stop, and preferably within walking distance to bars, restaurants, and stores. I also don't want to spend more than $1,000 in rent per month. Please put me in contact with a Realtor who can help me with this.

Thanks,
Sri Patel

20. Sample response:

Dear Robert,

Thank you for the notice that you are not going to be in the office. I have a few questions about the reports that are due Monday. The first is this: Would you like them turned in electronically, in hard copy, or both? I was also curious as to whether you prefer that the reports include a lot of graphs and images or you prefer straightforward text. Finally, will it be alright if my report exceeds the specified length by a page or two? I am having a little trouble cutting it down any further. Thanks and enjoy your trip!

Sincerely,
John Meadows

21. Sample response:

Dear Ms. Langly,

I am happy to help. Our office is located on the south side of town, about two miles past the Interstate on Highway 123. The address of the building is 4677 Highway 123, and we are in Suite 14. To get here from the downtown post office, you take Union Street south to the Interstate access road. Turn left at the access road, and get over into the left lane. Take an immediate left onto 123. You will pass several apartment complexes on the right and a small grocery store on the left. After you pass the grocery store, turn into the second driveway on the right. That is our building. If you reach the Airline Street stoplight, then you have gone too far. Feel free to call the office or me if you need any further help.

Sincerely,
Leon Graves

22. Sample response:

Dear Human Resources Department,

Thank you for contacting me. I do, in fact, have many questions about the job. Most of them, I am sure, will be answered in good time, but there are a couple of pressing questions that I would like to ask. First, how soon will I be eligible for the insurance coverage through the company's insurance provider? My wife is pregnant and I am wondering how the transition in health insurance will work with our July due date. Second, will I receive weekly, biweekly, or monthly paychecks? Knowing this will help me organize my budget. Thanks again for your concern. I look forward to working with you, too.

Sincerely,
Andres Alamillo

23. Sample response:

Great news, Marcia!

I am so happy for you. The job sounds perfect, and I think you'll do great. I have been on quite a few job interviews before (maybe too many!), and I do have many suggestions. Here are the most important things that come to mind. First off, I think it is always a good idea to wear a suit, even if the work environment seems casual. Suits make you look and feel more professional. Besides, it is better to be overdressed than underdressed.

You should also speak confidently and positively. Your answers should always focus on the things that you are competent and successful with. Try to steer the conversation back to your skills and successes whenever possible. And follow up with telling your interviewer how you think those skills will translate to the new job.

Last but not least, sit up straight and look your interviewer in the eye. Body language is very important. You will do great! Call me if you want talk more about it or even set up a practice interview.

Congratulations,
Liping

24. Sample response:

As with most things in life, there are stages and times when bringing work home from the office is a good idea, and stages and times in life when this is very dangerous. Young people should do everything that they can at the beginning of their careers to develop the skills that they need to make the years of work that they have ahead easy. For them, bringing work home is a good idea. However, once they have started a family, their work should stay at the office so that they can create a proper balance between work and family life.

Many young people don't want to bring work home with them. They would rather meet with coworkers at the bar after work or go out on the town. This is foolish. The beginning of a career is the perfect time to focus on developing the skills and tools that will make the years ahead smooth and easy. If someone puts in long hours and works hard at the beginning of his career, then by the time he is starting a family, work will be second nature. It is much more difficult to build a career or put in the extra time to prove oneself once life is complicated with such things as spouses and children. I have known several young people who really got ahead in their careers by showing great dedication early on.

Once a person starts a family, it becomes more difficult to work at home. Trying to work at home with the obligations and interruptions of a family can create stress for the worker and the family. Balancing home life and work life can be hard as it is, and bringing home work can make it almost impossible to either work or attend to domestic life. I have known many workers who found working at home very stressful in this situation. Especially during the childrearing years, it is good to designate spaces and times for things. When at work, work; when at home, be domestic. This relieves stress and helps establish the balance that is necessary for both good work and a good home life.

The final stage of life, after the children are out of the house, is still a mystery to me personally. I hope that at this point in life, a worker is in the position to decide what he wants to be the focus of his life, and do that when he clocks out. If he is very dedicated to work, and wants to work from home, he should. If he wants to take his wife to dinner, play racquetball, or tend his garden, he should have the time and space for that.

Looking at three stages of a worker's life and career, it is clear that taking work home from the office can be a good or a bad idea for a worker, depending on his circumstances, priorities, and age. Taking work home is only a good idea if does not create stress or disrupt life. It is a bad idea if it does.

25. Sample response:

Nothing in the world can completely rid someone's life of stress, but healthy lifestyle choices can help people manage and control their stress levels. Many people get trapped in a cycle of overeating and lounging in front of the television to escape their stress, but what they do not realize is that unhealthy lifestyles can create more stress than they had to begin with. Eating well, spending time outdoors, and exercising create a healthy body and a healthy

mind. A healthy lifestyle is the only real way to moderate stress.

When I was younger, I had a friend who was a single mother. She took care of three children, worked a full-time job, kept a clean home, put a home-cooked dinner on the table every night, and started each morning with yoga. She amazed me. At the time, I could hardly manage my job and my husband, much less the clean house, home-cooked dinner, and exercise. I asked her how she managed to balance it all. She explained to me that the clean house, dinner, and yoga were not extra work for her, but rather the foundation that made everything else possible.

I have seen the opposite extreme as well. My brother creates stress for himself, while he thinks that he is escaping it. He doesn't have time for a healthy meal because he is too busy at work, so he grabs a fast food hamburger for lunch instead of preparing something healthy. He goes home from work and needs to "blow off some steam" or "de-stress" in front of the TV. This has created a cycle of unhealthy living. Now he is getting overweight, which creates even more stress for him. His body is not well-nourished, so he can't think or work as well as he could if he took a little time to care for his body. His stress builds on itself.

I have also seen a few people in my life switch from high-stress unhealthy living to low-stress healthy living. The transition is amazing. My friend Gina started exercising and eating well in her 40s, after she had a health scare. She was upset at first about her strict doctor's orders. But after a few months of healthy living, she started to notice changes in all aspects of her life. She was happier, had more energy, and was less stressed. These three examples together have shown me that the best way to fight stress is with sanity. Healthy living is the best defense against stress.

By taking this first practice exam, you will get an idea of how much you already know and how much
you need to learn. This exam consists of questions modeled after the official TOEIC Listening, Reading, Speaking, and Writing sections.

1.	ⓐ ⓑ ⓒ ⓓ		46.	ⓐ ⓑ ⓒ ⓓ		91.	ⓐ ⓑ ⓒ ⓓ
2.	ⓐ ⓑ ⓒ ⓓ		47.	ⓐ ⓑ ⓒ ⓓ		92.	ⓐ ⓑ ⓒ ⓓ
3.	ⓐ ⓑ ⓒ ⓓ		48.	ⓐ ⓑ ⓒ ⓓ		93.	ⓐ ⓑ ⓒ ⓓ
4.	ⓐ ⓑ ⓒ ⓓ		49.	ⓐ ⓑ ⓒ ⓓ		94.	ⓐ ⓑ ⓒ ⓓ
5.	ⓐ ⓑ ⓒ ⓓ		50.	ⓐ ⓑ ⓒ ⓓ		95.	ⓐ ⓑ ⓒ ⓓ
6.	ⓐ ⓑ ⓒ ⓓ		51.	ⓐ ⓑ ⓒ ⓓ		96.	ⓐ ⓑ ⓒ ⓓ
7.	ⓐ ⓑ ⓒ ⓓ		52.	ⓐ ⓑ ⓒ ⓓ		97.	ⓐ ⓑ ⓒ ⓓ
8.	ⓐ ⓑ ⓒ ⓓ		53.	ⓐ ⓑ ⓒ ⓓ		98.	ⓐ ⓑ ⓒ ⓓ
9.	ⓐ ⓑ ⓒ ⓓ		54.	ⓐ ⓑ ⓒ ⓓ		99.	ⓐ ⓑ ⓒ ⓓ
10.	ⓐ ⓑ ⓒ ⓓ		55.	ⓐ ⓑ ⓒ ⓓ		100.	ⓐ ⓑ ⓒ ⓓ
11.	ⓐ ⓑ ⓒ		56.	ⓐ ⓑ ⓒ ⓓ		101.	ⓐ ⓑ ⓒ ⓓ
12.	ⓐ ⓑ ⓒ		57.	ⓐ ⓑ ⓒ ⓓ		102.	ⓐ ⓑ ⓒ ⓓ
13.	ⓐ ⓑ ⓒ		58.	ⓐ ⓑ ⓒ ⓓ		103.	ⓐ ⓑ ⓒ ⓓ
14.	ⓐ ⓑ ⓒ		59.	ⓐ ⓑ ⓒ ⓓ		104.	ⓐ ⓑ ⓒ ⓓ
15.	ⓐ ⓑ ⓒ		60.	ⓐ ⓑ ⓒ ⓓ		105.	ⓐ ⓑ ⓒ ⓓ
16.	ⓐ ⓑ ⓒ		61.	ⓐ ⓑ ⓒ ⓓ		106.	ⓐ ⓑ ⓒ ⓓ
17.	ⓐ ⓑ ⓒ		62.	ⓐ ⓑ ⓒ ⓓ		107.	ⓐ ⓑ ⓒ ⓓ
18.	ⓐ ⓑ ⓒ		63.	ⓐ ⓑ ⓒ ⓓ		108.	ⓐ ⓑ ⓒ ⓓ
19.	ⓐ ⓑ ⓒ		64.	ⓐ ⓑ ⓒ ⓓ		109.	ⓐ ⓑ ⓒ ⓓ
20.	ⓐ ⓑ ⓒ		65.	ⓐ ⓑ ⓒ ⓓ		110.	ⓐ ⓑ ⓒ ⓓ
21.	ⓐ ⓑ ⓒ		66.	ⓐ ⓑ ⓒ ⓓ		111.	ⓐ ⓑ ⓒ ⓓ
22.	ⓐ ⓑ ⓒ		67.	ⓐ ⓑ ⓒ ⓓ		112.	ⓐ ⓑ ⓒ ⓓ
23.	ⓐ ⓑ ⓒ		68.	ⓐ ⓑ ⓒ ⓓ		113.	ⓐ ⓑ ⓒ ⓓ
24.	ⓐ ⓑ ⓒ		69.	ⓐ ⓑ ⓒ ⓓ		114.	ⓐ ⓑ ⓒ ⓓ
25.	ⓐ ⓑ ⓒ		70.	ⓐ ⓑ ⓒ ⓓ		115.	ⓐ ⓑ ⓒ ⓓ
26.	ⓐ ⓑ ⓒ		71.	ⓐ ⓑ ⓒ ⓓ		116.	ⓐ ⓑ ⓒ ⓓ
27.	ⓐ ⓑ ⓒ		72.	ⓐ ⓑ ⓒ ⓓ		117.	ⓐ ⓑ ⓒ ⓓ
28.	ⓐ ⓑ ⓒ		73.	ⓐ ⓑ ⓒ ⓓ		118.	ⓐ ⓑ ⓒ ⓓ
29.	ⓐ ⓑ ⓒ		74.	ⓐ ⓑ ⓒ ⓓ		119.	ⓐ ⓑ ⓒ ⓓ
30.	ⓐ ⓑ ⓒ		75.	ⓐ ⓑ ⓒ ⓓ		120.	ⓐ ⓑ ⓒ ⓓ
31.	ⓐ ⓑ ⓒ		76.	ⓐ ⓑ ⓒ ⓓ		121.	ⓐ ⓑ ⓒ ⓓ
32.	ⓐ ⓑ ⓒ		77.	ⓐ ⓑ ⓒ ⓓ		122.	ⓐ ⓑ ⓒ ⓓ
33.	ⓐ ⓑ ⓒ		78.	ⓐ ⓑ ⓒ ⓓ		123.	ⓐ ⓑ ⓒ ⓓ
34.	ⓐ ⓑ ⓒ		79.	ⓐ ⓑ ⓒ ⓓ		124.	ⓐ ⓑ ⓒ ⓓ
35.	ⓐ ⓑ ⓒ		80.	ⓐ ⓑ ⓒ ⓓ		125.	ⓐ ⓑ ⓒ ⓓ
36.	ⓐ ⓑ ⓒ		81.	ⓐ ⓑ ⓒ ⓓ		126.	ⓐ ⓑ ⓒ ⓓ
37.	ⓐ ⓑ ⓒ		82.	ⓐ ⓑ ⓒ ⓓ		127.	ⓐ ⓑ ⓒ ⓓ
38.	ⓐ ⓑ ⓒ		83.	ⓐ ⓑ ⓒ ⓓ		128.	ⓐ ⓑ ⓒ ⓓ
39.	ⓐ ⓑ ⓒ		84.	ⓐ ⓑ ⓒ ⓓ		129.	ⓐ ⓑ ⓒ ⓓ
40.	ⓐ ⓑ ⓒ		85.	ⓐ ⓑ ⓒ ⓓ		130.	ⓐ ⓑ ⓒ ⓓ
41.	ⓐ ⓑ ⓒ ⓓ		86.	ⓐ ⓑ ⓒ ⓓ		131.	ⓐ ⓑ ⓒ ⓓ
42.	ⓐ ⓑ ⓒ ⓓ		87.	ⓐ ⓑ ⓒ ⓓ		132.	ⓐ ⓑ ⓒ ⓓ
43.	ⓐ ⓑ ⓒ ⓓ		88.	ⓐ ⓑ ⓒ ⓓ		133.	ⓐ ⓑ ⓒ ⓓ
44.	ⓐ ⓑ ⓒ ⓓ		89.	ⓐ ⓑ ⓒ ⓓ		134.	ⓐ ⓑ ⓒ ⓓ
45.	ⓐ ⓑ ⓒ ⓓ		90.	ⓐ ⓑ ⓒ ⓓ		135.	ⓐ ⓑ ⓒ ⓓ

136.	ⓐ	ⓑ	ⓒ	ⓓ
137.	ⓐ	ⓑ	ⓒ	ⓓ
138.	ⓐ	ⓑ	ⓒ	ⓓ
139.	ⓐ	ⓑ	ⓒ	ⓓ
140.	ⓐ	ⓑ	ⓒ	ⓓ
141.	ⓐ	ⓑ	ⓒ	ⓓ
142.	ⓐ	ⓑ	ⓒ	ⓓ
143.	ⓐ	ⓑ	ⓒ	ⓓ
144.	ⓐ	ⓑ	ⓒ	ⓓ
145.	ⓐ	ⓑ	ⓒ	ⓓ
146.	ⓐ	ⓑ	ⓒ	ⓓ
147.	ⓐ	ⓑ	ⓒ	ⓓ
148.	ⓐ	ⓑ	ⓒ	ⓓ
149.	ⓐ	ⓑ	ⓒ	ⓓ
150.	ⓐ	ⓑ	ⓒ	ⓓ
151.	ⓐ	ⓑ	ⓒ	ⓓ
152.	ⓐ	ⓑ	ⓒ	ⓓ
153.	ⓐ	ⓑ	ⓒ	ⓓ
154.	ⓐ	ⓑ	ⓒ	ⓓ
155.	ⓐ	ⓑ	ⓒ	ⓓ
156.	ⓐ	ⓑ	ⓒ	ⓓ
157.	ⓐ	ⓑ	ⓒ	ⓓ

158.	ⓐ	ⓑ	ⓒ	ⓓ
159.	ⓐ	ⓑ	ⓒ	ⓓ
160.	ⓐ	ⓑ	ⓒ	ⓓ
161.	ⓐ	ⓑ	ⓒ	ⓓ
162.	ⓐ	ⓑ	ⓒ	ⓓ
163.	ⓐ	ⓑ	ⓒ	ⓓ
164.	ⓐ	ⓑ	ⓒ	ⓓ
165.	ⓐ	ⓑ	ⓒ	ⓓ
166.	ⓐ	ⓑ	ⓒ	ⓓ
167.	ⓐ	ⓑ	ⓒ	ⓓ
168.	ⓐ	ⓑ	ⓒ	ⓓ
169.	ⓐ	ⓑ	ⓒ	ⓓ
170.	ⓐ	ⓑ	ⓒ	ⓓ
171.	ⓐ	ⓑ	ⓒ	ⓓ
172.	ⓐ	ⓑ	ⓒ	ⓓ
173.	ⓐ	ⓑ	ⓒ	ⓓ
174.	ⓐ	ⓑ	ⓒ	ⓓ
175.	ⓐ	ⓑ	ⓒ	ⓓ
176.	ⓐ	ⓑ	ⓒ	ⓓ
177.	ⓐ	ⓑ	ⓒ	ⓓ
178.	ⓐ	ⓑ	ⓒ	ⓓ
179.	ⓐ	ⓑ	ⓒ	ⓓ

180.	ⓐ	ⓑ	ⓒ	ⓓ
181.	ⓐ	ⓑ	ⓒ	ⓓ
182.	ⓐ	ⓑ	ⓒ	ⓓ
183.	ⓐ	ⓑ	ⓒ	ⓓ
184.	ⓐ	ⓑ	ⓒ	ⓓ
185.	ⓐ	ⓑ	ⓒ	ⓓ
186.	ⓐ	ⓑ	ⓒ	ⓓ
187.	ⓐ	ⓑ	ⓒ	ⓓ
188.	ⓐ	ⓑ	ⓒ	ⓓ
189.	ⓐ	ⓑ	ⓒ	ⓓ
190.	ⓐ	ⓑ	ⓒ	ⓓ
191.	ⓐ	ⓑ	ⓒ	ⓓ
192.	ⓐ	ⓑ	ⓒ	ⓓ
193.	ⓐ	ⓑ	ⓒ	ⓓ
194.	ⓐ	ⓑ	ⓒ	ⓓ
195.	ⓐ	ⓑ	ⓒ	ⓓ
196.	ⓐ	ⓑ	ⓒ	ⓓ
197.	ⓐ	ⓑ	ⓒ	ⓓ
198.	ⓐ	ⓑ	ⓒ	ⓓ
199.	ⓐ	ⓑ	ⓒ	ⓓ
200.	ⓐ	ⓑ	ⓒ	ⓓ

Listening

You will now begin the listening section. You will be asked to demonstrate how well you understand spoken English. The entire listening section should take approximately 45 minutes. There are four parts and directions are given for each part. Mark your answers—choice **a**, **b**, **c**, or **d**—on the answer sheet that begins on page 171.

When directed by the  icon, listen to the audio file at **http://www.learnatest.com/SpeakingGuides/ TOEIC_Test_Prep**. Or, if you do not have access to a computer, the complete transcripts are included in the appendix of this book. In that case, ask someone who speaks English fluently to read the material to you face-to-face or into a tape recorder. Be sure your reader speaks at a normal, conversational pace. It is highly recommended, however, that you use the audio files for a more authentic TOEIC experience.

Directions: For each question in this part, you will hear four statements about a picture. When you hear the statements, you must select the one statement that best describes what you see in the picture. Then find the number of the question on your answer sheet and mark your answer. The statements are available in audio files or written transcripts in the appendix of this book.

1.

Now, listen to Track 190.

2.

Now, listen to Track 191.

3.

Now, listen to Track 192.

4.

Now, listen to Track 193.

5.

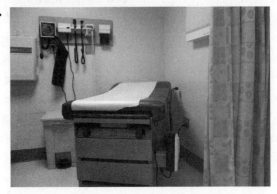

Now, listen to Track 194.

6.

Now, listen to Track 195.

7.

Now, listen to Track 196.

8.

Now, listen to Track 197.

9.

Now, listen to Track 198.

10.

Now, listen to Track 199.

Directions: 🎧 You will hear a question or statement and three responses spoken in English.

The question and statements are available in audio files or written transcripts in the appendix of this book. Select the best response to the question or statement and mark your choice—**a**, **b**, or **c**—on your answer sheet.

11. Now, listen to track 200.
    Mark your answer on the answer sheet.

12. Now, listen to track 201.
    Mark your answer on the answer sheet.

13. Now, listen to track 202.
    Mark your answer on the answer sheet.

14. Now, listen to track 203.
    Mark your answer on the answer sheet.

15. Now, listen to track 204.
    Mark your answer on the answer sheet.

16. Now, listen to track 205.
    Mark your answer on the answer sheet.

17. Now, listen to track 206.
    Mark your answer on the answer sheet.

18. Now, listen to track 207.
    Mark your answer on the answer sheet.

19. Now, listen to track 208.
    Mark your answer on the answer sheet.

20. Now, listen to track 209.
    Mark your answer on the answer sheet.

21. Now, listen to track 210.
    Mark your answer on the answer sheet.

22. Now, listen to track 211.
    Mark your answer on the answer sheet.

23. Now, listen to track 212.
    Mark your answer on the answer sheet.

24. Now, listen to track 213.
    Mark your answer on the answer sheet.

25. Now, listen to track 214.
    Mark your answer on the answer sheet.

26. Now, listen to track 215.
    Mark your answer on the answer sheet.

27. Now, listen to track 216.
Mark your answer on the answer sheet.

28. Now, listen to track 217.
Mark your answer on the answer sheet.

29. Now, listen to track 218.
Mark your answer on the answer sheet.

30. Now, listen to track 219.
Mark your answer on the answer sheet.

31. Now, listen to track 220.
Mark your answer on the answer sheet.

32. Now, listen to track 221.
Mark your answer on the answer sheet.

33. Now, listen to track 222.
Mark your answer on the answer sheet.

34. Now, listen to track 223.
Mark your answer on the answer sheet.

35. Now, listen to track 224.
Mark your answer on the answer sheet.

36. Now, listen to track 225.
Mark your answer on the answer sheet.

37. Now, listen to track 226.
Mark your answer on the answer sheet.

38. Now, listen to track 227.
Mark your answer on the answer sheet.

39. Now, listen to track 228.
Mark your answer on the answer sheet.

40. Now, listen to track 229.
Mark your answer on the answer sheet.

Directions: You will hear conversations between two people. You will be asked to answer four questions about what the speakers say in each conversation. Select the best response to each question and mark your choice—**a**, **b**, **c**, or **d**—on your answer sheet. The conversations are available in audio files or written transcripts in the appendix of this book.

Now, listen to track 230.

41. Now, listen to Track 231.
Why does the man need the new catalog?
   a. to buy a new sweater
   b. to look for a new supplier
   c. to complete the March order
   d. to be ready for the new year

42. Now, listen to Track 232.
What is the man worried about?
   a. that the supplier will not have the materials he needs in stock
   b. that the supplier has gone out of business
   c. that the supplier has raised prices
   d. that the new catalog is wrong

43. Now, listen to Track 233.
When do they decide is the best time to call about the new catalog?
   a. tomorrow
   b. today
   c. after checking on the backorder
   d. in March

Now, listen to Track 234.

44. Now, listen to Track 235.

How does the man feel about the company hiring a new worker?

a. excited

b. nervous

c. resentful

d. proud

45. Now, listen to Track 236.

When is the company interviewing?

a. next month

b. Interviews are over.

c. the end of the month

d. currently

46. Now, listen to Track 237.

Who was present at the interview?

a. the man

b. the woman

c. Fred

d. three new workers

Now, listen to Track 238.

47. Now, listen to Track 239.

What is the woman looking for?

a. information about major hotel chains

b. a new client

c. advice on where to eat out in Denver

d. a hotel recommendation

48. Now, listen to Track 240.

What is The Ridge?

a. a small independent hotel

b. a mountain

c. a coworker

d. a national hotel chain

49. Now, listen to Track 241.

Why is the woman going to Denver?

a. for a wedding

b. for a conference

c. to meet with a new client

d. to meet the regional director

Now, listen to Track 242.

50. Now, listen to Track 243.

What is the man's concern?

a. that the company forgot his bonus

b. that he got Peter's paycheck

c. that his paycheck bounced

d. that his paycheck was for the wrong amount

51. Now, listen to Track 244.

Why is Peter out of the office?

a. for a funeral

b. because his wife is having surgery

c. for a conference

d. because he is ill

52. Now, listen to Track 245.

In what department does Peter work?

a. sales

b. collections

c. accounting

d. human resources

Now, listen to Track 246.

53. Now, listen to Track 247.

Where is the new restaurant?

a. on the floor below the office

b. near Luke's apartment

c. near the office

d. across town

54. Now, listen to Track 248.

Why can't they go to lunch today?

a. The man brought his lunch from home.

b. The man has plans already.

c. It is not a nice day to walk.

d. The restaurant won't be open until tomorrow.

55. Now, listen to Track 249.

Who will invite Kristin?

   a. the man who is speaking

   b. the woman who is speaking

   c. Luke

   d. Sandra

Now, listen to Track 250.

56. Now, listen to Track 251.

Where is Meredith?

   a. at home in bed

   b. away on business

   c. in the office

   d. at the doctor's office

57. Now, listen to Track 252.

How long has Meredith been gone?

   a. all day

   b. all week

   c. two weeks

   d. all month

58. Now, listen to Track 253.

Which of the following is Meredith not doing to recover?

   a. resting

   b. taking antibiotics

   c. eating spaghetti

   d. drinking ginger tea

Now, listen to Track 254.

59. Now, listen to Track 255.

Why does the man buy vegetables at the farmers' market?

   a. because they are beautiful

   b. because they are fresh

   c. because they are inexpensive

   d. because they lack flavor

60. Now, listen to Track 256.

When does the man go to the farmers' market?

   a. after work on Thursdays

   b. Saturday mornings

   c. anytime he needs vegetables

   d. during the company party

61. Now, listen to Track 257.

What did the man bring to the company party?

   a. a fresh fruit tray

   b. vegetable dip

   c. pasta

   d. vegetable pastries

Now, listen to Track 258.

62. Now, listen to Track 259.

What does the company need to buy?

   a. umbrellas

   b. hard hats

   c. rain suits

   d. gloves

63. Now, listen to Track 260.

Why do the men need to hurry with their order?

   a. The inventory is incomplete.

   b. The rainy season is about to begin.

   c. The construction project is almost finished.

   d. The purchase orders are due.

64. Now, listen to Track 261.

Where can he look to find out what else the company needs to order?

   a. the warehouse

   b. online

   c. the inventory spreadsheet

   d. the list on his desk

Now, listen to Track 262.

65. Now, listen to Track 263.

Who did Pat call to try to resolve the problem?

a. the technical support line

b. the director

c. the administrative assistant

d. the archivist

66. Now, listen to Track 264.

Why might the man need to work late?

a. to fix the database

b. to fix the router

c. to finish the report

d. to wait for the technician

67. Now, listen to Track 265.

What does the man need in order to complete his work?

a. access to the archives

b. The most recent data from the database

c. a computer disk to back up his work

d. help from Pat

Now, listen to Track 266.

68. Now, listen to Track 267.

Where is the conference?

a. at a hotel

b. in a faraway city

c. close to where she lives

d. at the convention center

69. Now, listen to Track 268.

Why can't the woman drive home on Sunday?

a. She doesn't like to drive at night.

b. She has an important meeting at that time.

c. She doesn't have a car.

d. The hotels are all booked.

70. Now, listen to Track 269.

How does the coworker solve her problem?

a. by renting a car

b. by sharing a room

c. by carpooling

d. by leaving on Saturday

Directions: 🎧 You will hear some talks given by a single speaker. You will be asked to answer four questions about what the speaker says in each talk. Select the best response to each question and mark your choice—**a**, **b**, **c**, or **d**—on your answer sheet. The talks will not be printed in your test book and will be spoken only one time.

Now, listen to Track 270.

71. Now, listen to Track 271.

What is the main purpose of this talk?

a. to set the agenda of the April 7th staff meeting

b. to discuss changes to the insurance plan

c. to have staff mark important dates on their calendars

d. to talk about what the company has achieved during the month of April

72. Now, listen to Track 272.

Why is the health insurance representative coming to the office?

a. to report on his department's progress

b. to enroll people for the regional conference

c. to discuss the calendar for April

d. to talk about changes to insurance plans

73. Now, listen to Track 273.

What will staff need to bring to the April 21st meeting?

a. a new calendar

b. a departmental report

c. a completed enrollment form

d. a completed project

Now, listen to Track 274.

74. Now, listen to Track 275.

Where would you be likely to hear this announcement?

a. the weather service hotline

b. a department store

c. an airport

d. an office

75. Now, listen to Track 276.

What is the main message in the announcement?

a. that the office was hit by a tornado

b. that the computer network went down in the storm

c. that the office is closing early due to the storm

d. that the freeways will be crowded and dangerous

76. Now, listen to Track 277.

Which one of the following measures are office workers not asked to take?

a. making hard copies of their current projects

b. unplugging electronic devices

c. removing food from refrigerators

d. Taking home the emergency calling plan

Now, listen to Track 278.

77. Now, listen to Track 279.

Who is the telephone message from?

a. the receiving department

b. a shipping company

c. a supplier

d. a customer

78. Now, listen to Track 280.

What is the problem?

a. The order will not ship out tomorrow.

b. An item in the order is out of stock.

c. The billing statement is incorrect.

d. The shipping rates have changed.

79. Now, listen to Track 281.

Why does the caller need her phone call returned?

a. to let her know whether to cancel the backordered item or ship it later

b. to ensure that the billing statement is correct

c. to confirm that the original shipment was received

d. to reschedule the next day's shipment

Now, listen to Track 282.

80. Now, listen to Track 283.

To whom is this announcement directed?

a. the driver of a delivery truck

b. the driver of a green minivan

c. the workers at the unloading dock

d. everyone parked in the north parking lot

81. Now, listen to Track 284.

What is the problem?

a. A van has been towed.

b. Someone has left their lights on.

c. There has been an emergency on the unloading dock.

d. A van is illegally parked.

82. Now, listen to Track 285.

What is a possible consequence of this situation?

a. an injury

b. a fine

c. new parking assignments

d. The loss of a job

Now, listen to Track 286.

83. Now, listen to Track 287.

Who would most likely hear this message?

a. a person with a question about an invoice

b. a person with software problems

c. a person looking to register a software product

d. A person wanting to buy software

84. Now, listen to Track 288.

What should the listener have available?

a. the latest statement

b. the registration agreement

c. the reference number of the order

d. the license number of the product

85. Now, listen to Track 289.

When will the listener be helped?

a. in about nine minutes

b. in exactly nine minutes

c. in about five minutes

d. in exactly five minutes

Now, listen to Track 290.

86. Now, listen to Track 291.

Where is this talk being delivered?

a. in a staff development day

b. in a departmental meeting

c. in a conference convocation

d. in a report on Municipal Water Quality

87. Now, listen to Track 292.

What is a consequence of the floods in Indianapolis?

a. A workshop was canceled.

b. A workshop was postponed.

c. A workshop was moved.

d. A workshop was scheduled.

88. Now, listen to Track 293.

What workshop has changed rooms?

a. "From Rain to Faucet"

b. "The Toughest Microbes"

c. "The Future of Chlorine"

d. "Piping Solutions"

Now, listen to Track 294.

89. Now, listen to Track 295.

What is the overall tone of this speaker?

a. self-important and boastful

b. gracious and congratulatory

c. critical and demanding

d. hopeful and consoling

90. Now, listen to Track 296.

What is the main topic on which the speaker is reporting?

a. the increase in October sales

b. the decline in October sales

c. the company's failure to meet the sales goal

d. the quarterly sales figures

91. Now, listen to Track 297.

What will happen on Friday?

a. The figures for the report will be final.

b. The employees will take the boss to lunch.

c. The company will provide lunch for the staff.

d. The company will set new sales goals.

Now, listen to Track 298.

92. Now, listen to Track 299.

Who is the speaker of this message?

a. a bank president

b. a recording

c. the boss

d. a loan officer

93. Now, listen to Track 300.

What is the problem?

 a. The account has insufficient funds.

 b. The account has exceeded its credit limit.

 c. The credit card was stolen.

 d. There was irregular activity on the account.

94. Now, listen to Track 301.

How can the problem be resolved?

 a. by authorizing the purchase

 b. by correcting the purchase order

 c. by paying the fee

 d. by making a deposit

Now, listen to Track 302.

95. Now, listen to Track 303.

Where is this announcement being made?

 a. on board flight 472

 b. in the airport

 c. in a train station

 d. over the radio

96. Now, listen to Track 304.

What is the weather like in Baltimore?

 a. It is snowing lightly.

 b. It is clear.

 c. It is snowing heavily.

 d. It is raining hard.

97. Now, listen to Track 305.

What should passengers do with their boarding passes?

 a. Keep them until the flight is rescheduled.

 b. Turn them in at the gate.

 c. Give them to the flight attendant.

 d. Take them to the desk.

Now, listen to Track 306.

98. Now, listen to Track 307.

Which of the following best describes the talk?

 a. a briefing on the end-of-year reports

 b. a rant on the use of unnecessary graphs

 c. a projection of future marketing figures

 d. a strategy for improved communication between departments

99. Now, listen to Track 308.

Which of the following should be excluded from the report?

 a. success stories

 b. projections

 c. images

 d. useful graphs

100. Now, listen to Track 309.

How should the report be turned in?

 a. via e-mail

 b. on a floppy disk

 c. in hard copy and on a CD

 d. in hard copy and via e-mail

Reading

You will now begin the reading section. You will be asked to read a variety of texts and answer several different types of reading comprehension questions. The entire reading section should take approximately 75 minutes. There are three parts and directions are given for each part. Mark your answers on the answer sheet on pages 171–172.

Directions: A word or phrase is missing in each of the sentences below. Four answer choices are given below each sentence. Select the best answer to complete the sentence. Then mark your choice—**a**, **b**, **c**, or **d**—on your answer sheet.

101. Qi Ling Wong has made many significant _____ in the field of neuroscience and will receive an award from the Institute of Neuroscience of the University of Oregon.
   a. distinctions
   b. medals
   c. contributions
   d. research

102. Legal fees are considered _____ business expenditures, and, therefore, may be written off for tax purposes.
   a. legitimate
   b. preposterous
   c. unscrupulous
   d. profound

103. The director is planning to hire a candidate who _____ experience with marketing and web design.
   a. to have
   b. having
   c. has
   d. have

104. Of the three budgets presented for the new year, only _____ increases spending on advertising.
   a. a
   b. an
   c. these
   d. one

105. Scientists disagree as to _____ or not the dangers of chemical pesticides outweigh their benefits.
   a. whether
   b. when
   c. if
   d. why

106. The _____ of the city council's vote on the proposed change in zoning will figure heavily into our decision about relocating our business.
   a. quality
   b. procedure
   c. order
   d. outcome

107. Tomorrow, the board of directors _____ to approve the new budget.
   a. met
   b. meeting
   c. will meet
   d. are met

108. The new accounting software made preparing the annual report easier _____ ever before.
   a. as
   b. than
   c. of
   d. more

109. Some argue that the driving test for a California license is too easy, while others find it _____.
   a. obstacle
   b. challenging
   c. private
   d. fascinating

110. Ms. Sousa _____ this many employees before.
   a. has never managed
   b. hasn't never managed
   c. is never managing
   d. wasn't never managing

111. As _____ as I am offered the job, I'm going to apply for my visa.
    a. soon
    b. often
    c. usually
    d. early

112. Evelyn Nguyen _____ a promotion last week that she had to refuse for medical reasons.
    a. having been offered
    b. offered
    c. was offered
    d. being offered

113. Our sales team hasn't exceeded its annual goal _____ 1999.
    a. before
    b. since
    c. until
    d. after

114. We've _____ Dr. Francis Banks to speak about business ethics at the workshop.
    a. to invite
    b. inviting
    c. invite
    d. invited

115. In the interview, the director asked me several questions about my _____.
    a. designations
    b. resume
    c. entrepreneur
    d. recognition

116. The documentation for the accountant's financial audit was _____.
    a. absolute
    b. incomplete
    c. unreserved
    d. nervous

117. Tatiana and I _____ to see the new documentary film about the effects of industrialization on Chinese agriculture next Friday.
    a. am going
    b. will going
    c. are going
    d. have been going

118. While the consultant's advice helped cut unnecessary spending from the budget, it _____ cut some valuable and necessary items, and should be carefully reviewed.
    a. further
    b. neither
    c. similarly
    d. also

119. _____ never seems to be a shortage of bright and qualified applicants for entry level positions with our company; it is always hard to choose just one.
    a. There
    b. It
    c. They
    d. Because

120. The company's _____ for increasing the number of repeat customers has backfired, as many customers are put off by the aggressive marketing.
    a. market
    b. revenue
    c. purchase
    d. strategy

121. Traveling in the United States can be confusing since the 50 states _____ six time zones.
    a. consist of
    b. span
    c. are established by
    d. comprise

122. The e-mail reminded participants that the training session would begin at 5:30 P.M. _____ Tuesday.
  a. in
  b. the
  c. on
  d. of

123. He wrote the driving directions on the back of the agenda, but I am having trouble reading _____ handwriting.
  a. it
  b. its
  c. him
  d. his

124. We felt very lucky to be traveling with Mr. Ito; he _____ Seattle several times before and knew all of the best places to go.
  a. had visited
  b. has visited
  c. have visited
  d. has been visited

125. Janet's _____ accomplishment this year was doubling her number of accounts.
  a. more significant
  b. significanter
  c. most significant
  d. significantest

126. Moving to a new city can be stressful for the first few weeks, _____ once you know your way around, it is often an exciting and rewarding experience.
  a. moreover,
  b. because,
  c. however,
  d. also,

127. The extra cost of managing our accounting in-house is negligible _____ its benefits.
  a. equal to
  b. compared to
  c. seeing as
  d. outweighing of

128. The only thing that this report _____ is a general summary of the effectiveness of the new employee retention plan; please add that to the final draft.
  a. wants
  b. lacks
  c. keeps
  d. informs

129. Statistics show that the younger generation of professionals insists on balancing time and money, more than did their _____.
  a. parents
  b. older
  c. previous
  d. the older

130. The employees _____ by the CEO's announcement last week that she would take a personal pay cut to preserve administrative jobs.
  a. get inspired
  b. inspired
  c. are inspiring
  d. were inspired

131. You are required to attend the Thursday staff meeting _____ you are sick or have an emergency.
  a. unless
  b. because
  c. until
  d. but

132. Emily _____ late every night, but now that she is more familiar with the new software, she leaves at 5:30 every day.
  a. is working
  b. has to work
  c. works
  d. used to work

133. If I were starting over on this project, I _____ begin with the content and let the format follow.
  a. can
  b. would
  c. may
  d. should

134. Exercising _____ is a healthy, productive, and free way to manage stress.
  a. regularly
  b. regular
  c. regularness
  d. more regular

135. Ms. Sing _____ her new client right now; let's not disturb her.
  a. calls
  b. called
  c. is calling
  d. to call

136. We called the factory this morning because we are worried _____ the order won't arrive in time.
  a. when
  b. that
  c. if
  d. how

137. The August report details how the company can focus more energy on _____ a quality product, and less on soliciting new clients.
  a. providing
  b. provider
  c. to provide
  d. provision

138. Due to new environmental _____, we will have to update our waste management system by 2018.
  a. regulations
  b. services
  c. balances
  d. portfolios

139. The projections about how the product _____ in the Chinese market are based on surveys and test groups.
  a. performs
  b. performed
  c. is performing
  d. will perform

140. _____ the e-mail yet to confirm the hotel reservations for the regional conference?
  a. You have sent
  b. Have you sent
  c. Sended you
  d. You have to send

Directions: Read the texts that follow. A word or phrase is missing in some of the sentences. Four answer choices are given below each of the texts. Select the best answer to complete the text. Then mark your choice—**a**, **b**, **c**, or **d**—on your answer sheet.

Questions 141 through 144 refer to the following press release.

Press Release
Evergreen Bancshares, Inc.
FOR IMMEDIATE RELEASE
Evergreen Bank acquires Old Town Bank

Fairbanks, Alaska

In light of Old Town Bank's recent troubles, the struggling bank has (141) _____ a purchase offer from Evergreen Bank. Evergreen Bank is a locally owned and operated bank that has served Fairbanks and the surrounding areas for over 30 years. Evergreen happily welcomes the former Old Town banks into its own family of strong, solid, stable banks. While oversight has changed and some restructuring is necessary, Evergreen plans to make as few changes to branch operations at former Old Town banks as possible. Old Town Bank (142) _____ can expect to see the same friendly, familiar faces next week as they did last week. Evergreen is eager to meet all of its new customers' banking needs, and provides a full line of banking services, including home, business, and car loans, as well as online banking. Evergreen is committed to service and financial security. The bank also hopes (143) _____ this transition a positive experience for everyone involved. Evergreen is proud to introduce Norman Schmidt as the new director. Schmidt holds an MBA from The University of Indiana and has raised his three children in Fairbanks, where he has resided for 25 years. "I am excited to continue to serve the people of Fairbanks, and be a part of this (144) _____ merger," says Schmidt.

141. a. presumed
 b. accepted
 c. witnessed
 d. prepared

142. a. customers
 b. residents
 c. patron
 d. participants

143. a. making
 b. able to make
 c. it can making
 d. to make

144. a. portable
 b. traffic
 c. delicious
 d. promising

Questions 145 through 148 refer to the following letter.

Mr. Zhang Wei
Hua Huan Manufacturing, Inc.
10 Dong Street
Kumning City, 650031
Yuman Province
Republic of China
April 23, 2009
Dear Mr. Wei:

I am (145) _____ to inform you that the merchandise that we ordered from you on February 12, reference number 54681, was not delivered until April 17. We received it a week and a half after our spring sale had ended. My assistant placed several calls about the order, prior to the spring sale, and was consistently informed that the (146) _____ was on its way. This was obviously not the case, based on its arrival date. We had anticipated selling five or six cases of the T-shirts we ordered from your factory. The merchandise is now, (147) _____, out of season for retail purposes.

I have been informed that your factory underwent some changes in recent months, and I hope that the transition is now complete and your problems are resolved. Nonetheless, I cannot be expected keep merchandise that was delivered too late for sale. Please let me know how you (148) _____ like it returned and credit my account for the full price of the merchandise as well as the return shipping costs.

Thank you for your prompt attention to this matter.
Sincerely,

Francine Yeager
Purchasing Coordinator, Fabfash Retailers

145. a. excited
    b. writing
    c. regretted
    d. forgetting

146. a. shipment
    b. letter
    c. parceling
    d. casement

147. a. thankfully
    b. but
    c. otherwise
    d. however

148. a. can
    b. must
    c. ought to
    d. would

Questions 149 through 152 refer to the following e-mail.

TO: All Employees
FROM: Frank Gomez
DATE: October 12, 2009
RE: Change in Vacation Policy

As you know, over the summer the company experienced major disruptions due to the current vacation policy. We had a shortage of critical personnel during the second week of July, (149) _____ caused delays in some essential functions of our business. Management met on Friday to discuss this problem and draft a new company policy on vacations. This e-mail is to provide notice to all InfoTech employees of our new vacation policy.

(150) _____ November 1, 2009, employees must submit a vacation request to their immediate supervisors no less than two weeks in advance, if they plan to use three or more consecutive days of accumulated vacation time. The supervisor will either approve or decline the request within two business days. If an employee wishes to use two or fewer consecutive days of vacation time, the two-week rule (151) _____, but the employee is asked to notify his supervisor at least two days in advance. Management understands that it is sometimes necessary for employees use vacation time to attend to emergencies and urgent personal needs. In this case, you are exempt from the two-week rule, but please give your supervisor as much advance notice as possible.

Again, this policy this policy will go into effect on the first of the month.

This new policy will allow us to hire temporary help, when necessary, and ensure that vacations are scheduled in a way that will not be disruptive to the company.

Thank you for your (152) _____.
Thanks,
Frank Gomez
Human Resources

149. a. what
  b. instead
  c. but
  d. which

150. a. Effective
  b. Projected
  c. About
  d. Before

151. a. doesn't applies
  b. isn't applying
  c. does not apply
  d. wasn't applied

152. a. advice
  b. completion
  c. punctuality
  d. cooperation

Directions: In this part you will read a selection of texts, such as magazine and newspaper articles, letters, and advertisements. Each text is followed by several questions. Select the best answer for each question and mark your choice—**a**, **b**, **c**, or **d**—on your answer sheet.

Questions 153 through 157 refer to the following article.

While company layoffs often appear, at first glance, to be the most decisive and effective method by which a business can save money and recover costs, they provide only a short-term solution to a company's problems and may prove to be detrimental to a company in the long-term. The costs of downsizing can sometimes outweigh its benefits. Evidence repeatedly suggests that layoffs rarely reduce a company's costs by as much as expected and that layoffs can significantly reduce a company's performance. This can often lead to reduced stock values and insecurity among shareholders.

Employers, looking at salaries as strictly a budget item, may forget that employees are not merely an expense, but a long-term investment. Wages can be better understood as payments into an employee's capital of skill and commitment. The announcement of a round of layoffs can undermine this important investment. Layoffs not only affect those low-performing employees whose jobs have been cut, but they also create an atmosphere of uncertainty, which causes others to leave. Layoffs can therefore lead to a reduction in the quality and productivity of the overall staff.

If a reduction in payroll expenses does not already seem to be eclipsed by the reduction in performance, also consider the possible affect that this might have on shareholder morale. Layoffs communicate to the stockholders that a company is in severe crisis. They can therefore lead to a decline in stock value which often, in turn, compounds the very problem that the layoffs sought to resolve.

153. What is this article mainly about?
- **a.** the importance of budget analysis
- **b.** the negative effects of downsizing staff
- **c.** the best way for companies to increase stock value
- **d.** the various factors that contribute to shareholder morale

154. The word *detrimental*, in paragraph 1, is closest in meaning to
- **a.** positive
- **b.** temporary
- **c.** superficial
- **d.** harmful

155. According to the article, why does a company lose high-performing workers in a round of layoffs?
- **a.** They are usually the highest paid and therefore the first to be laid off.
- **b.** They often leave voluntarily due to the climate of uncertainty.
- **c.** They usually leave because they are worried about stock value.
- **d.** They become frustrated with their coworkers' lack of productivity.

156. According to the article, which of the following is least important to the overall success of a business?
- **a.** employee commitment
- **b.** payroll expenses
- **c.** shareholder confidence
- **d.** employee skill

157. The word *compounds* in the final sentence of the article is closest in meaning to
- **a.** multifaceted
- **b.** complex
- **c.** makes greater
- **d.** chemical combinations

Questions 158 through 160 refer to the following advertisement.

**The Fabrique Boutique
is having a
Going Out of Business Sale**
8:00 A.M. Monday, November 9 to 8:00 P.M.
Friday, November 13
116 Harney Road, Minneapolis
EVERYTHING MUST GO!
Clothing* Purses* Belts
as well as
Racks* Fixtures* Showcases
Even Our Mannequins Are for Sale!
All at Prices too Good to Be True!
We are closing our doors forever at 8:00 P.M.
on Friday and headed for retirement in Hawaii.
We must liquidate! Don't miss this
opportunity to stock up on all our funky,
hand-made, one-of-a-kind fashions!
For more information about this HUGE sale,
visit our website at www.fabriqueboutique.com
or call 872-8979.

158. What is the purpose of this advertisement?
- **a.** to advertise a business for sale
- **b.** to advertise a seasonal clearance sale
- **c.** to announce the owner's intention to retire
- **d.** to advertise a liquidation sale

159. What kind of store is this advertisement for?
- **a.** an independent clothing store
- **b.** an electrical fixture store
- **c.** a mannequin store
- **d.** a retail supply store

160. According to the advertisement, what can people find on the business's website?
- **a.** an online catalog
- **b.** a phone number
- **c.** information about the sale
- **d.** hours of operation

Questions 161 through 164 refer to the following letter.

Dear Mr. Jones:

Thank you for your recent phone call regarding your business banking account number 90089733. We are glad to be able to assist you in this matter. We were able to determine the source of the $1,348.78 discrepancy that you noticed in your checking account. We have tracked down our error and credited your account accordingly.

As of today, your business checking account balance is $5,678.93. The adjustment will appear on your next monthly statement. The adjusted balance is available for immediate withdrawal.

We value your business and we apologize for any inconvenience our error may have caused. If you have any questions or need any further assistance with the matter, please contact your local branch or our customer service line at 888-356-9087. Please retain this letter for your records as confirmation of the adjustment to your business checking account number 90089733.

Thank you for your business and your attention to your accounts.

Sincerely,

Margaret Reed
Highland National Bank, Springfield Branch Manager

161. What was the problem with Mr. Jones's account?
- **a.** Due to an error by the bank, his account was short by $1,348.78.
- **b.** Due to an error by the bank, his account was over by $1,348.78.
- **c.** Due to Mr. Jones's own error, his account was short by $1,348.78.
- **d.** Due to Mr. Jones's own error, his account was over by $1,348.78.

162. Why does Ms. Reed suggest that Mr. Jones keep the letter?
- **a.** to confirm his statement
- **b.** to remind him of the sincerity of her apology
- **c.** to correct his own accounting
- **d.** to serve as a record of the adjustment

163. The phrase *tracked down* at the end of the first paragraph is closest in meaning to
- **a.** placed
- **b.** located
- **c.** directed
- **d.** corrected

164. Which of the following best describes the tone of this letter?
- **a.** professional and apologetic
- **b.** conversational and friendly
- **c.** informal and unprofessional
- **d.** formal and accusatory

Questions 165 through 169 refer to the following article.

Radio frequency identification, or RFID, technology is not new, but as it becomes cheaper, it promises to change retail business significantly. Using RFID, a company can store vast amounts of information about a product on a microchip that attaches to the product itself like a bar code. Unlike a bar code, however, the RFID tag offers access to a database of information about the product. It can give an up-to-date history of where a product has traveled, and real-time inventory information, such as the sizes and colors currently available in any location. This technology may one day eliminate the necessity of having employees check inventory or track shipments. It also has the potential for numerous security and safety applications.

As major retailers begin to adopt this technology, concerns are arising about how RFID may affect the privacy of consumers and employees alike. Detractors worry about the implications of a business being able to track the movements of employees and customers in their stores and warehouses using the new technology. They fear that the technology might give businesses the ability to track customers' movements to determine their preferences. The potential for abuse, however, does not seem to be slowing down the demand and overall outlook for RFID.

165. Which of the following best states the purpose of this article?
- **a.** The article warns of the dangerous applications of RFID technology in various sectors of society.
- **b.** The article explains how RFID technology has replaced the bar code entirely.
- **c.** The article examines the promises and dangers of using RFID technology in the retail sector.
- **d.** The article illustrates how RFID favors major retailers over local retailers.

166. According to the article, how is an RFID tag superior to a barcode?
- **a.** It makes it necessary for employees to keep a closer watch on inventory.
- **b.** It protects consumer privacy.
- **c.** It contains more information about the product.
- **d.** It can be deactivated.

167. As used in the first sentence of the second paragraph, the word *adopt* means
- **a.** to take custody of a child
- **b.** to change in order to meet the needs of a situation
- **c.** to care for
- **d.** to choose and decide to use

168. According to the article, what ethical concerns does the rise of RFID technology raise?
- **a.** concerns about the loss of human jobs to machines
- **b.** concerns about consumer privacy
- **c.** concerns about outsourcing
- **d.** concerns about employee productivity

169. According to the article, what change in RFID technology has made it viable for use in retail applications?
- **a.** a change in speed
- **b.** a change in size
- **c.** a change in price
- **d.** a change in security standards

Questions 170 through 171 refer to the following business card.

HILLIARD CONSTRUCTION

Quality home building
from the foundation to the roof

Marcos Gil
General Contractor

4121 Las Palmas Ave.   TEL: 619-574-0835
San Diego, CA 92100   FAX: 619-574-0835
www.buildwithhilliard.com
E-MAIL: marcos.gil@buildwithhilliard.com

---

170. What information is not provided on this card?
   a. Marcos Gil's phone number
   b. Marcos Gil's title
   c. the hours of operation
   d. the company slogan

171. What does the company do?
   a. builds houses
   b. writes contracts
   c. makes websites
   d. constructs roads

Questions 172 through 176 refer to the following article excerpt.

Determining the success of a small business can be tricky. A business may show a good profit, but consistently run into cash flow problems, sometimes severe ones. The idea of profit refers to a sum of money earned at a fixed (but sometimes imaginary) point in time. As a reference point for a business' success, it is the standard. However, using cash flow as a reference point gives a more dynamic picture of a business' success based on a constant comparison of available cash to expenses. A business owner's understanding of his own success can depend on which of these models he works from.

The outlook on a business' financial situation can similarly depend on whether the business follows a cash method or an accrual method of accounting. In a cash method of accounting, income is reported only as payment is received, while the accrual method of accounting records income as soon as the sale is made. So, using the accrual method, if it takes a buyer three months to send a check for the goods and services provided, then a business may have trouble meeting its cash flow needs in the interim, while still showing a profit. For this reason, many small businesses prefer to use the cash method. The cash method is simpler and offers a more realistic picture of a business' finances at any given moment in time. The accrual system, however, allows for more sophisticated analysis, which can consolidate several facets of business management into a single operation.

172. What best states what this article is mostly about?
   a. how businesses can use different methods of accounting to look less profitable for tax purposes
   b. how the accrual method compares to the cash method of accounting
   c. how understandings of profitability and methods of accounting can alter perceptions of success
   d. how the idea of profit compares with the idea of cash flow

173. What is the major difference between the accrual method and cash method of accounting?
   a. what kinds of sales are recorded
   b. when a sale is recorded
   c. whether a business uses mostly cash or credit
   d. how many times a month sales are recorded

174. According to the article, what is an advantage of using an accrual system of accounting?
- **a.** It gives a more dynamic picture of a business's success.
- **b.** It is simpler.
- **c.** It reduces cash flow discrepancies.
- **d.** It allows for more sophisticated financial analysis.

175. According to the article, what problems can arise from looking strictly at profit?
- **a.** cash flow problems
- **b.** accrual problems
- **c.** accounting errors
- **d.** imaginary problems

176. The word *operation* in the final sentence is nearest in meaning to:
- **a.** a functioning state
- **b.** a medical procedure
- **c.** a controlled activity
- **d.** a military action

Questions 177 through 180 refer to the following e-mail message.

TO: Bob Schwartz
FROM: Ellen Sepeda
DATE: March 15, 2009
RE: Reservation Confirmation and Special Instructions

This e-mail confirms our recent telephone conversation regarding Martin Hamilton's stay at the Walford Hotel next week. He is an important client of our firm and we want to ensure that he is happy and comfortable during his stay. Any charges that Mr. Hamilton accrues are to be directed to me at Quesburger Enterprises, P.O. Box 1145, Newark, NJ 07101.

Mr. Hamilton's plane will land at Newark Liberty Airport on at 5:30 on March 21, and he should be checking in around 7:00 P.M.

As we agreed, the rate for his room will be $350 plus tax per day. He will probably be staying for three days.

Please have wine and appetizers in his room when he arrives, and please make certain that our important guest has everything he needs.

Thank you for your cooperation.

177. For whom does Bob Schwartz work?
- **a.** Quesburger Enterprises
- **b.** Walford Hotel
- **c.** Newark Liberty Airport
- **d.** Martin Hamilton

178. Who is going to pay for Mr. Hamilton's stay?
- **a.** Mr. Hamilton
- **b.** Mr. Schwartz
- **c.** Ms. Sepeda
- **d.** The stay is free.

179. When will Mr. Hamilton arrive at the hotel?
- **a.** around 5:30 P.M. on March 15
- **b.** around 7:00 P.M. on March 15
- **c.** around 5:30 P.M. on March 21
- **d.** around 7:00 P.M. on March 21

180. What is the relationship between Mr. Hamilton and Ms. Sepeda?
- **a.** He is her client.
- **b.** She is his client.
- **c.** He works at the hotel where her client is staying.
- **d.** She works at the hotel where his client is staying.

Questions 181 through 185 refer to the newspaper clipping and e-mail message.

Homes for Rent

2/2 South Central, $1500/mo.
641 Armstrong Street. Fantastic remodeled condo. Close to Donner Park and downtown. Modern kitchen with granite countertops, dishwasher, and gas stove. Both bedrooms have roomy bath and large closets. Central air and heat. Washer and dryer. Patio overlooks pool. Two reserved parking spots.

3/2 Walking Distance to University Campus! $2500/mo.
114 Lewis Street. Beautiful home near Pope Elementary School between Johnson and 1st St. This home is close to everything! The large master bedroom has its own spacious bathroom. The two other bedrooms are connected by the other smaller bathroom. Wood floors. Plenty of yard and storage space. Central heat and air conditioning. Shed for tools and equipment. Recently painted. Well kept. Separate utility room off kitchen with washer and dryer. The refrigerator, washer and dryer will stay with the tenant. Available August 15. A must-see!

4/3 Suburban Dream! $2000
14902 Highland Estates Drive. Brand New Construction! Huge lot! WOW! GRANITE, STAINLESS, ON-DEMAND HOT WATER, VARIABLE LIGHT DIMMERS, and MORE! Great schools. Community pool. Walking distance to neighborhood parks and schools.

To: Mr. Nazim
From: Arjun Patel
Date: July 6, 2009
Re: Relocation Questions

Dear Mr. Nazim,

Thank you for giving me the opportunity to prove my capabilities with your firm. I am very excited about the opportunity to work with such a respected name in the field of biotechnology. I am also excited to come to Berkeley. I have sent in the final paperwork for my visa, which I expect to arrive early in August. I will be able to begin work on August 22.

I am, however, unfamiliar with the city of Berkeley and have a few questions about relocating. I understand that I will be doing some work at the university lab and some at the BioLead office. I like to walk to work and am hoping to find a house to rent that is either near the university or near the downtown office. I have two children who will be attending elementary school and a wife who does not drive, so it would be nice to be near an elementary school. I also would like to have a yard for the children to play in. Could you recommend a neighborhood, or let me know if you see a house that would meet my needs at a reasonable price for the area?

Thanks again. I look forward to meeting you in person and getting to work on my first project.

Sincerely,
Arjun Patel

181. Of the three real estate listings above, which house or houses would meet all of Mr. Patel's needs?
  a. 641 Armstrong
  b. 114 Lewis
  c. 14902 Highland Estates Drive
  d. more than one of the homes

182. Why is Mr. Patel coming to Berkeley?
  a. He is going to attend the university.
  b. He was offered a job.
  c. He has to wait for his visa.
  d. He is looking for a new house.

183. What might be a concern for Mr. Patel about the home at 14902 Highland Estates Drive?
  a. He can't walk to work.
  b. It has no yard.
  c. It is far from the schools.
  d. More than one of the above is true.

184. What will happen in early August?
  a. Mr. Patel will move into the house.
  b. Mr. Patel will begin his new job.
  c. Mr. Patel will get his visa.
  d. The company will have a position for Mr. Patel.

185. Which of the following does the house on Lewis Street not have?
  a. air conditioning
  b. a bedroom for each of Patel's children
  c. a refrigerator
  d. a pool

Questions 186 through 190 refer to the following policy and receipt.

Allowable Business Expenses
Travel

For reimbursable and non-reimbursable expenses related to travel, including transportation, lodging, meals (in travel status), etc., see separate Travel Policy.

Business Meals

We will reimburse a business meal expense when it is deemed to be necessary, reasonable, and appropriate by a supervisor. We will reimburse meals only when they are an essential part of a business meeting or activity, not when they are a matter of personal convenience. You must submit the original itemized receipt and include the provider's name and date, the name(s) of any other person included on the bill, and the purpose of the meeting; this information may be attached to the bill on another sheet of paper as necessary.

Employee Morale

Many expenses for employee recognition and morale activities can be reimbursed. This includes food and related expenses for events such as birthdays, holiday parties, births, and farewell parties. Receipts must be submitted along with an explanation of the purchases for such events. If a receipt includes both personal and work-related expenses, the work-related expenses should be circled and a separate page attached, which totals and explains the reimbursable expenses. Receipts must be submitted within 30 days of the purchase. Most personal gifts, such as farewell gifts, shower gifts, or birthday gifts are not allowable expenses; the members of a department must purchase gifts for fellow employees out-of-pocket. The company, however, will reimburse for the purchase of a condolence gift or get-well-soon gift for a coworker, in the case of a family death or personal hospitalization.

Telephone Calls

Long distance phone charges on a personal home phone or cellular phone for business purposes can be reimbursed. A copy of the bill showing the charges must be attached along with an explanation of the business purpose of any call.

Conference/Registration Fees

The company will reimburse employees for the registration fees of any approved conference or professional meeting.

SUPER Z MARKET

111 Main Street
San Antonio, TX 78789
****

10/20/09   8:53:08pm
Your Cashier: Adrian
CASH TRANSACTION

****

Party hats
    3@3.99ea   11.97 T
Eggs $1.99
Milk $4.99
Bread $2.29
Bakery Cake (15 servings) $29.95
Plates
    3@2.50ea   7.50 T
Cups
    2@4.00ea   8.00 T
Soda Pop Variety Pack
    2@7.50ea   15.00
TAX $2.25

Balance	$73.94
Cash Tendered	$75.00
Change	$1.06

TOTAL ITEMS SOLD   14

****

186. This receipt is from an employee who bought food for a coworker's birthday party at the supermarket. He also bought eggs, milk, and bread for his own home. According to the company policy on business expenses, how should he distinguish between the two before turning in his receipt for reimbursement?
   a. He should put a star next to party hats, bakery cake, plates, cups, and soda pop.
   b. He should put a star next to eggs, milk, and bread.
   c. He should draw a circle around party hats, bakery cake, plates, cups, and soda pop.
   d. He should draw a circle around eggs, milk, and bread.

187. What is important about the date November 19, 2009 in this situation?
   a. November 19, 2009 is the day of the party.
   b. November 19, 2009 is the day the new reimbursement policy goes into effect.
   c. November 19, 2009 is the day he made the purchase.
   d. November 19, 2009 is the last day he can turn in his receipt.

188. Where should he write the total price of the items purchased for the work party?
   a. at the bottom of the receipt
   b. at the top of the receipt
   c. in the margin of the receipt
   d. on a different sheet of paper

189. Under the company expense reimbursement policy, which of the following can't be reimbursed?
   a. an unexplained long-distance call
   b. an approved business lunch
   c. a conference registration fee
   d. a bouquet of flowers for a worker in the hospital

190. Which of the following does not need to be provided for an employee to be reimbursed for a business meal?
   a. the reason for the meeting
   b. an itemized bill
   c. the names of all people at the meal
   d. a supervisor's signature

Questions 191 through 195 refer to the following resume and letter.

Tina Flores
987 West 3rd St.
Louisville, KY 88979
782-999-0909
tina.jones@zzombo.com

Objective:
A warehouse management position in Oklahoma.

Skills:
Bilingual English/Spanish. Experience with all major office software. Experience with network and database management (WareInfo Software, 8 years).

Experience:
2001–present
Team Manager, Super Z Regional Distribution Center and Warehouse
Duties:
Managing workers, training workers, maintaining inventory database (WareInfo Software)

1999–2001
Office Assistant and Receptionist, J and J Home Insurance
Duties:
Light bookkeeping, recordkeeping, filing, managing customer communication

Education:
BA, 1999 Sul Ross University, Alpine, Texas (Major: Spanish Language; Minor: Information Sciences)

Certifications:
2003 Certified Bilingual, 2005 Certified WareInfo Administrator

Ms. Tina Flores
987 West 3rd St.
Louisville, KY 88979

Dear Ms. Flores,

We regret to inform you that the position for which you have applied, as a team manager at the MegaMart Distribution Warehouse, has been filled. We ended up filling the position in-house. It is difficult to have to turn away an applicant with your qualifications and experience. Looking over your resume, I see that you may be an excellent candidate for a position opening in the near future.

Over the summer we are changing our warehouse management software. We will be switching to the WareInfo Software Database and will be hiring three trainers in the program. I will keep your resume on file for one of those positions.

You will need to fill out another application for the position, which will be posted on our website in mid-May. We will be looking for a bilingual (English/Spanish) trainer who is already familiar with the software. I think your qualifications are ideal for this job.

Thank you for your interest in working with the MegaMart. I hope to be in contact with you again in May.

Sincerely,

Frank Jones
Human Resources, MegaMart Distribution Warehouse

191. For what position did Ms. Flores apply?
    a. WareInfo Software Trainer
    b. WareInfo Software Adminsitrator
    c. MegaMart Distribution Warehouse Team Manager
    d. MegaMart Distribution Warehouse Office Assistant

192. Which if the following is does not qualify Ms. Flores for the training position mentioned in the letter?
    a. her language skills
    b. her software experience
    c. her bookkeeping experience
    d. her experience training workers

193. Where is the MegaMart Distribution Center most likely located?
    a. Texas
    b. Kentucky
    c. Oklahoma
    d. Arkansas

194. According to the letter, what does Ms. Flores need to do in May?
    a. fill out another job application
    b. send in another résumé
    c. update the job postings on the website
    d. call Mr. Jones on the telephone

195. What kind of degree does Ms. Flores hold?
    a. an associate degree in Information Sciences
    b. a bachelor degree in Spanish
    c. a WareInfo Administration Certificate
    d. This information is not given.

Questions 196 through 200 refer to the following article and website.

Business Today, February 10, 2008
What is an MBA really worth?
Is it worth the time and money to pursue a Masters in Business? Does it really advance your career? Does it increase your salary? Does it increase your job security?

According to a recent study of the highest ranked business schools in the country, the average cost for a 2-year MBA has almost doubled since 1998. The average cost at the top ten ranked schools jumped from $52,000 in 1998, to almost $95,000 in 2008. During the same period, the average differential between pre-MBA and post-MBA salaries dropped significantly. MBAs from the top-ranked schools could expect a salary jump of more than $51,000 a year in 1998. That number was below $31,000 a year by 2008.

However, for many people, an MBA is more than a matter of money. Sure, an MBA can help you move up in your current job in regard to pay, but just as importantly, it can help you move up in terms of responsibility. It can help you earn the responsibility and power you need to make important changes and contributions in your field. An MBA can, of course, be of huge benefit to anyone who wants to start his own business. And perhaps most importantly, an MBA is a good way to increase your knowledge, skills, and general competency. It will help you do a better job, not just get a better job. It can help you stay up-to-date with the issues and technologies of the day. Aren't these better reasons to pursue a degree than money, anyway?

Boulean University
Morgan School of Business

Online Business Programs
We offer Master Certificates in Today's Most Important Business
    Subjects!
Build your Career Online with Boulean University
Boulean University's online master certificate programs are suited to
    professionals who are looking to stay sharp and competitive. It
    is a program for people who want to stay at the top of their
    fields and hone their skills by mastering the most critical MBA
    subject areas. Certificates will have a focus on marketing,
    management, finance, or human resources. Our online
    programs allow students flexibility to pursue their dreams.
Choose from these programs:
Marketing—The marketing MBA gives you
    the tools, technology, and knowledge to reach your audience
    and sales. More Details →
Management—A management MBA will
    make you a better manager and make your company more
    successful. More Details →
Finance—An MBA in finance will help you manage your money,
    and analyze your finances to make your business grow
    and flourish. More Details →
Human Resources—The human resources MBA will make you a
    better communicator and teach you to
    protect your business from liabilities. More Details →

Home

Online Classrooms

Online Business Programs

Tuition and Aid

Contacts

Apply Online

Success Stories

FAQs

196. Both the website and the article mention which of the following as a benefit of an MBA?
- **a.** increased flexibility
- **b.** increased pay
- **c.** increased skill
- **d.** increased confidence

197. How many online MBA programs does Boulean University offer?
- **a.** one
- **b.** four
- **c.** eight
- **d.** This information is not given.

198. Using the website (the page shown and its links) and article together, which of the following could one do?

    a. compare the tuition of Boulean with the average tuition of the nation's top ten MBA programs

    b. determine by how much an MBA at Boulean would increase an applicant's salary

    c. figure out which Boulean program would increase one's pay by the greatest margin

    d. compare online classrooms to regular classrooms

199. Which of the following best summarizes the *Business Today* article?

    a. Getting an MBA is a waste of money and time in the new economy, as salaries can't make up for the cost of losing two years of work.

    b. An MBA might not be worth the energy if you are just interested in the money, but is very valuable if you are interested in the learning.

    c. An MBA is the best, and perhaps only, way to increase your earning potential and advance in your career.

    d. It is better to do the right thing for the wrong reason than not to do the right thing at all.

200. In the webpage's introduction to Boulean's online MBA programs, the word *flexibility* is closest in meaning to

    a. ability to bend the body

    b. ability to adapt to circumstances

    c. ability to be influenced by other people

    d. ability to retain shape

Speaking

This section tests your skills for the TOEIC Speaking Test. It includes 11 questions that measure different aspects of your speaking ability. The test lasts approximately 20 minutes.

For each type of question, you will be given specific directions, including the time allowed for preparation and speaking. It is to your advantage to say as much as you can in the time allowed. It is also important that you speak clearly and that you answer each question according to the directions.

Directions: In this part of the test, you will read aloud the text on the screen. You will have 45 seconds to prepare. Then you will have 45 seconds to read the text aloud. Use a stopwatch or clock to keep track of your time.

201. Every day more and more people are changing their lifestyles in minor, and sometimes major, ways to minimize their environmental impact. Such small gestures as bringing reusable shopping bags to the grocery store, turning down the thermostat on the hot water heater, or hanging laundry outside to dry on sunny days can save millions of tons of fossil fuels a year. Some people are even making major investments in a greener future by installing solar panels in their homes or purchasing cars that run on alternative fuels. I am doing my part by switching my investment portfolio to Greensense Investments, where I can choose between several environmentally friendly mutual funds.

202. Could your business stand to save thousands of dollars a year? How would it change your bottom line to hold all your business meetings online? Take our free trial to find out. You have nothing to lose! Business meetings require hours of employee planning, expenditures on food and refreshments, and wasted time in transit. It all adds up. For $55 a month you could cut those costs and save that time. Subscribe to our service and hold unlimited business meetings online for $55 a month. Setup is easy and the savings are huge. Visit netmeet.com for details.

Directions: In this part of the test, you will describe the picture on your screen in as much detail as you can. You will have 30 seconds to prepare your response. Then you will have 45 seconds to speak about the picture. Use a stopwatch or clock to keep track of your time.

203.

Directions: In this part of the test, you will answer three questions. For each question, begin responding immediately after you hear a beep. No preparation time is provided. You will have 15 seconds each to respond to questions 204 and 205, and 30 seconds to respond to question 206. Use a stopwatch or clock to keep track of your time.

Imagine that you are speaking with a financial advisor about your spending habits and preferences. The advisor is asking you how you feel about using credit cards.

204. How often do you buy things using a credit card?

205. What kinds of things do you usually buy with a credit card?

206. Tell me whether you think using a credit card is a good idea or not, and why.

Directions: In this part of the test, you will answer three questions based on the information provided. You will have 30 seconds to read the information below. Then, you will have 15 seconds to respond to questions 207 and 208, and 30 seconds to respond to question 209. Use a stopwatch or clock to keep track of your time.

Hello, I'm calling because I want to make a donation to your foundation. I do not have a pledge form, so I need to pledge my donation over the phone. I do have a few questions about becoming a member.

Care and Share Foundation
Supporting our local food banks, homeless shelter, afterschool enrichment programs, and coats for tots programs and many other worthy community-based charities since 1978

Make Your Tax-Deductible Donation Today!
Pledge a donation at any of the following membership levels, and receive a thank you gift:

___$20 Care and Share Membership (you will receive a subscription to our monthly newsletter)

___$50 Care and Share Great Neighbor (you will receive a subscription to our monthly newsletter and a "Great Neighbor" T-shirt)

___$100 Care and Share Community Leader (you will receive a subscription to our monthly newsletter and an "I Take Care of my Community" coffee mug)

___$500 Care and Share Local Hero (you will receive a subscription to our monthly newsletter, a "Great Neighbor" T-shirt, and an "I Take Care of my Community" coffee mug)

We also accept donations of any other amount!

☐ Yes, I want to support my local food banks, homeless shelter, afterschool enrichment programs, and coats for tots programs and many other worthy community-based charities by becoming a member of the Care and Share foundation at the $_____ level.

I want to make my payment using:

☐ Personal Check (check #_____).

☐ Major Credit Card (Type of Card_____ Card #_____).

☐ Please bill me later.

New Member Information:

Name_____

Address_____

Phone Number_____

207. What is the minimum pledge to become a supporting member of your foundation?

208. What are my payment options for a donation?

209. Can you tell me a little about the kinds of programs that your organization supports?

Directions: In this part of the test, you will be presented with a problem and asked to propose a solution. You will have 30 seconds to prepare. Then you will have 60 seconds to speak. Use a stopwatch or clock to keep track of your time.

210. Reply as though you worked for the company that owns the website.
As you reply, be sure to:
- show that you recognize the problem
- propose a way of dealing with the problem
Now, listen to Track 310.

Directions: In this part of the test, you will give your opinion about a specific topic. Be sure to say as much as you can in the time allowed. You will have 15 seconds to prepare. Then you will have 60 seconds to speak. Use a stopwatch or clock to keep track of your time.

211. Some people are willing to move from place to place to take better jobs and advance quickly in their fields. Other people prefer staying in one location or community to pursue their careers, even if they cannot advance as quickly that way. What is your opinion about transferring from place to place to advance more quickly in a career? Give reasons for your opinion.

Writing

This is the TOEIC Writing Test. This test includes eight questions that measure different aspects of your writing ability. The test lasts approximately one hour. For each type of question, you will be given specific directions, including the time allowed for writing.

Directions: In this part of the test, you will write ONE sentence that is based on a picture. With each picture, you will be given TWO words or phrases that you must use in your sentence. You can change the forms of the words and you can use the words in any order.

Your sentence will be scored on:

- the appropriate use of grammar
- the relevance of the sentence to the picture

You will have eight minutes to complete this part of the test. Use a stopwatch or clock to keep track of your time.

212.

freeway exit, realize

_____

_____

213.

presentation, after

_____

_____

214.

decide on, when

_____

_____

215.

imagine, finally

_____

_____

216.

weekend, beside

_____

_____

Directions: In this part of the test, you will show how well you can write a response to an e-mail.

Your response will be scored on:

- the quality and variety of your sentences
- vocabulary
- organization

You will have 10 minutes to read and answer each e-mail. Use a stopwatch or clock to keep track of your time.

> From: Nancy Jones, Administrative Assistant
> To: Staff
> Sent: August 8
> Re: Purchase of Office Supplies
> Hello, everyone! Tomorrow I am going to place our monthly order for office supplies for the department. Please reply to me before noon tomorrow and let me know if you are running low on any supplies. Please tell me what you need and how much of it to order. Thanks.

Directions: Respond to the e-mail. Respond as if you were an employee of this company. In your e-mail, let Ms. Jones know at least TWO items you need.

Please respond to Ms. Jones's e-mail by asking her to order at least two things for you.

217. _____

_____

_____

_____

Directions: In this part of the test, you will show how well you can write a response to a letter.

Your response will be scored on:

- the quality and variety of your sentences
- vocabulary
- organization

You will have 10 minutes to read and answer each e-mail. Use a stopwatch or clock to keep track of your time.

> Dear Sir or Madam,
> Your former boss has applied for a job with our company. You were listed as a reference on your former boss's resume. Could you please tell us a little about your former boss's character, work ethic and management skills, as well as how long you worked together. We appreciate your taking the time to provide us with this information.
>
> Thank you,
> Elton Harris
> Human Resources, North Co., Inc.

Directions: Reply to the letter, providing a reference for a former boss. In your response, provide the requested information, including at least TWO reasons you liked working for this person.

218. _____

_____

_____

_____

_____

Directions: In this part of the test, you will write an essay in response to a question that asks you to state, explain, and support your opinion on an issue. Typically, an effective essay will contain a minimum of 300 words.

Your response will be scored on

- whether your opinion is supported with reasons and/or examples
- grammar
- vocabulary
- organization

You will have 30 minutes to plan, write, and revise your essay. Use a stopwatch or clock to keep track of your time.

Many people believe that happy workers are more productive and perform better at their jobs. Many factors contribute to workers' happiness: feeling appreciated, being challenged, having a sense of purpose in their work, feeling secure in their position. What do you think is the most important factor in a worker's happiness? Give reasons and examples to support your opinion.

219. _____

_____

_____

_____

_____

_____

_____

_____

_____

_____

_____

_____

_____

_____

_____

_____

_____

Answers

1. b. The man is on an airplane flight. The man is using the device without any indication that it is broken, so the answer is not choice **a**. He is on an airplane, not a bus, so choice **c** is incorrect. The coffee is upright on the table, so choice **d** is not correct.

2. d. The woman is preparing to give her check and credit card to the waiter. The women are inside the restaurant, so it is not closed, making choice **c** incorrect. The answer is not choice **a** because the woman is paying the check and so did not forget it. The answer is not choice **b** because the food is already on the table.

3. b. The photo shows a businessman taking inventory in a warehouse. None of the boxes appears to be damaged, so choice **d** is not correct. The shelves are functioning correctly, making choice **a** incorrect. There is no injured woman in the photo, so choice **c** is not an appropriate answer.

4. a. The children are smiling and splashing in the pool. They seem to be happy and having fun. Choice **b** is incorrect because the photo does not show a picnic. The picture does not indicate that a hotel has good rates, so the answer is not choice **c**. Choice **d** is also incorrect because no one in the picture is running.

5. d. There are no people inside the examining room at the doctor's office, making choices **b** and **c** both incorrect. The curtain is open, so choice **a** is not correct.

6. b. The woman is exercising using a machine at the gym. She is not playing soccer or preparing a healthy meal, so choices **c** and **d** are incorrect. The two women shown seem to be exercising independently, so they are not cooperating, and choice **a** is not the correct answer choice.

7. d. She is giving a presentation. She has already prepared for the meeting so choice **a** is not the answer. She is neither closing a book nor ironing her suit, so choices **b** and **c** are also incorrect.

8. a. The receptionist is talking on the telephone, or is "on the phone," as Americans say. She has not hung up the phone yet in this photograph, so choice **b** is incorrect. She is not turning off the computer; she is typing on it, so choice **c** is also incorrect. You can not tell from the picture anything about an appointment cancellation, so choice **d** is not the correct one.

9. c. This family is playing a board game. They are not eating dinner together or shopping for a sofa, so choices **b** and **a** are both incorrect. The family is also not putting away any toys, so choice **d** is also incorrect.

10. b. The woman is inside a grocery store. She is not buying furniture; she is buying groceries, so the answer is not choice **c**. There are no bananas in her cart, making choice **d** incorrect.

11. b. The statement, "Yes, I am fine here," appropriately responds to a question about whether someone is comfortable. Choice **a** gives a location, not a yes or no answer and choice **c** answers an unrelated question.

12. c. Choice **c** gives directions on how to get to the post office, while choice **a** tells who takes the mail, and choice **b** talks about buying stamps.

13. a. This choice gives a time that the manager will probably be back. Choice **b** talks instead about when the speaker will leave. Choice **c** is completely unrelated.

14. b. Choice **b** gives the location of the tickets. Choice **c** is not correct because it tells what the tickets are for and choice **a** tells where they came from.

15. c. An appropriate answer about how long the trip took gives a length of time. Choice **a** is about how the speaker traveled, not how long it took. Choice **b** is unrelated.

16. a. Thirty minutes is not long, so they must hurry to get there before the bank closes. Choice **b** talks about what the speaker is doing at the bank, but does not respond to the fact that the bank closes in 30 minutes. Choice **c** is unrelated.

17. b. Choice **b** responds correctly to the question, by telling when the speaker was in Chicago. Choice **a** refers to "him," indicating that it is about a person, rather than a place. Choice **c** answers an unrelated question.

18. a. "Yes, it was definitely a success" is a good answer to a question about whether the meeting went well. Choice **b** and choice **c** do not seem to be about the success of the meeting.

19. c. Telling someone that he or she has messages is a good way to answer a question about whether anyone called while the person was away. Choice **b** gives the time, and choice **a** refers to an explanation.

20. b. Choice **b** agrees with the statement about the flu, making it the best choice. Choice **a** asks a question about a person who is ill, but does not respond appropriately to the statement. Choice **c** is unrelated to the statement.

21. c. Choice **c** tells us that the copier is still broken, or not working yet. Choice **a** speaks about a person rather than a machine. Choice **b** talks about the weight of the machine, but not whether it is working.

22. b. The question asks for a yes or no response to the question of whether the traffic was bad. Choice **b** gives the answer, "yes," with some elaboration. Choice **a** tells when the speaker leaves for work, and choice **c** talks about the train, neither of which answers the question.

23. a. It tells how the trip was—wonderful. Choice **c** is incorrect because it tells how long the trip was. Choice **b** is unrelated.

24. c. Choice **c** gives the time that the flight arrived. Choice **a** is incorrect because it tells how long the flight was, and choice **b** is incorrect because it gives the flight number.

25. a. The question asks where the listener prefers to wait, and choice **a** responds with a suggestion that they wait in the lobby. Choices **b** and **c** are incorrect. Choice **c** talks about a cancelled reservation and choice **b** answers an unrelated question.

26. b. The speaker responds to the statement about the parade by commenting that he would like to see it. Choice **a** makes a nonsensical comment about the mayor and answer c asks an unrelated question.

27. a. "I haven't seen it" is an appropriate response to the question of whether someone left her purse in the room. "It was very interesting" does not respond to the question, nor does "I am missing several."

28. c. In choice **c** the speaker gives permission to borrow the book, along with a reminder to return it. Choice **a** is incorrect because, instead of answering the question, it talks about something that the speaker probably will not do. Choice **b** does not answer the question about the book.

29. a. The answer implies that the speaker does not know whether he likes it because he has never tried it. Choice **b** and choice **c** give information about sushi, but offer no indication of whether the speaker likes it.

30. c. The speakers agree that the data is confusing; one uses the word "confusing" while the other says that it is "difficult to analyze." Choice **c** does not answer the question; it talks about the frequency with which the speaker uses the data. Choice **b** talks about how current the data is, not whether it is confusing.

31. b. Only choice **b** answers the past tense "when" question with a definite time.

32. c. Choice **c** is the best answer; it politely declines the invitation. Choice **a** talks about leaving something at the restaurant, and choice **b** talks about the weather.

33. a. In the question, the speaker offers help in finding what the listener is looking for. In choice **a**, a woman responds by telling what she is looking for. Choice **b** and choice **c** are unrelated to the question.

34. c. The two speakers agree that the new printer is better. Choice **b** tells what printers use, but makes no comparison between this printer and the old one. Choice **a** also offers no comparison, but offers to lend something to the speaker.

35. c. This question asks for a location, which choice **c** gives. Choice **a** doesn't give a location, rather it tells when the train leaves. Choice **b** compares the speed of the train to that of the bus.

36. b. Choice **b** tells what the speaker will wear to the party. The party is in the future, as is indicated by the words "going to" in the question. Choice **a** talks about a party in the past. Choice **c** expresses a dislike for ironing, but doesn't answer the question.

37. a. Choice **a** gives the price of the tickets. Choice **b** talks about not understanding the rules of baseball, but doesn't give the price of game tickets. Choice **c** accepts an invitation that was not offered.

38. a. "Not yet" is a good response to a question about whether the mail has come. Choice **c** is incorrect because it talks about a problem with the mail, but not whether it has come or not.

39. b. An appropriate response to someone who is having trouble with the Internet is a suggestion that they check the connection. Choice **a** suggests calling a doctor, but doctors do not have much to do with an Internet problem. Choice **c** talks about uses of the Internet, not what to do if there is a problem with it.

40. b. The question is looking for the reason that the listener was not at work on the previous day. Choice **b** gives the reason, an appointment. Choice **a** gives an unrelated response, and choice **c** tells what is happening now, not what happened yesterday.

41. c. The man needs the new catalogue to complete the March order. Immediately after asking whether the catalogue has come yet, he goes on to explain that he is putting together the March order. Choice **b** is incorrect because, while he does mention looking for a new supplier, that idea comes up in a different context. Choices **a** and **d** are also incorrect because the man does not mention the new year or buying a sweater.

42. a. The man expresses concern that J&R Supply "often run[s] out of stock." The man says that J&R has the best prices, so choice **c** is incorrect. The dialogue mentions nothing about the supplier going out of business or the catalog being wrong, so choices **b** and **d** are also incorrect.

43. b. At the end of the dialogue the man says that he will call about the catalog today. All other answers are incorrect.

44. a. When he hears about the candidate for the position, the man says, "I am excited to hear that. It is always nice to have new ideas around." He does not mention feeling nervous, resentful or proud, making choices **b**, **c**, and **d** incorrect.

45. d. The woman tells the man that the company has already started interviewing. This means that they have started and have not finished. Choices **a** and **c** respond as if they have not started, and choice **b** responds as if they have finished, making these three choices incorrect.

46. c. The woman is telling the man about the interviews based on what she heard from Fred. She begins talking about the candidates by saying, "Fred told me." This means that she was not there, and the fact that he is asking means that the man speaking was not there, so choices **a** and **b** are incorrect. The three new workers have not yet been hired, so they could not have been at the interview either.

47. d. The woman asks, "Can you recommend a hotel?" Choice **a** is incorrect because when the second woman mentions the major hotel chains, the first woman responds that the small independent hotel is what she had in mind. Choice **b** is not the best choice because the woman already has a new client and is going to Denver to meet with him. Choice **c** is not a good choice because the woman is asking where to stay, not where to eat.

48. a. The woman says that she stayed in a "small independent hotel called The Ridge." A small independent hotel is not a national chain, so choice **d** is wrong. Choices **b** and **c** are also incorrect, as neither is mentioned in reference to The Ridge.

49. c. The woman states, "I am flying to Denver next month to meet with a new client." She explicitly gives that as her reason for going to Denver. No other answer choice gives that as the reason, so all other answer choices are incorrect.

50. d. The man is worried because his paycheck was for the wrong amount. He says, "I was overpaid by two hundred dollars." Choice **a** is not correct because he received more than he expected, not less. He does not mention that he got the wrong person's paycheck, or that it bounced, making choices **b** and **c** incorrect.

51. b. Peter is out of the office because his wife is having surgery. The first man says, "I thought that Peter was out this week. Isn't his wife having surgery?" And the second man responds, "You're right." The dialogue does not mention a funeral, a conference, or illness, so the other choices are incorrect.

52. d. Peter works in the human resources department, as the second speaker indicates by saying, "talk to Peter in the human resources department." While it sounds logical that a person in accounting might know about a paycheck, the speaker explicitly states that Peter is in human resources, thus choice **c** is incorrect. The dialogue does not mention anything about the sales or collections departments, so the answer is not choice **a** or **b**.

53. c. The woman says the restaurant is "down the street" and the man suggests that they walk to the restaurant. Both of these indicate that the restaurant is near their office. These same two quotes rule out the possibility that the restaurant is on the floor below or across town, so the answer is not choice **a** or **d**.

54. b. The man can't go to lunch today because he has plans already. He is having lunch with a client. He did not bring his own lunch, so choice **a** is incorrect. The dialogue says nothing about whether it is a nice day to walk, so choice **c** is incorrect. The dialogue begins with the woman noticing that the restaurant is open, so choice **d** is also wrong.

55. b. The woman will invite Kristin. She says at the end that she will invite all three of the office friends that they mention. The other three answer choices are people who have not volunteered to invite the others.

56. a. The second speaker says that Meredith is sick and resting in bed, with her husband caring for her. She is not away on business; the first speaker asks if she is away on business and gets the reply "No," so choice **b** is not correct. She is not in the office; the first speaker states that he has not seen her all week. She is not at the doctor's office; the reported conversation suggests that she went to the doctor and returned home with antibiotics, so choice **d** is not the best one.

57. b. The first speaker says that he hasn't seen Meredith all week. The dialogue does not mention that she has been gone for two weeks or a month, so choices **c** and **d** are both incorrect.

58. c. Meredith is not eating spaghetti to recover from her illness. He husband has made her chicken noodle soup and ginger tea, but not spaghetti. The dialogue does mention that she is resting, taking antibiotics, and that her husband made her ginger tea, so choices **a**, **b** and **d** are incorrect choices.

59. b. The man states, "I like to shop at the farmers' market. It doesn't have the same variety as the supermarket, but the vegetables are always fresh." Choices **a** and **d** are incorrect because the woman, not the man, mentions the beauty and lack of flavor at the supermarket, not the farmers' market. No one mentions the price of the vegetables, so choice **c** is also not correct.

60. a. The man says about the market, "It's in the lot across the street from the public library on Thursday evenings. I usually stop in there right after work." Markets often take place on Saturday mornings, but this one is on Thursday, so choice **b** is not right. The man brought food to the party, so he was not at the market then, making choice **d** incorrect. He gives a specific time that he shops at the market, so choice **c** is also not right.

61. d. The man brought vegetable pastries to the party. We know this because the woman says, "The vegetable pastries you brought to the company party were wonderful." None of the other answer choices are mentioned in the dialogue, so the others are incorrect.

62. c. The company needs to buy rain suits. The first speaker says that he noticed that the company was running low on rain suits and needed to reorder. He does not mention umbrellas, hard hats, or gloves.

63. b. The man says, "With the rainy season just around the corner, we had better hurry up and reorder." He does not mention whether the inventory is complete, so choice **a** is incorrect. Nowhere in the dialogue is there mention of a construction project or purchase order, so choices **c** and **d** are also not good choices.

64. d. When the second speaker asks if there is anything else the company needs, the first speaker replies, "I made a list and left it on your desk." He does not mention an inventory spreadsheet, so choice **c** is incorrect, and he has already checked the warehouse, so choice **a** is not the best choice.

65. a. The dialogue states, "Pat has been on the phone with the technical support person all morning trying to get it fixed." It does not mention that Pat has called the director, administrative assistant, or archivist, so the other choices are incorrect.

66. c. The man needs access to the data on the database to finish his report, and says that he will have to stay late to finish if the server does not get fixed soon. He does not mention fixing the database or the router, nor does he mention staying late to wait for the technician, so choices **a**, **b**, and **d** are not correct.

67.. b. The man says, "I need some of that information to finish my report. I am working from an archive right now, but I will need the most recent data to finish it." He already has an archive to work from, so choice **a** is incorrect. He doesn't mention needing a disk or help from Pat, so choice **c** and choice **d** are also incorrect.

68. d. The dialogue begins with a coworker asking, "Are you going to the conference at the convention center next weekend?" The woman also mentions that the conference center is a long way outside of town, not in another city, so the answer is not choice **b**. The problem hinges on the convention center being far away, so choice **c** is not a good choice.

69. a. When asked why she can't drive back Sunday night, she says, "I prefer not to drive at night." Her meeting is on Monday, so choice **b** is not a good choice. She does not mention not having a car or the hotels being booked as her reason for not driving, so choices **c** and **d** are incorrect.

70. c. When two people decide to ride together, it is called *carpooling*. They use this word in the dialogue to talk about sharing a ride. None of the other answer choices is mentioned in the dialogue as a solution to the problem.

71. c. The speaker wants the workers to mark important dates for April on their calendars. While the speaker does mention the staff meeting on the 7th, he doesn't set the agenda, so choice **a** is not the best choice. Choice **b** is not the correct answer because the memo mentions two meetings. Choice **d** is also incorrect.

72. d. The speaker says, "On the 16th there will be a representative here from our insurance provider. He will discuss changes to our health insurance packages." The other topics are mentioned in the speech, but not in reference to the insurance representative.

73. b. The speaker says, "Please prepare a brief report on your department's current project for the April 21st meeting." None of the other answers is mentioned as something that should be brought to the meeting.

74. d. The announcement is being made in an office. It is addressed to the staff and lists the preparations that those working in the office must make for the office's early closure. While the message does mention the weather service warning, it is unlikely that a message like this would be heard on a weather service hotline.

75. c. The main message in the announcement is that the office is closing. It then tells the staff what precautions to take. The message does not mention that the computer network is down or that the office was hit by a tornado, making choices **a** and **b** incorrect. The announcement does ask employees to drive safely, but that is not the main message of the announcement, so choice **d** is not the best choice.

76. a. Nowhere in the announcement does it mention making hard copies of work as a precaution. The announcement says, "Please shut down and unplug all computers and other major electronic equipment. Please take home your laptops, the emergency calling procedures from your employee handbook, and any perishable food you may have in the refrigerators," which does ask workers to take the precautions mentioned in choices **b**, **c**, and **d**.

77. c. The message is from a supplier. A supplier is what you call anyone from whom you order the necessary materials to do a job. The supplier is delivering a message about a product that will ship the next day and one that is on backorder, but is not calling from the shipping company, so choice **b** is not correct. She is not in charge of receiving the item; she is in charge of sending it, so choice **a** is also incorrect.

78. b. Pamela is calling about is an item that is out of stock. The rest of the order will ship tomorrow, so choice **a** is not a good choice. Pamela says that she has adjusted the billing statement, so choice **c** is not a good choice. The message doesn't mention a change in shipping rates, so the answer is not choice **d**.

79. a. Pamela says, "Please call me back at 972-772-8301 at your convenience to confirm that you have received this message, and to let me know if you want to cancel the backordered item or have it shipped at the later date." None of the other answers is given as a reason that she needs her call returned, so choices **b**, **c**, and **d** are incorrect.

80. b. The announcement begins, "Would the owner of a green minivan, license plate number XHB-78S4 please report to the north parking lot immediately?" The problem involves a delivery truck, but the announcement is not directed to the delivery truck, so the answer is not choice **a**. The message does not mention the unloading dock workers, so the answer is not choice **c**. Only one car is causing the problem and the message is directed at the owner of one car, so the answer is not choice **d**.

81. d. The problem is that a van is illegally parked. While the message threatens to tow the van if it is not moved, it has not yet been towed so the answer is not choice **a**. The announcement does not mention a car with its lights on or an emergency on the loading dock, so choices **b** and **c** are also incorrect.

82. b. The announcement says, "Failure to move your vehicle in the next ten minutes will result in towing and possible fines." The announcement does not mention parking assignments, injuries, or the loss of a job as possible consequences of the situation, so choices **c**, **a**, and **d** are not right.

83. b. The recording is on a technical support line for a software company. People usually call technical support when they are having problems with technology or equipment. Technical support personnel do not handle invoices, registration of products, or sales, so choices **a**, **c**, and **d** are incorrect.

84. d. The message says, "You will be asked for the license number of your product. Please have this information on hand." The message does not mention that the caller needs a statement, a registration agreement, or a reference number for an order, so choices **a**, **b**, and **c** are incorrect.

85. a. The message says, "Your approximate wait time is nine minutes." English uses the word *about* to show approximation or estimation. Choice **b** gives an exact rather than an approximate time.

86. c. The talk is from the introductory speech at the convocation for a conference. It begins, "Welcome to our 12th Annual Regional Conference on Municipal Water Quality." The other answers are incorrect, as they are not mentioned in the speech.

87. b. The speaker says, "The workshop entitled the 'The Future of Chlorine' has been postponed. Due to the floods in Indianapolis, our presenter's flight was delayed." The speaker makes no indication that this workshop was canceled or moved, so choices **a** and **c** are incorrect. The scheduling of the workshop was not a result of the flooding, so choice **d** is also incorrect.

88. d. The speaker says that the workshop called "Piping Solutions" has changed locations. The workshop called "The Future of Chlorine" was postponed, so the answer is not choice **c**. The other two workshops were not mentioned in the speech.

89. b. The speaker congratulates the whole staff on the success and commends everyone's work. Such expressions are neither self-important nor critical, so choices **a** and **c** are incorrect. Choice **d** is not a good one because someone usually takes a consoling tone when trying to make some one feel better about something bad that has happened; this is a happy situation, with no need for consoling.

90. d. The speaker is talking about an overall increase in sales for the quarter. Choices **a** and **b** both refer only to the month of October, which is a small part of what he is reporting on. Choice **c** is incorrect because the company actually did meet its sales goals.

91. c. The speaker says, "Thank you for your hard work. To celebrate, the company will provide lunch for the whole staff on Friday." None of the other choices is mentioned in the speech, so choices **a**, **b**, and **d** are incorrect.

92. b. The message says, "This is an automated message," which means a recording. The message does not mention being from the bank president or a loan officer, who would probably not call about irregular account activity, so choices **c** and **d** are not correct answer choices.

93. d. The message says "we are calling to inform you of irregular account activity taking place on October 2." The message does not mention insufficient funds, an exceeded credit limit, or a stolen credit card, so choices **a**, **b**, and **c** are incorrect.

94. a. The message asks that the listener to call to authorize the purchase. The message doesn't mention an incorrect purchase order, so choice **b** is not a good choice. The message also does not ask the listener to make a deposit or pay a fee, so choices **c** and **d** are also incorrect.

95. b. The announcement says, "Attention, passengers waiting to board Flight 472 to Baltimore." Passengers usually wait to board a plane in the airport. Choice **a** is incorrect because the passengers are not yet on the plane. Such messages would probably not be heard in a train station or on the radio, so choices **c** and **d** are incorrect.

96. c. It is snowing heavily in Baltimore, as the announcement indicates by saying, "due to heavy snowfall in the Baltimore area, Flight 472 has been canceled." Light snow and clear conditions would not cause a flight cancellation, and the message does not mention rain at all, so the other choices are incorrect.

97. d. The announcement asks that passengers "turn in [their] boarding passes at the desk for a voucher that [they] can use on the rescheduled flight or another flight." The other answer choices are not consistent with this part of the message and so are incorrect.

98. a. A *briefing* is a short talk or update that gives directions and details. The speaker is giving a briefing about the reports. A *rant* is an angry, impassioned speech, so choice **b** is not right. The speaker also doesn't seem to be giving a strategy or projections about the future, so choices **c** and **d** are also incorrect.

99. c. The speaker makes clear that the report should not have any images when he says, "Please do not include any images, or unnecessary graphs or charts." The speaker does ask that the reports contain success stories and projections, so choices **a** and **b** are both incorrect choices. The speaker only asks that unnecessary graphs be excluded from the report, so the answer is not choice **d**.

100. c. The speaker gives instructions "to turn in a hard copy and a copy saved to a CD." The other answers are inconsistent with these directions and so are wrong.

101. c. Usually someone receives an award for the *contributions* they make to a field. *Distinctions* are usually made between two things, so choice **a** is not right. *Research* is a non-count noun so can't be modified by the word many, therefore choice **d** is also incorrect.

102. a. For something to be written off for tax purposes it must be a *legitimate* expense. *Preposterous* and *unscrupulous* expenses are not legitimate and so those words do not make sense in the sentence, making choices **b** and **c** incorrect. The adjective *profound* is generally not used in talking about expenses, so choice **d** is also not the right choice.

103. c. The subject of this verb is the candidate, so the correct form of the verb is the third person singular indicative form, *has*. The other forms of the verb given in the other answer choices are incorrect. *To have* and *having* are not indicative verb forms of the verb and *have* is not conjugated in the third person singular.

104. d. The word *one* correctly completes the sentence. *Only* is used to indicate singularity; choice **c** is plural and therefore incorrect. The articles *a* and *an* are always used with nouns and cannot stand alone.

105. a. The word *whether* correctly completes the sentence. The words *when*, *if*, and *why* cannot be used in combination with *or not*. So choices **b**, **c**, and **d** are incorrect.

106. d. The outcome of the vote is something that might figure into the decision. The words *quality*, *procedure*, and *order* could all make sense grammatically in the sentence, but logically the quality, procedure, or order of a vote is not as important as its outcome, and not something to base a major decision on.

107. c. The sentence calls for the future form of the verb, as it is talking about something that will happen tomorrow. Choice **a** is the past tense of the verb. Choice **b** is a gerund. Choice **d** is the present passive form of the verb.

108. b. The comparative form of the adjective is used with the word *than*. The word *as* is used to make equative, not comparative, statements so the answer is not choice **a**. The word *of* is a preposition that does not fit into the comparison, so choice **c** is incorrect.

109. b. The word *challenging* correctly completes the sentence. The structure of the sentence sets up an opposition; *challenging* appropriately opposes *easy*. *Obstacle* cannot complete the opposition because it is a noun and *easy* is an adjective so choice **a** is incorrect. Choices **b** and **c** are adjectives, but do not logically oppose the idea *easy*.

110. a. The use of the word *before* shows that the sentence requires a verb in the present perfect. Choices **a** and **b** are both in the present perfect, but choice **b** contains a double negative, which is incorrect in English.

111. a. The phrase, "as soon as," indicates that the instant one thing happens, another thing will or can happen immediately. "As often as" means that every time one thing happens, another thing happens, too; this doesn't make sense in the sentence, so choice **b** is incorrect. The words *usually* and *early* are not commonly used in an "as ___ as" construction, so choices **c** and **d** are not correct.

112. c. The sentence calls for the past tense, passive form of the verb. Choice **b** is incorrect because it is not passive. Choices **a** and **d** are incorrect because they are not past tense.

113. b. The word *since* is used to show that something has not happened during an interim time. The other prepositions do not make sense in this construction.

114. d. *We've*, a contraction of *we have*, requires a past participle of the verb to complete the present perfect tense. The word *have* cannot be contracted when used with an infinitive to express necessity, so choice **a** is incorrect. Choice **b** is a present, not a past, participle. Choice **c** is an indicative form, which can't be used with the auxiliary verb *have*.

115. b. A *resume* is what employers usually ask about in interviews. While some of the other answers work grammatically, they don't fit into the logical context.

116. b. The only adjective on the list of choices that can logically modify the noun *documentation*, is *incomplete*. The adjectives *unreserved* and *nervous* usually describe people. The adjective *absolute* usually modifies an idea or concept.

117. c. In this sentence the present progressive is being used to talk about the future. *Will go* could also correctly complete the sentence, but *will going* is an incorrect and nonexistent verb form, so choice **b** is not a good choice. Choice **a** is incorrect because *am going* can only be used with a first person singular pronoun. Choice **d** is not right because the present perfect progressive form of the verb is not used to talk about the future.

118. d. The sentence begins with the word *while*, which indicates that it should contain a dichotomy. The word *also* is the only choice that preserves that sense of dichotomy. *Further* and *similarly* have continuative sense, so choices **a** and **c** are incorrect.

119. a. This is an existential *there* used with *seems to be* to talk about the existence or, in this case, seeming existence, of something. The use of *there is* is the best way to talk about existence in English.

120. d. A *strategy* contains plans that may not always go as hoped, so it makes good sense in the sentence. Neither *markets* nor *revenues* can backfire, so choices **a** and **b** are incorrect. A *purchase* cannot be used to increase the number of repeat customers, so choice **c** does not make sense.

121. b. The best verb to complete this sentence is *span*, which means *to stretch across*. Choice **a** is wrong because the states are not made of time zones. Choice **d** is wrong because the time zones are not made of the states. Choice **c** is wrong because the time zone did not set up the states.

122. c. The preposition *on* is used with days of the week in English. The other choices contain incorrect prepositions or an article.

123. d. The subject of the sentence is the pronoun *he*. Because *he* wrote the directions, they are in *his* handwriting. The possessive pronoun his correctly completes the sentence. Choice **c** is an object pronoun, not a possessive one, so it does not indicate that the handwriting belongs to someone. The other two answer choices are forms of the pronoun *it*, which is not generally used to refer to people.

124. a. The past perfect form of the verb is correct here. The speaker is speaking about the trip in the past tense, at which time Mr. Ito had already visited Seattle several times before. This is the appropriate time to use the past perfect tense of the verb.

125. c. The sentence calls for the superlative form of *significant*. Because *significant* is a four syllable word, you form the superlative form with the word *most*, rather than the ending *-est*. Choices **a** and **b** are comparative rather than superlative.

126. c. The sentence requires a conjunction that provides a sense of opposition. The only conjunction listed that sets up an opposition is *however*.

127. b. The idea of the sentence is comparison of the costs and benefits of managing accounting in-house. The use of the word *negligible* in reference to the costs keeps choices **a** and **d** from making sense.

128. b. The verb *lacks* makes the best sense in this sentence. *Wants* and *keeps* in English generally refer to human actions, so choices **a** and **d** are not good choices. A report can inform, but informs does not work with the object in this sentence.

129. a. The sentence requires a noun to complete it. The word *their* must modify a noun. *Parents* is the only noun listed in the answer choices.

130. d. The sentence needs a past tense, passive form of the verb. Choices **b** and **c** are not passive. Choice **a** is not in the past tense.

131. a. The word *unless* is used to introduce an exception. Illness and emergencies are reasonable exceptions to the requirement. The answer is not choice **b**; illness and emergencies are reasonable causes for the requirement. The answer is not choice **c**; the word *until* is used to note the end of a time period.

132. d. The structure of the sentence sets up a contrast between the past and the present. The present situation is that she does not have to work late anymore. The past situation was that she did. *Used to work* is the best way to express that this was something that happened regularly in the past. None of the other verb forms can be used to talk about the past.

133. b. This is a present unreal conditional construction. English uses the modal *would* in these constructions. *Can*, *may*, and *should* are also modals, but they are used in different situations and constructions. The only other modal that is used in conditional statements is *could*, which is not one of the answer choices.

134. a. The sentence should be completed with the adverb, *regularly*. The adverb *regularly* modifies the gerund *exercising*. A gerund can not be modified by an adjective, such as *regular* in choice **b**, or a comparative adjective, such as *more regular* in choice **d**. Choice **c** is incorrect because it is not an actual word.

135. c. English uses the present progressive form of the verb to talk about something that is happening *right now*. Choice **a** is the simple present form of the verb, which is used to talk about things that happen regularly or as a rule. Choice **b** is the past tense of the verb, which is used to talk about the past. Choice **d** is the infinitive form of the verb, which is unmarked and has no time.

136. b. The word *that* correctly completes the sentence; it is used as a function word to introduce the subordinate clause. None of the other answer choices correctly introduces such a clause.

137. a. The gerund *providing* correctly completes the sentence; the appropriate way to make a verb such as *to provide* function as a noun in a sentence is by adding the *-ing* ending.

138. a. Environmental *regulations* could logically call for updating a waste management system. New environmental *services*, *balances*, or *portfolios* would not logically call for such an update, so choices **b**, **c**, and **d** are not correct.

139. d. *Projections* deal with the future, so this sentence calls for a verb in the future tense. Choice **a** is in the simple present tense. Choice **b** is in the past tense. Choice **c** is in the present progressive tense.

140. b. This is a question. The only beginning of the sentence with the proper word order for a question is choice **b**. In choice **c**, the verb form *sended* is incorrect. The past tense of *to send* is *sent*. In choices **a** and **d** the word order is not appropriate for a question.

141. b. The verb *accepted* correctly completes the sentence. The verbs *presumed* and *witnessed* do not make sense in the sentence, so choice **a** and choice **c** are incorrect. The verb *prepared* would be appropriate if Old Town was the bank buying not being bought, so choice **d** is also incorrect.

142. a. The noun *customers* fits best into the sentence. A bank does not have *residents* or *participants*, so choices **b** and **d** are not good choices. Choice **c** will not work because *patron* is a singular, not a plural, noun.

143. d. The verb *hopes* is indicative and, in this context, takes the infinitive form of the verb *to make*. The other verb forms can't be used in combination with *hopes*.

144. d. The adjective *promising* best modifies *merger*. A merger can't logically be *portable* or *delicious*, so choices **a** and **c** are not good choices. A *traffic merger* is a different thing than a business merger, so this answer will not work in the context.

145. b. The word *writing* completes the idea logically and grammatically by correctly forming the present progressive of the verb *write*. Grammatically, choice **a** could work in the sentence, but logically this choice doesn't work because the situation is not a good one, so the speaker is not excited about it. The verb *forgetting* is in the correct form grammatically, but the speaker is obviously not forgetting to inform his vendor of the problem.

146. a. The problem is with a *shipment*. The problem is not with a *letter* or a *casement*, which is a type of window. The gerund *parceling* is a noun formed of an action, which is not a physical thing that can be sent.

147. d. The conjunction *however* creates a sense of contrast with the idea expressed in the previous sentence. The conjunction *but* can also create this sense, but the word is in the incorrect word order in this sentence, so choice **b** is not the best choice. The woman is not thankful that the merchandise is out of season, so choice **a** will not work in the sentence. *Otherwise* means in a different way or situation, which is not the relationship that the sentence is trying to express.

148. d. The modal *would* combines with the word *like* to politely express the idea of wanting. The other modals do not create this sense and therefore do not correctly complete the idea of the sentence.

149. d. *Which* correctly introduces the relative clause. The words in the other answer choices do not appropriately fill this function in the sentence.

150. a. "Effective November 1," means beginning on that date, or taking effect on that date. The word, *projected* is used to talk about an indefinite or estimated time in the future, and the word *about* also introduces an estimation. He gives a definite day that the policy begins, so the writer of this e-mail is not estimating.

151. c. The sentence requires a negative, present tense form of the verb *apply*. The correct way to form this construction is *does not apply*. Choice **a** is incorrect because in a negative construction, only the verb *do* is conjugated. The other two choices are in the wrong tense for the sentence.

152. d. While the other answer choices work grammatically in the sentence, the idea of the sentence is that Mr. Gomez wants and expects the employees to cooperate with management on the new policy.

153. b. The article is mostly about the negative impact that layoffs can have on performance, stock value, and worker morale. The article mentions budget analysis briefly, and factors that contribute to stockholder morale briefly, but it is not mainly about either of those subjects, so choices **a** and **d** are not correct choices. Choice **c** is not mentioned in the article.

154. d. *Detrimental* means *harmful*. The other answer choices are not close in meaning to *detrimental*.

155. b. The article states, "Layoffs not only affect those low-performing employees whose jobs have been cut, but they also create an atmosphere of uncertainty, which causes others to leave." This idea is best summarized by choice **b**.

156. b. The article contends that a reduction in payroll expenses is eclipsed by the reduction in performance and blows to shareholder morale. So it does deem choices **a**, **c**, and **d** to be important.

157. c. *Compound* is word with several meanings. When used as a verb, as in this article, it means *to make greater* or *increase*. When it is used as an adjective, it is similar in meaning to choices **a** and **b**. When it is used as a noun it is similar in meaning to choice **d**.

158. d. A *liquidation sale* is the kind of sale that a business has when it is going out of business and selling everything, not just merchandise. They are not selling the business itself, so choice **a** is not correct. A seasonal sale happens at the end of a season, not when the business is closing, so choice **b** is not right. This is definitely an advertisement of an event, so choice **c** is not the best choice.

159. a. The ad says, "Don't miss this opportunity to stock up on all of our funky, handmade, one-of-a-kind fashions" and also mentions that there are clothing, purses and belts for sale. It is a clothing store. The store is selling its fixtures, racks, showcases, and mannequins because it is closing and selling everything, not because it normally sells those things.

160. c. The advertisement says, "For more information about this HUGE sale, visit our website at www.fabriqueboutique.com or call 872-8979." The other information is likely to be on the website as well, but only the information about the sale is specified in the ad.

161. a. The letter says that the bank *credited* the account to compensate for the error, so the account was short. The letter also apologizes and refers to the error as "our error," so the bank committed the error.

162. d. The letter says, "Please retain this letter for your records as confirmation of the adjustment to your business checking account number 90089733." This idea is best restated in answer choice **d**.

163. b. *Tracked down* is an English colloquialism that means *to find* or *to locate*. The other answer choices could also be eliminated by context; they do not fit with the idea of the sentence.

164. a. The correct answer is choice **a**. The tone is professional and apologetic. Nothing in this letter is conversational, unprofessional, or accusatory, so choices **b**, **c**, and **d** are incorrect.

165. c. The article is evenly split between talking about the promise and the dangers of RFID technology. Choices **b** and **d** are not in the article, and choice **a** refers to only part of the overall idea of the article.

166. c. The article states, "Unlike a bar code, however, the RFID tag offers access to a database of information about the product." Choices **a** and **b** contradict information in the article and choice **d** is not mentioned in the article.

167. d. *Adopt* is a word with multiple meanings. The sense in which it is used here is *to choose and decide to use. Adopt* can also mean *to take custody of and care for another's child*, but this meaning does not make sense in the context of the article. A similar word, *adapt*, means to change to meet the needs of a situation.

168. b. The article says, "As major retailers begin to adopt this technology, concerns are arising about how RFID may affect the privacy of consumers and employees alike." While some of the other choices are conceivable concerns about the new technology, the question specifically asks which concern the article brings up.

169. c. The article says, "Radio frequency identification, or RFID, technology is not new, but as it becomes cheaper, it promises to change retail business significantly." The article does not mention speed, size, or security standards as factors that have made the technology available to retailers.

170. c. The company's hours of operation are not on the card. Choice **a** is not the correct choice because Gil's phone number is listed on the card where it says, TEL: 619-574-0835. Marcos Gil's title, General Contractor, appears below his name, so choice **b** is not the answer. The company slogan, "quality home building from the foundation to the roof," appears below the company name, so choice **d** is not a good choice.

171. a. The correct answer is choice **a**. The company builds houses, as the slogan, "quality home building from the founda-tion to the roof," indicates. The card does not suggest that it does any of the jobs listed in the other answer choices.

172. c. The article is mostly about the factors that can skew a business owner's perception of his business' success. The article discusses two factors: profit versus cash flow understanding of profitability, and cash versus accrual systems of accounting. These ideas are listed separately as answer choices **b** and **d**. These are, however, not good answer choices because the article is about how both of these things can influence a business owner's understanding of his success.

173. b. The article says, "In a cash method of accounting, income is reported only as payment is received, while the accrual method of accounting records income as soon as the sale is made." The difference given is in when a sale is recorded. The other answer choices are not listed as differences between the two systems.

174. d. In comparing the advantages of the two methods, the article says that the accrual system "allows for more sophisticated analysis, which can consolidate several facets of business management into a single operation." Choices **a** and **b** are listed as advantages of a cash system. Choice **c** is an implied advantage of a cash system.

175. a. The article says, "a business may show a good profit, but consistently run into cash flow problems, sometimes severe ones." The other answer choices are not listed as problems with looking only at profit to determine success.

176. c. The word *operation* has many meanings. Based on the context of the sentence, it is nearest in meaning to *a controlled activity*. The sentence is talking about doing several jobs with just one activity. Military actions and medical procedures have no relevance to the article or sentence, so choices **b** and **d** are not good choices. Choice **a** does not make sense because the sentence is talking about an action, not a functioning state.

177. b. The e-mail is directed to Bob Schwartz with special instructions about a hotel reserva-tion, so we can assume that Bob Schwartz works for the hotel. Ms. Sepeda works for Quesburger Enterprises and Mr. Hamilton is the hotel guest about whose stay she is writing, so choices **a** and **d** are not good choices.

178. c. The e-mail is from Ms. Sepeda and says, "Any charges that Mr. Hamilton accrues are to be directed to me." The e-mail does not mention that the stay will be free or that Mr. Schwartz or Mr. Hamilton will pay for the stay.

179. d. According to the e-mail, "Mr. Hamilton's plane will land at the Newark Liberty Airport on at 5:30 on March 21, and he should be checking in around 7:00 P.M." The phrase *checking in* is used to talk about arriving at a hotel.

180. a. Mr. Hamilton is Ms. Sepeda's client. She refers to him as an important client of her firm. Choice **b** reverses the masculine and feminine pronouns, which confuses the relationship and makes the choice incorrect. Choice **c** describes the relationship between Ms. Sepeda and Mr. Schwartz.

181. b. The house at 114 Lewis has a yard, is close to elementary schools, and is walking distance to the university. The house on Highland Estates Drive is suburban, and therefore too far from downtown and the university to walk, so choice **c** is not a good choice. The listing on Armstrong is a condo and so has no yard, only a patio, so choice **a** is also not the right answer.

182. b. Mr. Patel was offered a job, as can be understood from the opening paragraph of the letter. He will do some work at the university, but is not coming to Berkeley to attend the university, so choice **a** is incorrect. He is also looking for a house, but that is not the reason he is moving, so choice **d** is also incorrect.

183. a. The suburban home is far from his work, and he can't walk there. It has a large yard (lot) and is close to the schools, so the other answers are incorrect.

184. c. The letter says, "I have sent in the final paperwork for my visa, which I expect to arrive early in August." Mr. Patel has already been offered the job and accepted it, so choices **b** and **d** are incorrect. He doesn't mention when he will be able to move into the new house, so choice **a** is not the best answer.

185. d. The listing for the house on Lewis mentions that it has three bedrooms, air conditioning, and a refrigerator, but not a pool.

186. c. The policy states, "If a receipt includes both personal and work-related expenses, the work-related expenses should be circled and a separate page attached, which totals and explains the reimbursable expenses." There is no mention of starring any item.

187. d. The date on the receipt is October 20, 2009 and the policy states that receipts must be submitted within 30 days of the purchase. So November 19 is the last day to submit the receipt. Neither document mentions the day of the party or when this policy began, so choices **a** and **b** are incorrect. The day of the purchase is on the receipt, so choice **d** is not the right choice.

188. d. The policy states that a separate sheet of paper should be attached to the receipt "which totals and explains the reimbursable expenses." While the total cost of all items purchased is generally found at the bottom of a receipt, this total does not indicate which items were purchased for the work party, making choice **a** incorrect. Choices **b** and **c** were not mentioned in the policy.

189. a. The policy reads, "A copy of the bill showing the charges must be attached along with an explanation of the business purpose of any call." The policy says that the company will reimburse approved business lunches, registration fees for conferences, and get-well-soon gifts, making choices **b**, **c**, and **d** incorrect.

190. d. The policy says in regard to business meals, "You must submit the original itemized receipt and include the provider's name and date, the name(s) of any other person included on the bill, and the purpose of the meeting." The policy does not ask that the supervisor sign anything.

191. c. The correct answer is choice **c**. The letter tells Ms. Flores, "the position for which you have applied, as a team manager at the MegaMart Distribution Warehouse, has been filled." Her resume shows that she is a trained administrator of WareInfo Software, and Mr. Jones suggests that the company might be looking for a trainer in this software, but the letter does not indicate that she has applied for either such job, making choices **a** and **b** incorrect.

192. c. Mr. Jones says in the letter, "We will be looking for a bilingual (English/Spanish) trainer who is already familiar with the software. I think your qualifications are ideal for this job." The position seems to require training, speaking two languages, and knowing the software, all skills appear on her resume, so choices **a**, **b** and **d** are not correct. He, however, does not mention bookkeeping. So choice **c** is the best choice.

193. c. Ms. Flores's resume states that she is looking for a position in Oklahoma, so it can be inferred that the MegaMart distribution center is in that state. She currently lives in Kentucky and wants to move from there, so choice **b** is not the best choice. She went to college in Texas, but doesn't indicate that she is looking for a job there, so choice **a** is not the right answer.

194. a. The letter says, "You will need to fill out another application for the position" in reference to the job opening in May. Mr. Jones says he will keep her resume on file, so choice **b** is incorrect. He does not indicate that she will be responsible for updating the postings on the website or that she should call him on the phone, so c and choice **d** are also incorrect.

195. b. Her resume lists her degree as a B.A. from Sul Ross University with a Spanish Language major. She had a minor in Information Sciences, but that is not a degree. A software administrator certificate is also not a degree.

196. c. Both sources mention the increase in skill and performance that can come from an MBA. The website talks about the flexibility of its programs, but doesn't mention flexibility as a benefit of an MBA, so choice **a** is not correct. The article, but not the website, mentions increased pay as a benefit of an MBA.

197. b. Boolean lists four MBA programs: Marketing, Management, Finance, and Human Resources.

198. a. The Boolean webpage has a link for tuition, and the article gives the statistics about the nation's top ten MBA programs, so these could be compared. None of the other tasks could be achieved by looking at these two sources.

199. b. The article downplays the financial benefit of an MBA, but praises getting an MBA as a way to increase skills and knowledge. Choice **a** is not correct, because salary comparison is a small part of the article and so an answer focusing only on salary is not a good summary. Choice **c** is not the best choice, because the article does not take a stance on the subject that is listed in the answer choice. Choice **d** is an adage that may or may not apply to the article, but is not a good summary of the article.

200. b. The word *flexibility* has several meanings; here it is closest in meaning to *ability to adapt to circumstances*. The Web page suggests that the MBA program allows students to pursue their dreams even given a variety of personal circumstances. The physical meanings in choices **a** and **b** are not appropriate to the context.

201. **To hear this passage, listen to Track 311.** In the first sentence be sure to pause at the commas, which are very important to the flow and intelligibility of ideas. The second sentence lists small ways that people can save fossil fuels; the items in the list are separated by commas. Be sure to pause at each comma to create the spoken sense of the list. The end of this same sentence should have a rising inflection. The last sentence should put emphasis on the pronoun "I" to show that the subject is changing. Some of the more difficult words to pronounce are:

> minimize—MIN-i-mize
> thermostat—THUR-mo-stat
> mutual—MYOO-choo-al

202. **To hear this text, listen to Track 312.** This text begins with a string of questions, which should end on a rising pitch and have an interrogative tone. *Bottom line* is a business term that basically means profit. It should be pronounced as a single word, even though it shows up as two words in writing. The fifth sentence lists the hidden expenses of holding business meetings; the items in the list are separated by commas. Be sure to pause at each comma to break up the long sentence, and create the spoken sense of the list. In the sixth sentence, the emphasis should be on the word *all*. The seventh sentence has a natural pause after the word *month*. In giving a Web address aloud, the punctuation (a period) is spoken as *dot*, so here you would say, "netmeet dot com." One of the more difficult words to pronounce is:

> expenditures—ik-SPEND-i-churs

203. Sample Response: The couple is standing outside a home that is for sale. They are waiting while the Realtor talks on the phone. They seem nervous and excited, like maybe they are waiting for news. I think that they probably want to buy the house and the Realtor is calling about the price or to set up a tour.
To hear this sample response, listen to track 313.

204. Sample Response: I use a credit card about once or twice a week. I pay for most of my regular monthly expenses with checks, and use cash for most daily purchases.
To hear this sample response, listen to track 314.

205. Sample Response: I sometimes put gasoline on my credit card because it is convenient. I also use it for big purchases, like appliances or nice gifts.
Don't worry about being truthful on questions like this. If you need to invent things that you buy on credit, that's better than fumbling for words while trying to think of a true response.
To hear this sample response, listen to track 315.

206. Sample Response: I don't think it is a good idea to use it so much that I can't pay it off at the end of the month. I think that people can get into financial trouble when they have too much debt. It makes sense to have a little debt if it improves your quality of life or makes important pursuits possible, but having a lot of debt is dangerous.
To hear this sample response, listen to track 316.

207. Sample Response: The minimum pledge to become a member is $20. We have four suggested membership levels, but you can donate another amount if you like.
To hear this sample response, listen to track 317.

208. Sample Response: We accept checks and major credit cards. We can also bill you later if you prefer.
To hear this sample response, listen to track 318.

209. Sample Response: The Care and Share Foundation supports a number of local charities. We have been working since 1978 to help meet the critical needs of our community. We support local food banks, the homeless shelter, afterschool programs for children, and many other causes.
To hear this sample response, listen to track 319.

210. Sample Response: Hello, Ms. Boyd, this is Mr. Doe returning your call about the problem with our online order form. I am sorry about the inconvenience. We have been having problems with our website all week and are working with our web team to resolve them. I will be happy to take your order over the phone. If it is more convenient for you, you can fax the order and I will be sure that it posts today. I understand that the order is important and I will be sure that you get a rush delivery. Would you like to place the order with me now?
To hear this sample response, listen to track 320.

211. Sample Response: At this point in my life, I would be happy to move around to get ahead in my career. I think it is important to do this when you are young, so you can get a lot of experience before you have a family. Moving can be hard after you have a family. It is also hard to make any real civic contributions in a community if you are always moving, because by the time you know the politics and issues of a place, it's time to move again. At some point you have to settle down and commit to a place even if it means that you can't get ahead in your career as easily. I hope to be settled down by the time I'm 35.
To hear this sample response, listen to track 321.

212. Sample answer: When he realized that he missed the freeway exit, the man tried to change lanes and crashed his car.

213. Sample answer: After he finishes making the copies for the presentation, he will rush down to the conference room.

214. Sample answer: When everything is moved into the new house, she can decide on where to put the rug.

215. Sample answer: He is imagining what the house is going to look like when the crew finally finishes the construction.

216. Sample answer: They are spending the weekend riding bikes on the trail beside the park.

217. Sample answer:

Thank you for letting me know before you placed the order, Ms. Jones. I am running low on several essential supplies. I need a box of one-inch, white, three-ring binders with clear plastic over the cover for the department reports. I also need a toner cartridge for my printer and a box of highlighter markers. If it is not too much trouble, would you also order a new three hole punch? Mine has broken and I don't want to have to continue borrowing yours.

218. Sample answer:

Dear Mr. Harris,

I am glad you contacted me a reference because I have many wonderful things to say about my former boss. My former boss, Mary Springs, is kind, thoughtful, and professional. She is a leader. I worked for her for six years and I never once felt that she was unclear about a project or an expectation. She is a superb communicator, and her friendly, caring demeanor inspires those around her to succeed. I think that what made her so effective with our company was that everyone was happy to do what she asked. She seemed to really respect us as workers, and as human beings with lives outside the office. On a more personal level, she is also a great cook and has a brilliant sense of humor. Please contact me if you have any more questions.

Sincerely,

Mandy Martinez

219. The opinion essay should be well organized. Clear details and supporting statements should back up the opinion. Words should be spelled correctly and the grammar should be correct. An example of a sample response is:

A worker needs a clear sense of purpose in his work to be truly happy in his job. He needs to know why he is doing what he is doing, and he needs to feel good about what his work accomplishes. Some people have jobs where the purpose and meaning are clear; they might be working to save lives, help those in need, or further human knowledge. Others find the purpose for their work outside the work itself; they might be feeding their children, paying their parents' medical bills, or funding the meaningful work that they pursue outside the office. The reason behind the work is what makes a worker happy.

My brother is an emergency room doctor. He has a stressful job, with demanding hours and pay that is lower than that of most other doctors. He is happier with his work than almost anyone I know. Although it is sometimes hard and thankless, he always knows why he is doing his job: to help people in emergency situations, often to save lives or attend to critical injuries. He falls into the category of workers whose jobs are inherently meaningful. He can be grouped with teachers, scientists, social workers, and workers at nonprofit organizations, the meaning of whose work is obvious and built into the work itself. They seem to be generally happy at work, as long as no other factors stand in the way of their mission.

My good friend Ismael works on a road crew. He has a physically demanding job and comes home exhausted each day. He sometimes has to spend weeks away from his wife and children. He is happy about and very grateful for his job, not because he knows how important roads are to society, but because he lifted his family out of poverty and is sending a son to college. He supports his children and sends money to his parents in Mexico. The meaning in his work is clear. He wants to make a better life for his children, and he is succeeding at this goal. I think that most happy workers are more like Ismael than my brother. Their purpose in work is, for them, external to the job itself. They have some other important thing that they are doing with their lives and their jobs fund it. These workers seem to become unhappy if their work stands in the way of the purpose that exists for them outside of it. For this kind of workers to stay happy, their employers must be understanding about how important their lives outside of work are to them, and give them the leeway to attend to their personal needs.

Happy workers are good for a business. It is important to understand what makes workers happy and put structures in place to ensure that they stay happy. A good employer should know what drives his workers, and do the things in his power to keep his workers' sense of purpose alive and at the forefront of their minds during work.

CHAPTER

9 ▶ PRACTICE EXAM 2

Listening

You will now begin the listening section. You will be asked to demonstrate how well you understand spoken English. The entire listening section should take approximately 45 minutes. There are four parts and directions are given for each part. Mark your answers on the answer sheet starting on page 231.

When directed by the 🎧 icon, listen to the audio file at **http://www.learnatest.com/SpeakingGuides/**. Or, if you do not have access to a computer, the complete transcripts are included in the appendix of this book. In that case, ask someone who speaks English fluently to read the material to you face-to-face or into a tape recorder. Be sure your reader speaks at a normal, conversational pace. It is highly recommended, however, that you use the audio files for a more authentic TOEIC experience.

1.	ⓐ	ⓑ	ⓒ	ⓓ
2.	ⓐ	ⓑ	ⓒ	ⓓ
3.	ⓐ	ⓑ	ⓒ	ⓓ
4.	ⓐ	ⓑ	ⓒ	ⓓ
5.	ⓐ	ⓑ	ⓒ	ⓓ
6.	ⓐ	ⓑ	ⓒ	ⓓ
7.	ⓐ	ⓑ	ⓒ	ⓓ
8.	ⓐ	ⓑ	ⓒ	ⓓ
9.	ⓐ	ⓑ	ⓒ	ⓓ
10.	ⓐ	ⓑ	ⓒ	ⓓ
11.	ⓐ	ⓑ	ⓒ	
12.	ⓐ	ⓑ	ⓒ	
13.	ⓐ	ⓑ	ⓒ	
14.	ⓐ	ⓑ	ⓒ	
15.	ⓐ	ⓑ	ⓒ	
16.	ⓐ	ⓑ	ⓒ	
17.	ⓐ	ⓑ	ⓒ	
18.	ⓐ	ⓑ	ⓒ	
19.	ⓐ	ⓑ	ⓒ	
20.	ⓐ	ⓑ	ⓒ	
21.	ⓐ	ⓑ	ⓒ	
22.	ⓐ	ⓑ	ⓒ	
23.	ⓐ	ⓑ	ⓒ	
24.	ⓐ	ⓑ	ⓒ	
25.	ⓐ	ⓑ	ⓒ	
26.	ⓐ	ⓑ	ⓒ	
27.	ⓐ	ⓑ	ⓒ	
28.	ⓐ	ⓑ	ⓒ	
29.	ⓐ	ⓑ	ⓒ	
30.	ⓐ	ⓑ	ⓒ	
31.	ⓐ	ⓑ	ⓒ	
32.	ⓐ	ⓑ	ⓒ	
33.	ⓐ	ⓑ	ⓒ	
34.	ⓐ	ⓑ	ⓒ	
35.	ⓐ	ⓑ	ⓒ	
36.	ⓐ	ⓑ	ⓒ	
37.	ⓐ	ⓑ	ⓒ	
38.	ⓐ	ⓑ	ⓒ	
39.	ⓐ	ⓑ	ⓒ	
40.	ⓐ	ⓑ	ⓒ	
41.	ⓐ	ⓑ	ⓒ	ⓓ
42.	ⓐ	ⓑ	ⓒ	ⓓ
43.	ⓐ	ⓑ	ⓒ	ⓓ
44.	ⓐ	ⓑ	ⓒ	ⓓ
45.	ⓐ	ⓑ	ⓒ	ⓓ

46.	ⓐ	ⓑ	ⓒ	ⓓ
47.	ⓐ	ⓑ	ⓒ	ⓓ
48.	ⓐ	ⓑ	ⓒ	ⓓ
49.	ⓐ	ⓑ	ⓒ	ⓓ
50.	ⓐ	ⓑ	ⓒ	ⓓ
51.	ⓐ	ⓑ	ⓒ	ⓓ
52.	ⓐ	ⓑ	ⓒ	ⓓ
53.	ⓐ	ⓑ	ⓒ	ⓓ
54.	ⓐ	ⓑ	ⓒ	ⓓ
55.	ⓐ	ⓑ	ⓒ	ⓓ
56.	ⓐ	ⓑ	ⓒ	ⓓ
57.	ⓐ	ⓑ	ⓒ	ⓓ
58.	ⓐ	ⓑ	ⓒ	ⓓ
59.	ⓐ	ⓑ	ⓒ	ⓓ
60.	ⓐ	ⓑ	ⓒ	ⓓ
61.	ⓐ	ⓑ	ⓒ	ⓓ
62.	ⓐ	ⓑ	ⓒ	ⓓ
63.	ⓐ	ⓑ	ⓒ	ⓓ
64.	ⓐ	ⓑ	ⓒ	ⓓ
65.	ⓐ	ⓑ	ⓒ	ⓓ
66.	ⓐ	ⓑ	ⓒ	ⓓ
67.	ⓐ	ⓑ	ⓒ	ⓓ
68.	ⓐ	ⓑ	ⓒ	ⓓ
69.	ⓐ	ⓑ	ⓒ	ⓓ
70.	ⓐ	ⓑ	ⓒ	ⓓ
71.	ⓐ	ⓑ	ⓒ	ⓓ
72.	ⓐ	ⓑ	ⓒ	ⓓ
73.	ⓐ	ⓑ	ⓒ	ⓓ
74.	ⓐ	ⓑ	ⓒ	ⓓ
75.	ⓐ	ⓑ	ⓒ	ⓓ
76.	ⓐ	ⓑ	ⓒ	ⓓ
77.	ⓐ	ⓑ	ⓒ	ⓓ
78.	ⓐ	ⓑ	ⓒ	ⓓ
79.	ⓐ	ⓑ	ⓒ	ⓓ
80.	ⓐ	ⓑ	ⓒ	ⓓ
81.	ⓐ	ⓑ	ⓒ	ⓓ
82.	ⓐ	ⓑ	ⓒ	ⓓ
83.	ⓐ	ⓑ	ⓒ	ⓓ
84.	ⓐ	ⓑ	ⓒ	ⓓ
85.	ⓐ	ⓑ	ⓒ	ⓓ
86.	ⓐ	ⓑ	ⓒ	ⓓ
87.	ⓐ	ⓑ	ⓒ	ⓓ
88.	ⓐ	ⓑ	ⓒ	ⓓ
89.	ⓐ	ⓑ	ⓒ	ⓓ
90.	ⓐ	ⓑ	ⓒ	ⓓ

91.	ⓐ	ⓑ	ⓒ	ⓓ
92.	ⓐ	ⓑ	ⓒ	ⓓ
93.	ⓐ	ⓑ	ⓒ	ⓓ
94.	ⓐ	ⓑ	ⓒ	ⓓ
95.	ⓐ	ⓑ	ⓒ	ⓓ
96.	ⓐ	ⓑ	ⓒ	ⓓ
97.	ⓐ	ⓑ	ⓒ	ⓓ
98.	ⓐ	ⓑ	ⓒ	ⓓ
99.	ⓐ	ⓑ	ⓒ	ⓓ
100.	ⓐ	ⓑ	ⓒ	ⓓ
101.	ⓐ	ⓑ	ⓒ	ⓓ
102.	ⓐ	ⓑ	ⓒ	ⓓ
103.	ⓐ	ⓑ	ⓒ	ⓓ
104.	ⓐ	ⓑ	ⓒ	ⓓ
105.	ⓐ	ⓑ	ⓒ	ⓓ
106.	ⓐ	ⓑ	ⓒ	ⓓ
107.	ⓐ	ⓑ	ⓒ	ⓓ
108.	ⓐ	ⓑ	ⓒ	ⓓ
109.	ⓐ	ⓑ	ⓒ	ⓓ
110.	ⓐ	ⓑ	ⓒ	ⓓ
111.	ⓐ	ⓑ	ⓒ	ⓓ
112.	ⓐ	ⓑ	ⓒ	ⓓ
113.	ⓐ	ⓑ	ⓒ	ⓓ
114.	ⓐ	ⓑ	ⓒ	ⓓ
115.	ⓐ	ⓑ	ⓒ	ⓓ
116.	ⓐ	ⓑ	ⓒ	ⓓ
117.	ⓐ	ⓑ	ⓒ	ⓓ
118.	ⓐ	ⓑ	ⓒ	ⓓ
119.	ⓐ	ⓑ	ⓒ	ⓓ
120.	ⓐ	ⓑ	ⓒ	ⓓ
121.	ⓐ	ⓑ	ⓒ	ⓓ
122.	ⓐ	ⓑ	ⓒ	ⓓ
123.	ⓐ	ⓑ	ⓒ	ⓓ
124.	ⓐ	ⓑ	ⓒ	ⓓ
125.	ⓐ	ⓑ	ⓒ	ⓓ
126.	ⓐ	ⓑ	ⓒ	ⓓ
127.	ⓐ	ⓑ	ⓒ	ⓓ
128.	ⓐ	ⓑ	ⓒ	ⓓ
129.	ⓐ	ⓑ	ⓒ	ⓓ
130.	ⓐ	ⓑ	ⓒ	ⓓ
131.	ⓐ	ⓑ	ⓒ	ⓓ
132.	ⓐ	ⓑ	ⓒ	ⓓ
133.	ⓐ	ⓑ	ⓒ	ⓓ
134.	ⓐ	ⓑ	ⓒ	ⓓ
135.	ⓐ	ⓑ	ⓒ	ⓓ

136.	ⓐ	ⓑ	ⓒ	ⓓ
137.	ⓐ	ⓑ	ⓒ	ⓓ
138.	ⓐ	ⓑ	ⓒ	ⓓ
139.	ⓐ	ⓑ	ⓒ	ⓓ
140.	ⓐ	ⓑ	ⓒ	ⓓ
141.	ⓐ	ⓑ	ⓒ	ⓓ
142.	ⓐ	ⓑ	ⓒ	ⓓ
143.	ⓐ	ⓑ	ⓒ	ⓓ
144.	ⓐ	ⓑ	ⓒ	ⓓ
145.	ⓐ	ⓑ	ⓒ	ⓓ
146.	ⓐ	ⓑ	ⓒ	ⓓ
147.	ⓐ	ⓑ	ⓒ	ⓓ
148.	ⓐ	ⓑ	ⓒ	ⓓ
149.	ⓐ	ⓑ	ⓒ	ⓓ
150.	ⓐ	ⓑ	ⓒ	ⓓ
151.	ⓐ	ⓑ	ⓒ	ⓓ
152.	ⓐ	ⓑ	ⓒ	ⓓ
153.	ⓐ	ⓑ	ⓒ	ⓓ
154.	ⓐ	ⓑ	ⓒ	ⓓ
155.	ⓐ	ⓑ	ⓒ	ⓓ
156.	ⓐ	ⓑ	ⓒ	ⓓ
157.	ⓐ	ⓑ	ⓒ	ⓓ

158.	ⓐ	ⓑ	ⓒ	ⓓ
159.	ⓐ	ⓑ	ⓒ	ⓓ
160.	ⓐ	ⓑ	ⓒ	ⓓ
161.	ⓐ	ⓑ	ⓒ	ⓓ
162.	ⓐ	ⓑ	ⓒ	ⓓ
163.	ⓐ	ⓑ	ⓒ	ⓓ
164.	ⓐ	ⓑ	ⓒ	ⓓ
165.	ⓐ	ⓑ	ⓒ	ⓓ
166.	ⓐ	ⓑ	ⓒ	ⓓ
167.	ⓐ	ⓑ	ⓒ	ⓓ
168.	ⓐ	ⓑ	ⓒ	ⓓ
169.	ⓐ	ⓑ	ⓒ	ⓓ
170.	ⓐ	ⓑ	ⓒ	ⓓ
171.	ⓐ	ⓑ	ⓒ	ⓓ
172.	ⓐ	ⓑ	ⓒ	ⓓ
173.	ⓐ	ⓑ	ⓒ	ⓓ
174.	ⓐ	ⓑ	ⓒ	ⓓ
175.	ⓐ	ⓑ	ⓒ	ⓓ
176.	ⓐ	ⓑ	ⓒ	ⓓ
177.	ⓐ	ⓑ	ⓒ	ⓓ
178.	ⓐ	ⓑ	ⓒ	ⓓ
179.	ⓐ	ⓑ	ⓒ	ⓓ

180.	ⓐ	ⓑ	ⓒ	ⓓ
181.	ⓐ	ⓑ	ⓒ	ⓓ
182.	ⓐ	ⓑ	ⓒ	ⓓ
183.	ⓐ	ⓑ	ⓒ	ⓓ
184.	ⓐ	ⓑ	ⓒ	ⓓ
185.	ⓐ	ⓑ	ⓒ	ⓓ
186.	ⓐ	ⓑ	ⓒ	ⓓ
187.	ⓐ	ⓑ	ⓒ	ⓓ
188.	ⓐ	ⓑ	ⓒ	ⓓ
189.	ⓐ	ⓑ	ⓒ	ⓓ
190.	ⓐ	ⓑ	ⓒ	ⓓ
191.	ⓐ	ⓑ	ⓒ	ⓓ
192.	ⓐ	ⓑ	ⓒ	ⓓ
193.	ⓐ	ⓑ	ⓒ	ⓓ
194.	ⓐ	ⓑ	ⓒ	ⓓ
195.	ⓐ	ⓑ	ⓒ	ⓓ
196.	ⓐ	ⓑ	ⓒ	ⓓ
197.	ⓐ	ⓑ	ⓒ	ⓓ
198.	ⓐ	ⓑ	ⓒ	ⓓ
199.	ⓐ	ⓑ	ⓒ	ⓓ
200.	ⓐ	ⓑ	ⓒ	ⓓ

Directions: For each question in this part, you will hear four statements about a picture. When you hear the statements, you must select the one statement that best describes what you see in the picture. Then mark your choice—**a**, **b**, **c**, or **d**—on the answer sheet. The statements are available in audio files or written transcripts in the appendix of this book.

1.

Now, listen to Track 322.

2.

Now, listen to Track 323.

3.

Now, listen to Track 324.

4.

Now, listen to Track 325.

5.

Now, listen to Track 326.

6.

Now, listen to Track 327.

7.

Now, listen to Track 328.

8.

Now, listen to Track 329.

9.

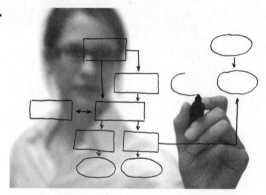

Now, listen to Track 330.

10.

Now, listen to Track 331.

Directions: You will hear a question or statement and three responses spoken in English. The question and statements are available in audio files or written transcripts in the appendix of this book. Select the best response to the question or statement and mark your choice—**a**, **b**, or **c**—on your answer sheet.

11. Now, listen to Track 332.
Mark your answer on your answer sheet.

12. Now, listen to Track 333.
Mark your answer on your answer sheet.

13. Now, listen to Track 334.
Mark your answer on your answer sheet.

14. Now, listen to Track 335.
Mark your answer on your answer sheet.

15. Now, listen to Track 336.
Mark your answer on your answer sheet.

16. Now, listen to Track 337.
Mark your answer on your answer sheet.

17. Now, listen to Track 338.
Mark your answer on your answer sheet.

18. Now, listen to Track 339.
Mark your answer on your answer sheet.

19. Now, listen to Track 340.
Mark your answer on your answer sheet.

20. Now, listen to Track 341.
Mark your answer on your answer sheet.

21. Now, listen to Track 342.
Mark your answer on your answer sheet.

22. Now, listen to Track 343.
Mark your answer on your answer sheet.

23. Now, listen to Track 344.
Mark your answer on your answer sheet.

24. Now, listen to Track 345.
Mark your answer on your answer sheet.

25. Now, listen to Track 346.
Mark your answer on your answer sheet.

26. Now, listen to Track 347.
Mark your answer on your answer sheet.

27. Now, listen to Track 348.
Mark your answer on your answer sheet.

28. Now, listen to Track 349.
Mark your answer on your answer sheet.

29. Now, listen to Track 350.
Mark your answer on your answer sheet.

30. Now, listen to Track 351.
Mark your answer on your answer sheet.

31. Now, listen to Track 352.
Mark your answer on your answer sheet.

32. Now, listen to Track 353.
Mark your answer on your answer sheet.

33. Now, listen to Track 354.

Mark your answer on your answer sheet.

34. Now, listen to Track 355.

Mark your answer on your answer sheet.

35. Now, listen to Track 356.

Mark your answer on your answer sheet.

36. Now, listen to Track 357.

Mark your answer on your answer sheet.

37. Now, listen to Track 358.

Mark your answer on your answer sheet.

38. Now, listen to Track 359.

Mark your answer on your answer sheet.

39. Now, listen to Track 360.

Mark your answer on your answer sheet.

40. Now, listen to Track 361.

Mark your answer on your answer sheet.

Directions: You will hear conversations between two people. You will be asked to answer four questions about what the speakers say in each conversation. Select the best response to each question and mark your choice on your answer sheet. The conversations are available in audio files or written transcripts in the appendix of this book.

Now, listen to Track 362.

41. Now, listen to Track 363.

What are the man and woman discussing?
a. where the service shop is
b. an upcoming business trip
c. what the software is for
d. why his car needs to be serviced

42. Now, listen to Track 364.

What problem does the man have?
a. The software program has not been tested enough.
b. He needs to buy a new car for his business trip.
c. He needs to have someone pick him up at the shop.
d. The woman will not give him a ride from the shop.

43. Now, listen to Track 365.

How long will the man be away?
a. one week
b. two weeks
c. three weeks
d. four weeks

Now, listen to Track 366.

44. Now, listen to Track 367.

What is the woman's problem?
a. Her computer is broken.
b. She doesn't know her ID number.
c. She can't log on to the company's website.
d. She can't figure out how to fill out a help ticket.

45. Now, listen to Track 368.

What does the man ask the woman?
a. whether she called the tech people
b. whether she restarted her computer
c. whether she knows the company's web address
d. whether she has filled out a help ticket

46. Now, listen to Track 369.

Why does the man need the woman's ID number?
a. so he can identify her
b. so he can fix her computer
c. so he can call the tech people
d. so he can restart her computer

Now, listen to Track 370.

47. **Now, listen to Track 371.**

What are the man and woman discussing?

a. the upcoming product training

b. the number of trainers

c. what changes occurred in the product

d. how long the training will last

48. **Now, listen to Track 372.**

Why does the woman think she doesn't need to take the training?

a. She doesn't like the product.

b. She is too busy with work.

c. She will be on vacation.

d. She took it last year.

49. **Now, listen to Track 373.**

What can you infer about the man?

a. He is the president of the company.

b. He is organizing the training.

c. He doesn't want to take the training.

d. He is one of the trainers.

Now, listen to Track 374.

50. **Now, listen to Track 375.**

What is the woman's problem?

a. She can't find a coupon for a car rental.

b. She has to go on a business trip.

c. She doesn't want to rent a car.

d. She doesn't like her job.

51. **Now, listen to Track 376.**

Why doesn't the woman use the coupon on the Internet?

a. It is for less than the one she lost.

b. She cannot find it on the Internet.

c. It is for a two-week rental.

d. It cannot be downloaded.

52. **Now, listen to Track 377.**

Why is the woman going to the Tri-City area?

a. To rent a car

b. To see store managers

c. To see her supervisor

d. To pick up a computer

Now, listen to Track 378.

53. **Now, listen to Track 379.**

What does the woman's supervisor want the woman to do?

a. Write a memo about saving paper.

b. Ask employees to save energy.

c. Come up with ways to be greener.

d. Create a carpooling plan.

54. **Now, listen to Track 380.**

What is the woman's problem?

a. She can't think of ways to be greener.

b. The man doesn't want to help her.

c. She is afraid she will lose her job.

d. She doesn't want to save resources.

55. **Now, listen to Track 381.**

What can you infer about the man?

a. He drives a bike rather than a car.

b. He works for another company.

c. He wants the woman's job.

d. He likes the idea of being greener.

Now, listen to Track 382.

56. **Now, listen to Track 383.**

What are the man and woman discussing?

a. a meeting to introduce a new management team

b. what the new regulations consist of

c. their supervisor and what he wants them to do

d. how to use the new intercom system

57. Now, listen to Track 384.

What problem does the man have?

a. He doesn't want to go to the meeting on the regulations.

b. He has a conflict between two meetings.

c. He feels the woman is treating him unfairly.

d. He doesn't care for his supervisor.

58. Now, listen to Track 385.

What is the man going to do to resolve the problem?

a. Talk to the person doing the regulations training.

b. Attend the mandatory meeting in the morning.

c. Ask the woman to talk to his supervisor.

d. Ask his supervisor what to do.

Now, listen to Track 386.

59. Now, listen to Track 387.

What does the man ask the woman to do?

a. to find out where he has to go

b. to get him a rental car

c. to book plane reservations for him

d. to come to the conference with him

60. Now, listen to Track 388.

What can you infer about the woman?

a. She does travel bookings for the man's company.

b. She wants to go on the trip with the man.

c. She is the man's only client.

d. She is organizing the conference.

61. Now, listen to Track 389.

Why does the woman say that the man is lucky?

a. because he doesn't have to drive

b. because he is getting a raise

c. because he is going on a business trip

d. Because he can get back on Sunday

Now, listen to Track 390.

62. Now, listen to Track 391.

What are the man and woman discussing?

a. employee attitudes

b. a new security system

c. where to buy keypads and ID cards

d. the person who heads up security

63. Now, listen to Track 392.

Why is the keypad system being replaced?

a. It could be unsafe.

b. It is broken.

c. Employees don't like it.

d. The keypads are expensive.

64. Now, listen to Track 393.

What can you infer about the man?

a. He thinks the keypad system is adequate.

b. He is a security expert.

c. He believes security is unnecessary.

d. He works with the woman.

Now, listen to Track 394.

65. Now, listen to Track 395.

Why is the woman going to Wisconsin?

a. She got a promotion.

b. She is picking up a GPS unit.

c. The man asked her to go.

d. She quit her job.

66. Now, listen to Track 396.

Why did the woman get a GPS unit?

a. Her boss told her to get one.

b. The man gave her his GPS unit.

c. She was given one by a friend.

d. She doesn't want to get lost.

67. Now, listen to Track 397.

What can you infer about the man?

  a. He is upset that the woman got a promotion.
  b. He doesn't know what a GPS unit is.
  c. He is probably a friend of the woman's.
  d. He works in Wisconsin, too.

Now, listen to Track 398.

68. Now, listen to Track 399.

What are the man and woman discussing?

  a. another name for the company's website
  b. which design choice is best for the company's website
  c. the progress that is being made on the company's website
  d. the committee that oversees the development of the website

69. Now, listen to Track 400.

What problem do the man and the woman have?

  a. The website name was already taken.
  b. The website designs are not ready.
  c. The website will be late.
  d. The committee cannot come up with a new name.

70. Now, listen to Track 401.

What do the man and woman think about the website?

  a. They are not in favor of creating one.
  b. They worry that the volume of sales will go down.
  c. They believe the company is too new to have one.
  d. They think it is a good idea and will help the company.

Directions: You will hear some talks given by a single speaker. You will be asked to answer four questions about what the speaker says in each talk. Select the best response to each question and mark your choice—**a**, **b**, **c**, or **d**—on your answer sheet. The talks will not be printed in your test book and will be spoken only one time.

Now, listen to Track 402.

71. Now, listen to Track 403.

Where would this announcement be heard?

  a. on a plane
  b. in a school
  c. in a supermarket
  d. on a ship

72. Now, listen to Track 404.

What is the purpose of this announcement?

  a. to explain how to use snorkeling equipment
  b. to tell passengers what will happen during the day
  c. to remind the crew that they need to help passengers
  d. to alert passengers to the dangers of snorkeling

73. Now, listen to Track 405.

What time is lunch served?

  a. noon
  b. 1:00 P.M.
  c. 12:30 P.M.
  d. 11:45 A.M.

Now, listen to Track 406.

74. Now, listen to Track 407.

Where does this announcement take place?

  a. on television
  b. at a track meet
  c. in a high school
  d. in a museum

75. Now, listen to Track 408.

What is the purpose of the announcement?

a. to give an overview of the facility

b. to explain the languages of Native Americans

c. to tell what happens in the film

d. to remind visitors that they need tickets

76. Now, listen to Track 409.

What does the gift shop have?

a. books on Native Americans

b. films of Native Americans

c. items made by Native Americans

d. traditional Native American dress

Now, listen to Track 410.

77. Now, listen to Track 411.

What is the purpose of this announcement?

a. to explain to passengers what a club car is

b. to inform passengers about their eating options

c. to tell passengers the special of the day

d. to let passengers know that trains serve food

78. Now, listen to Track 412.

How does the dining room differ from the club car?

a. The dining car serves wine.

b. The dining car serves snacks.

c. The dining car has full meals.

d. The dining car has sandwiches.

79. Now, listen to Track 413.

What are the conductors about to do?

a. take food orders

b. sell tickets

c. give out menus

d. collect tickets

Now, listen to Track 414.

80. Now, listen to Track 415.

Who is making this announcement?

a. a pilot

b. a train conductor

c. a tour guide

d. a salesman

81. Now, listen to Track 416.

Which city is the first stop?

a. Orlando

b. Washington, DC

c. Savannah

d. Boston

82. Now, listen to Track 417.

What should someone with a problem do?

a. Raise his or her arm.

b. Tell the problem before leaving.

c. Write a note and give it to the leader.

d. Talk to the leader during a break.

Now, listen to Track 418.

83. Now, listen to Track 419.

Who is making this announcement?

a. a travel agent

b. a college administrator

c. an English professor

d. a parent

84. Now, listen to Track 420.

What advice does the announcer give the applicants?

a. to spend time with other applicants

b. to visit the dormitories but not the library

c. to be on time for their interviews

d. to eat the snacks that have been prepared

85. Now, listen to Track 421.

How long do the interviews take?

a. 15 minutes

b. 20 minutes

c. 45 minutes

d. one hour

Now, listen to Track 422.

86. Now, listen to Track 423.

Where does this announcement take place?

a. in a park

b. in a department store

c. on television

d. over the phone

87. Now, listen to Track 424.

What is the purpose of the announcement?

a. to help callers reach the person they want

b. to explain how to reach the resort

c. to give information about a resort

d. to make reservations for units

88. Now, listen to Track 425.

Where are the units located?

a. near the water

b. on a golf course

c. next to tennis courts

d. on a hillside

Now, listen to Track 426.

89. Now, listen to Track 427.

Who is making the announcement?

a. a farmer

b. a police office

c. a store manager

d. a weatherman

90. Now, listen to Track 428.

Why is wildlife threatened?

a. The citrus crop is at risk.

b. The temperatures are unusually cold.

c. The turtles do not have food.

d. The citrus crop may freeze.

91. Now, listen to Track 429.

What does the announcer tell listeners?

a. to stay inside

b. to buy citrus fruit

c. to help the turtles

d. to bundle up

Now, listen to Track 430.

92. Now, listen to Track 431.

Where does this announcement take place?

a. in a store

b. at a restaurant

c. in an auditorium

d. on the radio

93. Now, listen to Track 432.

What is causing the traffic to back up?

a. the closing of Route 16

b. rush hour

c. a car accident

d. a car that broke down

94. Now, listen to Track 433.

Where is the traffic backed up?

a. Third Street

b. Sturgeon Bridge

c. Route 16

d. Route 25

Now, listen to Track 434.

95. Now, listen to Track 435.

What is the purpose of the announcement?

a. to remind passengers that the variety show will be after dinner

b. to let passengers know all the events that are planned for them

c. to reassure passengers that the band is well-known

d. to explain to passengers why they will be on their own for lunch

96. Now, listen to Track 436.

Where does the announcement probably take place?

a. in a Los Vegas hotel

b. on an international flight

c. on a train

d. on a cruise ship

97. Now, listen to Track 437.

What is named Dupree?

a. an island

b. a variety show

c. a band

d. a nightclub

Now, listen to Track 438.

98. Now, listen to Track 439.

Who is making the announcement?

a. an announcer on television

b. a passenger on a ship

c. an airline employee

d. a train conductor

99. Now, listen to Track 440.

Why is the plane delayed?

a. There is bad weather.

b. It has a maintenance problem.

c. It needs to be refueled.

d. It is waiting final takeoff approval.

100. Now, listen to Track 441.

When will the information about the delay be updated?

a. in a half hour

b. in one hour

c. in two hours

d. in three hours

Reading

You will now begin the listening section. You will be asked to read a variety of texts and answer several different types of reading comprehension questions. The entire reading section should take approximately 75 minutes. There are three parts and directions are given for each part. Mark your answers on the answer sheet beginning on page 231.

Directions: A word or phrase is missing in each of the sentences below. Four answer choices are given below each sentence. Select the best answer to complete the sentence. Then mark your choice—**a**, **b**, **c**, or **d**—on your answer sheet.

101. After you dial the number you will hear a message that _____ you where the meeting will be held.

a. told

b. tells

c. tell

d. was telling

102. The new department will come up with ways _____ communication between the various agencies.

a. was improved

b. is improving

c. having improved

d. to improve

103. We will be giving advice to everyone who
_____ registered for the seminar on how to
prepare a better resume.
a. has
b. will
c. have
d. were

104. _____ you can do to speed the production of
the new software will be much appreciated.
a. Nothing
b. Whichever
c. Unless
d. Whatever

105. Two of the new inventions were introduced last
month and _____ available for inclusion in the
new catalog, too.
a. is being
b. has been
c. were
d. was

106. Most volunteers _____ found that it is a good
idea to read through all the manuals that tell
the history of the institution prior to starting.
a. was
b. have
c. were
d. been

107. When you meet Tory Staton, be sure to ask her
about why she has not responded to the _____
memo that management sent.
a. simple
b. medium
c. typical
d. last

108. A large international company _____ a study
into the possibility of creating new technology
to build medical equipment.
a. have instituted
b. has instituted
c. was instituted
d. to institute

109. When the new rules regarding office dress
_____, few people realized the full extent of
them.
a. was adopted
b. adopting
c. will be adopted
d. were adopted

110. We are very proud of our new _____, which
will allow two employees to share one full-time
position.
a. theory
b. note
c. policy
d. production

111. Whenever you _____ the new sales promotion
plan, please send it to me as soon as you can so
we can critique it.
a. have finished
b. having finished
c. will finishing
d. finishing

112. The number of products that our company is
able _____ is based strictly on the number of
hours that we spend working.
a. was manufactured
b. is manufactured
c. to manufacture
d. manufacturing

113. _____ the new regulations regarding internal communications have been adopted, they have not yet been put fully into place.
   a. Consequently,
   b. For example,
   c. Although
   d. However,

114. Generally, the best way to identify faulty logic is to look for errors in reasoning and then _____ them.
   a. highlights
   b. highlighted
   c. is highlighting
   d. highlight

115. It is extremely important to dress in a professional manner when you_____ going on an interview for a new position.
   a. were
   b. are
   c. is
   d. was

116. The winner of the sales competition will receive an expense-free trip to Florida, where the _____ will be held in January.
   a. probability
   b. scene
   c. convenience
   d. convention

117. We _____ a new website to make it much more user-friendly so we can boost the number of people who visit it.
   a. developing
   b. is developing
   c. are developing
   d. to develop

118. When it is time to buy a new smartphone, you should definitely research all the information that is available about them in order to get the _____ one possible.
   a. better
   b. best
   c. good
   d. goodest

119. Offices that _____ well designed and pleasant to be in report less absenteeism than those that are uncomfortable and poorly designed.
   a. are
   b. is
   c. has
   d. have

120. If you _____ questions about our vacation policy, you can check the company handbook under Additional Information.
   a. is having
   b. having
   c. have
   d. was have

121. After you prepare a budget for your project, run it by your supervisor to make sure it is _____ with our guidelines.
   a. efficient
   b. capacity
   c. consistent
   d. careful

122. Please be _____ that the company will close for the entire week during the first week of July in order to cut down on the use of energy.
   a. advised
   b. advises
   c. is advised
   d. advising

123. SUMA Operation _____ forces with its affiliate company, LESD, to come up with an entirely new product line.
   a. has joining
   b. had joining
   c. is joining
   d. are joining

124. _____ is ample time for you to report your expenses for your last business trip to our New York City branch.
   a. When
   b. How
   c. There
   d. Which

125. The Oliver Institute has hired a new facilitator to help train employees so they will be up-to-date on all recent studies that _____ done.
   a. will being
   b. is being
   c. has been
   d. have been

126. _____ the company party will begin after the last speaker has completed her assessment of last quarter's revenues.
   a. Remember
   b. Remembering
   c. Remembered
   d. Is remembered

127. The Rochet Organization _____ on expanding its scope of operations into the international market.
   a. are planned
   b. is planning
   c. will planning
   d. to plan

128. The program is not in complete compliance with our standards, ___ there is no reason for concern about that aspect.
   a. but
   b. until
   c. in spite of
   d. neither

129. A full list of products that _____ developed can be found at our website, so there is no need to include that information in your presentation.
   a. will been
   b. was
   c. are been
   d. are being

130. If anyone needs a ride to the upcoming training seminar, they should notify the customer service office since they _____ it.
   a. was organizing
   b. are organizing
   c. were organized
   d. have organizing

131. We offer instructional films to new employees _____ them in understanding our overall goals for the coming year.
   a. assisted
   b. was assisting
   c. is assisting
   d. to assist

132. The new company gym is now open to all employees and management _____ everyone to make use of it.
   a. urge
   b. is urging
   c. urged
   d. are urged

133. _____ of the people who prefer to travel by train will not be able to arrive in time for the opening lecture.
  a. More
  b. One
  c. Best
  d. Most

134. We have two very capable candidates who _____ for the position of Sales Manager and they are about to undergo the final interview process next week.
  a. are applying
  b. is applying
  c. are applied
  d. was applying

135. Any employees who _____ not attended the seminar on sensitivity in the workplace should do so before the end of the month.
  a. has
  b. have
  c. are having
  d. having

136. Our international branch is not in sync with the trends that exist in the United States, but that problem can be easily _____.
  a. resolved
  b. resolving
  c. having resolved
  d. to resolve

137. Ever since September, employees _____ to log in and out at our company's website so we could keep track of the hours that they were working.
  a. requiring
  b. will be required
  c. have been required
  d. was required

138. The company talent competition will continue every Friday _____ the 27th of February.
  a. such as
  b. yet
  c. and
  d. until

139. Our department's duties include, but are not limited to, _____ information about possible duplication of materials.
  a. to research
  b. researching
  c. researches
  d. are researching

140. Last winter, we _____ interviews on an hourly basis in order to give each prospective employee the time to complete an exam as well as the interview.
  a. were scheduling
  b. was scheduling
  c. is scheduled
  d. will be scheduled

Directions: Read the texts that follow. A word or phrase is missing in some of the sentences. Four answer choices are given below each of the sentences. Select the best answer to complete the text. Then mark your choice—**a**, **b**, **c**, or **d**—on your answer sheet.

Questions 141 through 144 refer to the following e-mail.

To: All Employees:
From: Janet Toulons, President, KHG Shoe Corporation: "We Love Shoes—Do You?"

Re: Fall Fashion Show

We are preparing for our (141) _____ in the upcoming Fall Fashion Show and I wanted to update you all on our progress. We have been fortunate enough to come up with a new line of (142) _____ shoes that will appeal to older clients as well as younger ones. Thanks to our inventive designers, these shoes are both classic and comfortable. They will be the main feature of the fashion show and I am confident that they will be a huge success. The best (143) _____ is that they are all manufactured and ready to go and they look terrific! As you know, not all of you will be attending the show, but I want to extend my heartfelt thanks for the hard work you have done this past year. Our revenues show us that we have achieved the (144) _____ we set earlier in the year. As a result, you will each be receiving a bonus, based on your salary. I am sure this is good news for all. Again, I am very happy with our progress. We are definitely a leader in this field.

141. a. defeat
   b. compensation
   c. devotion
   d. participation

142. a. funny
   b. awkward
   c. fabulous
   d. fragile

143. a. ideas
   b. awards
   c. news
   d. offerings

144. a. goals
   b. beliefs
   c. testimony
   d. credit

Questions 145 through 148 refer to the following letter.

Dear Mr. Nickerson:

We are contacting you to interest you about our new convention center, which was completed just last month. This state-of-the-art facility includes everything a (145) _____ such as yours would need to have a successful convention. We have more than 40,000 square feet of space available for meeting rooms as well as display areas. We are wired in all possible ways and have beautiful (146) _____ of the Carter River and Bird Preserve. Adjacent to our facility is the five-star Grandson Hotel. This hotel features all the (147) _____ guests want including restaurants and lounges, in-room dining, a business center, spa and beauty facility, and a fitness center. This 400-room hotel is attached to the conference center through a second floor passageway. We hope you will think of us when you arrange for your corporation's annual convention. We would be happy to meet with you and explain other (148) _____ of using our facility. Please do not hesitate to contact me with your needs.

Sincerely,

Francine Gammer
Director
Kure Convention Center

145. a. level
   b. world
   c. corporation
   d. community

146. a. transportation
    b. possession
    c. connections
    d. views

147. a. treasures
    b. amenities
    c. fantasies
    d. changes

148. a. advantages
    b. problems
    c. worries
    d. attitudes

Questions 149 through 152 refer to the following e-mail.

To: All Employees
From: Kenneth Mayer
Subject: Company Fundraiser

We are organizing a company fundraiser to benefit Habitat for Humanity. We will be having a silent auction at the Vista Resort on June 1 and we need volunteers to help organize and run the event as well as individuals to seek (149) _____ for our silent auction. This is a great (150) _____ for many of you to give back to the community. As you know, Habitat does a wonderful job of building and rehabbing houses that become homes to people who never thought they would be able to afford one. Items that we would like to see (151) _____ for our silent auction include coupons from restaurants, beauty salons, and retail shops as well as baskets from artists and craftspeople. If you have a connection with a possible candidate, please do your best to convince this party that this is a very worthy cause. There is a sign-up

sheet in the lunchroom and I do hope that I will see many of your names on it. My name is (152) _____ there and I plan to donate a week's stay at my condo in Florida. Thanks for all your help.

149. a. welcomes
    b. parties
    c. notices
    d. donations

150. a. provision
    b. opportunity
    c. agreement
    d. certainty

151. a. carried
    b. stolen
    c. obtained
    d. wondered

152. a. already
    b. probably
    c. usually
    d. narrowly

Directions: In this part you will read a selection of texts, such as magazine and newspaper articles, letters, and advertisements. Each text is followed by four questions. Select the best answer for each question and mark your choice—**a, b, c,** or **d**—on your answer sheet.

Questions 153 through 156 refer to the following article.

Being fit has become an obsession for many people in modern society. Some individuals will go to great lengths to become and stay in good condition. While the idea of being in good shape spans back to the ancient Greeks and earlier, it has reached a high point in today's society with the large number of ways to become fit.

Jogging became popular in the 1970s at the same time that aerobic workouts made their debut. Yoga and Pilates are choices for those people who want to build inner core strength. In addition, yoga provides a way into meditation and regulated breathing. Others prefer to use exercise machines that exist thanks to newer technology, such as treadmills, exercise bikes, chest and shoulder presses, leg extension machines, and butterfly machines, to name a few. Some people go to the gym to exercise and others have gyms in their homes.

Whatever the choice—circuit machines, bicycling, or swimming—exercise plays an important part in a person's emotional life as well. Besides helping you keep fit by toning the body, exercise can also be mentally uplifting, say the experts.

Working out makes you feel better, gives you more energy, and may prevent illness and extend your life, according to its advocates. It may also cause injury to various joints, although that doesn't stop all those who have fallen in love with exercise.

153. What is the article mainly about?
  a. how most people prefer to exercise
  b. the various kinds of exercise machines
  c. the fact that so many people are into exercising
  d. how working out may hurt you

154. What do people gain from practicing Pilates?
  a. stronger body core
  b. stronger joints
  c. healthier heart
  d. better breathing techniques

155. The word "advocates" in paragraph 5, line 2, is closest in meaning to:
  a. providers
  b. inventors
  c. customers
  d. supporters

156. According to the article, what do the experts say about exercising?
  a. Yoga can improve posture.
  b. Exercise also benefits your mood.
  c. Exercise should be done on a daily basis.
  d. Bicycling is safer for your body than running.

Questions 157 through 160 refer to the following advertisement.

Veronica's Pet Spa Annual Sale
All Pet Grooming 15% off—
All Pet Grooming Tools 25% off

Offer Good through End of Month
Have Two Pets?
"Special Saturdays Offer"
Buy one grooming and get the other free!
Make an appointment today for your furry friend.
A groomed pet is a happy pet
2188 Castle Street
310-2920

157. What is the purpose of this advertisement?
  a. to announce a sale and boost business
  b. to list the various pet grooming tools that are for sale
  c. to tell where the business is located
  d. to explain how long it takes to groom a pet

158. The word "spa" as used in the advertisement is closest in meaning to:

   a. shelter

   b. house

   c. salon

   d. hospital

159. What is the Special Saturdays Offer?

   a. Two pets can get 15 % off the cost of grooming.

   b. Two pets can be groomed for the cost of one.

   c. Two pets can only be groomed on Saturdays.

   d. Two pets need to be groomed on the same day.

160. What happens at the end of the month?

   a. The Special Saturdays Offer will end.

   b. The sale on the price of grooming and tools is over.

   c. The spa will close for vacation.

   d. Prices for grooming two pets will go up.

Questions 161 through 164 refer to the following article.

We have asked you here today to explain our new sales campaign policy. We will be starting a new approach to reaching out to our clients. We are calling it "Customer Service Week."

Each of you will spend a week in your territory visiting all your customers. We have decided on the week of September 20–26, so you will all need to make appointments to see your customers during that time period. When you make your appointments, be sure to tell your clients that you will be doing a presentation on our new user-friendly software. This software is a second generation of our earlier software program and has some remarkable improvements. If you are not already familiar with the updated software, please check the training schedule. We want you all to be knowledgeable about all the changes that were made.

We are hoping to increase sales by 20% with this innovative sales approach. Most of our selling has previously been done over the phone or the Internet, so this will mark a significant shift from that policy. We believe that one-on-one selling is most effective—that's why we are willing to underwrite the cost of all sales reps spending a week on the road.

If you have any questions, see me during our break this afternoon.

161. What is the article mainly about?

   a. why sales are going up

   b. which territories the company's sales reps cover

   c. what the upgraded software can do

   d. the launch of a new sales campaign

162. If the sales reps are not familiar with the upgraded software, what are they supposed to do?

   a. take a training session

   b. call their clients

   c. ask other sales reps for help

   d. review the software after hours

163. Who will pay for the sales reps' trips?

   a. the sales reps

   b. the software developer

   c. the company

   d. the clients

164. The word "innovative" in paragraph 13 line 1 is closest in meaning to

   a. complicated

   b. challenging

   c. inventive

   d. delicate

Questions 165 through 168 refer to the following advertisement.

Race for Food

The annual Race for Food fundraiser will take place next Saturday at 8 A.M. at Greenfield Park. This four-mile race raises money for the Samara Food Pantry, where the number of needy has risen significantly in the past few months. Those interested in participating are asked to call 815-9097 before Wednesday to reserve a spot. Runners will need to be sponsored by individuals or businesses. Organizers are suggesting that sponsors pledge $10 per mile, but any donation is welcomed.

165. What is the purpose of the news brief?
  a. to explain what a food pantry does
  b. to discuss why fundraisers are important
  c. to encourage people to join the Race for Food
  d. to get people to watch the fundraiser in Greenfield Park

166. Why does the brief include a telephone number?
  a. so sponsors can contact the race organizers
  b. so runners can sign up for the race
  c. so the food pantry can contact the sponsors
  d. so the racers can find sponsors

167. Why do runners need to be sponsored?
  a. to raise money for the food pantry
  b. to ensure they show up for the race
  c. to pay for the T-shirts runners will wear
  d. to buy insurance needed for the run

168. The word "significantly" in line 3 of the news brief is closest in meaning to
  a. a little
  b. narrowly
  c. somewhat
  d. a great deal

Questions 169 through 172 refer to the following article.

Those of you who are to be in charge of our teenaged employees need to be aware of the many restrictions that are placed on the work they can do. Federal regulations dictate that 14- or 15-year-old teens may work as long as the job does not interfere with school. Other rules say that this age group is not allowed to operate heavy or dangerous machinery or to work after 10 P.M. Teenagers between 16 and 17 may work until 12 midnight, but they must have a parent consent form to do so. No parent consent form is needed for those teens over the age of 18.

But here at ComDotCom Publications, we have developed even stricter guidelines that we want implemented. Unlike the federal guidelines, we do not hire anyone under the age of 16, and we require a parent consent form to be signed by a legal guardian until the teenager turns 18.

Also, we do not allow any teens to work later than 9 P.M. and we do not allow any teenagers under the age of 18 to use heavy or dangerous equipment.

Teenagers under the age of 18 may not work more than six consecutive hours and a total of no more than 20 hours a week. Please review our regulations and if you have any questions, contact me.

169. What is the purpose of this article?
   a. to give guidelines for working with heavy or dangerous equipment
   b. to introduce the employees who will oversee teenaged employees
   c. to explain a company's rules regarding teenage employees
   d. to review the federal government laws for teens who work

170. How are the company's rules regarding teens and the federal government's rules similar?
   a. Teens under the age of 16 cannot work.
   b. Teens under the age of 18 cannot work more than six consecutive hours.
   c. A parent consent form is required until a teen is 18.
   d. No parent consent form is needed for teens 18 and over.

171. Under the company's rules, how many hours can teens under 18 work a week?
   a. six hours
   b. twelve hours
   c. twenty hours
   d. There is no restriction.

172. The word "dictate" in paragraph 1 line 2 of the article closest in meaning to:
   a. desire
   b. choose
   c. speak
   d. require

Questions 173 through 176 refer to the following advertisement.

Winter Luggage Sale
15 to 25% off all existing inventory*

All types and sizes: lightweight, plastic, canvas

We specialize in carry-on bags.

New luggage line will be available in May.

Carriers for golf clubs are also available while they last.

*Leather luggage is excluded from the sale.

173. What is the purpose of the advertisement?
   a. to let people know about a luggage sale
   b. to encourage people to buy leather luggage
   c. to explain how large a carry-on bag is
   d. to inform people about the different types of luggage

174. Why do you suppose leather luggage is not included?
   a. because leather luggage is not popular
   b. because leather luggage doesn't go out of style
   c. because leather luggage is old-fashioned
   d. because there isn't much leather luggage left

175. What will happen in May?
   a. The sale will continue.
   b. The leather luggage will go on sale.
   c. Golf carriers will be discontinued.
   d. New luggage will be showcased.

176. What does the advertisement suggest about the golf club carriers?
   a. The store has a limited number of them.
   b. They are made of plastic or canvas.
   c. They are not large enough for a full set of clubs.
   d. They can be carried onto a plane.

Questions 177 through 180 refer to the following memo.

Memo: To All Employees
From: Andre Kang, Chief Security Officer
Subject: New Security Measures

We are no longer going to issue ID swipe cards that can be used on a 24-hour, 7-day-a-week basis to employees. Instead, the swipe cards will be coded only for the hours that an employee is scheduled to work. We feel this will cut down on inappropriate use of these cards.

In addition, we are now asking employees to wear their ID swipe cards at all times.

All visitors to our facility will now be required to sign in and out in the reception area. While on-site, guests must wear their visitor cards at all times. Visitor cards will only work during business hours. Visitors must return their visitor cards before leaving the building.

Employees should avoid letting anyone into the building who does not have an ID swipe card. Instead, employees should ask the person who they are here to see and offer to call that person for them. Anyone who senses that there is something out of the ordinary should call security.

We are sure that these new security measures will make for a safer work area.

177. What is the article mainly about?
   a. how to use an ID swipe card
   b. why ID cards are necessary
   c. a new security policy
   d. where guests should sign in

178. What has changed about the ID swipe cards?
   a. They will only be given out to visitors.
   b. They will not be valid all the time.
   c. They will have a photo and ID number.
   d. They will be turned in at the end of the day.

179. Why is the new security plan being put into place?
   a. Guests were taking the ID swipe cards home.
   b. Employees were misusing their ID swipe cards.
   c. Employees kept losing their ID swipe cards.
   d. Guests were not allowed in the building.

180. What should employees do if they see someone trying to get in without an ID swipe card?
   a. Call the receptionist.
   b. Ask the person who they want to see.
   c. Tell the person to leave the area.
   d. Tell the person to go to the reception area.

Questions 181 through 185 refer to the following magazine article and advertisement.

Three Top Tips for Getting a Job
So you are looking for a job. You are not alone. There are a lot of you out there and the competition is fierce. To help, we have compiled a list of the three top tips for finding suitable employment. You may or may not be aware of the tips, but it doesn't hurt to review.

■ **Number 1: Make Your Resume Stand Out**
Make your resume shine. Keep it brief, not pages long. Open with a statement about your talents and your goals. Use headers and explain briefly what each position consisted of. Add information about your education and any volunteer activities you are involved in. Don't use jargon, but do use language that is similar to what the job description used.

■ Number 2: Do Your Homework

Before you go on an interview, make sure to find out everything you can about the company. What are the company's goals? What are its needs? How do you mesh with its philosophy?

■ Number 3: Wow Your Interviewer

Be confident. Dress comfortably but professionally. Put your hand out as you enter the room. Smile and make eye contact. Be alert and be prepared to tell your interviewer why you would be an asset to this company.

We feel confident that if you follow these easy suggestions, you will land the job you want.

Wetrainyou.com presents:

How to Interview

Looking for a job?

Come to our training session and you will learn everything you need to know to shine at your interview.

We cover the following:

- how to be confident
- what to wear
- how to act
- what questions to ask
- what not to do

Training Sessions Available Both During the Day and Evenings

Only $45 for three-hour session

Call 765-934-1234 or visit wetrainyou.com for more information and to sign up.

181. What is the main purpose of the magazine article?
   a. to tell how to get a job
   b. to explain that jobs are difficult to get
   c. to give advice on how to dress for an interview
   d. to advise people on what not to say at an interview

182. Why does the article suggest putting out your hand when you go into the interview room?
   a. so you will look professional
   b. so you can impress the interviewer
   c. so you can shake hands
   d. so you can grab a chair

183. What does the advertisement leave out?
   a. what will be covered in the training session
   b. where the training session takes place
   c. a contact number
   d. the price of the training session

184. What topic is covered in the advertisement but not in the article?
   a. how to be confident
   b. how to research a company
   c. how to dress for an interview
   d. what not to say during an interview

185. In what way are the article and the advertisement similar?
   a. They both want to help people do better at interviews.
   b. They both talk about the benefits of taking interview training.
   c. They both list helpful sites on the Internet.
   d. They both emphasize having a good resume.

Questions 186 through 190 refer to the following e-mail and menu.

From: Marilyn Cantarella
To: Jason Kaplan
Subject: Menu changes

Hello, Jason,

Our board of directors met last week to discuss what changes we want to make in the menu for our popular Dixie Grill restaurants. They were of the opinion that we need to make our food more appealing to those people looking for less fat and fewer calories.

I agreed with their decision and they asked me to develop some new food ideas that reflect this decision. I came up with some recommendations, which they have reviewed, but before acting on anything, they wanted to know what you thought of them. They specifically want to know how difficult it would be to incorporate some of the new dishes and what we should charge for them. You can see that I haven't put any prices on anything.

I think in the future more and more restaurants will want to target people concerned with how much fat and how many calories they are consuming in their diet. Even fast food restaurants are acting on this trend.

I have another question for you. Do you think we should include a breakdown of all entrees in terms of nutrition, including amount and kinds of fat and calories, or do you think this be a turnoff to many customers? We want people to continue to think of us as friendly.

I look forward to getting your response.

The Dixie Grill

The Popular Choice: Where the Costs Are Down and the Flavor Up!

Salads and Sandwiches

Keep It Simple Tossed Salad
Iceberg and romaine with tomatoes

Romaine and More
Romaine salad with black olives, tomatoes, cucumbers, and blue cheese

Dixie's Special Salad
Organic baby mixed greens, cherry tomatoes

All salads can be topped with your choice of:
roast turkey
shrimp
tuna

Build a Sandwich
Choose any Cold Cut: Roast Beef, Turkey, Ham
Add any Cheese: Swiss, Cheddar, Provolone
Pick a Bread: White, Wheat, Pumpernickel
And Tell Us What Else You Want on It:
Mayo, Mustard, Lettuce, Tomato, Pickles

186. What is the e-mail mainly about?
a. what the board of directors of the Dixie Grill like to eat
b. why the Dixie Grill menu has dishes that are high in fat
c. where the Dixie Grill restaurants are located
d. introducing dishes with less fat and calories at the Dixie Grill

187. Why are salads and soups recommended as new menu dishes?
- **a.** They are tastier.
- **b.** They tend to be easier to make.
- **c.** They have fewer calories and less fat.
- **d.** They are usually less expensive.

188. Which food can you top a salad with?
- **a.** shrimp
- **b.** provolone
- **c.** roast beef
- **d.** ham

189. Which can you get both on a salad and in a sandwich?
- **a.** turkey
- **b.** shrimp
- **c.** provolone
- **d.** tuna

190. How is the Dixie Grill described in both the e-mail and the menu?
- **a.** as being clean
- **b.** as being friendly
- **c.** as being popular
- **d.** as being reasonable

Questions 191 through 195 refer to the following letter and coupon.

Dear New Club Member:

We welcome you as a new member of our hotel club and congratulate you on your good taste. As you know we have a wonderful facility here, complete with tennis courts, pools, putting green, and business centers. We hope you will be staying with us on a regular basis.

By joining the club, you are guaranteed the best price for rooms as long as you commit for at least one week per year. Of course, you have the option of staying here much more frequently than that. Just call our reservation desk and book your space.

Because you have recently joined our club, we want to reward you with a $50 gift certificate to our lovely Italian Restaurant, Spesso. This fine eatery offers exquisite Northern Italian cuisine, so we know you will be pleased to dine there. It is on the top floor of the hotel and offers spectacular views as well as delicious food.

If you should require anything out of the ordinary during your stay here, please contact me personally and I will ensure that any of your needs are met. Remember, our motto here is "The guest comes first," and we intend to do just that.

Again, please drop by my office and say hello. I enjoy meeting all our guests.

Sincerely,

Bobby Bryant, Manager
Gloriana Hotel Club

Coupon
Spesso Restaurant

Featuring the best Northern Italian food available outside Italy
$50 toward dinner for two or more
Valid Tuesday through Sunday (closed Monday)

Located on the top floor of the Gloriana Hotel Club
Our name is Italian for "often."
And we hope you will visit us "spesso."

191. What is the main purpose of the letter?
   a. to greet a new member of the Gloriana Hotel Club
   b. to describe what the Gloriana Hotel Club looks like
   c. to discuss which times of the year a club member can visit
   d. to let club members know that Spesso Restaurant is open

192. Why is the coupon included with the letter?
   a. The restaurant owner asked to have it included.
   b. The hotel club wants to give its new members a gift.
   c. The hotel club just opened the restaurant.
   d. The hotel club doesn't want the restaurant to contact its members directly.

193. What is the reason the coupon cannot be used on Mondays?
   a. The restaurant hosts private parties on Mondays.
   b. Less expensive meals are served on Mondays.
   c. On Mondays the restaurant is very crowded.
   d. The restaurant is closed on Mondays.

194. What do you learn about Spesso in the letter that is not learned in the coupon?
   a. that it serves Italian food
   b. that it has wonderful views
   c. that it is on the top floor
   d. that it is very intimate

195. What piece of information is found in the coupon but not the letter?
   a. The value of the coupon
   b. What type of restaurant Spesso is
   c. where the restaurant is located
   d. What the name Spesso means

Questions 196 through 200 refer to the following agenda and e-mail.

Chamberlain Arts Council

January 10 Board Meeting Agenda

Greeting: Chamberlain Arts Council Director Fredericka Hodges

Minutes of December Board Meeting: Jorge Ruiz

Treasurer's Report: Berry Dunmore

Members' Comments

Publicity Drive: Dahlia Everton

Update on Newsletter: Jan Gies

Group Art Show: Terri Mann

From: Fredericka Hodges [fhodges@CAC.org]
To: tmann@yahoo.com
Subject: Arts Council Meeting

Hey, Terri,

I meant to mention to you at the last board meeting that I think we should go ahead with the art show you were going to talk about Monday evening. Because the meeting ran so late, we didn't have time to talk about it. We never seem to be able to finish our agenda.

I think it would be a fine thing for our organization to have a group show of its members' art. Certainly we can get some good press out of it, since publicity is one of our main goals. And because there will be many people's works being shown, including your own, we are guaranteed good attendance at the show's opening.

By the way, what do you think about the newsletter? I see it as an important step in getting the word out about our activities. We could send it not just to members, but to our mailing list. I think we have everyone's e-mail as well as home address.

Anyway, let me know what date you think would work for the show. We will have a lot of work to organize it. If you know of people who you think would be willing to help out on the show, let me know who they are and I will contact them.

Best,

Freddi

196. What is the purpose of the agenda?
   a. to tell what will be covered at the meeting
   b. to show that many people will attend the meeting
   c. to encourage members of the arts council to attend
   d. to increase the membership of the arts council

197. Why does Fredericka Hodges e-mail Terri Mann?
   a. to inform her that the organization has a newsletter
   b. to tell her that she wants to go ahead with the group art show
   c. to ask her to write a press release
   d. to get her to help on more projects

198. What does the e-mail suggest about Terri Mann?
   a. that she has organized an art show before
   b. that she is probably an artist
   c. that she is a member of the board
   d. that she wasn't at the board meeting

199. What topic is found in the agenda, but not in the e-mail?
   a. the newsletter
   b. the group art show
   c. the publicity drive
   d. the meeting's minutes

200. Based on the information in both the agenda and e-mail, what immediate goal does the chamber have?
   a. to have many more art shows
   b. to get a lot of publicity
   c. to encourage artists
   d. to locate more artists

Speaking

This section tests your skills for the TOEIC Speaking Test. It includes 11 questions that measure different aspects of your speaking ability. The test lasts approximately 20 minutes.

For each type of question, you will be given specific directions, including the time allowed for preparation and speaking. It is to your advantage to say as much as you can in the time allowed. It is also important that you speak clearly and that you answer each question according to the directions.

Directions: In this part of the test, you will read aloud the text on the screen. You will have 45 seconds to prepare. Then you will have 45 seconds to read the text aloud. Use a stopwatch or clock to keep track of your time.

201. If you have never experienced the warm waters of Puerto Rico, you should definitely plan a visit to this magical tropical island where the beaches are wide and the surf comforting. At Palmas del Sol you will enjoy every amenity under the sun, including a world-class golf course, tennis courts, a spa, and more. Ride the waves of the Caribbean or lie aimlessly on the beach under your private shade tree. This resort offers five different restaurants, each one more inviting than the next. You will never forget your stay with us, so come play with us!

202. Although the new city law has good intentions, I do not believe it will benefit our fair metropolis. Granting tax exemptions to entice a business to relocate here might help unemployment rates, but the rates in our city—and our state, for that matter—are already very low. What our city needs is to have everyone pay a fair share of the tax burden. Letting a large company pay less means that regular citizens will have to pay more, by comparison. Our city offers many benefits to a company; there's no need to add corporate tax breaks to this list.

Directions: In this part of the test, you will describe the picture on your screen in as much detail as you can. You will have 30 seconds to prepare your response. Then you will have 45 seconds to speak about the picture. Use a stopwatch or clock to keep track of your time.

203. Describe the photo in as much detail as possible.

Directions: In this part of the test, you will answer three questions. For each question, begin responding immediately after you hear a beep. No preparation time is provided. You will have 15 seconds to respond to questions 204 and 205, and 30 seconds to respond to question 206.

Imagine that a German camera company is doing a survey in the United States and you agree to participate.

204. What kind of camera do you have?

205. How often do you use your camera?

206. Describe what you use your camera for.

Directions: In this part of the test, you will answer three questions based on the information provided. You will have 30 seconds to read the information below. Then you will have 15 seconds to respond to questions 207 and 208, and 30 seconds to respond to question 209. Use a stopwatch or clock to keep track of your time.

I am calling about an advertising copywriting seminar that will take place on July 6. Could you give me some information?

WordWrite.com Presents
All about Ad Copy Writing

Date: July 6

Location: Coastal Community College

Training Seminars:

9 A.M.	What Is Ad Copy?
10 A.M.	Getting to the Heart of the Copy
	or
	Best Quips Copy
11 A.M.	Writing Your First Advertisement
12 noon	Lunch Break
1 P.M.	Practice Makes Perfect
2 P.M.	Panel with Advertising Copywriters
	Moderated by
	Jon Murchison, CEO,
	WordWrite.com
Topic:	The Purpose of Advertising
3 P.M.	The Art of Perfect Copy
4 P.M.	Closing Statement and Questions

Registration Fee: $100 all day; $55 half day

Lunch can be purchased at several nearby restaurants.

207. Can you please tell me how much the ad copy seminar is?

208. Is lunch included in the price of the seminar?

209. Can you tell me what the morning session will include?

Directions: In this part of the test, you will be presented with a problem and asked to propose a solution. You will have 30 seconds to prepare. Then you will have 60 seconds to speak. Use a stopwatch or clock to keep track of your time.

210. Respond as if you work at a salon.
As you reply, be sure to:
■ show that you recognize the problem
■ propose a way of dealing with the problem

Now, listen to Track 442.

Directions: In this part of the test, you will give your opinion about a specific topic. Be sure to say as much as you can in the time allowed. You will have 15 seconds to prepare. Then you will have 60 seconds to speak. Use a stopwatch or clock to keep track of your time.

211. Some people think that builders should be required to use green materials in new construction or face fines. What is your opinion about requiring builders to use green materials and fining them if they don't? Give reasons for your opinion.

Writing

This is the TOEIC Writing Test. This test includes eight questions that measure different aspects of your writing ability. The test lasts approximately one hour. For each type of question, you will be given specific directions, including the time allowed for writing.

Directions: In this part of the test, you will write ONE sentence that is based on a picture. With each picture, you will be given TWO words or phrases that you must use in your sentence. You can change the forms of the words and you can use the words in any order.

Your sentence will be scored on:

■ the appropriate use of grammar
■ the relevance of the sentence to the picture

You will have eight minutes to complete this part of the test. Use a stopwatch or clock to keep track of your time.

212.

waitress, salad

_____

_____

213.

smiling, dancing

_____

_____

214.

class, hands up

_____

_____

215.

sneakers, white

_____

_____

216.

happy, jumping

_____

_____

Directions: In this part of the test, you will show how well you can write a response to an e-mail.

Your response will be scored on:

- the quality and variety of your sentences
- vocabulary
- organization

You will have 10 minutes to read and answer each e-mail. Use a stopwatch or clock to keep track of your time.

> From:17th Street Delicatessen
> To: Our Valued Customers
> Subject: Free Sides
> Sent: July 2
>
> Happy Fourth of July! To celebrate our country's founding the 17th Street Delicatessen is awarding our valued customers two free sides when you order one of our great sandwiches. We have a variety of sides and we know you will enjoy them. Try our three bean salad or pasta salad. We also have potato salad and cucumber salad. You will enjoy two of these great salads with any of our sandwiches if you come in between the hours of 11:00 A.M. and 2:00 P.M. We are open every day except Sunday, so it's up to you when you want to take advantage of our offer. Just print out this e-mail and bring it along with you.
>
> The Management

Reply to the e-mail as though you were a customer of the 17th Street Delicatessen. In your e-mail, let management know two reasons you shop there.

217. _____

_____

_____

_____

_____

_____

Directions: In this part of the test, you will show how well you can write a response to a letter.

Your response will be scored on:

- the quality and variety of your sentences
- vocabulary
- organization

You will have 10 minutes to read and answer each letter. Use a stopwatch or clock to keep track of your time.

> Dear Mr. Farran:
>
> We are contacting you to tell you that you are eligible for an upgrade of our software. In the past two years, you have been a good customer and we want to reward your loyalty with this opportunity. Please go to our website at www.newworld.com and make out an

application for this free upgrade. If you have any questions, do not hesitate to contact me.

Lucille Minion, Manager
New World Software

Reply to the letter as though you were a customer of the software company. In your e-mail, ask two questions about the software.

218. _____

_____

_____

_____

_____

Directions: In this part of the test, you will write an essay in response to a question that asks you to state, explain, and support your opinion on an issue. Typically, an effective essay will contain a minimum of 300 words.

Your response will be scored on:

- whether your opinion is supported with reasons and/or examples
- grammar
- vocabulary
- organization

You will have 30 minutes to plan, write, and revise your essay. Use a stopwatch or clock to keep track of your time.

People have many different goals. Some people want to earn a lot of money while others think it is more important to do good deeds. Which goal do you see as the most important? Give reasons or examples to support your opinion.

219. _____

_____

_____

_____

_____

_____

_____

_____

_____

_____

_____

_____

Answers

1. b. They are looking at a computer. Choice **a** is not correct since they are not eating dinner. They are not looking out the window, although there is one behind them. They are not walking down a hall, so choice **c** and choice **d** are not correct.

2. c. They are all clapping. Choice **a** is not correct. They are neither talking nor are they sitting at their desks, so choice **b** is incorrect. It is possible they are listening to a speech, but we can't be sure, so choice **d** is not the best answer.

3. b. They are playing soccer. They are not swimming or watching a film, so choice **a** and choice **c** are incorrect. They are running, but they are not running a race, so choice **d** is wrong, too.

4. d. The man is eating. Choice **a** is not correct. He is not walking. He is not laughing or talking either, so choices **b** and choice **c** are incorrect, too.

5. a. He is playing golf. He is not watching TV, so choice **b** is incorrect. He is not running a race or hiking outside, so choice **c** and choice **d** are incorrect also.

6. c. They are taking a walk. They are ⟨not at⟩ a house, so choice **a** is wro⟨ng. There is no⟩ evidence they are sho⟨pping⟩, so choice **b** is incorrect, as is ⟨ch⟩oice **d**.

7. d. They are in a meeting. They are not laughing, so choice **a** is not correct. One person is standing up, but not all of them, so choice **b** is incorrect also. They are not having lunch, so choice **d** is wrong, too.

8. a. She is riding a bike. She is not walking a dog or singing a song, so choice **b** and choice **c** are incorrect. She is not at a computer either, so choice **d** is also wrong.

9. b. The woman is drawing a diagram. Choice **a** is not correct. She is not sitting at a table. She is not waiting in a line or stretching out either, so choice **c** and choice **d** are incorrect, too.

10. b. He is skiing. He is not eating or typing so choice **a** and choice **c** are incorrect. He is not sitting, either, so choice **d** is wrong also.

11. a. It responds to the question. Choice **b** talks about a mailroom and choice **c** asks a question, but neither one responds to the question about where the meeting room is.

12. c. Choice **c** is the only response that makes sense. Choice **a** asks a question that has nothing to do with the topic. Choice **b** is a statement that doesn't answer the question about where the desk is.

13. a. This is the appropriate response to the statement. Choice **b** talks about a conference room and choice **c** talks about a social security number. Neither one has anything to do with the statement about being the first ones to arrive.

14. c. Choice **c** responds to the question about ⟨. . . . .⟩ ⟨. . . . .⟩ makes a statement that doesn't have to do with the topic, either.

15. b. It is the only choice that responds to the question about what supplies are needed. Choice **a** is a question that does not relate to the topic. Choice **c** has nothing to do with the topic, either.

16. a. It answers the question of how long the meeting will be. Choice **b** and choice **c** are statements that are unrelated to the topic, so they are both incorrect.

17. b. It responds to the statement about upgrading a computer. Choice **a** and choice **c** are statements that are unrelated to the main topic.

18. c. It is an appropriate response to the question. Choice **a** asks a question that is unrelated to the topic of applying for the position. Choice **b** is a statement that has nothing to do with the topic.

19. a. Choice **a** responds to the question about when a person started to work at a new place. Choice **b** is about a computer and choice **c** is about an elevator, so they are not related.

20. a. Choice **a** is the best response to the statement about keeping a door closed. Choice **b** and choice **c** talk about topics unrelated to keeping a door closed, so they are incorrect.

21. b. Choice **b** responds to the question correctly. Choice **a** and choice **c** talk about things that are unrelated to when the trainees are returning.

22. b. Choice **b** answers the question that is asked. Choice **a** asks an unrelated question, and choice **c** gives directions to something.

23. c. It answers the question about where new employees sign in. Choice **a** is about being late for a sales conference and choice **b** talks about a software program, so neither one is relevant.

24. a. Choice **a** relates to the statement about the office being closed. Choice **b** and choice **c** both talk about things that are not related to the topic.

25. b. Choice **b** is the correct response since it answers the question about which building the conference is in. Choice **a** and choice **c** are both statements, but they are about unrelated topics.

26. a. Choice **a** tells the location of the lunchroom. Choice **b** talks about leaving for a meeting and choice **c** about telephoning someone, so neither one is related to the topic.

27. c. Choice **c** is the only one that responds to the question about what papers the publicity department needs. Choice **a** talks about errors in a text and choice **b** is about a memo, so they are incorrect.

28. b. Choice **b** relates to having a lunch meeting. The other choices do not. Choice **a** is about expenses, while choice **c** is about a CEO going to England.

29. a. Choice **a** is correct because it responds to the question about where the supervisor is. Choice **b** asks a question about getting help on a project and choice **c** is a statement about an e-mail. Neither one is related to the topic.

30. c. Choice **c** is the only answer that relates to the topic about a conference on increasing sales. Choice **a** talks about an extension number and choice **b** asks an unrelated question, so they are both incorrect.

31. b. Choice **b** is the correct response to the question. Choice **a** is not related to the topic of having an interview and choice **c** talks about taking mail to the mail room, so that is not related either.

32. b. This question is related to the topic of having to do research. Choices are not related. They talk about personnel department and the main conference room, not about doing research for a project.

33. c. It responds to the information in the statement that a supervisor is waiting for an employee. Choice **a** talks about working on Saturday and choice **b** asks an unrelated question, so they are both incorrect.

34. a. Choice **a** is correct because it responds to the statement about renting a car. Choice **c** is about an e-mail and choice **c** about being late. Neither of them relate to the topic.

35. c. Choice **c** is correct becuase it relates to the question about finding a cell phone. Choice **a** and choice **b** are about unrelated topics.

36. a. Choice **a** is the correct response to the question. Choice **b** is about someone being on a phone and choice **c** is asking an unrelated question, so they are both incorrect.

37. c. This responds to the statement that more forms need to be ordered. Choice **a** has nothing to do with the topic. It is about going to a restaurant. Choice **b** talks about a plan being well organized and is unrelated to the topic.

38. b. Choice **b** answers the question that is asked about the name of a supervisor. Choice **a** tells you that a Mrs. Martinez is sick, but there is no mention of her being a supervisor. Choice **c** is unrelated also.

39. c. This question is related to the statement that a person is driving to a meeting. Choice **a** talks about restarting a computer and choice **b** asks an unrelated question, so they are incorrect.

40. a. Choice **a** is correct becuase it answers the question about where the cafeteria is located. Choice **b** talks about asking a favor, and choice **c** tells someone what to do, but neither one is related to the topic.

41. b. Choice **b** is correct because the man tells the woman that he is "going on a road trip next Monday" and that he needs to go "to four cities in two different states." The service shop is mentioned, but nothing is stated about its location. There is no mention of what the software is for or why his car needs to be serviced, either.

42. c. Choice **c** is the correct response. The man asks the woman is she can pick him up at the shop. That is his problem. Choice **a** is not correct since the man says the software was tested 10,000 hours. Choice **b** is not correct. There is no mention of the man buying a new car for his trip. The woman tells the man that she would be happy to pick him up, so choice **d** is not correct, either.

43. c. The man tells the woman that he will be away three weeks, so choice **c** is the correct answer. Other numbers were mentioned relating to other things, but they were not the number of weeks he will be away.

44. c. Choice **c** is correct because the woman tells the man she "can't seem to logon to our company site." She does not say her computer is broken, so choice **a** is incorrect. She knows her ID number, so choice **b** is not correct. There is no mention of her not being able to figure out how to fill out a help ticket, only that she can't get on the company's site to get one.

45. b. The man asks the woman, "Did you restart your computer?" He doesn't ask whether she called the tech people, if she knows the company's web address, or has filled out help ticket, so choices **a**, **c**, and **d** are incorrect.

46. a. There is no mention of the man fixing her computer. He tells her that they are not supposed to call the tech people so choice **c** is incorrect. She has already restarted her computer, so choice **d** is incorrect also.

47. a. The man and woman are discussing the training, so choice **a** is correct. There is no mention of the number of trainers, so choice **b** is not correct. They mention that changes did occur, but they do not discuss what they are, so choice **c** is incorrect. The man and woman do not discuss how long the training will last, so choice **d** is also wrong.

48. d. Choice **d** is correct because the woman said, "I took that training last year. I don't see why I need to take it again." There is no mention of her not liking the product or being too busy with work, so choice **a** and choice **b** are incorrect. The woman never mentions going on vacation, so choice **c** is also wrong.

49. b. Choice **b** is the correct one since the man says, "I've arranged it so there will only be six people in a class." This clue helps you infer that he is organizing the training. There is no evidence that he is the president of the company or that he is one of the trainers. And he doesn't sound as though he doesn't want to take the training, so choice **c** is incorrect.

50. a. The woman says she cut out a coupon and put it on her desk, "but it's not there now." She doesn't say anything about not wanting to go on a business trip or that she doesn't want to rent a car, so choice **b** and choice **c** are wrong. She doesn't appear to dislike her job, either, so choice **d** cannot be correct.

51. a. The woman says that the coupon online "was only for a 10% discount. I remember that the discount I had was for 20% off a weekly rental," so choice **a** is the correct answer. There was no mention of her not finding it on the Internet or that it was for a two-week rental or that it cannot be downloaded, so the other choices are incorrect.

52. b. In the conversation, the woman says, "I have to see all the managers of our stores in the Tri-City Area," so we know that choice **b** is the correct answer. None of the other choices were mentioned, so they cannot be correct.

53. c. Choice **c** is correct since the woman says, "My supervisor wants me to come up with a list of ways that we can save energy and be greener." There is no mention of her writing a memo or asking employees for ideas, although she does do that. Nor did her supervisor ask her to come up with a carpooling plan.

54. a. The woman tells the man that she can't think of any ways to be greener," so choice **a** is correct. The man seems very helpful, so choice **b** cannot be correct. There is no evidence that she is afraid she will lose her job or that she doesn't want to save resources, so those choices are incorrect also.

55. d. The man has ideas about being greener, so it's likely that he likes the idea. There is no evidence that either choice **a** or choice **c** is correct. And the man seems to work for the same company that the woman works for, so choice **b** is incorrect.

56. a. The woman begins the conversation telling the man about a meeting that he needs to go to. The topic of new regulations is mentioned, but there is no mention of what they consist of. The supervisor is mentioned, but not what he wants them to do, so choice **c** is incorrect. There is no mention of an intercom. Therefore, choice **d** is also incorrect.

57. b. The man says tells the woman that he is supposed to go to another meeting. There is no indication that any other choice is correct.

58. d. This is what the man says at the end of the conversation. There is no mention of choice **a** or choice **c**, and choice **b** is not correct because he says he has another training to go to.

59. c. The man says at the start of the conversation, "I need you to book my trip for the book marketing conference." There is no mention of her finding out where he has to go or booking a rental car. He does not ask her to come with him, either, so all the other choices are incorrect.

60. a. She probably does travel bookings for the company that the man works for. Choice **b** is not suggested in any way, nor is choice **c**. It is fairly clear that she is not organizing the conference.

61. d. The other choices are not suggested in the conversation. Yes, he is going on a business trip, but that is not why she tells the man he is lucky. It is because he will be able to get back Sunday night.

62. b. The woman asks the man if he has heard about the new security system. That is what they are discussing. There is no mention of employee attitudes, where to buy keypads, ID cards, or the person who heads up security, so those choices are all incorrect.

63. a. The woman says, "The keypad system worries management," so choice **a** is the correct answer. It could be unsafe. There is no mention of the system being broken or that the employees don't like it, so choice **b** and choice **c** are incorrect. We are not told whether the keypads are expensive or not, so this choice is wrong, too.

64. d. We can infer that the man and woman work together. They are discussing the new security system, so that is one clue. There is no evidence for choice **a** or choice **b**, and it appears he believes a security system is needed, so choice **c** is wrong as well.

65. a. The woman says, "I've got a promotion but it means moving to Wisconsin." Choice **b** is incorrect. The woman already picked up the GPS unit. There is no mention of the man asking her to go or that she quit her job.

66. d. She says it herself. There is no suggestion that choice **a** or choice **b** are correct. Maybe she was given the GPS unit by a friend, but this is not mentioned, so it is not correct, either.

67. c. We can't be sure, but it would appear that the man and woman are friends. There is nothing in the conversation to indicate that the man is upset and it appears he knows exactly what a GPS unit is, so those two can be eliminated. Again, there is nothing to suggest that he works in Wisconsin. Maybe he does, but he doesn't tell us this.

68. c. The man and woman are discussing the progress that is being made on the company's website. Choice **a** is mentioned, but not discussed. The woman does say the designs will be ready for review, but there is no discussion of which one is best. Again, the committee is mentioned, but only in passing. This is not the topic of the discussion.

69. a. Choice **a** is correct because the woman tells the man that the design company hadn't "been able to register our name. It's already been taken." Choice **b** is not correct since the woman said the designs were ready. There is no mention of the website being late or the committee being unable to come up with a new name.

70. d. The woman says that the website "is going to make a big difference," and the man says, "We believe it will help us meet our goals for this year," so it is clear that they both like the idea of the new website. None of the other choices are suggested by the conversation.

71. d. Choice **a** is a possibility since the announcement welcomes people aboard and says they are going to Monkey Island. But the fact that they are serving lunch in the main cabin and are going to be at the island all day snorkeling suggests a ship rather than a plane. This announcement would not be heard in a school or in a supermarket.

72. b. The overall purpose of the announcement is to tell passengers what to expect. The announcement does mention snorkeling equipment and it does say that the crew will answer questions, but these are not the purpose of the announcement. There is no mention of the dangers of snorkeling, so choice **d** is incorrect also.

73. a. Lunch will be served at 12:00 noon. The announcement says that lunch will be over at 1:00 P.M., so choice **b** is not correct. The other choices are not mentioned at all.

74. d. You can rule out choice **a** and choice **b** since this announcement would not be heard at either one. While the announcement does talk about learning the lore and wisdom of Native Americans, other clues are not consistent with a high school. Display areas and films and gift shops all suggest a museum.

75. a. This is the overall purpose of the announcement. There is no mention of the languages of Native Americans. The film is mentioned, but the announcement doesn't tell what happens in it. There is no mention of tickets, so choice **d** is incorrect also.

76. c. This is what the announcement says. It does not mention books on Native Americans. While a film is shown, it is not for sale nor is the traditional Native American dress.

77. b. The announcement does tell the special of the day, but that is not the overall purpose. Choice **a** and choice **d** are not correct. These do not tell the purpose of the announcement.

78. c. The dining car has a full menu and complete meals, while the club car has snacks and sandwiches. Although the announcement doesn't specifically say that the dining car serves wine, it stands to reason it does, since the club car serves wine, so choice **a** is not correct either.

79. d. This is what the announcement says. None of the other choices are mentioned in connection with the conductors.

80. c. You can tell that this is a tour from the many clues, so it stands to reason a tour guide would make the announcement. These people are not traveling on a plane, so choice **a** is incorrect. Nor are they on a train. You can tell this since they are traveling on Route 95, not on tracks. Choice **d** is incorrect also.

81. b. The announcement says that the first stop will be Washington, D.C., so choice **b** is correct. The final destination is Orlando and the second stop is Savannah. Boston is where the tour is leaving from, so the other choices are all incorrect.

82. d. This is what the leader tells the people on the tour. None of the other choices are mentioned.

83. b. The announcement is given by someone who works for the college. A travel agent wouldn't be familiar with a college campus or asked to make this announcement. An English professor is likely on the staff of a college, but would not be asked to do this kind of job and a parent would be listening to this announcement, not giving it.

84. c. This is the advice the announcer gives the applicants. There is no mention of spending time with other applicants. The announcement tells the applicants that they will be seeing both the dormitories and the library, so choice **b** is not correct. While the announcement does mention there will be snacks, the announcer does not advise the applicants to eat them.

85. b. The tour is supposed to last an hour and the room where students should register is 15, but the tour is 20 minutes.

86. d. The announcement says, "Thank you for calling our reservation desk." None of the other choices would be a reasonable choice given the clues.

87. c. There is nothing in the announcement about helping callers reach someone nor is there any information about how to get to the resort. This announcement cannot make reservations, but it does mention them.

88. a. The units have a view of the marina, which tells you water is nearby. There could reasonably be a golf course and tennis courts at the resort, but there is nothing to suggest that the units are located near them. Nothing is said about a hill either, so choice **d** is incorrect.

89. d. The announcement is about the weather. Farmers are mentioned, but a farmer wouldn't be making this announcement. Choice **b** and choice **c** are also unlikely.

90. b. This is what the announcement says. While choice **a** and choice **d** are true, they are not the reason that the wildlife is threatened. There is no suggestion that the turtles do not have food, so choice **c** is not correct.

91. d. This is what the announcer says at the end of the announcement. None of the other choices are correct.

92. d. The announcement says, "We interrupt this program to let you know that there has been a traffic accident on the Sands River Bridge, which suggests this is either on the radio or on TV. The other choices aren't likely because of that clue.

93. c. This is what the announcement says. There is no mention of choice **a** or choice **b**. While choice **d** might be possible, it is not the reason.

94. a. This is what the announcement says. The other locales are all mentioned, but not for this reason.

95. b. This is the overall purpose of the announcement. True, the variety show will be after dinner, but that is not the overall purpose of the announcement. Nor is it to reassure passengers about the band or to explain to them why they will be on their own for lunch.

96. d. There are many clues. They are approaching the equator, they are putting in to an island, and they have entertainment on board. Although the name of the variety show has "Vegas" in it, none of the other clues fit a Las Vegas hotel. The clues don't suggest an international flight or a train, either.

97. a. This is the name of the island where they will be putting in. The other choices all have names in the announcement, but the names are not Dupree.

98. c. There are many clues that suggest this. The other choices, such as a flight being delayed and instructions for those passengers who will miss connecting flights, are not suggested by the information in the announcement.

99. b. This is what the announcement says. There is no reference to bad weather or to the plane needing to be refueled. There is no mention of waiting for final takeoff approval, either.

100. a. The announcement says that information about the delay will be updated in a half hour, so choice **a** is correct. Choice **b** and choice **d** are not mentioned, while choice **c** is the amount of time the plane will probably be delayed.

101. b. Choice **b** is the correct verb since it is a singular form of the verb. Choice **a** is a past tense rather than a present one, which is called for. Choice **c** is the plural form of the verb, which is incorrect, and choice **d** is an incorrect past tense.

102. d. Choice **d** is the correct verb form since it is an infinitive, which is called for here. Choice **a** is an incorrect past tense, as is choice **c**. Choice **b** is an incorrect present tense form.

103. a. Choice **a** is the correct form of helping verb since it is singular and in the present tense. Choice **b** is a future tense helping verb, which is incorrect. Choice **c** is incorrect because it is a plural form of the helping verb, and choice **d** is an incorrect past tense.

104. d. It is the correct conjunction. Choice **b** and choice **c** do not work grammatically and choice **a** changes the meaning of the sentence.

105. c. Choice **c** is the correct verb form, which is a plural past tense. Choice **a** and choice **b** are incorrect singular verbs and choice **d** is an incorrect singular past tense.

106. b. Choice **b** is the correct helping verb. It is in the past tense and is plural. Choice **a** is a singular form of the past tense, so it is not correct. Choice **c** and choice **d** are improper forms of the verb.

107. d. This adjective makes sense in the context of the sentence. The others do not fit into the context and don't make sense.

108. b. It is past tense and singular, since the subject is singular. Choice **a** is past tense, but it is a plural form. Choice **c** is incorrect since it is a passive form of the verb. Choice **d** is an incorrect infinitive form of the verb.

109. d. The action was in the past and a plural verb is required. Choice **a** is in the past tense, but is singular. Choice **c** is an incorrect verb form. Choice **c** is in the future, and the action here was in the past.

110. c. It fits with the meaning of the sentence. None of the other nouns make sense in the context of the sentence.

111. a. Choice **a** is the correct verb form. It is in the past tense. Choice **b**, choice **c**, and choice **d** are all incorrect verb forms.

112. c. Choice **c** is the correct verb choice, since an infinitive form is called for here. All the other choices are incorrect verb forms.

113. c. This conjunction makes sense because it suggests a contrast to the previous information in the sentence. Choice **a** suggests a cause and effect relationship that doesn't exist. Choice **b** and choice **d** do not fit into the context of the sentence.

114. d. This sentence calls for a plural verb in the present tense. Choice **a** is incorrect because it is singular form, although it is correctly in the present tense. Choice **b** is in the past tense, so it is incorrect. Choice **c** is also a singular form of the verb.

115. b. Choice **b** is the correct form of the helping verb, since it is in a present tense and is plural. Choice **a** is plural, but in an incorrect past form. Choice **c** is present but in a singular form. Choice **d** is also singular, which is incorrect, and in a past tense, which is also incorrect.

116. d. People typically attend a *convention*. One doesn't attend a *probability* or a *convenience*. You might see a *scene*, but it usually isn't attended.

117. c. Choice **c** is plural an in the present tense. Choice **a** is an incorrect verb form. Choice **b** is in the present tense, but it is singular. Choice **d** is the infinitive form of the verb, which is not called for here.

118. b. The superlative form of the adjective is called for here. Choice **a** is a comparative form. Choice **c** is not a comparative. Choice **d** is an incorrect superlative.

119. a. The verb should be in the present tense since the action is happening now and be plural. Choice **b** is singular present tense and the others are incorrect verbs. They do not fit into the context of the sentence.

120. c. It is plural and in the present tense, which is called for here. Choice **a** is a singular verb form as is choice **d**. Choice **b** is an incorrect verb form.

121. c. Choice **c** is the correct adjective. It fits with the context of the sentence. Choices **a** and choice **d** change the meaning of the statement. Typically, a budget is not *efficient* so choice **d** does not make sense.

122. a. Choice **a** is the correct form of the verb. Choices **b**, **c**, and **d** are incorrect. They do not make sense in the context of the sentence.

123. c. It is in the present tense and is singular. Choice **a** has an incorrect helping verb, as does choice **b**. Choice **d** is incorrect because it is a plural form of the verb.

124. c. Choice **c** is the only answer that makes sense in the context of the sentence. Choice **a**, choice **b**, and choice **d** do not and are often used at the start of a question rather than a statement.

125. d. Choice **d** is the proper verb form. It is past tense and plural, which is called for here. Choice **a** is an incorrect verb form. Choice **b** and choice **c** are both singular forms of the verb, so they are incorrect.

126. a. This sentence calls for the imperative form of the verb. None of the other choices is a correct form for the context of this sentence.

127. b. This sentence requires a singular verb in the present tense. Choice **a** is an incorrect plural form of the verb. Choice **c** is an incorrect future tense form and choice **d** is an infinitive, which is not called for here.

128. a. The word *but* indicates a contrast between the information in one part of the sentence and the other. The other choices do not make sense in the context of the sentence.

129. d. This sentence requires a plural helping verb. Choice **a** and choice **c** are incorrect forms of helping verbs. Choice **b** is singular, so it is incorrect.

130. b. Choice **b** is the correct verb form. It is plural and in the present tense. Choice **a** is singular and in a past tense. Choice **c** and choice **d** are incorrect verb forms.

131. d. The sentence calls for the infinitive of *assist*. None of the other choices fit into the context of the sentence, so they are incorrect.

132. b. Choice **b** is the correct verb form. It is singular and in the present tense. Choice **a** is a plural verb form and choice **c** is a past verb form. Choice **d** is incorrect as well.

133. d. This is a superlative form that fits with the context of the sentence. Choice **a** is a comparative form, which is incorrect. Neither choice **b** nor choice **c** make sense in the sentence.

134. a. Choice **a** is the correct verb form. It is plural and in the present tense. Choice **b** is a singular form. Both choice **c** and choice **d** are incorrect forms as well.

135. b. Choice **b** is the correct helping verb. It agrees with the plural subject. Choice **a** is singular, so it is not correct. Choice **c** and choice **d** are incorrect verb forms.

136. a. It is a past tense of the verb *resolve*. Choice **b** and choice **c** are incorrect verb forms. Choice **d** is an infinitive and is not called for here.

137. c. This verb is plural and in the past tense that the sentence requires. Choice **a** is an incorrect verb form. Choice **b** is a future tense. Choice **d** is a singular verb form.

138. d. The other connecting words do not fit into the context of the sentence. They do not make sense.

139. b. Choice **b** is the correct verb form. Choice **a** is an uncalled-for infinitive. The others do not fit the context of the sentence.

140. a. This verb is correctly in the past tense and is plural. Choice **b** is in the past tense, but it is singular. Choice **c** is in an incorrect present tense and choice **d** is in an incorrect future tense.

141. d. Choice **a** and choice **c** are also nouns, but they do not fit into the context of the sentence. Choice **b** might be considered at first, but is not consistent with the following information.

142. c. This fits in with the meaning of the sentence. Choice **a** would hardly be what the president of a shoe company would call her shoes, nor would she call them awkward or fragile, so those choices are wrong.

143. c. Choice **c** is the one that makes the most sense. Choice **a** is an abstract noun and doesn't fit in.

144. a. Choice **a** is the noun that fits best in the context of this sentence. Choices **b** and **c** could be considered, but they are too abstract. Choice **d** does not make sense.

145. c. Choice **c** fits in with the context of the sentence. You might consider choice **d**, but *corporation* is a better answer. Choice **a** and choice **b** do not make sense.

146. d. Choice **a** doesn't fit the context of the sentence. Choice **b** is possible, but highly unlikely when compared to choice **d**. Choice **c** doesn't make sense.

147. b. It fits in with the context of the sentence. Choice **a** might be possible, but choice **b** better fits with the rest of the sentence.

148. a. It fits in with the meaning of the sentence. Choice **b** is not what someone who is trying to impress another person would say, nor is choice **c**. Choice **d** doesn't make sense.

149. d. This is what is needed for the silent auction. The other choices do not fit into the context of the sentence.

150. b. All the others do not fit into the context of the sentence.

151. c. Choice **a** doesn't make sense. Choice **b** is also not correct.

152. a. All the other choices change the meaning of the sentence in a way that is not in line with the information in the e-mail.

153. c. Choice **c** is what the article is mainly about. Choice **a** is not correct. The article talks about a variety of ways to exercise, but not how most people prefer to do it. The article does talk about the different kinds of exercise machines, but that is not what it is mostly about. Choice **d** is incorrect also. This is mentioned, but only in passing.

154. a. This is stated in the article. Choice **b** is not correct. The only mention of joints in the article is that exercise might hurt them. Choice **c** is not mentioned in the article. Choice **d** is mentioned in relationship to yoga, not Pilates.

155. d. This word is closest in meaning to *advocates*. Choice **a**, choice **b**, and choice **c** are all incorrect since they all mean something else.

156. b. This is what the article tells us. Choice **a** may be true, but it is not mentioned in the article. Choice **c** could be correct, but that is not covered in the article either. Choice **d** is incorrect also. There is no mention of one being better than the other.

157. a. Choice **a** is the best answer. It is the main purpose of the advertisement. While the ad does talk about a sale on grooming tools, it does not list them. The ad does say where the business is located, but that is not its purpose. The ad does not mention how long it takes to groom a pet, so choice **d** is incorrect also.

158. c. Choice **c** is the closest in meaning to spa. Choice **a**, choice **b**, and choice **d** all mean something else.

159. b. This is the special that is available on Saturdays. Choice **a** is incorrect since all pets get 15% off, not just two pets. Choice **c** is incorrect. The ad does not say that two pets can only be groomed on Saturdays, but that the special is only on Saturdays. Choice **d** is also incorrect.

160. b. This is what happens at the end of the month. There is no suggestion that choice **a** is correct nor is there any suggestion that choice **c** is correct. Choice **d** is not mentioned and so it is incorrect also.

161. d. This is what the article is about. The fact that the sales reps have territories is mentioned, but that is not the main idea. The other choices are not included in the article, so they are incorrect as well.

162. a. That is what the article says employees should do if unfamiliar with the upgraded software. They are supposed to call their clients to set up appointments, so choice **b** is incorrect. Choice **c** and choice **d** are not mentioned.

163. c. This is stated in the article. None of the other choices are suggested in any way.

164. c. Choice **c** is the word that means nearly the same as *innovative*. Choices **a** and **b** are incorrect. The software program may or may not be complicated or challenging. It most likely is not delicate, so choice **d** is wrong as well.

165. c. This is the purpose of the news brief. While the food pantry is mentioned, the brief does not say what food pantries do, nor does it discuss why fundraisers are important, so choice **a** and choice **b** are not correct. There is no mention of people watching the fundraiser in Greenfield Park, so choice **d** is not correct, either.

166. b. That is the purpose of the phone number. None of the other choices is correct.

167. a. The sponsors pledge money for each person running the race. This is how money is raised for the food pantry. The other choices are incorrect.

168. d. This choice is the closest in meaning to *significantly*. Choice **a** and choice **d** mean the opposite of *significantly*. Choice **b** is not correct, either.

169. c. This is the article's overall purpose. Choice **a** is mentioned, but is not the main purpose. Choice **b** is not the purpose of the article. While the federal government laws for teens who work are discussed, that is not the main purpose of the article.

170. d. This is the only way the company and federal government regulations are similar. According to the article, teens under the age of 16 can work. There do not seem to be any restrictions on the number of consecutive hours a teen under 18 can work, so that is not the correct choice either. The federal government does not require a parent consent form for teens until they are 18, although it is required for teens between 16 and 18 to work until midnight.

171. c. Choice **a** is the number of hours that a teen under 18 can work consecutively. Choice **b** and choice **d** are also incorrect.

172. d. As used in the article, choice **d** is the closest in meaning. Choice **a** might be considered, but *dictate* means more than desire. It means it is required. Choice **b** is incorrect. This isn't a matter of choosing. Choice **c** is another meaning of the word *dictate*, but context clues tell us this is not the correct choice.

173. a. This is what the advertisement's purpose is. Leather luggage and carry-on bags are both mentioned, but only in passing. Choice **d** is also incorrect.

174. b. Choice **a** doesn't make sense. If it is not popular, why not put it on sale? Choice **c** is not accurate. Leather luggage is generally a more expensive and desirable option. There is nothing in the ad to suggest choice **d** is correct.

175. d. The sale is called a Winter Sale, so it probably would not still be on in May. There is no reason to believe that choices **b** or **c** are correct either.

176. a. Choice **a** is the best answer. This is suggested by the advertisement, which says they are available "while they last." The other choices are not suggested by the advertisement.

177. c. This is what the article is mostly about. There is no mention of choice **a** or choice **b**. While the policy asks guests to sign in, this is not what the whole article is about.

178. b. This is what the article says. Choice **a** doesn't make sense. Choice **c** is probably true of both the old and new ID cards. There is no mention of choice **d**.

179. b. This is what the article says. There is no mention of the other choices, so they are all incorrect.

180. b. This is what the article says an employee should do. There is no mention of calling the receptionist, nor is there any mention of telling the person to leave or having them go to the reception area.

181. a. This is what the article is mostly about and its purpose. Choice **b** is mentioned, as is choice **c**, but they are not the main purpose of the article.

182. c. This is what the article suggests. The other choices are not correct. You might consider choice **a**, but choice **c** is the better answer.

183. b. All the other information is included in the advertisement.

184. d. This is covered only in the advertisement. Choice **a** is mentioned in the article, as is choice b, but not in the advertisement. Both the article and advertisement mention choice **c**.

185. a. While the advertisement suggests choice **b**, the articles does not mention the topic. Choice **c** is not correct since neither one provides helpful sites on the Internet. Only the article talks about resumes, so choice **d** is not correct either.

186. d. This is what the e-mail is mostly about. The other choices are not mentioned in the e-mail.

187. c. This is why soups and salads were recommended. There is no reason to believe that choice **a**, choice **b**, or choice **d** is correct.

188. a. This is one of the three foods that can go on top of a salad. Choice **b**, choice **c**, and choice **d** are all available for sandwiches only.

189. a. This is the only item that can go both on a salad and in a sandwich. Choice **b** and choice **c** can go on salads but not in a sandwich. Choice **c** can only go in a sandwich.

190. c. This is how the restaurant is described in both the e-mail and the menu. Choice **a** is not mentioned in either the e-mail or the menu. Choice **b** is mentioned in the e-mail, but not the menu, while choice **d** is mentioned in the menu but not the e-mail.

191. a. This is the main purpose of the letter. There is no mention of what the hotel club looks like, so choice **b** is wrong. Choice **c** is not mentioned, either. While the letter mentions Spesso Restaurant and there is a coupon enclosed, this is not the main purpose of the letter.

192. b. Choice **a** may be true, but we cannot tell from the letter. Neither choice **c** nor choice **d** is suggested by the letter, either.

193. d. Choice **a** might be true, but it seems unlikely, as does choice **b**. Choice **c** is doubtful as well.

194. b. Both choice **a** and choice **c** are learned in the letter and coupon. Choice **d** is not mentioned in either one.

195. d. This is the only piece of information found only in the coupon. All of the other choices are found in both the letter and the coupon.

196. a. This is the purpose of the agenda. It is not to show that many people will attend the meeting. There is nothing to suggest that either choice **c** or choice **d** is correct.

197. b. This is why she e-mailed Terri Mann. Choice **a** is not correct because although there is mention of the newsletter, Terri Mann was at the meeting, so she already knew about it. There is no mention of either choice **c** or choice **d**, so they are incorrect as well.

198. b. This is suggested by Fredericka Hodges when she says that the show will include Terri Mann's artwork. There is no mention of Terri Mann organizing an art show before or that she is a member of the board. We know that she was at the board meeting, so choice **d** is also incorrect.

199. d. This is the only topic found in the agenda that is not mentioned in the e-mail. All the other choices are mentioned in the e-mail and the agenda.

200. b. This seems to be the main concern in the e-mail and is also on the agenda. There is no mention of choices **a**, **c**, or **d**, so they are all incorrect.

201. To hear this passage, listen to Track 443. This passage is about visiting Puerto Rico. Some of the more difficult words to pronounce are:
experienced—ik-SPIR-e-ensd
Puerto—POR-to
Palmas—PAM-as
Caribbean—ker-e-BEE-en

202. To hear this passage, listen to Track 444. This passage is about a new city law. Some of the more difficult words to pronounce are:
intentions—in-TEN-shuns
metropolis—muh-TROP-oh-liss
entice—enn-TICE
benefits—benn-nuh-FITZ

203. Sample response: The photo shows two women sitting across a table from a man. They seem to be discussing something. The man's laptop is open. They all seem happy. He could be selling them something or explaining something to them.

To hear this sample response, listen to Track 445.

204. Sample response: I have a Canon EOS Rebel. It's brand new.

To hear this sample response, listen to Track 446.

205. Sample response: I use it quite a lot of the time, at least two or three times a week.

To hear this sample response, listen to Track 447.

206. Sample response: I use it to take pictures of my family and of animals that I see in the zoo and at the park. I also use it for school since I am studying photography and hope to become a photojournalist.

To hear this sample response, listen to Track 448.

207. Sample response: The cost of the seminar is $100 for the whole day or $55 for a half day.

To hear this sample response, listen to Track 449.

208. Sample response: Lunch is not included in the price of the seminar, but there are nearby restaurants.

To hear this sample response, listen to Track 450.

209. Sample response: There are seminars every hour. At ten you can choose between two seminars about writing ad copy. The last seminar of the morning is about writing your first advertisement.

To hear this sample response, listen to Track 451.

210. Hello. Is that Jessica Anson? This is Martin Castelli at Ocean Salon. I am sure you must be upset about your necklace, especially since it is gold. I understand completely. But I wanted to let you know right away that Diana found it and put it in a safe place. She said it was sitting right there on the table. She tried to catch you, but you had already driven away. Anyway, we have it here, so any time you want to pick it up just ask for me. We are open every day except Monday, from 10 in the morning until 7 in the evening. If you want, call me first to make sure I am here. The phone number here is 673-9090. Again, my name is Martin.

To hear this sample response, listen to Track 452.

211. I think builders should be required to use green materials in new construction because it is important to use materials that don't pollute or hurt the environment and the people who live or work in the buildings. The only way you can get builders to comply would be by fining them, so I think that is important as well. Nowadays, there are enough green materials that are reasonably priced, so builders wouldn't be facing higher costs than they would with materials that are not green.

To hear this sample response, listen to Track 453.

212. Sample answer: A smiling waitress is serving salad on two plates.

213. Sample answer: A smiling couple is dancing.

214. Sample answer: People in an exercise class have their hands up.

215. Sample answer: A man with sneakers and a white shirt is running.

216. Sample answer: A happy young girl is jumping in the air.

217. Sample answer:

> Thanks so much for your nice gift. I love your salads, so I will certainly take advantage of your offer. In fact I think your salads and sandwiches are the best in town. I particularly like your roast turkey sandwich because you use cranberry sauce instead of mayonnaise. Your homemade bread is terrific, too. Thanks again.

218. Sample answer:

> Dear Ms. Minion:
>
> Thank you for your letter. I am very excited about receiving an upgrade on the software I bought from you last year. Can you tell me in what way the software was improved? Also, how much memory will I need to run the upgraded software? You can reach me at afarran@yahoo.com. I look forward to your answer.

219. The opinion essay should be well organized. Clear details and supporting statements should back up the opinion. Words should be spelled correctly and the grammar of each sentence should be correct. An example of a sample response is:

> I think it is more important to do good deeds than to earn a lot of money. I know I may be in the minority, but when all is said and done and you look back on your life, isn't it more important to have done something meaningful than to just have a lot of money? Take my father, for example.

He's been a schoolteacher for over 40 years. He makes a fairly good living, but is by no means rich. But he has enjoyed his work and when he meets former students, you can see that they respect him a great deal.

He has had an effect on so many young people and he really takes his job seriously. If students aren't doing well, he goes out of his way to find out why and tries to help them achieve the best that they can. But it's not just his job as a teacher that makes him special; it is other things as well.

He has been a great father to me and my sister and brother. He is patient with us, even when he doesn't have to be. He takes an interest in everything we do and is encouraging when we are down.

Seeing the way he lives has had an extreme influence on me. That is why right after college I joined the Peace Corps, so I could help people. I had a great experience living in Africa and working with people who had so little in terms of possessions. The experience was so rich in rewards. it made me feel as though I was making a difference.

So, that is why I say it is more important to do good deeds than to make a lot of money. Money is fine, but it doesn't give you the kind of gratification you receive from helping someone else.

10 ▶ PRACTICE EXAM 3

By taking this third practice exam, you will get additional practice in each section of the TOEIC—Listening, Reading, Speaking, and Writing.

	a	b	c	d
1.	a	b	c	d
2.	a	b	c	d
3.	a	b	c	d
4.	a	b	c	d
5.	a	b	c	d
6.	a	b	c	d
7.	a	b	c	d
8.	a	b	c	d
9.	a	b	c	d
10.	a	b	c	d
11.	a	b	c	
12.	a	b	c	
13.	a	b	c	
14.	a	b	c	
15.	a	b	c	
16.	a	b	c	
17.	a	b	c	
18.	a	b	c	
19.	a	b	c	
20.	a	b	c	
21.	a	b	c	
22.	a	b	c	
23.	a	b	c	
24.	a	b	c	
25.	a	b	c	
26.	a	b	c	
27.	a	b	c	
28.	a	b	c	
29.	a	b	c	
30.	a	b	c	
31.	a	b	c	
32.	a	b	c	
33.	a	b	c	
34.	a	b	c	
35.	a	b	c	
36.	a	b	c	
37.	a	b	c	
38.	a	b	c	
39.	a	b	c	
40.	a	b	c	
41.	a	b	c	d
42.	a	b	c	d
43.	a	b	c	d
44.	a	b	c	d
45.	a	b	c	d

	a	b	c	d
46.	a	b	c	d
47.	a	b	c	d
48.	a	b	c	d
49.	a	b	c	d
50.	a	b	c	d
51.	a	b	c	d
52.	a	b	c	d
53.	a	b	c	d
54.	a	b	c	d
55.	a	b	c	d
56.	a	b	c	d
57.	a	b	c	d
58.	a	b	c	d
59.	a	b	c	d
60.	a	b	c	d
61.	a	b	c	d
62.	a	b	c	d
63.	a	b	c	d
64.	a	b	c	d
65.	a	b	c	d
66.	a	b	c	d
67.	a	b	c	d
68.	a	b	c	d
69.	a	b	c	d
70.	a	b	c	d
71.	a	b	c	d
72.	a	b	c	d
73.	a	b	c	d
74.	a	b	c	d
75.	a	b	c	d
76.	a	b	c	d
77.	a	b	c	d
78.	a	b	c	d
79.	a	b	c	d
80.	a	b	c	d
81.	a	b	c	d
82.	a	b	c	d
83.	a	b	c	d
84.	a	b	c	d
85.	a	b	c	d
86.	a	b	c	d
87.	a	b	c	d
88.	a	b	c	d
89.	a	b	c	d
90.	a	b	c	d

	a	b	c	d
91.	a	b	c	d
92.	a	b	c	d
93.	a	b	c	d
94.	a	b	c	d
95.	a	b	c	d
96.	a	b	c	d
97.	a	b	c	d
98.	a	b	c	d
99.	a	b	c	d
100.	a	b	c	d
101.	a	b	c	d
102.	a	b	c	d
103.	a	b	c	d
104.	a	b	c	d
105.	a	b	c	d
106.	a	b	c	d
107.	a	b	c	d
108.	a	b	c	d
109.	a	b	c	d
110.	a	b	c	d
111.	a	b	c	d
112.	a	b	c	d
113.	a	b	c	d
114.	a	b	c	d
115.	a	b	c	d
116.	a	b	c	d
117.	a	b	c	d
118.	a	b	c	d
119.	a	b	c	d
120.	a	b	c	d
121.	a	b	c	d
122.	a	b	c	d
123.	a	b	c	d
124.	a	b	c	d
125.	a	b	c	d
126.	a	b	c	d
127.	a	b	c	d
128.	a	b	c	d
129.	a	b	c	d
130.	a	b	c	d
131.	a	b	c	d
132.	a	b	c	d
133.	a	b	c	d
134.	a	b	c	d
135.	a	b	c	d

136.	ⓐ	ⓑ	ⓒ	ⓓ
137.	ⓐ	ⓑ	ⓒ	ⓓ
138.	ⓐ	ⓑ	ⓒ	ⓓ
139.	ⓐ	ⓑ	ⓒ	ⓓ
140.	ⓐ	ⓑ	ⓒ	ⓓ
141.	ⓐ	ⓑ	ⓒ	ⓓ
142.	ⓐ	ⓑ	ⓒ	ⓓ
143.	ⓐ	ⓑ	ⓒ	ⓓ
144.	ⓐ	ⓑ	ⓒ	ⓓ
145.	ⓐ	ⓑ	ⓒ	ⓓ
146.	ⓐ	ⓑ	ⓒ	ⓓ
147.	ⓐ	ⓑ	ⓒ	ⓓ
148.	ⓐ	ⓑ	ⓒ	ⓓ
149.	ⓐ	ⓑ	ⓒ	ⓓ
150.	ⓐ	ⓑ	ⓒ	ⓓ
151.	ⓐ	ⓑ	ⓒ	ⓓ
152.	ⓐ	ⓑ	ⓒ	ⓓ
153.	ⓐ	ⓑ	ⓒ	ⓓ
154.	ⓐ	ⓑ	ⓒ	ⓓ
155.	ⓐ	ⓑ	ⓒ	ⓓ
156.	ⓐ	ⓑ	ⓒ	ⓓ
157.	ⓐ	ⓑ	ⓒ	ⓓ

158.	ⓐ	ⓑ	ⓒ	ⓓ
159.	ⓐ	ⓑ	ⓒ	ⓓ
160.	ⓐ	ⓑ	ⓒ	ⓓ
161.	ⓐ	ⓑ	ⓒ	ⓓ
162.	ⓐ	ⓑ	ⓒ	ⓓ
163.	ⓐ	ⓑ	ⓒ	ⓓ
164.	ⓐ	ⓑ	ⓒ	ⓓ
165.	ⓐ	ⓑ	ⓒ	ⓓ
166.	ⓐ	ⓑ	ⓒ	ⓓ
167.	ⓐ	ⓑ	ⓒ	ⓓ
168.	ⓐ	ⓑ	ⓒ	ⓓ
169.	ⓐ	ⓑ	ⓒ	ⓓ
170.	ⓐ	ⓑ	ⓒ	ⓓ
171.	ⓐ	ⓑ	ⓒ	ⓓ
172.	ⓐ	ⓑ	ⓒ	ⓓ
173.	ⓐ	ⓑ	ⓒ	ⓓ
174.	ⓐ	ⓑ	ⓒ	ⓓ
175.	ⓐ	ⓑ	ⓒ	ⓓ
176.	ⓐ	ⓑ	ⓒ	ⓓ
177.	ⓐ	ⓑ	ⓒ	ⓓ
178.	ⓐ	ⓑ	ⓒ	ⓓ
179.	ⓐ	ⓑ	ⓒ	ⓓ

180.	ⓐ	ⓑ	ⓒ	ⓓ
181.	ⓐ	ⓑ	ⓒ	ⓓ
182.	ⓐ	ⓑ	ⓒ	ⓓ
183.	ⓐ	ⓑ	ⓒ	ⓓ
184.	ⓐ	ⓑ	ⓒ	ⓓ
185.	ⓐ	ⓑ	ⓒ	ⓓ
186.	ⓐ	ⓑ	ⓒ	ⓓ
187.	ⓐ	ⓑ	ⓒ	ⓓ
188.	ⓐ	ⓑ	ⓒ	ⓓ
189.	ⓐ	ⓑ	ⓒ	ⓓ
190.	ⓐ	ⓑ	ⓒ	ⓓ
191.	ⓐ	ⓑ	ⓒ	ⓓ
192.	ⓐ	ⓑ	ⓒ	ⓓ
193.	ⓐ	ⓑ	ⓒ	ⓓ
194.	ⓐ	ⓑ	ⓒ	ⓓ
195.	ⓐ	ⓑ	ⓒ	ⓓ
196.	ⓐ	ⓑ	ⓒ	ⓓ
197.	ⓐ	ⓑ	ⓒ	ⓓ
198.	ⓐ	ⓑ	ⓒ	ⓓ
199.	ⓐ	ⓑ	ⓒ	ⓓ
200.	ⓐ	ⓑ	ⓒ	ⓓ

Listening

You will now begin the listening section. You will be asked to demonstrate how well you understand spoken English. The entire listening section should take approximately 45 minutes. There are four parts and directions are given for each part. Mark your answers on the answer sheet on pages 281–282.

When directed by the icon, listen to the audio file at **http://www.learnatest.com/SpeakingGuides/**. Or, if you do not have access to a computer, the complete transcripts are included in the appendix of this book. In that case, ask someone who speaks English fluently to read the material to you face-to-face or into a tape recorder. Be sure your reader speaks at a normal, conversational pace. It is highly recommended, however, that you use the audio files for a more authentic TOEIC experience.

Directions: For each question in this part, you will hear four statements about a picture. When you hear the statements, you must select the one statement that best describes what you see in the picture. Then mark your choice—**a**, **b**, **c**, or **d**—on your answer sheet. The statements are available in audio files or written transcripts in the appendix of this book.

1.

Now, listen to Track 454.

2.

Now, listen to Track 455.

3.

Now, listen to Track 456.

4.

Now, listen to Track 457.

5.

Now, listen to Track 458.

6.

Now, listen to Track 459.

7.

Now, listen to Track 460.

8.

Now, listen to Track 461.

9.

Now, listen to Track 462.

10.

Now, listen to Track 463.

Directions: You will hear a question or statement and three responses spoken in English. The question and statements are available in audio files or written transcripts in the appendix of this book. Select the best response to the question or statement and mark your choice—**a**, **b**, or **c** on your answer sheet.

11. Now, listen to Track 464.
Mark your answer on the answer sheet.

12. Now, listen to Track 465.
Mark your answer on the answer sheet.

13. Now, listen to Track 466.
Mark your answer on the answer sheet.

14. Now, listen to Track 467.
Mark your answer on the answer sheet.

15. Now, listen to Track 468.
Mark your answer on the answer sheet.

16. Now, listen to Track 469.
Mark your answer on the answer sheet.

17. Now, listen to Track 470.
Mark your answer on the answer sheet.

18. Now, listen to Track 471.
Mark your answer on the answer sheet.

19. Now, listen to Track 472.
Mark your answer on the answer sheet.

20. Now, listen to Track 473.
Mark your answer on the answer sheet.

21. Now, listen to Track 474.
Mark your answer on the answer sheet.

22. Now, listen to Track 475.
Mark your answer on the answer sheet.

23. Now, listen to Track 476.
Mark your answer on the answer sheet.

24. Now, listen to Track 477.
Mark your answer on the answer sheet.

25. Now, listen to Track 478.
Mark your answer on the answer sheet.

26. Now, listen to Track 479.
Mark your answer on the answer sheet.

27. Now, listen to Track 480.
Mark your answer on the answer sheet.

28. Now, listen to Track 481.
Mark your answer on the answer sheet.

29. Now, listen to Track 482.
Mark your answer on the answer sheet.

30. Now, listen to Track 483.
Mark your answer on the answer sheet.

31. Now, listen to Track 484.

Mark your answer on the answer sheet.

32. Now, listen to Track 485.

Mark your answer on the answer sheet.

33. Now, listen to Track 486.

Mark your answer on the answer sheet.

34. Now, listen to Track 487.

Mark your answer on the answer sheet.

35. Now, listen to Track 488.

Mark your answer on the answer sheet.

36. Now, listen to Track 489.

Mark your answer on the answer sheet.

37. Now, listen to Track 490.

Mark your answer on the answer sheet.

38. Now, listen to Track 491.

Mark your answer on the answer sheet.

39. Now, listen to Track 492.

Mark your answer on the answer sheet.

40. Now, listen to Track 493.

Mark your answer on the answer sheet.

Directions: You will hear conversations between two people. You will be asked to answer four questions about what the speakers say in each conversation. Select the best response to each question and mark your choice—**a**, **b**, **c**, or **d**—on your answer sheet. The conversations are available in audio files or written transcripts in the appendix of this book.

Now, listen to Track 494.

41. Now, listen to Track 495.

What are the man and the woman trying to figure out?

a. who is going to cook dinner

b. when they can each get a haircut

c. who will pick up the kids from school

d. how the woman is going to get to her meeting

42. Now, listen to Track 496.

Why can't the woman pick up the kids from school?

a. She has a meeting.

b. She has a dinner date.

c. She has to get her hair cut.

d. She has a job interview.

43. Now, listen to Track 497.

What was the man supposed to be doing at 3 o'clock?

a. attending a meeting

b. getting his hair cut

c. cooking dinner

d. going to work

Now, listen to Track 498.

44. Now, listen to Track 499.

What is the relationship between these two people?

a. They are a teacher and a student.

b. They are students in the same class.

c. They are two people who work together.

d. They are a professor and a college president.

45. Now, listen to Track 500.

What does the woman want to know about?

a. why her grade is so low

b. whether she can join the class

c. when the exam is going to take place

d. what the essay portion of the exam will be like

46. Now, listen to Track 501.

What is going to take place in class on Monday?

a. a test

b. a guest speaker

c. a three-part discussion

d. an in-class presentation

Now, listen to Track 502.

47. Now, listen to Track 503.

What is the relationship between these two people?

a. They are brother and sister.

b. They are a boss and her employee.

c. They are a customer and a clerk in a store.

d. They are two people who work together in a store.

48. Now, listen to Track 504.

What does the man want?

a. He wants to complain about bad service.

b. He wants to find a shirt to match his pants.

c. He wants to get money back for a purchase he made.

d. He wants to return a pair of pants that don't fit.

49. Now, listen to Track 505.

What does the man decide he is going to do?

a. He is going to buy a new pair of pants.

b. He is going to exchange his pants for another item.

c. He is going to purchase a gift for his sister.

d. He is going to get a refund for pants that don't fit.

Now, listen to Track 506.

50. Now, listen to Track 507.

What describes the situation of these two people?

a. They are trying to buy some novels.

b. They work together in a book store.

c. They are competing for the same job.

d. They are deciding what books to read.

51. Now, listen to Track 508.

What task do these two people have to accomplish?

a. They have to decide which books to put on sale.

b. They have to figure out which of them is going to go on break.

c. They have to put a bunch of novels in a new order on the shelves.

d. They have to find room on the shelves for a new shipment of books.

52. Now, listen to Track 509.

How do they decide to approach their task?

a. They agree to split up the job and both work on it at the same time.

b. They decide that the woman will work first and the man will finish later.

c. They figure out a way to get a different employee to work on this task.

d. They determine that they have more important things to do first.

Now, listen to Track 510.

53. Now, listen to Track 511.

What are these two people doing?

a. packing for a trip they're taking together

b. deciding on wallpaper for their living room

c. arguing about always being late to the airport

d. getting dressed to go out to dinner with friends

54. Now, listen to Track 512.

Why does the woman want to finish packing later?

a. She needs to do laundry first.

b. She is supposed to meet a friend.

c. She has second thoughts about taking the trip.

d. She has to wallpaper the living room before they leave.

55. Now, listen to Track 513.

What is one thing they will be doing during their trip?

a. buying clothes

b. going to a meeting

c. picking out wallpaper

d. going to a formal dinner

Now, listen to Track 514.

56. Now, listen to Track 515.

What does the man want?

a. to buy a car

b. to have his car fixed

c. to get a job fixing cars

d. to sell his car to the woman

57. Now, listen to Track 516.

What is the woman's job?

a. She's a salesperson.

b. She's a receptionist.

c. She's an auto mechanic.

d. She's a parking lot attendant.

58. Now, listen to Track 517.

What is one problem the man has with his car?

a. It is difficult to get started.

b. The car phone can't make calls.

c. It stalls after he's been driving it.

d. There's a strange noise when he drives it.

Now, listen to Track 518.

59. Now, listen to Track 519.

What is the relationship between these two people?

a. a professor and a student

b. a teacher and a student's mother

c. two parents of a school-age child

d. two teachers discussing a student

60. Now, listen to Track 520.

What does the man tell the woman?

a. Her mother has died.

b. She has very low test scores.

c. She has been accepted into college.

d. Her son is having a problem in school.

61. Now, listen to Track 521.

Why do they think the student hasn't been doing all his homework?

a. He is having difficulty reading the questions.

b. He is upset because his grandmother died recently.

c. He has been too sick to keep up with his schoolwork.

d. He has been skipping school during the past few weeks.

Now, listen to Track 522.

62. Now, listen to Track 523.

What is the relationship between these two people?

a. husband and wife

b. boss and employee

c. coworkers in a store

d. customer and salesperson

63. Now, listen to Track 524.

What does the man want?

a. a job at a store

b. a new cell phone

c. a better computer

d. an electronic calendar

64. Now, listen to Track 525.

What is the man looking for in a new cell phone?

a. more power
b. a smaller device
c. longer battery life
d. a wireless connection

Now, listen to Track 526.

65. Now, listen to Track 527.

Where are these people speaking with each other?

a. in a grocery store
b. at a cooking class
c. on a farm
d. at home

66. Now, listen to Track 528.

What does the woman want to know?

a. techniques for chopping vegetables
b. a good way to cook Brussels sprouts
c. whether Brussels sprouts are on sale
d. nutritional information about Brussels sprouts

67. Now, listen to Track 529.

About how long does the man say it will take to prepare his recipe?

a. six minutes
b. eight minutes
c. fifteen minutes
d. thirty minutes

Now, listen to Track 530.

68. Now, listen to Track 531.

What is the woman helping the man do?

a. fix his camera
b. decide on a gift for someone
c. figure out where to buy batteries
d. exchange his camera for a new one

69. Now, listen to Track 532.

What is the problem here?

a. The batteries in the man's camera have died.
b. The woman won't let the man get his money back.
c. The man's camera doesn't work the way he wants it to.
d. The store won't exchange the man's camera.

70. Now, listen to Track 533.

What does the man decide to do in this situation?

a. get a refund on his camera purchase
b. try a new battery to see if that works
c. come back to the store another day
d. let the flash on his camera recharge

Directions: You will hear some talks given by a single speaker. You will be asked to answer four questions about what the speaker says in each talk. Select the best response to each question and mark your choice—**a**, **b**, **c**, or **d**—on your answer sheet. The talks will not be printed in your test book and will be spoken only one time.

Now, listen to Track 534.

71. Now, listen to Track 535.

When would someone hear this message?

a. after pressing zero
b. after speaking with an operator
c. after calling the main number at a college
d. after typing a name into the name directory

72. Now, listen to Track 536.

What is the purpose of this message?

a. to direct callers to the correct number

b. to indicate a problem with phone service

c. to get people to wait to speak to an operator

d. to give students advice about getting services

73. Now, listen to Track 537.

What happens if the caller does not press any number?

a. The call will be ended.

b. The message will be repeated.

c. The call will be put through to an operator.

d. The name directory announcement will play.

Now, listen to Track 538.

74. Now, listen to Track 539.

Where would this talk be heard?

a. in a college lecture hall

b. at a dedication ceremony

c. in the lobby of a new building

d. at an information desk in a library

75. Now, listen to Track 540.

What is the purpose of this announcement?

a. to introduce a speaker

b. to detail emergency procedures

c. to give people a topic for discussion

d. to provide an overview of activities at an event

76. Now, listen to Track 541.

What should someone who is interested in attending a particular event do?

a. look on the board in the lobby

b. find the building's chief architect

c. go into an office and ask for help

d. wait until 9 o'clock for the reception to start

Now, listen to Track 542.

77. Now, listen to Track 543.

This talk is most likely a part of what?

a. a lecture for a history class

b. a guided tour of the Capitol building

c. an introduction for a keynote speaker

d. an orientation for new members of the Senate

78. Now, listen to Track 544.

Why is the Rotunda the main circulation space in the Capitol?

a. It is extremely tall.

b. It was created in two stages.

c. It was conceived by a famous architect.

d. It connects the two sides of the building.

79. Now, listen to Track 545.

Why was the Rotunda not completed until 1824?

a. It was not designed until 1818.

b. The Senate did not first meet until that year.

c. Construction was delayed for various reasons.

d. Charles Bulfinch challenged the results of the design competition.

Now, listen to Track 546.

80. Now, listen to Track 547.

What is the purpose of this message?

a. to argue a position

b. to introduce a documentary

c. to describe an economic problem

d. to give background for a speaker

81. **Now, listen to Track 548.**

What will the program this message describes do?

a. explain how lobbyists do their job

b. give advice about avoiding credit card debt

c. describe procedures for declaring bankruptcy

d. examine the way credit card companies operate

82. **Now, listen to Track 549.**

Who will ask most of the questions in this program?

a. bankers

b. citizens

c. journalists

d. politicians

Now, listen to Track 550.

83. **Now, listen to Track 551.**

Where would this message most likely be heard?

a. at a food bank

b. at a grocery store

c. in a family nutrition class

d. in a documentary about the food industry

84. **Now, listen to Track 552.**

Which of these foods should people eat least?

a. oats

b. meat

c. fruits

d. potatoes

85. **Now, listen to Track 553.**

What advice does this speaker give?

a. Try to cook from scratch.

b. Eat a lot of processed food.

c. Consume as much meat as you do potatoes.

d. Plan all your family's meals around vegetables.

Now, listen to Track 554.

86. **Now, listen to Track 555.**

Where would you most likely hear this talk?

a. at a zoo

b. at a museum

c. in a college classroom

d. in an elementary school auditorium

87. **Now, listen to Track 556.**

What kind of animal is the emperor penguin?

a. a fish

b. a bird

c. a squid

d. a mammal

88. **Now, listen to Track 557.**

What are emperor penguins best known for?

a. taking long journeys in the antantarctic winter

b. using their wings as flippers to swim in icy waters

c. flying hundreds of miles to feed their offspring

d. being larger than all other types of penguin

Now, listen to Track 558.

89. **Now, listen to Track 559.**

Where is this talk being given?

a. At a town recycling facility

b. At a business being given an award

c. At the future site of a new building

d. At the offices of the city building department

90. Now, listen to Track 560.

What is the purpose of this talk?

a. To introduce a tour of local businesses

b. To outline environmentally friendly building techniques

c. To describe the mayor's new economic revitalization program

d. To explain the choice of the site for the new city hall building

91. Now, listen to Track 561.

What is one reason this site was chosen?

a. its view of the town

b. its relatively low price

c. its central location in the town

d. its proximity to the town dump

Now, listen to Track 562.

92. Now, listen to Track 563.

Who would have given this talk?

a. a local sculptor

b. a Native American interpreter

c. a history professor from the town

d. a representative of the local arts council

93. Now, listen to Track 564.

What is this talk introducing?

a. the opening of an art exhibition

b. the dedication of a new cultural center

c. the beginning of a series of history lectures

d. the winners of a contest among local artists

94. Now, listen to Track 565.

What kind of art will appear in this exhibition?

a. historical photographs

b. Native American artifacts

c. local landscape paintings

d. sculpture and three-dimensional paintings

Now, listen to Track 566.

95. Now, listen to Track 567.

When would someone hear this message?

a. when calling a movie theater

b. when ordering at a drive-through

c. when buying tickets at a box office

d. when opening a movie theater website

96. Now, listen to Track 568.

What is the purpose of this message?

a. to give driving directions to a movie theater

b. to list showtimes, prices, and location for a movie

c. to announce the launch of a movie theater's webpage

d. to explain why tickets are a different price for adults and children

97. Now, listen to Track 569.

What is the earliest that someone can buy a ticket to one of these movies?

a. noon

b. 12:30

c. 3:15

d. 5:00

Now, listen to Track 570.

98. Now, listen to Track 571.

Who would hear this message?

a. someone driving a snow route school bus

b. someone calling a school district phone number

c. someone looking for updated weather information

d. someone who has children who are stranded at school

99. **Now, listen to Track 572.**

What is the purpose of this message?

a. to provide an updated weather forecast

b. to list all of the regions in the school district

c. to explain where to go to ride a snow route bus

d. to make an announcement about school closures

100. **Now, listen to Track 573.**

Schools in which part of the district will open late?

a. southeast

b. southwest

c. downtown

d. north Portland

Reading

You will now begin the listening section. You will be asked to read a variety of texts and answer several different types of reading comprehension questions. The entire reading section should take approximately 75 minutes. There are three parts and directions are given for each part. Mark your answers on the answer sheet on page 283.

Directions: A word or phrase is missing in each of the sentences that follow. Four answer choices are given for each sentence. Select the best answer to complete the sentence. Then mark your choice—**a, b, c,** or **d**—on your answer sheet.

101. _____ an oil change every 3,000 miles is an important part of keeping your car in good running shape.

a. To get

b. Gotten

c. Getting

d. To be getting

102. The tour bus was _____ to leave at 5 P.M., but it was delayed by the late arrival of some members of the tour.

a. anticipated

b. scheduled

c. attempted

d. delayed

103. The new mayor faced a major scandal _____ after taking office.

a. calmly

b. happily

c. frequently

d. immediately

104. It takes a lot of workers to see a major construction project _____ to completion.

a. over

b. around

c. through

d. up

105. Mary's new computer was supposed _____ delivered on Monday, but it did not arrive until Wednesday.

a. to be

b. going to be

c. having been

d. to have been

106. In 2009, Barack Obama _____ the first African American president of the United States.

a. became

b. becomes

c. had become

d. was to become

107. The company announced the development of a new type of coffee _____ that would both grind the beans and brew the coffee.
a. maker
b. process
c. beverage
d. production

108. Although she claimed to be very methodical, Susie could never explain the _____ behind her seemingly odd decisions.
a. names
b. reasons
c. debates
d. perspectives

109. _____ completing his law degree, Pablo decided not to become a lawyer after all.
a. Only
b. After
c. During
d. Whenever

110. The United States consumes the world's _____ share of energy despite having a relatively small population.
a. large
b. larger
c. largest
d. largely

111. The play was canceled because of the snowstorm, _____ the actors who had managed to make it to the theater decided to put on a performance nonetheless.
a. but
b. and
c. despite
d. consequently

112. The children _____ an argument over a toy when their father entered the room.
a. had had
b. have had
c. having had
d. were having

113. The sign stated that there would be a maximum _____ of $500 for throwing litter on the highway.
a. fine
b. waste
c. hazard
d. indication

114. Eileen had worked as the assistant director for five years before she was promoted to take her boss's place as _____ of the department.
a. auditor
b. associate
c. head
d. aide

115. Callie was disappointed to _____ that her new shirt had a hole in the sleeve that she hadn't noticed in the store.
a. discover
b. discovered
c. discovering
d. be discovered

116. The recipe stated that the flour, salt, and baking powder should be _____ before adding them to the milk-and-egg mixture.
a. melted
b. diluted
c. combined
d. separated

117. The mechanic told Mr. Horowitz that he _____ replace his brake pads before his car would be safe to drive again.
   a. have to
   b. is having to
   c. had had to
   d. would have to

118. Although she is very skilled as a carpenter, Lily can neither do electrical wiring _____ can she do plumbing.
   a. but
   b. and
   c. nor
   d. however

119. The final _____ of the movie left the audience wondering what had actually happened.
   a. idea
   b. scene
   c. conflict
   d. perspective

120. An umbrella provides much _____ protection against rain than most rain hats.
   a. best
   b. better
   c. of a good
   d. more good

121. _____ mountain climbing can be a dangerous sport, many people find that it is extremely rewarding.
   a. Yet
   b. When
   c. However
   d. Although

122. While most dogs have an extremely powerful sense of smell, many breeds have _____ eyesight.
   a. poor
   b. keen
   c. acute
   d. decisive

123. The trees that lose their leaves in the autumn do so _____ the lack of sunlight during the short winter days means their leaves wouldn't do them much good anyway.
   a. despite
   b. because
   c. since neither
   d. in response to

124. A dictionary is only a useful tool if you already _____ a certain amount of knowledge about words.
   a. entail
   b. acquire
   c. announce
   d. possess

125. The whole is sometimes _____ than the sum of its parts, but in many cases, the whole is the same as the sum of its parts.
   a. about
   b. greater
   c. higher
   d. more pure

126. Larry's doctor told him that he _____ to exercise more if he wants to maintain a healthy heart.
   a. need
   b. needs
   c. is needing
   d. will be needing

127. One trait of a good craftsman is knowing which _____ is best suited to each specific job.
   a. tool
   b. idea
   c. outfit
   d. assembly

128. Because of the traffic jam, the musicians arrived late for the _____.
   a. play
   b. trial
   c. concert
   d. seminar

129. There is no such thing as a _____ parenting situation; all parents face completely unique challenges.
   a. mild
   b. mobile
   c. typical
   d. reliable

130. Journalists who work for daily newspapers must meet tight _____ nearly every day of their working life.
   a. criteria
   b. borders
   c. scrutiny
   d. deadlines

131. High school teachers have to impart knowledge and sometimes deal with the challenge of _____ their students.
   a. admiring
   b. coaching
   c. calculating
   d. disciplining

132. Many people find job interviews _____ extremely stressful.
   a. to be
   b. had been
   c. are being
   d. to have been

133. _____ in doubt, it is best to ask questions rather than make assumptions.
   a. As
   b. Yet
   c. When
   d. Although

134. Li wanted to get a new cell phone, but because of her _____ with the phone company, she would have had to pay an extra $100 to do so.
   a. message
   b. contract
   c. argument
   d. affiliation

135. Some people are very good at growing plants, but others have a _____ time keeping even a cactus alive.
   a. major
   b. bright
   c. struggle
   d. difficult

136. The Nestors had to borrow chairs from their next-door neighbors _____ they ended up having more dinner guests than they expected.
   a. after
   b. because
   c. although
   d. however

137. White clothes are much _____ to keep clean than black or other dark clothes.
- **a.** harder
- **b.** hardest
- **c.** as hard
- **d.** more harder

138. Marcus's trip into New York City took almost two hours because one of the _____ over the Hudson River was closed for repairs.
- **a.** canals
- **b.** bridges
- **c.** tunnels
- **d.** skyscrapers

139. Firefighters have to respond _____ there is a fire alarm in a building even though many of these alarms turn out to be pranks or errors.
- **a.** since
- **b.** however
- **c.** whenever
- **d.** promptly

140. Celeste thinks that it is _____ to send thank-you notes within two days of receiving a gift from someone.
- **a.** important
- **b.** importance
- **c.** importantly
- **d.** more important

Directions: Read the texts that follow. A word or phrase is missing in some of the sentences. Four choices are given for each blank. Select the best answer to complete the text. Then mark your choice—**a**, **b**, **c**, or **d**—on your answer sheet.

Questions 141 t hrough 144 refer to the following letter.

To Whom It May Concern:

I am writing to (141) _____ my dissatisfaction with the condition of a product I received from your company recently. I ordered a lighted globe, but when I opened the package, the globe was scratched and the bulb was missing. I can easily replace the bulb, but the scratches are (142) _____. I would like to have the product replaced with an undamaged version.

The box arrived in fine condition with no apparent damage, indicating to me that shipping was not the cause of the problem. I have come to the conclusion that the product was packed in the box in (143) _____ condition, and I am writing in the hopes that you will take full responsibility for the damage as well as pay for return shipping. I spoke to one of your customer service representatives, who informed me that I would have to pay for return shipping in order to have my globe (144) _____. This is unacceptable. Since your company is clearly at fault, I would hope that you would take it upon yourself to pay for the return shipping.

141. a. view
- **b.** ignore
- **c.** express
- **d.** handle

142. a. unsightly
- **b.** permanent
- **c.** noticeable
- **d.** temporary

143. a. defective
b. malignant
c. inconsiderate
d. irresponsible

144. a. determined
b. inspected
c. refunded
d. replaced

Questions 145 through 148 refer to the following brochure.

Every musician is unique, and at High Wire Records, we treat them that way. We only sign musicians with a (145) _____ artistic vision that sets them apart from everyone else. We do our part to bring out the exceptional qualities of each musician we work with. Our studio in Los Angeles provides musicians with a comfortable and (146) _____ environment, and our sound engineers have the skills and equipment to bring out the best in every recording.

We have achieved (147) _____ success with our approach. Four out of five of our musicians have (148) _____ over 100,000 records, and our most successful artists have gone on to sell nearly a million records. High Wire Records is poised to achieve even greater success in the future.

145. a. variable
b. qualified
c. distinctive
d. cooperative

146. a. austere
b. natural
c. inspiring
d. ingenious

147. a. remarkable
b. undaunted
c. limited
d. understandable

148. a. used
b. sold
c. made
d. held

Questions 149 through 152 refer to the following.

For this project, you will be following a three-step (149) _____ to write the chapters for a technical manual instructing new employees in important policies and procedures. The first step is to align the learning outcomes listed in the appendix for each chapter you have been assigned with the outline provided. This involves (150) _____ which learning outcomes will be met in that chapter and describing how these outcomes will be met in the text. When this is completed, you will submit your work to an editor for review. The second step occurs after receiving feedback from the editor; in this step, you will write the content of each chapter, making sure that you (151) _____ each of the learning outcomes you have identified. Again, you will submit your work to an editor for review once you have completed this step. The final step is to make (152) _____ to your first draft according to the feedback your editor has provided.

149. a. idea
  b. verse
  c. process
  d. standard

150. a. clarifying
  b. correcting
  c. identifying
  d. managing

151. a. meet
  b. state
  c. grasp
  d. elaborate

152. a. revisions
  b. conclusions
  c. collaborations
  d. explanations

Directions: In this part you will read a selection of texts, such as magazine and newspaper articles, letters, and advertisements. Each text is followed by several questions. Select the best answer for each question and mark your choice—**a**, **b**, **c**, or **d**—on your answer sheet.

Questions 153 through 156 refer to the following article.

Introduction to the New Edition of James Madison's *Constitutional Convention*

The men who wrote the U.S. Constitution in 1787 worked in secrecy so that they could have a free exchange of ideas without worrying about what outsiders would say. Producing a document such as the U.S. Constitution can be messy work, and the delegates wanted to make sure that opponents of the Constitution wouldn't have ammunition to use against the final plan. They wanted the constitutional system judged on its own merits. The official journal of the convention, which recorded the votes taken, was only published 30 years later. James Madison's more thorough journal, which included speeches and debates, remained out of the public eye until 1839. Once Madison's journal was published, it became apparent to Americans that their Constitution had been formed by many difficult compromises.

153. How was the U.S. Constitution written?
  a. in secrecy
  b. without debate
  c. by hundreds of men
  d. at a public convention

154. When was the official journal of the Constitutional Convention published?
  a. 1776
  b. 1787
  c. 1817
  d. 1839

155. What fact was revealed by the publication of Madison's journal?
  a. that the U.S. Constitution was written in secrecy
  b. that the official journal was not a complete record
  c. that some Americans were opposed to the Constitution
  d. that the U.S. Constitution contained many compromises

156. What is the purpose of this passage?
- **a.** to explain how the U.S. Constitution was written
- **b.** to highlight the importance of James Madison's journal
- **c.** to argue against the ratification of the U.S. Constitution
- **d.** to report on the debates and speeches at the Constitutional Convention

Questions 157 through 160 refer to the following flier.

Huge Computer Sale

End-of-Year Computer Liquidation
All computers must go!

Laptop Special—only $499! (regularly $999)
15-inch screen
100 Gb hard drive
1.4 mhz processor
Built-in wireless card
Removable combo CD/DVD drive
Long-life battery

Desktop Special—only $249! (regularly $749)
Custom-built desktop
21-inch monitor
500 Gb hard drive
1.2 mhz processor
CD/DVD drive
Wireless receiver
Microsoft Windows 7 installed
Microsoft Office Suite included

157. What is the purpose of this flier?
- **a.** to advertise a low price for certain computers
- **b.** to compare the features of laptops and desktops
- **c.** to make customers aware of a new line of computers
- **d.** to provide publicity for the opening of a new computer store

158. How does the desktop special compare to the laptop special?
- **a.** It offers a factory-guaranteed computer.
- **b.** It offers a computer with a larger monitor.
- **c.** It offers a computer with wireless capability.
- **d.** It offers a more expensive but faster computer.

159. Why is this company having a computer sale?
- **a.** to attract new customers
- **b.** to help sell software packages
- **c.** to clear out its stock at the end of the year
- **d.** to promote computers with wireless capability

160. What makes the laptop on sale different from the desktop on sale?
- **a.** It has a larger hard drive.
- **b.** It has a removable CD/DVD drive.
- **c.** It comes with more software included.
- **d.** It is marked down a larger amount.

Questions 161 through 164 refer to the following plaque.

James Knox Polk

James K. Polk was the 11th president of the United States, serving from 1845 to 1849. Born in North Carolina, Polk moved as a boy to Tennessee. He returned to North Carolina for his university education, graduating in 1818 at the top of his University of North Carolina class. He returned to Tennessee to study law and begin a political career. Polk was a unique president, announcing that he had four goals for his administration and that he would serve only a single term if those goals were met. Remarkably, he fulfilled all his goals and stuck to his promise not to run again, for which he is generally regarded as a near-great president. Relatively unknown today, Polk's administration is notable because of its role in expanding

U.S. territory. During his term, Polk saw the United States spread to the Pacific Ocean as a result of the Oregon Treaty with Britain and the Mexican Cession.

161. What is the purpose of this plaque?
   a. to track Polk's remarkable political rise
   b. to list some of Polk's major accomplishments
   c. to question that Polk was a near-great president
   d. to celebrate the political history of North Carolina

162. Why did Polk serve only one term as president?
   a. He died in office.
   b. He lost his reelection campaign.
   c. He was too unpopular to run for reelection.
   d. He retired after one term as he had promised.

163. What territory did the United States acquire while Polk was president?
   a. Oregon
   b. Mexico
   c. Tennessee
   d. North Carolina

Questions 165 through 168 refer to the following passage.

Throughout history, humans have tended to settle near water because of the many advantages it provides. Water routes such as rivers and seas provide natural transportation routes, and provide humans with access to supplies of water and seafood. The Mediterranean is one of the world's most important water-centered regions. Although the Mediterranean Sea is filled with salt water that can't be used for drinking or irrigation, it can be used for transportation. The

Mediterranean Sea is the meeting point for three continents: Europe, Asia, and Africa. It is the only location in the world where three continents are tied so closely together. The long seacoast of the Mediterranean, combined with a mild climate and relatively calm seas, made this region the perfect setting for the development of sailing and navigation.

The Mediterranean was one of Earth's earliest transportation routes. Ancient peoples traveled the Mediterranean by sea looking for new lands to settle and other peoples to trade with. Although the Mediterranean naturally links three continents, the absence of an eastern outlet limited its connection to the rest of the world, particularly South and East Asia. Humans remedied this in the late 1800s by constructing the Suez Canal. This canal links the Mediterranean Sea to the Indian Ocean through the Red Sea. With the Suez Canal open, people from the Mediterranean region have access to South and East Asia without having to go over land or sail all the way around Africa.

164. What is the purpose of this passage?
   a. to point out the importance of the Suez Canal
   b. to list the similarities between Europe and Asia
   c. to explain why humans tend to settle near water
   d. to describe the traits of the Mediterranean region

165. What word best describes the Mediterranean climate?
   a. mild
   b. harsh
   c. extreme
   d. accessible

166. What makes the Mediterranean region unique in the world?

  a. It is the only sea without an eastern outlet.

  b. It is the only region linking three continents.

  c. It is the only sea with a canal linking it to the ocean.

  d. It is the only region with a mild climate and calm seas.

167. What does the Suez Canal do?

  a. It provides transportation between East and South Asia.

  b. It gives the Red Sea an eastern outlet.

  c. It creates a direct link connecting three continents.

  d. It links the Mediterranean Sea with the Indian Ocean.

168. What trait of the Mediterranean facilitated the development of sailing and navigation?

  a. the large population

  b. the mild climate and calm seas

  c. the plentiful supply of seafood

  d. the construction of the Suez Canal

Questions 169 through 172 refer to the following passage.

Political sociologists study the way people develop their political ideas. One thing many political sociologists agree on is that political attitudes tend to run in the family. Not that families are factories for identical political opinions—people in families disagree all the time, especially about politics. Members of the same family don't always vote the same way, and it's common for people in the same family to support different sides on major issues. But when it comes to political participation, the family is a big influence. The family often shapes a person's level of political activity. If people in your family vote regularly, you are

likely to do so as well. If your family is active in political groups, then you are likely to join in also. And if your family discusses politics a lot, you'll most likely know more about the issues.

169. What do members of the same family tend to do?

  a. vote the same way

  b. agree on major issues

  c. vote with the same frequency

  d. agree on how important family is

170. What political behavior do political sociologists think the family shapes?

  a. a person's position on the issues

  b. the candidates a person votes for

  c. a person's level of political activity

  d. the political offices a person runs for

171. What is most likely to lead a person to know a lot about political issues?

  a. A family that votes regularly

  b. A family that rarely disagrees

  c. A family that agrees about politics

  d. A family that frequently discusses politics

Questions 172 through 175 refer to the following letter.

To Whom It May Concern:

I saw your ad for a writer of a companion book for the PBS program *History Detectives*, and I wanted to send you my resume and writing samples right away. I believe that my education and experience make me the ideal candidate for this position.

I'm a freelance writer who specializes in social science education writing. I have experience working on contract projects that involve tight deadlines and the kind of learning objectives that you outlined in your ad. I have the research and computer resources needed to start immediately, and I'm excited about the possibility of working on this project.

In addition to my resume, I have attached two writing samples from book-length work-for-hire projects I have completed. These projects both involved taking a large amount of material and making it accessible to a general audience in an interesting and educational way. Let me know if you would like to find out more about these projects or see further sample materials. Thank you for your attention in this matter, and I look forward to hearing from you soon.

Sincerely,

John Doe

172. What is the purpose of this letter?
   a. to apply for a job
   b. to dispute an idea
   c. to lodge a complaint
   d. to describe a project

173. What does John Doe do for a living?
   a. He is a freelance writer.
   b. He is a private detective.
   c. He is a high school teacher.
   d. He is a computer programmer.

174. What kind of experience does John Doe have that is relevant to this position?
   a. producing PBS programs
   b. writing resumes for people
   c. studying audience behavior
   d. working on writing projects

175. Which of these is NOT included in the envelope John Doe is sending to PBS?
   a. a resume
   b. a cover letter
   c. a photograph
   d. a writing sample

Questions 176 through 180 refer to the following letter to the editor.

Dear Editor:

I applaud your article on the New SAT (Oct. 27), another initiative in a long line of attempts to battle the decline of the American educational system. The most dismaying thing about this latest effort to improve America's schools is that it indicates how strongly we want a quick fix that costs little, even if it does nothing to improve the real situation. While the New SAT may succeed in pushing the curriculum in a positive direction (though the article raises legitimate doubts that even this will happen), the bigger problem—the fatal problem—is the classroom, not the curriculum. American classrooms are inhabited by a swarming population of students overseen by a weary cadre of overworked, underappreciated, an unincentivized teachers.

Instead of looking for the source of the problem in bad tests and wrongheaded curricula, we need to focus on what really hurts American classrooms: underfunding. Without proper funding, schools cannot hire enough teachers. Fewer teachers means a high student-teacher ratio that precludes personalized attention and a burdensome work load that leads to battle fatigue and burnout. Without proper funding, schools cannot afford or attract enough intelligent, proficient, and more importantly, inspired teachers.

176. What position does this letter take?
- **a.** Schools need better funding.
- **b.** Teachers need to work harder.
- **c.** The New SAT needs to be rewritten.
- **d.** The American educational system needs a quick fix.

177. What is the purpose of this letter?
- **a.** to discuss an issue raised in a article published earlier
- **b.** to argue that the American educational system is beyond repair
- **c.** to explain why the New SAT will no push the curriculum in a positive direction
- **d.** to point out why American classrooms have such a large population of students

178. What is one of the problems that the author of the letter thinks results from underfunding?
- **a.** a large student population
- **b.** a high student-teacher ratio
- **c.** a poorly designed curriculum
- **d.** a reliance on standardized testing

179. What does the author think is the biggest problem with the American educational system?
- **a.** the teachers
- **b.** the students
- **c.** the classroom
- **d.** the curriculum

180. What does this author think the American educational system needs?
- **a.** more high-tech classrooms
- **b.** a new, more positive curriculum
- **c.** students who are not overworked
- **d.** smart, effective, and inspired teachers

Questions 181 through 185 refer to the following e-mail and webpage.

To: All Faculty
From: Safety and Risk Department
Re: Evacuation and Lockdown Procedures

Dear Faculty:

1. Please talk with your classes about the difference between evacuation and lockdown alerts and how to respond to each of them. If you are not sure what the lockdown alert is, or how to respond to either of the alarms, please read about them on the Safety and Risk Department webpage.

2. Know where the Area of Refuge and Safe Assembly areas are for each building in which you teach.

3. If an alert sounds, please assist in guiding your students and others to follow procedures.

4. Alerts are sounded in the event of an emergency and sound no different from assessment alerts. Please respond to each and every alert as a real situation.

5. Be aware that the college schedules assessment alerts at least once per term.

Lockdown Protocol
(formerly called "Active Shooter")

- If you are in a classroom, lab, or office, employees will direct others within that area to *conceal and cover.*
- If you are in an indoor, non-classroom, student, or public gathering area, Building and Floor Monitors will direct all employees, students and campus visitors to the safest place possible and direct them to *conceal and cover.*

181. What is the purpose of the e-mail?
  a. to schedule a practice evacuation for later in the term
  b. to describe procedures for different kinds of lockdowns
  c. to ask instructors to talk about evacuations and lockdowns
  d. to define the difference between an evacuation and a lockdown

182. Why does the e-mail refer to the Safety and Risk Department webpage?
  a. to justify the urgency of the e-mail's contents
  b. to explain to faculty more about why the department exists
  c. to provide a schedule mentioned but not given in the e-mail
  d. to point out where to find information not contained in the e-mail

183. What difference does the webpage explain?
  a. the difference between an evacuation and a lockdown
  b. the difference between a lockdown and an active shooter
  c. the difference between lockdown procedures for different areas
  d. the difference between an area of refuge and a safe assembly area

184. What should faculty and students do when there is an assessment lockdown alert?
  a. conceal and cover
  b. continue class as normal
  c. leave for a Safe Assembly area
  d. read the Safety and Risk Department webpage

185. What is the difference, if any, between an emergency alert and an assessment alert?
  a. There is no difference.
  b. They are given by different departments.
  c. Emergency alerts are scheduled once per term.
  d. One requires a lockdown, the other an evacuation.

Questions 186 through 190 refer to the following book and webpage.

Online books are digital versions of printed books. There are several advantages this format offers over traditional books. Online books can be viewed with a Web browser at any time from any computer connected to the Internet. This means that they are available as needed; there is no need to be on campus or wait until an item is returned to a library to borrow it. Online books generally include the full text along with the graphics, illustrations, charts, and photographs of the print counterpart. Online book collections can be searched by title, topic, or keyword with results displayed in order of relevance. Like print books, online books are protected by copyright and other laws. Use does not permit unauthorized reproduction, republishing, or transfer. Systematic or programmatic copying or downloading is not allowed.

Welcome to The Zither University Library Help Page.

Many of your questions can be answered using the online information tools available. Help is just a mouse click away. Follow the links below or contact a librarian to get help accessing our extensive collection of print and online materials.

- User Guide
- Login Help
- Introductory Tour
- Frequently Asked Questions
- Tips for Searching the Online Catalogue

186. How can a student at Zither University get access to an online book?
   a. by downloading it from the Internet
   b. by using a printer available at the library building
   c. by getting login help from a Zither University librarian
   d. by clicking the User Guide link on the Library Help Page

187. What is one of the disadvantages of a traditional book compared to an online book?
   a. It cannot be copied without permission from the publisher.
   b. It does not contain all the graphics available in the online book.
   c. Librarians are not available to help you search for them in the catalogue.
   d. You have to wait for it to be returned if someone else has checked it out.

188. How do online books differ from traditional print books?
   a. They are not protected by copyright laws.
   b. They do not contain charts, tables, or other graphics.
   c. There is no need to go to a physical location to retrieve them.
   d. They can be duplicated without permission from the publisher.

189. Which of these links should students follow if they are not sure how to search an online book collection using a keyword search?
   a. User Guide
   b. Introductory Tour
   c. Frequently Asked Questions
   d. Tips for Searching the Online Catalogue

190. Which of these links would NOT contain further information about online books?
   a. Login Help
   b. User Guide
   c. Introductory Tour
   d. Frequently Asked Questions

Questions 191 through 196 refer to the following e-mail and table.

To: Michael Barnes
From: Nancy Barnes
Re: Summer Trip Options

Michael,

I've been doing some research on the Internet to get prices and options for our trip this summer. I've attached a document with a table that compares the information I've compiled. It's so hard to make a decision. I would like to go to Hawaii for a week, but it seems so expensive compared to the other options, and a shorter trip seems like a waste. For the same amount of money, we could go to Paris for 10 days. My sensible side says we should spend a week in Paris and save ourselves a little money, but it would be nice to go to Palm Springs. We wouldn't have to rent a car because there's a shuttle from the airport and we wouldn't need to leave the resort—and our meals would be included at the hotel there, too. Or would you rather go to Hawaii? I know we've been dying to go to New York again, but it hardly seems worth the money to me. Let's talk this over when you get back from your business trip.

Nancy

	HAWAII	NEW YORK CITY	PALM SPRINGS	PARIS
Airfare (round-trip per person)	$ 555	$ 279	$ 425	$ 389
Hotel (per night)	$ 250	$ 225	$ 300	$ 189
Car rental (per day)	$ 49	$ 25	—	$ 32
Food and other expenses (estimated per day)	$ 200	$ 200	$ 100	$ 150
Total cost for a 7-day trip	$4,603	$3,708	$3,650	$3,375

191. What are Michael and Nancy Barnes trying to decide about?
- **a.** where to move
- **b.** where to go on vacation
- **c.** where to send their kids to college
- **d.** where to locate their business office

192. Why does Nancy write this e-mail to Michael?
- **a.** to get him to make a difficult decision for her
- **b.** to urge him to cut his business trip short and come home
- **c.** to give him information to help them make a decision together
- **d.** to demonstrate why they cannot afford to take their vacation in Hawaii

193. About what are the daily expenses for the trip to Hawaii?
- **a.** $200
- **b.** $250
- **c.** $500
- **d.** $1,050

194. What is one of the benefits of the Paris option?
- **a.** It is the least expensive overall.
- **b.** The airfare is the least expensive.
- **c.** Meals are included with the hotel.
- **d.** Paris is closer to the Barnes's home.

195. What destination is Nancy's last-choice for this trip?
- **a.** Hawaii
- **b.** New York
- **c.** Palm Springs
- **d.** Paris

196. Why is there no car rental expense entered in the Palm Springs column?
- **a.** Nancy forgot to enter the number in her table.
- **b.** There is no place to rent a car in Palm Springs.
- **c.** Nancy could not get an estimated cost for that expense.
- **d.** There is no need for them to rent a car for that trip.

Questions 197 through 200 refer to the following passage and table.

There are two main types of economic system: free market and command. The main difference between these systems centers around how involved the state gets and how much private individuals are left alone to make economic decisions for themselves. When private individuals get to decide freely what they will produce, buy, and sell, there's a free-market system. In this system, economic decisions are made by the free choices of producers and consumers. This system, which is also referred to as capitalism, is the most common economic system on earth. A command system is one in which most economic decisions are made by the government. Even in a free-market system, the government plays a role. The role of the government in the free-market system is to make sure that producers and consumers can make free choices. This is done by making and enforcing laws that stop theft, fraud, and coercion; that protect private property; and that guarantee competition.

COUNTRIES WITH A FREE-MARKET SYSTEM	COUNTRIES WITH A COMMAND ECONOMY
United States	China
Japan	Cuba
India	Vietnam
South Korea	North Korea

197. What is one of the differences between the two main types of economic system?
- **a.** how many different companies there are
- **b.** how many goods are produced, bought, and sold
- **c.** how much theft, fraud, and coercion takes place
- **d.** how free people are to make decisions for themselves

198. Which of these countries makes most of the economic decisions in its economy?
- **a.** Cuba
- **b.** Japan
- **c.** India
- **d.** South Korea

199. Which of these jobs is done by the Japanese government?
- **a.** guaranteeing competition
- **b.** deciding on what gets produced
- **c.** making sure everyone has basic necessities
- **d.** preventing the economy from going into recession

200. Generally speaking, where can consumers make mostly free choices about their purchases?
- **a.** China
- **b.** Vietnam
- **c.** North Korea
- **d.** South Korea

Speaking

This section tests your skills for the TOEIC Speaking Test. It includes 11 questions that measure different aspects of your speaking ability. The test lasts approximately 20 minutes.

For each type of question, you will be given specific directions, including the time allowed for preparation and speaking. It is to your advantage to say as much as you can in the time allowed. It is also important that you speak clearly and that you answer each question according to the directions.

Directions: In this part of the test, you will read aloud the text on the screen. You will have 45 seconds to prepare. Then you will have 45 seconds to read the text aloud. Use a stopwatch or clock to keep track of your time.

201. Improvements in communication have enabled and stimulated global economic growth. Improved communication networks facilitate the coordination of transportation and logistics, making transport chains flow much more smoothly. The cost of communications has dropped substantially in recent decades. Developments like fiber optics and the Internet make communications smoother and more useful as well as less expensive. The rise of outsourcing has contributed to a rapid expansion in the international trade of labor services, such as technical consulting and call center services. As a result, international trade includes a widening variety of services that were previously fixed to regional markets.

202. The beauty and size of the Grand Canyon is humbling, but the Grand Canyon you visit today is more than just an awe-inspiring natural formation. It is a gift from past generations that have preserved it and helped develop it in a sustainable way. As you visit the canyon, take time to enjoy this gift, but always keep in mind that this gift must continue to be passed on. We all have the responsibility to ensure that future generations have the chance to experience the same Grand Canyon that we can see today.

Directions: In this part of the test, you will describe the picture on your screen in as much detail as you can. You will have 30 seconds to prepare your response. Then you will have 45 seconds to speak about the picture. Use a stopwatch or clock to keep track of your time.

203.

Directions: In this part of the test, you will answer three questions. For each question, begin responding immediately after you hear a beep. No preparation time is provided. You will have 15 seconds to respond to questions 204 and 205, and 30 seconds to respond to question 206. Use a stopwatch or clock to keep track of your time.

Imagine that a person has come to your front door to ask you questions for a political study.

204. How much do you pay attention to politics and current events?

205. Are you satisfied with the political leadership in this country?

206. What kind of changes would you most like to see in the country in the coming year?

Directions: In this part of the test, you will answer three questions based on the information provided. You will have 30 seconds to read the information that follows. Then, you will have 15 seconds to respond to questions 207 and 208, and 30 seconds to respond to question 209. Use a stopwatch or clock to keep track of your time.

Student: I was thinking about taking your course, but I have some questions before I sign up.

GRADES

Grades are based on a 400-point system. The course letter grade is determined by the point values below:

above 360:	A
320–359:	B
280–319:	C
240–279:	D
below 240:	F

Points are distributed as follows:

- Attendance—80 points (20%)
- 3 Short Papers—40 points each/120 points (30%)
- Midterm Exam: Multiple-choice and short answer—100 points (25%)
- Final Exam: Essay Only—100 points (25%)

Late Work and Makeups

Timely submission of all required work is an essential component of this course. Students will be given extensions and/or makeups only with a documented and legitimate excuse of a medical or personal emergency. The terms of all makeup work will be discussed with the professor on an individual basis. Students without a documented excuse who miss an in-class assignment may be given a makeup assignment at the instructor's discretion.

207. How much are the exams worth, and what is the format of the exams?

208. What other work expectations do you have for this class?

209. I may have to miss one week in the middle of the term for a business trip. Will I be able to do that, and if so, how will it impact my grade?

Directions: In this part of the test, you will be presented with a problem and asked to propose a solution. You will have 30 seconds to prepare. Then you will have 60 seconds to speak. Use a stopwatch or clock to keep track of your time.

210. Reply as though you are attending a surprise birthday party.
As you reply, be sure to:

- explain that you understand the probem
- propose a solution

Now, listen to Track 574.

Directions: In this part of the test, you will give your opinion about a specific topic. Be sure to say as much as you can in the time allowed. You will have 15 seconds to prepare. Then you will have 60 seconds to speak. Use a stopwatch or clock to keep track of your time.

211. Some people think that all the technology of modern life has made life more hectic and stress-filled and that we would all be happier if we were living a simpler life without all the gadgets that we're come to depend on. What's your opinion about this? Give reasons for your opinion.

Writing

This is the TOEIC Writing Test. This test includes eight questions that measure different aspects of your writing ability. The test lasts approximately one hour. For each type of question, you will be given specific directions, including the time allowed for writing.

Directions: In this part of the test, you will write ONE sentence that is based on a picture. With each picture, you will be given TWO words or phrases that you must use in your sentence. You can change the forms of the words and you can use the words in any order.

Your sentence will be scored on:

- the appropriate use of grammar
- the relevance of the sentence to the picture

You will have eight minutes to complete this part of the test. Use a stopwatch or clock to keep track of your time.

212.

computer, credit card

_____

_____

213.

couple, market

_____

_____

214.

carpenters, house

_____

_____

215.

girl, playground

_____

_____

216.

applicant, three people

_____

_____

Directions: In this part of the test, you will show how well you can write a response to an e-mail.

Your response will be scored on:

- the quality and variety of your sentences
- vocabulary
- organization

You will have 10 minutes to read and answer each e-mail. Use a stopwatch or clock to keep track of your time.

> We received your request to refund your money for your recent guided tour through the zoo. Your satisfaction is important to us, and we would be happy to refund your money. In order to serve you and other zoo patrons better in the future, we would like to know what you found unsatisfying about your zoo experience.

217. _____

_____

_____

_____

_____

Directions: In this part of the test, you will show how well you can write a response to a letter.

Your response will be scored on:

- the quality and variety of your sentences
- vocabulary
- organization

You will have 10 minutes to read and answer each letter. Use a stopwatch or clock to keep track of your time.

Thank you for your job application. We have looked over your resume, and we are impressed with your experience. You are one of a great number of well-qualified applicants, so we are writing to solicit more information before making a decision about whom to interview. To aid us in this process, please write back to us with a brief description of your ideal workplace and your ideal boss.

218. _____

_____

_____

_____

_____

Directions: In this part of the test, you will write an essay in response to a question that asks you to state, explain, and support your opinion on an issue. Typically, an effective essay will contain a minimum of 300 words.

Your response will be scored on:

- whether your opinion is supported with reasons and/or examples
- grammar
- vocabulary
- organization

You will have 30 minutes to plan, write, and revise your essay. Use a stopwatch or clock to keep track of your time.

Some people think happiness is more important than success, while others feel that you cannot truly be happy unless you are successful. What do you think is the relationship between happiness and success? Give reasons or examples to support your opinion.

219. _____

_____

_____

_____

_____

_____

_____

_____

_____

_____

_____

_____

_____

_____

_____

_____

_____

_____

_____

_____

_____

_____

_____

_____

_____

Answers

1. b. The two people are working together with a laptop in front of them. You can't tell what they're working on or whether the computer or telephone is broken.

2. d. All the people are listening and watching someone, probably at a meeting.

3. c. A large backhoe is in the process of moving dirt to dig a hole. The sky is clear, so it will not rain soon, and the dirt will not turn to mud. There is nothing broken that needs to be fixed.

4. b. The two people are looking at a questionnaire, and the younger woman is filling in the answers the older woman is giving.

5. a. The cars on the road are not moving, but there are no signs indicating that there is any construction or that the cars are for sale.

6. c. The waiter is smiling as the woman looks at her menu, while the man is ordering their meal.

7. a. One of the kids is putting cheese on top of the pizza that already has vegetables on it. There is not much of a mess, and we can't tell whether the hats are new.

8. d. The only things you can see are the sun and the ocean. There is not sight of a beach or a boat or someone who is lost.

9. b. A bird has landed in a birdbath to clean itself. It is not looking for food or escaping from a cat.

10. a. A clerk is handing a woman her credit card after she has paid for the items in the bags.

11. a. A person without a watch would not likely know what time it is. Choice **b** talks about a gift, not the time, and choice **c** doesn't give an answer to the question.

12. c. This question asks a yes-or-no question. Neither choice **a** nor choice **b** replies with a yes or no.

13. b. The question asks about a time, and choice **b** gives a time. Neither of the other answers mentions a time.

14. b. When someone mentions that something isn't hot, they probably want it to be. Choice **a** brings up cake, which often goes with coffee, but this choice doesn't address the issue of heat. Neither does choice **c**.

15. a. This choice addresses the question of whether someone is ready to go by giving a time when she will be ready. Choice **b** adds new information by talking about where they're going, not when, and choice **c** does not address a time or a place at all.

16. b. A person who is going to miss the bus probably needs a ride. He doesn't need dinner or someone to order for him.

17. c. This question asks for a list of people, which choice **c** gives. Choice **b** mentions people, but tells what they don't like rather than just listing them. Choice **a** does not list any people.

18. b. The question is a request for something put as a yes-or-no question. Choice **b** gives a yes choice **by** saying, "Sure." Choice **a** may look like a yes answer stated as "Thanks," but it's about taking something, not giving something to someone to borrow. Choice **c** does not give any kind of yes-or-no answer.

19. a. The question asks for a yes-or-no answer, which choice **a** gives by saying, "It is," instead of simply "Yes." Neither of the other answers gives a yes-or-no answer.

20. c. The question asks about a news program, but choice **a** talks about a cat and choice **b** talks about boots, neither of which is related to a news program.

21. a. This question asks for a reason, which choice **a** gives. Choice **b** is a statement, not an explanation, and choice **c** is a denial.

22. c. This question asks for a yes-or-no answer, which choice **c** gives directly, along with a suggestion for what to do instead. Choice **b** gives a yes answer, but it's about babysitting, not a problem, and choice **a** does not give a yes-or-no answer.

23. c. The question asks for someone to agree or disagree, which choice **c** does. Choice **a** changes the subject, and choice **b** is unrelated.

24. a. The first statement is a compliment, and the proper response to a compliment is to thank the person. Choice **b** is about glasses but does not address the compliment, and choice **c** is unrelated.

25. b. This answer provides a reason that is directly related to the question. Choice **a** gives a reason, but filling up the tank is unrelated to car insurance. Choice **c** makes a statement instead of giving a reason.

26. c. This question asks about location, and choice **c** gives a location. Neither choice **a** nor choice **b** gives a location.

27. b. The question is about a noise, and this answer refers to a source of the noise. Choice **a** does not talk about a noise, and choice **c** changes the subject.

28. a. This is a yes-or-no question, and choice **a** gives a yes by saying, "Good idea." Choice **b** does not give a yes or a no. Choice **c** gives a yes by saying "Thanks," but the reason is not related.

29. a. The question asks about a location. Neither choice **b** nor choice **c** gives a location.

30. b. The statement refers to hot food, and choice **b** mentions peppers, which are hot. Neither choice **a** nor choice **c** refers to hot food, or even food at all.

31. c. The question asks for a yes-or-no answer. Choice **a** does not give a yes or a no. Choice **b** gives a yes, but the reason is unrelated.

32. c. The question asks for a yes-or-no answer. Neither choice **a** nor choice **b** gives a yes or a no.

33. a. The question asks for a yes-or-no answer. Neither choice **b** nor choice **c** gives a yes or a no.

34. b. The question is about a job interview, and choice **b** references the job. Neither choice **a** nor choice **b** mentions a job.

35. a. The question asks for a yes-or-no answer. Neither choice **b** nor choice **c** gives a yes or a no.

36. c. The question asks about going to the dentist, and this answer tells when the appointment happened. Choice **a** is about teeth, but it does not refer to an appointment, and choice **b** is not about teeth or a dentist.

37. c. The question asks about a length of time. Neither choice **a** nor choice **b** mentions anything about time.

38. a. This choice agrees with the statement made by the original speaker. Choice **b** is not related to basketball, and choice **c** does not address the statement made.

39. b. This question asks for a yes-or-no answer. Choice **a** gives a yes answer, but the reason does not address whether there is a problem. Choice **c** implies a no answer, but the reason is not about computers at all.

40. a. The question is about a garden, and choice **a** mentions tomatoes. Neither choice **b** nor choice **c** brings up anything related to a garden.

41. c. The woman begins by asking if the man can pick up the kids from school, and they continue to discuss this plan. The meeting, haircut appointment, and cooking of dinner are obstacles to solving this problem.

42. a. The woman stated, "I have a 3 o'clock meeting that I can't reschedule."

43. **b.** The man said, "I was supposed to get my hair cut at 3 o'clock."

44. **a.** The woman is asking about an exam, and the man is answering. Thus, he is the teacher who knows what will be on the exam, and she is the student.

45. **d.** The woman's questions revolve around the essay portion of the exam. She does not ask about her grade, the day of the exam, or joining the class.

46. **a.** The woman starts by saying, "I have some questions about the exam on Monday."

47. **c.** When a person is trying to return an item, he is a customer at a store, and someone helping him make the return is a clerk in a store. Choice **d** is not correct even though it mentions working in a store, because coworkers would not discuss returning pants unless there was a third person present who was trying to return them.

48. **d.** The man begins by saying, "I would like to return these pants," and he later tells the clerk why: "they're too small."

49. **b.** The man asks, "Can I exchange them for something else?" The clerk tells him that he can, and he decides to do that.

50. **b.** The two people are working together on a task, which is putting novels on the shelves in a bookstore; people who work together would discuss a task of this kind. Although they are discussing novels, they are not trying to buy novels, as choice **a** states, and they never talk about reading the books, as choice **d** states.

51. **d.** The woman starts by stating, "We need to make space on the shelves for these new books that just arrived." Although these are novels, as choice **c** states, they are trying to make room for them, not put them in a new order.

52. **a.** After discussing what they need to do and agreeing on an approach, the woman states, "I'll start at the beginning of the alphabet and you start at the end." This means they are both going to do part of the job, as choice **a** states. They are not going to take turns, as choice **b** states, get someone else to do it, as choice **c** states, or do something else first, as choice **d** states.

53. **a.** The woman begins by saying, "Can we finish packing later?" This indicates that they are in the middle of packing. Both of them are choosing clothes, so they are taking the trip together.

54. **b.** The woman states, "I have to meet my friend to help her pick out wallpaper for her living room." Choice **d** is incorrect since it is someone else's living room that needs wallpaper, not her own.

55. **d.** The woman reminds the man to pack his black suit to wear for a formal dinner on Saturday, so that is one thing we know they will be doing. The meeting and picking out wallpaper are things they have to do that are getting in the way of packing before the trip.

56. **b.** The man states, "I'm having a problem with my car," and the woman is asking him questions about what is wrong. This shows that she is trying to help him get his car fixed. He is not trying to sell or buy a car, as choice **a** and choice **d** state, and he never asks about getting a job, as choice **c** states.

57. c. The woman is asking the man questions about what is wrong with his car in an attempt to figure out what the problem is so that the car can be fixed. This shows that she's a mechanic who will work on the car's problem. Choice **d** is not correct since she is not parking his car, and choice **a** is not correct since she is not selling him a car. She is also not a receptionist, as choice **b** states, because she tells him to leave the keys and cell phone number at the front desk; if she were a receptionist, she would work at the front desk and would take his keys and cell phone number herself.

58. a. In response to the woman's question, "What kind of problem have you been having?" the man answers, "It's difficult to start." He also talks about the car stalling, as choice **c** states, but the problem is that it stalls before he drives it, not after. He does not mention a strange noise, as choice **d** does, or complain about a car phone.

59. b. The man talks about the woman's son and his difficulties in school, so she is a student's mother and he is a teacher. Choice **c** is not correct because two parents would not know what a student was doing in class without a teacher telling them. Choice **d** is not correct since the man starts by saying, "your son," showing that one of them is a parent. Choice **a** is not correct since the woman is discussing her son's performance in school, not her own.

60. d. The man begins by saying, "Your son has been having some difficulty in school." Choice **a** is not correct since it is the woman who mentions the death in the family. Choice **b** and choice **c** are not correct because the woman is not the student; she is the mother of a student.

61. b. When the man asks, "Are there any problems at home that might be affecting his work?" the woman tells him about the death in the family. There is no mention of difficulty reading, illness, or skipping school.

62. d. The man wants to buy a new cell phone, and the woman is asking him questions and offering to show him a new model, so he is a customer and she is a salesperson.

63. b. The man begins by saying, "I'm thinking about getting a new cell phone." Choice **c** and choice **d** are not correct; the man mentions computers and an electronic calendar, but these are features he wants in a cell phone, not things he wants to buy.

64. a. At the beginning of the conversation, the man states that he wants a cell phone "that's more powerful than the one" he currently owns. Choice **b** is not correct since the man states that "the screen is too small" on his old phone. Choice **c** is not correct because he does not mention battery life. Choice **d** is not correct because the man does not ask about a wireless connection; the woman offers a model that has a wireless connection, but the man did not ask for that feature before she brought it up.

65. a. The woman notices that the man is buying Brussels sprouts; people buy Brussels sprouts in a grocery store, not at a cooking class. Brussels sprouts may be sold on a farm, but it is unlikely that these people would meet on a farm.

66. b. The woman asks, "Do you have a good recipe?" She does not ask about the price or nutritional information.

67. c. The man says, "it's only about fifteen minutes total." Choice **a** and choice **b** are not correct since these are the times the man says you need to cook the Brussels sprouts, but there is additional time needed to cut up the Brussels sprouts and chop the garlic.

68. d. The man says, "I want to return this camera." The woman gives him different options, including the option leave the camera he doesn't want and look for a new one. Choice **a** is not correct even though the woman does offer some suggestions about fixing the camera, because the man does not want the camera fixed.

69. c. The man wants the flash to recharge more quickly than this camera does. Choice **a** is not correct since the batteries are not dead, just slow. Choice **b** and choice **d** are not correct since the woman offers to give the man his money back or exchange the camera for another one.

70. a. The man states, "I think I'll get the refund right now." Choice **b** is not correct since the man already tried a new battery, and choice **d** is not correct since he has let the flash recharge but is not satisfied with the speed of recharging.

71. c. The message begins by stating, "You have reached the main switchboard at Portland Community College." Pressing zero, speaking with an operator, and typing a name into the name directory are all options available *after* hearing the message.

72. a. The message gives callers various options to get them to the correct number. Choice **b** is not correct since there is no mention of problems. Choice **c** is not correct even though one of the options is to speak to an operator, because callers have other options. Choice **d** is not correct even though reaching student services or an academic advisor are options, because callers have even more options.

73. c. The message states that callers who stay on the line will be helped by an operator.

74. c. At one point, the speaker says, "here in the lobby," indicating that the listeners are in the lobby of a building. The speaker also mentions "new offices," so the building is a new one.

75. d. The speaker mentions several activities that are available and states, "We have a few events planned throughout the evening, which you can see here on this board." Choice **a** is not correct even though the architect will be speaking because that speaker will not be giving a talk until late, and that is only one of the events mentioned.

76. a. The speaker points out that the events planned for the evening are on a board in the lobby. Choice **b** is not correct since the chief architect will be giving a talk about the building's architectural history.

77. b. The talk opens with a welcome, so the listeners are actually in the Rotunda receiving information about it. This is not a history class, and there is no indication that a keynote speaker will follow.

78. d. After mentioning that the Rotunda is the main circulation space in the Capitol, the speaker goes on to give a reason for this: "It connects the House and Senate sides."

79. c. The speaker points out that even though the Rotunda was conceived in 1793, construction did not begin until 1818 because of certain delays, namely "a shortage of funds and materials and the fire set by the British in 1814."

80. b. This talk begins by stating, "You're about to watch a documentary," and then goes on to describe what the program will show.

81. d. The talk states that the documentary is about "credit card companies and the kinds of practices they employ." Choice **a** is incorrect even though lobbyists are mentioned, because they are only one small part of the program, not the focus. Every part of the description focuses on credit card companies.

82. c. The talk states that "our correspondents interview industry insiders, lobbyists, politicians, and consumer advocates." Correspondents are journalists, and interviewing involves asking questions, so journalists ask most of the questions in this program.

83. c. This talk discusses making good choices about nutrition for planning family meals. This kind of information would most likely be given in a class about family nutrition. Choice **d** is not correct even though a documentary about the food industry would cover similar topics, because such a documentary would not focus on these choices exclusively.

84. b. The speaker states that certain foods "should be eaten in moderation," and meat is on this list, while the diet should be heaviest in fruits and vegetables and basic starches, which includes oats and potatoes. Since meat should be eaten in moderation and the others the heaviest part of the diet, meat should be eaten the least.

85. a. The speaker advises listeners to "try to avoid processed foods as much as possible." Avoiding processed foods involves cooking from scratch.

86. a. The speaker mentions that there are penguins behind her, and a zoo is a place where penguins are kept. Penguins are not usually found in museums, college classrooms, or elementary school auditoriums.

87. b. The speaker states that "the emperor penguin is actually a flightless bird." Penguins eat fish and squid, and mammals are never mentioned.

88. a. The speaker says, "The emperor penguin is best known for the long journeys the adults make each year to feed their offspring." This feeding takes place during the antarctic winter. Choice **b** and choice **d** are not correct even though these traits are mentioned, because they are not the things the emperor penguin is best known for. Choice **c** is not correct because penguins cannot fly.

89. c. The talk begins by stating that "this is the planned site for our new city hall building," so the speaker is giving this talk at the site itself.

90. d. The speaker spends most of the talk describing the reasons for choosing this site. Choice **a** is not correct because local businesses are only mentioned in passing. Choice **b** is not correct because the use of environmentally friendly building techniques is only a small part of the talk. Choice **c** is not correct because there is no revitalization program mentioned.

91. c. The speaker states that the site "is centrally located in our town." There is no mention of the view, the price, or proximity to the town dump.

92. d. The speaker begins by saying, "Tonight we are proud to bring you a new exhibition," and finishes by saying that "The town arts council is proud to sponsor this exhibition." This indicates that the "we" is the arts council.

93. a. The speaker begins by introducing "a new exhibition." There is no mention of a cultural center, a series of lectures, or a contest.

94. d. The exhibition is the work of Mark Gunderson, who "has been creating three-dimensional paintings and sculpture for two decades." Gunderson worked with a Native American artist, but there is no mention of Native American artifacts in the description of either artist or of the exhibition.

95. a. The message lists movie times for today's movie. The message also mentions the box office and the movie theater's website, so this message would not be heard at the box office or on the website.

96. b. The message lists showtimes, prices, and the location of the movie theater. There are no driving directions or explanation of the different ticket prices provided. The movie theater's webpage is mentioned as a reference, not as a newly launched site.

97. a. The message states, "Our box office opens at noon every day." The other choices are all movie times that start after the box office opens.

98. b. This message gives details about snow closures and delays for the Multnomah County School District. Choice **a** is not correct because it provides very little information for a bus driver. Choice **c** is not correct because no weather information is given other than the mention of snowy conditions.

99. d. This messages details which schools are closed, delayed, and open on this day. Choice **a** is not correct because no weather information is given other than the mention of snowy conditions. Choice **b** is not correct even though all the regions are listed, because these regions are listed in order to describe their status. Choice **c** is not correct because snow routes are mentioned but not detailed.

100. b. The message states, "Schools in southwest Portland with the exception of those schools downtown will open three hours late." Schools in downtown and north Portland are closed, while schools in southeast are open at the regular time.

101. c. The other choices use the wrong verb tense.

102. b. The bus was delayed, which means it was not running according to the regular plan or schedule.

103. d. Choice **a** and choice **b** are not relevant because there is no reason in the sentence to think the mayor was calm or happy.

104. c. A project is not taken over, around, or up.

105. d. Choice **d** is correct because the delivery is in the past tense. The other choices are in the wrong tense.

106. a. Choice **a** is correct because 2009 is in the past tense. The other choices are in the wrong tense.

107. a. Choice **a** is correct because a coffee maker is what turns beans into brewed coffee. A process or production would not grind the beans, and a beverage is what comes out of the machine, not what makes the coffee.

108. b. People have reasons behind their decisions, not names, debates, or perspectives.

109. b. Pablo made a decision about being a lawyer after finishing his degree, not during.

110. c. Choice **b** is not correct because there is no comparison made to another country; a comparison is needed to determine if something is larger. A claim that something is largest does not need to refer to anything else.

111. a. The word "but" indicates a change in direction for a sentence, and this sentence changes direction after the comma as indicated by the word "nonetheless."

112. d. Choice **d** is correct because the argument is in the past tense. The other choices are in the wrong tense.

113. a. The penalty for littering is a fine. Someone is not charged $500 as a waste, hazard, or indication.

114. c. Someone who takes their boss's place becomes the head of something.

115. a. The other choices are in the wrong tense.

116. c. Ingredients such as flour, salt, and baking power are mixed together, or combined, not melted, diluted, or separated.

117. d. The "would" later in the sentence indicates that something would have to be done.

118. c. The word "neither" is always paired with "nor."

119. b. A movie ends with a final scene. There are ideas, conflicts, and perspectives in a movie, but none of these words matches well with "final" in this sentence.

120. b. A comparison between umbrellas and rain hats is being made, so one can be better than the other.

121. d. The word "although" indicates a contrast between parts of the sentence. In this sentence danger is contrasted with rewarding.

122. a. The word "while" indicates that the second half of the sentence will be different from the first. A powerful sense of smell is different from bad or poor eyesight.

123. b. The second half of the sentence provides an explanation for the fact that trees lose their leave in the autumn; the word "because" is used to indicate an explanation.

124. d. To use a dictionary, you must have some knowledge. The word "possess" means the same as "have."

125. b. Purity and height are not useful measures of a quantity. Choice **a** is not correct because "about" and "the same" are similar, and this sentence makes a contrast in ideas.

126. b. The sentence is in the present tense because of "wants." The other answers are in the wrong tense.

127. a. A craftsman uses tools to complete a job. Although a craftsman has an outfit and ideas, they are not part of completing a job.

128. c. Musicians give concerts, not plays, trials, or seminars.

129. c. This sentence presents a contrast between something "unique" and its opposite, which is "typical."

130. d. Journalists are writers who have deadlines for submitting their work. They have criteria, but these are not met every day.

131. d. Teachers have to discipline students who are unpredictable. They might coach them, but disciplining them is a better fit in this sentence.

132. a. The other choices are in the wrong tense.

133. c. Doubt occurs in a time, which is indicated by the word "when."

134. b. A penalty of $100 results from a contract, not an affiliation, argument, or message.

135. d. The word "but" indicates a contrast; the opposite of being good at something is having a difficult time doing it. The word "struggle" might work, but the phrase "struggle time" is awkward.

136. b. The second half of the sentence offers an explanation for the need to borrow chairs, and the word "because" is used to introduce explanations.

137. a. This sentence compares white with black or dark clothes, so a comparative statement such as "harder" is appropriate.

138. b. A bridge goes over a river. Canals are waterways like rivers, and tunnels go under rivers.

139. c. Responding happens at a time, which is indicated by "whenever."

140. a. The missing word describes the sending of thank-you notes. Importance is something on its own, not a description. Importantly is an adverb that describes an action, not a thing. There is no comparison between two or more things, so "more" should not be used.

141. c. A person expresses his or her own dissatisfaction. People may view, ignore, or handle someone else's dissatisfaction but not their own.

142. b. The bulb can be replaced, but the scratches cannot be fixed, so they are permanent. Scratches may be unsightly, noticeable, or temporary, but in the context of this sentence, none of those words fits as well as permanent.

143. a. The letter eliminates shipping as a cause of the damage, so the globe must have been damaged, or defective, when packed. Malignant does not describe an object like a globe, and inconsiderate and irresponsible describe people or actions, not inanimate objects.

144. d. In the first paragraph, the letter states, "I would like to have the product replaced with an undamaged version." The writer wants a replacement, not a refund or inspection.

145. c. The company thinks of musicians as "unique," so they are looking for that quality; distinctive is the closest in meaning to unique.

146. c. This word is paired with "comfortable," so it must match the tone and meaning of this word. Something austere is not comfortable. Something natural is not necessarily well paired with something comfortable, and something ingenious has no relationship.

147. a. Success can be remarkable, not undaunted. Success can be understandable, but since there is nothing done to show why it should be understandable, this word does not fit well here. Limited success is incorrect because most of the musicians are successful.

148. b. This sentence later states that musicians "sell" records.

149. c. Something with three steps is a process, not an idea, a verse, or a standard.

150. c. Before something can be described, it must be identified. You do not clarify, correct, or manage something prior to describing it.

151. a. After identifying and describing an outcome, the next step is to meet it, not state, grasp, or elaborate.

152. a. The purpose of feedback is to help someone revise.

153. a. The passage states that the men who wrote the Constitution "worked in secrecy."

154. c. The official journal was published 30 years after the convention, which took place in 1787, so the journal was published in 1817.

155. d. The passage states that Madison's journal made it apparent that the "Constitution had been formed by many difficult compromises."

156. b. This passage is from an introduction to a new edition of Madison's journal, so the purpose is to introduce that publication. The introduction discusses how and why the journal was important.

157. a. The computers listed in this flier are on sale for much less than the regular price. The flier does show the features of two computers, but the purpose is to sell them, not to compare them.

158. b. The desktop monitor is 21 inches while the laptop monitor is only 15 inches. Both computers have wireless capabilities, and neither has a factory guarantee. The desktop is less expensive.

159. c. The flier states that this is an "End-of-Year Computer Liquidation," so the company is trying to get rid of its computers.

160. b. Both computers have a CD/DVD drive, but only the laptop's drive is removable. The laptop has a smaller hard drive and no software. Both computers are marked down by $500.

161. b. The plaque lists some of Polk's accomplishments but does not go into much about his political rise. It states facts without making an argument and does not talk about North Carolina's political history on its own.

162. d. The passage states that Polk promised to serve only a single term if his goals were met and that he stuck to his promise not to run again.

163. a. The Oregon Treaty gave Oregon to the United States. Mexico is not part of the United States. Tennessee and North Carolina were important places in Polk's early life, not acquisitions during his term as president.

164. d. The passage lists various traits of the Mediterranean region and explains their importance. The Suez Canal is a detail, not the overall purpose. The passage begins by mentioning that humans tend to settle near water, but this fact is not pursued throughout the passage.

165. a. The passage states that the Mediterranean has a "mild climate."

166. b. The passage states that the Mediterranean "is the only location in the world where three continents are tied so closely together."

167. d. The passage states that the Suez Canal "links the Mediterranean Sea to the Indian Ocean through the Red Sea."

168. b. The passage states, "The long seacoast of the Mediterranean, combined with a mild climate and relatively calm seas, made this region the perfect setting for the development of sailing and navigation."

169. c. The passage states, "If people in your family vote regularly, you are likely to do so as well."

170. c. The passage states, "The family often shapes a person's level of political activity."

171. d. The passage states that "if your family discusses politics a lot, you'll most likely know more about the issues."

172. a. The person who wrote the letter states that he is the ideal candidate for a job, so the purpose is to get that job.

173. a. The second paragraph begins by stating, "I'm a freelance writer who specializes in social science education writing."

174. d. The letter states, "I have experience working on contract projects that involve tight deadlines and the kind of learning objectives that you outlined in your ad."

175. c. This is a cover letter, so that is included. The letter states that "In addition to my resume, I have attached two writing samples," so a resume and writing sample are also included. There is no mention of a photograph.

176. a. The second paragraph argues that underfunding is the problem, which implies that schools need better funding.

177. a. This letter to the editor references an earlier article published by this newspaper or magazine. The author of the letter uses the issue raised there to discuss the problem of underfunding.

178. b. The letter states that schools do not have enough teachers because of underfunding, and that "Fewer teachers means a high student-teacher ratio." This high ratio does not allow for personal attention, and it leads to battle fatigue and burnout.

179. c. The letter states that the "fatal problem" is the classroom, not the curriculum. Students are not blamed. Teachers are extensively discussed as part of the problem, but the problems faced by teachers result from underfunding, not the teachers themselves.

180. d. The letter ends by stating, "Without proper funding, schools cannot afford or attract enough intelligent, proficient, and more importantly, inspired teachers." The letter argues for more funding so that schools can attract smart, effective, and inspired teachers.

181. c. The first point in the e-mail requests that faculty "talk with your classes about the difference between evacuation and lockdown alerts and how to respond to each of them."

182. d. The e-mail does not describe what a lockdown alert is, and this information might be needed by someone reading the e-mail. The Safety and Risk Department webpage contains information about this kind of alert.

183. c. The webpage focuses on lockdown alerts and gives procedures for dealing with such an alert depending on your location at the time of the alert.

184. a. The Web Page describing lockdown alerts indicates that no matter where you are, you should "conceal and cover." The e-mail points out that there is no difference between an emergency and an assessment alert.

185. a. Point #4 of the e-mail states, "Alerts are sounded in the event of an emergency and sound no different from assessment alerts. Please respond to each and every alert as a real situation."

186. a. The first passage states, "Online books can be viewed with a Web browser at any time from any computer connected to the Internet."

187. d. The first passage states that with an online book, there is no need to "wait until an item is returned to a library to borrow it," but with a traditional print book, if someone has checked it out, you have to wait until it is returned to get it yourself.

188. c. The first passage states that online books are available as needed, and "there is no need to be on campus or wait until an item is returned to a library to borrow it."

189. d. This link will give information about making a keyword search. The User Guide and Frequently Asked Questions links might include this as well, but the best place to start for advice on searching is a link that directly refers to searching.

190. a. The Login Help link will provide information about getting into the online library system, but it will not contain information about the kinds of books—traditional or online—that the library contains.

191. b. The information in the table includes vacation expenses, not the expenses for moving, going to college, or opening a business office.

192. c. Nancy has done research related to a decision that she and Michael will make together. She does not ask him to make the decision for her or urge him to cut his trip short. She does indicate that the trip to Hawaii is more expensive, but she does not argue that they cannot afford it.

193. c. The hotel is $250 per night, the car rental about $50 per day, and food and other expenses another $200, for a total of $500.

194. a. At a total cost of $3,375 for a seven-day drip, the overall expenses for the Paris option are less than any other choice.

195. b. Nancy prefers Hawaii and gives good reasons for going to Paris or Palm Springs, and she says that New York hardly seems worth the money.

196. d. Nancy states that "we wouldn't have to rent a car because there's a shuttle from the airport and we wouldn't need to leave the resort."

197. d. The passage states, "The main difference between these systems centers around how involved the state gets and how much private individuals are left alone to make economic decisions for themselves."

198. a. Cuba has a command economy, which the passage describes as a system "in which most economic decisions are made by the government."

199. a. Japan is listed as a free-market system. The passage states that the government in a free-market system is supposed to make and enforce laws that guarantee competition.

200. d. South Korea has a free-market system, which the passage defines as one where "producers and consumers can make free choices."

201. **To hear this passage, listen to Track 575.** This passage is about improvements in the communications industry. Here is a list of some of the tougher words and how they should be pronounced:

    Communication—kuh-myoo-ni-KAY-shun
    Facilitate—fuh-SILL-ih-tayt
    Logistics—loh-JIS-tiks

202. **To hear this passage, listen to Track 576.** This passage is about the Grand Canyon. Here is a list of some of the tougher words and how they should be pronounced:

    Formation—for-MAY-shun
    Sustainable—suh-STAYN-uh-bul
    Responsibility—ri-spon-suh-BIL-ih-tee

203. Sample response: There is a large snow-covered mountain in the background set against a clear sky. In front of the mountain is a large barn surrounded by a fence. The fence also encloses a pasture. Behind the barn is a row of tall evergreen trees.

To hear this sample response, listen to Track 577.

204. Sample response: I don't pay much attention to politics. I don't feel like the things politicians do have much impact on my life. I do pay attention to current events, though, because I like to know what's going on in the world around me.

To hear this sample response, listen to Track 578.

205. Sample response: I'm mostly satisfied because I feel like the country is doing pretty well, but of course I have some problems. I think political leaders are sometimes too distant from the people. They need to know more about what it's like to live like the rest of us.

To hear this sample response, listen to Track 579.

206. Sample response: I think the economy needs to be turned around. The unemployment rate keeps going up, and that's hurting a lot of people. The government should do something about it, but so should big companies. They're the ones firing and laying off people just to save money. Companies need to know that they're hurting real people just to get a little boost in their profit margin.

To hear this sample response, listen to Track 580.

207. Sample response: There are two exams that are each worth 25% of the grade, so the two exams together are worth half of the course grade. The midterm exam has multiple-choice and short answer questions. The final exam only has essay questions, no multiple-choice or short answers.

To hear this sample response, listen to Track 581.

208. Sample response: Students are expected to attend all the classes, and class attendance is 20% of the grade. There are also three short papers that must be turned in on time.

To hear this sample response, listen to Track 582.

209. Sample response: It is never good to miss too many classes, and you will lose some points for the classes you miss, but one week won't kill your grade. It's very important that you don't miss any paper deadlines because of your trip. You should also check the course schedule to make sure you won't be gone during the midterm or final. A business trip is not a medical excuse or a personal emergency, so you won't be given a makeup or extension because of this trip.

To hear this sample response, listen to Track 583.

210. Sample response: I appreciate that you're concerned about our missing the beginning of a surprise birthday party. I would like to avoid being late, but these things do happen. If you want, I can drive down to the bus stop and pick you up. That will probably save some time. I can leave immediately, but I may not get there before your bus arrives. If you bus does arrive before I get there, don't get on it. I'll call you on your cell phone when I'm almost there. See you soon.

To hear this sample response, listen to Track 584.

211. Sample response: I do think that technological gadgets make our lives more hectic and stressed. Just because we're able to be in constant communication with everybody, people expect that you'll be available whenever they call, text, or e-mail, and they often get upset if you don't answer immediately or get back to them quickly. Employers are particularly demanding. You're not just at work when you're in the office. Because you can always be reached, they think they can ask you to do more work outside the office. But even with all of that said, I still wouldn't want to do without technology. A simpler life might be less hectic, but I also think it would be more boring. I'll take the stress of a gadget-filled life over the boredom of a simpler life any day.

To hear this sample response, listen to Track 585.

212. Sample answer: Two people are using a credit card to shop online with their laptop computer.

213. Sample answer: A couple is shopping for apples at a farmer's market.

214. Sample answer: Two carpenters are putting a new roof on a house.

215. Sample answer: A girl is about to go down a slide at a playground.

216. Sample answer: A job applicant is having an interview with three people.

217. Sample answer:

I had been led to believe that a guided tour through the zoo would enrich my zoo experience, but I did not find that to be the case. I expected to learn things about the animals, as well as the history of the zoo, that I would not be able to learn unless I took the tour, but this was not the case. The tour guide was very friendly and somewhat amusing, but all the information she gave us is also contained in the various brochures and signs available for free throughout the zoo. Your guided tours should provide something that is not already available to all zoo patrons. Otherwise they're just a waste of money.

218. Sample answer:

My ideal workplace is one where I feel like I'm part of a team. I want to know that I and my coworkers are all working toward the same goals and feel like success depends on all of us and belongs to all of us. My ideal boss is a person who is able to foster this kind of team spirit in his or her workers. To do this, the boss should be willing to do everything that the rest of us do and should be able, when necessary, to fill in for a team member who is absent for some reason. Another trait of my ideal boss is someone who is able to inspire his or her workers to do their best on every project. I want a boss who can bring out the best in me and those I work with.

219. The opinion essay should be well organized. Clear details and supporting statements should back up the opinion. Words should be spelled correctly and the grammar of each sentence should be correct. An example of a sample response is:

To me, happiness is the most important thing. There are many things to strive for in the world, but the reason people strive for them is because they think those things will make them happy. Everything that people are trying to do is ultimately aimed at making them happy.

Financial and personal success is means to an end. They can make a person happy, but they can also make a person unhappy. Rich people may not have the same problems that poor people have, but they still have problems. Wealth is no guarantee of happiness. But people who strive for wealth do so because they believe that money will bring them happiness, and in some cases, they are right.

However, it's easy to get caught up in the things you're striving for, the success you're trying to achieve, and forget that the purpose of striving for them is to bring happiness. If happiness comes from something simple like watching a sunset or playing with your children, then you should focus on doing these things rather than missing out on them because you are striving for success that might or might not bring you the happiness that you desire.

Chapter 3: Diagnostic Exam

Track 1
a. The man is presenting at today's seminar.
b. Please take a seat now.
c. He is attaching a name tag for the event.
d. He can prepare for a business seminar ahead of time.

Track 2
a. She is shopping at a grocery store.
b. She is asking questions about her food.
c. The woman is considering grapes at an outdoor market.
d. It is Sunday and the grocery store is closed now.

Track 3
a. She is learning more about her food.
b. This woman is on a diet.
c. She likes the box of cereal.
d. This woman will buy the pasta.

Track 4
a. The woman is ready to speak or listen.
b. She is taking part in a business meeting.
c. She is talking on the telephone.
d. The woman is listening to music while she works.

Track 5
a. Friends like to shop together.
b. They are surprised to have met in the store.
c. The sisters like to shop.
d. They like to talk about their purchases.

Track 6
a. The dog will require his rabies vaccination.
b. Dog bites can happen every day.
c. The vet is examining the dog's head.
d. Pets make excellent companions.

Track 7
a. The man is preparing for a meeting.
b. He is analyzing information.
c. The computer is not working correctly.
d. A file has been erased from the hard drive.

Track 8

a. These are the successful tools of any business.
b. Every business person needs to be professional and organized.
c. It is time for a meeting.
d. These are some ways to communicate in business.

Track 9

a. This couple is surfing together.
b. They are ready to go surfing.
c. This married couple is taking a vacation.
d. They need more than one surfboard.

Track 10

a. She is holding the dog on her lap.
b. She must be careful when picking up the dog.
c. She cannot take a picture because she is standing on one leg.
d. She is going to pick some flowers from the window box.

Track 11

Where are the washrooms?
a. The cafeteria is closed now.
b. They are just down the hall.
c. When can you visit us?

Track 12

I would like to hold the meeting at 3 o'clock.
a. Great, I'll meet you at three.
b. Is it lunchtime now?
c. The bathrooms are over there.

Track 13

Please finish this report by tomorrow morning.
a. Sure, that would be no problem.
b. When did you want to visit?
c. I should leave now.

Track 14

When is the office open?
a. Every day is a good day to visit.
b. When can we travel to see him?
c. Every day from eight to five.

Track 15

The deadline for the project is fast approaching.
a. Why should he do all the work?
b. We should work more quickly on the project.
c. Why change the budget on the project?

Track 16

Would you like to visit the park during lunch?
a. Where is the office?
b. Let's make an appointment now.
c. Sure, I'd love to eat there.

Track 17

I am having computer problems.
a. I can call the IT department.
b. Where is the report?
c. Is the file due now?

Track 18

Where can I find the executive assistant?
a. You can see our printers here.
b. His office is just down the hall.
c. Where is the washroom?

Track 19

I would like to make an appointment for tomorrow.
a. Sure, what time is convenient?
b. No, thank you, I'd rather not.
c. Let's try the office later.

Track 20

Would you like to come back later to have lunch?
a. Sure, we could finish typing the draft.
b. Sure, maybe it will be less busy.
c. When can we make an appointment?

Track 21

Where could we find resources for this project?

- **a.** The airplane leaves from that gate.
- **b.** Why should we make a reservation?
- **c.** The library has many good sources.

Track 22

When are the sales reports due?

- **a.** Where is the manager?
- **b.** Lunch is being served.
- **c.** I was told by three this afternoon.

Track 23

Is this a dress event or a casual event?

- **a.** Where can I find a suit?
- **b.** You should wear business casual.
- **c.** This suit doesn't fit.

Track 24

Where did you park the car?

- **a.** I think I am late for lunch.
- **b.** Let's go over the meeting notes.
- **c.** I think I am in Lot 3.

Track 25

I can't remember where I parked the car.

- **a.** This parking garage is underground.
- **b.** We should have lunch.
- **c.** We should look for a parking attendant.

Track 26

Would you like a newspaper to read?

- **a.** I don't like eggs.
- **b.** That would be nice, thank you.
- **c.** When can I expect to see him?

Track 27

How can I send a fax on this printer?

- **a.** Here is the instruction booklet.
- **b.** I would like to print five sheets, please.
- **c.** I do not need to make copies now.

Track 28

Could you help me with this copy machine, please?

- **a.** I prefer not to sit here.
- **b.** Where are they going?
- **c.** I would be glad to.

Track 29

Who is responsible for the catering at this event?

- **a.** Why is he leaving?
- **b.** I think the company is called Acme Food Services.
- **c.** I am feeling unwell.

Track 30

What can I expect at the conference?

- **a.** Should I wear a tie?
- **b.** I can arrive no later than four.
- **c.** There will be three speakers.

Track 31

Where can I put this letter for the accountant?

- **a.** I can give it to him.
- **b.** Yes, please, I would like that.
- **c.** I'd rather fax it, anyway.

Track 32

When is the auditor available?

- **a.** There is an appointment available at two.
- **b.** No, he is not.
- **c.** I think the office is here.

Track 33

Why is the vice-president upset?

- **a.** He will see you now.
- **b.** I think he got some bad news.
- **c.** What a busy day I had.

Track 34

Where did you get that coat?

- **a.** I'd like to celebrate this event.
- **b.** Blue is the most flattering color.
- **c.** At the new store downtown.

Track 35

Who is in charge of ordering food for this meeting?

   a. We have plenty of time to order meals.

   b. Where is the reception room?

   c. I think the receptionist will do that.

Track 36

Where should we meet to discuss the new project?

   a. How about the library?

   b. Which flight is he on?

   c. I don't like early mornings.

Track 37

What should we do about the new deadline?

   a. I have an idea for lunch.

   b. We will have to work late tonight now.

   c. Why is he in a hurry?

Track 38

Let's go to the concert tonight.

   a. That sounds like fun.

   b. Where is the car?

   c. I think I lost my file.

Track 39

When should we have the birthday party?

   a. Why have a party for her?

   b. How about Sunday night?

   c. How about my house?

Track 40

Why do you want to throw a party for him?

   a. She is happy to see us.

   b. I'd be happy to attend the party.

   c. It's his birthday.

Track 41

(*Man*) I think I'm going to volunteer.

(*Woman*) Oh, really? Where?

(*Man*) I was thinking of volunteering at my local library. They have a program for people who are new to this country.

(*Woman*) What will you be doing?

(*Man*) I would sit around and talk to newcomers to offer them encouragement.

(*Woman*) That sounds like a great opportunity.

(*Man*) I think it will be.

(*Woman*) I look forward to hearing about the people you meet.

Track 42

What does the man plan to do?

Track 43

What does the woman suggest will be discussed in future conversations?

Track 44

Where will the man meet people?

Track 45

(*Woman*) My instructor didn't show up for my evening class yesterday.

(*Man*) What happened?

(*Woman*) We sat around for half an hour and then everyone left.

(*Man*) Maybe he was sick.

(*Woman*) That's possible. Many of us in the class have had the flu.

(*Man*) That's annoying.

(*Woman*) Yes, it is. I hope next time there's a note on the class door if he's absent.

(*Man*) A note would be helpful.

Track 46

What problem is the woman having?

Track 47

What can we assume the woman would have preferred?

Track 48

Why does the woman think it's likely the instructor was ill?

Track 49

(*Woman*) I don't know where to get some sources for this work project.

(*Man*) What is it about?

(*Woman*) It's about whether our customers enjoy our new perfume.

(*Man*) You could interview some customers.

(*Woman*) Yes, but I'm shy.

(*Man*) You could ask customers through an online poll.

(*Woman*) I'm not good with computers.

(*Man*) You could go to a store and watch customers in the perfume aisle buying the product.

(*Woman*) That's a good idea. I'll try that.

Track 50

Why does the woman not take the first two pieces of advice the man offers her?

Track 51

Why can we assume the woman takes the man's final piece of advice?

Track 52

What does the woman hope to find out?

Track 53

(*Man*) Our accountant seems in a bad mood.

(*Woman*) He is. He got a big dent in his new car.

(*Man*) Oh, no! What happened?

(*Woman*) His daughter drove the car into a garbage can.

(*Man*) Well, at least no one was hurt.

(*Woman*) Yes, but he'll have to pay for the damage.

(*Man*) That will be expensive.

(*Woman*) He could always ask for a raise.

Track 54

What is implied about the accountant's daughter?

Track 55

What is bothering the accountant?

Track 56

What did the accountant's daughter hit?

Track 57

(*Man*) I'm so tired today.

(*Woman*) Why is that?

(*Man*) I was up late working on the final sales report.

(*Woman*) At least you got it done.

(*Man*) Yes, but it was really hard to do; my printer broke.

(*Woman*) I heard the vice-president say it was really good, though.

(*Man*) Really?

(*Woman*) Yes, and that should be good news for your promotion.

Track 58

What good news does the woman give to the man?

Track 59

Why did the man have trouble finishing his sales report?

Track 60

How does the man feel after finishing his sales report?

Track 61

(*Woman*) I'm going to France next week for a wedding.

(*Man*) That's exciting. Have you ever been there before?

(*Woman*) Yes, I studied there for three years.

(*Man*) Me, too. I studied art there six years ago.

(*Woman*) I love the food in France.

(*Man*) I loved the art galleries most.

(*Woman*) It's fun to travel.

(*Man*) Just as long as you don't have to wake up early for a flight.

Track 62

What does the man enjoy about France?

Track 63

Who has been to France before?

Track 64

Why is the woman traveling to France?

Track 65

(Woman) I hate Mondays.

(Man) They are not so bad.

(Woman) They're pretty bad. I hate to wake up early after sleeping in.

(Man) If we didn't have to come back on Monday, we'd still have to come back to work on Tuesday.

(Woman) That would be just as bad.

(Man) At least we get two days off on the weekend.

(Woman) That's true. That gives me lots of time to go boating.

(Man) Me, I like to stay in and read on weekends.

Track 66

Why does the woman hate Mondays?

Track 67

What does the woman like to do on weekends?

Track 68

What argument does the man use to show the woman Mondays are not so bad?

Track 69

(Man) I'm going back to school.

(Woman) Really? What will you study?

(Man) I'm going to take a business degree so that I can get a better job.

(Woman) My cousin did that and now he works for a big company.

(Man) Does he like it?

(Woman) Yes, but it was hard for him to take four years off. He has big student loans.

(Man) I'm going to night school so that won't happen.

(Woman) That's probably a good idea, although you'll have to find time for homework, too.

Track 70

Why does the man want to go back to school?

Track 71

What problem does the woman's cousin have?

Track 72

Why does the man decide to go to night school?

Track 73

(Woman) I'm going to get involved in local politics this year.

(Man) Really? What will you do?

(Woman) I will go door-to-door to talk to voters about the next general election.

(Man) Why would you do that?

(Woman) I believe in my local parties and I think more voters would vote if they could talk to a party representative about it.

(Man) I don't vote.

(Woman) Well, I'll come to your house to convince you to vote, then.

(Man) But I don't vote because I'm not a citizen yet.

Track 74

What will the woman be doing to support her local political party?

Track 75

Why does the man not vote?

Track 76

Why does the woman want to take part in politics?

Track 77

(Woman) I think my computer is broken.

(Man) What makes you say that?

(Woman) My screen goes blank and I can't get my mouse to work.

(Man) Are you sure you don't have your monitor set on a timer so it turns off after a while?

(Woman) Maybe. I don't know. I'm not very good with my new computer.

(Man) You got a new computer at work, then?

(Woman) Yes, and I still have to read the manual for it.

(Man) I'll stop by your office after lunch to help you.

Track 78

What does the woman need to do about her new computer?

Track 79

What solution does the man offer the woman?

Track 80

Does the man think the computer is the problem?

Track 81

This year, at the company, we would like to create a new workshop. This workshop will be called "Creating Team Players" and will take place during the annual sales meeting in July. Every employee will be grouped into a team, consisting of employees across all departments. Each team will have a mentor, who will guide participants through activities that will help employees learn how to work together. We hope that the workshop will allow everyone in the company to get to know each other. Other companies have had very good success with this type of workshop, so we hope we will also see improved productivity and cooperation after this workshop. If the first workshop is successful, "Creating Team Players" will be held every year. Let's have fun at this first workshop in July!

Track 82

What is the purpose of the workshop?

Track 83

For whom is the workshop?

Track 84

Who will be in each group?

Track 85

I would like to introduce Andrew Smith. Mr. Smith is a motivational speaker, an author, and a global expert on creativity in the workplace. We all know that creative thinking is important in creating new ideas, in marketing and in every area of business. Mr. Smith helps companies reach success by teaching employees, management, and all people within a company how to be more creative. Having studied in Stanford University, Mr. Smith founded his own business, Creative Works, which provides seminars, workshops, and creativity programs for businesses. Mr. Smith has helped small businesses and Fortune 500 companies in the United States, Canada, Japan, and Europe become more creative and profitable. Here at this year's "Reaching the Stars" business conference, Mr. Smith will be talking about the role of creative thinking in business. There will be a question period after his talk.

Track 86

Where is this speech taking place?

Track 87

Who is Mr. Smith?

Track 88

Why is the topic of the talk *creativity*?

Track 89

For those of us who are new to the "Better Sales Today" conference, I'd like to welcome you to this year's conference. As you may know, our conference helps sales and marketing professionals develop their skills. Through workshops, discussions, and lectures, we help professionals learn the latest news in the world of sales and marketing. Of course, we also provide opportunities for networking. Please register for the workshops you are interested in at the registration desk to my right. Each participant may select up to ten workshops, lectures, and discussion panels. Please look over all the conference opportunities and select up to ten discussions, lectures and workshops that you feel will be most helpful to you. Then, fill out your registration sheet, checking off the events you will participate in.

Track 90

What are the three goals of the conference?

Track 91

How can participants take part?

Track 92

How is the conference organized?

Track 93

Hello, class, I am your new instructor for this class, "History 101." Dr. Stevens, your former instructor, has asked me to take over this class. My name is Dr. Terry and my specialty at this university is Modern Western History. Even though we will be working together from now on, the class will proceed much as it would under Dr. Stevens. We will begin where you left off—with a discussion of World War I. The final exam will still cover everything you will have learned during the year, which means it will cover everything from the Ottoman Empire to the Cold War. The only significant change is that your final term papers will be due on April 8 instead of March 31. I look forward to working with you and if you have any questions, please see me after class.

Track 94

How would you describe this speech?

Track 95

Where is this talk most likely to take place?

Track 96

What is one change that is announced?

Track 97

Hello, passengers, and welcome to Cloud 9 Airlines, flight 767, with nonstop service to London. As we prepare for our flight, we ask that you avoid using your cell phones or your laptops, as these devices prevent airplane systems from working correctly. Please wait until we have landed in London to use your mobile devices. Please store your carry-on luggage in the overhead compartments or under the seat in front of you. If you need assistance, our flight attendants would be happy to help. This is a nonsmoking flight

and we will be offering a film as well as lunch. If you like, you can purchase headphones from one of the flight attendants to view the movie. The flight safety demonstration will begin shortly.

Track 98

What is happening in this talk?

Track 99

When can passengers use mobile devices?

Track 100

What entertainment is offered on the flight?

Track 101

Hello, class, I am your guest lecturer today and I will be speaking about the Romantic Era. The Romantic Era, or the Age of Romanticism, began in the late 1700s in Western Europe. During this age, many famous composers and writers created masterpieces that we still enjoy today. Romanticism was a reaction to the Age of Enlightenment, which emphasized science and reason. The Romantics praised art instead. During the Age of Romanticism emotion was something to be proud of. Artists and writers considered nature in a spiritual or emotional sense rather than through science. They looked to foreign countries for inspiration and new topics.

Track 102

Where is this conversation likely taking place?

Track 103

What is the speaker discussing?

Track 104

What was Romanticism a reaction to, according to the speaker?

Track 105

Attention, travelers. Train 7707 with service to Boston has been delayed due to bad weather. There is a storm system moving into our current location and this has resulted in delays. We ask that all passengers remain in the terminal and await further instructions. We will announce any changes or updates over the intercom system as information becomes available. If you wish to get a refund for your ticket, please go to the refund desk near the clock. We hope to get you on your way soon. We apologize for the delay and thank you for your patience.

Track 106
Why is there a delay?

Track 107
What options are presented to passengers?

Track 108
What will be offered to passengers?

Track 109
Welcome back, listeners. Today on CRKC Radio Boston, we will be playing your favorite songs of today and yesterday. But first, the traffic report. Traffic is heavy on Highway 101, due to a tractor trailer accident. There is a stalled car on Windmill Road, and we'd like to thank callers for reporting that to our studios. Our CRKC Radio Boston helicopter crew reports that there is heavy traffic through the downtown area, where congestion seems to be a problem. Construction work is slowing traffic in the East End, near Main Street. Stay safe on the roads, listeners, and call in your traffic reports as you see them. Our telephone number here at CRKC is 555-6567.

Track 110
Where does the speaker get his information?

Track 111
What problems are there on the roads?

Track 112
What does the speaker request?

Track 113
Welcome, neighbors. I'm not sure how many of you know me, but my name is Victor Patel and I am running for local office. Like many of you, I believe in our community and I feel that we need to make changes. I am asking for your vote today because I know I can make some positive changes here. I am tired of local politicians not taking care of my concerns. I understand your concerns because I share them. If you vote for me, I will work very hard to improve our schools, our hospitals, and the safety of our streets. I have worked as an attorney in this neighborhood for 20 years and I am ready to start making some positive changes, with your help.

Track 114
What is the speaker's current job?

Track 115
What is the speaker trying to do?

Track 116
What does the speaker think he can change in the community?

Track 117
We'd like to thank the viewers of TV 101 New York for sending in pictures of the current weather conditions. My name is Stacey Abbot and here is your local weather. A low pressure system is moving in, bringing with it wintry conditions. Over the next 24 hours, expect strong winds, blowing snow, cold temperatures, and accumulation of 20 inches. It's our first major snowstorm of the season, so get ready, New York. We can expect delays and cancellations, so if you are traveling, call ahead. Once the snow starts, avoid driving if possible, since blowing snow is expected to create very poor visibility.

Temperatures will drop rapidly overnight, so dress warmly and make sure to keep your pets indoors.

Track 118

What is the best way to describe this short conversation?

Track 119

What is being forecast?

Track 120

What should viewers do?

Track 121

Buying your first home can be a challenge, but there are many people and services to help you. Your real estate agent, for example, can help you find a home that suits your needs and budget and will guide you through the process of buying the home. A mortgage professional will help you get the loan you need to buy your home. Many banks have workshops and offer free services to first-time homebuyers, too. These seminars and workshops cover all the basics and help you understand what you need to do to buy your home. It can seem challenging to buy a property, but it can be done.

Track 122

London Spa Services provides all the modern technology and tools you need for looking your best. Spa services include full hair services, makeup application, massage, and many relaxation services that help you ease away stress and look your best. You may want to book a waxing appointment or a nail appointment for a special occasion. Maybe you would like to buy a gift certificate to treat that someone special to a little pampering. London Spa Services has the professionals, the products, the services, and the facilities to make it happen. At London Spa Services, we are ready to help you feel and look your best.

Track 123

The woman, man, and two boys are fishing outdoors. The boys are holding the fishing rods. Everyone is looking at the camera and smiling. The weather is bright and the adults are wearing sunglasses.

Track 124

I have worked with computers three years and have studied them in school. I am familiar with them and use them every day.

Track 125

I prefer laptop computers with a Windows system. I like to be able to travel with my computer.

Track 126

I most often use my computer for word processing and e-mail at work. I surf the Internet each day, so the Internet is important to me. Once a week, I create a presentation using PowerPoint. A few times a month, I use a spreadsheet to calculate sales.

Track 127

We have a vegetarian stir-fry made with grilled vegetables and tofu. If you enjoy seafood, we offer a salmon dinner with vegetables or seafood pasta.

Track 128

Our prices range from $9 for a child's dinner to $30 for a steak dinner.

Track 129

Our child menu items are $9. We offer fish and chips, hamburger and French fries, or sandwiches for children under twelve. Your son will also receive an ice cream with his choice of dinner.

Track 130

Hello, My name Stacey Williams, and I saw an ad for your company, Wilson Recruiters. I understand that you help people find work. Well, I am a receptionist. I used to work for a dentist's office downtown but I am now looking for work. I have never used a recruiter service before. I went on your company website and noticed that I can upload my resume to your website. Is that how this service will work? You can reach me at 555-6888. If you could get back to me with more details of how to apply, that would be great.

Track 131

Hello, Stacey, my name is Anna and I work for Wilson Recruiters. You are correct—you can apply for any position by uploading your resume to our website. Once we have your resume, we pair you with companies who ask us to find them good employees. We sometimes call to ask for additional information about your experience and education, so that we can better help you find a job. You can also choose to come in to the offices to drop off your resume in person. That way, we can discuss your work search further. If I can be of any assistance, please feel free to call.

Track 132

I think that both natural medicine and modern medicine have their place, because they are not two different things. Many modern medicines are based on old practices. Modern scientists are always finding new herbs and plants that cure diseases, and plants have been used for a long time to make us healthy. Not all plants and natural cures are healthy, either, while many modern medicines have side effects. I think that trying to stay healthy with good diet and exercise is important, even though diet and exercise are not very modern ideas. However, if someone gets sick it is very useful to be able to run accurate tests with modern scanners and equipment to find the cause of the problem. I would not want to choose between natural and modern medicine, because both are important and both work together to keep us healthy.

Chapter 4: Listening Comprehension Review

Track 133

  a. This woman has a medical condition.
  b. This woman works in a clothing store.
  c. This woman is a laboratory assistant.
  d. This woman is speaking on the telephone.

Track 134

  a. The woman is pointing something out to the man.
  b. These coworkers are sharing a joke.
  c. They are studying.
  d. The man and woman are preparing a report.

Track 135

  a. These people are preparing for a presentation.
  b. These people are examining some paperwork.
  c. They are reading a newspaper.
  d. These businesspeople are worried.

Track 136

  a. The people are waiting for the business seminar to begin.
  b. The business seminar room has been changed.
  c. The business seminar has been cancelled.
  d. Where is the washroom?

Track 137

  a. The man is afraid his strategies will not work.
  b. What time is it?
  c. He is creating a plan.
  d. He is late.

Track 138

  a. The people are late for a meeting.
  b. They are late because the meeting room has been changed.
  c. There is no time for lunch.
  d. They are hurrying.

Track 139

a. These peppers are for sale.
b. These vegetables are not fresh.
c. Vegetables help lower the risk of heart disease.
d. Is spicy food bad for you?

Track 140

Has the train schedule changed since last month?

a. I think the washrooms are still over here.
b. No, the flight is still leaving from the same gate.
c. Yes, the Boston train now leaves twice a day.

Track 141

This shirt would look great with that tie.

a. Yes, I think white and blue go together well.
b. I don't think this item is on sale.
c. What time do we need to get there?

Track 142

How can we get the presentation done sooner?

a. When can we have lunch?
b. We could work on the project in the evenings.
c. Let's see a later movie.

Track 143

This amusement ride looks too scary.

a. I love horror movies, so I think I'd really like it.
b. I don't think our accountant would approve.
c. Let's go outside, since it is such a nice day.

Track 144

Where is the sales seminar this year?

a. Tuscon
b. Three o'clock
c. Next week

Track 145

Let's try the new Italian restaurant for lunch.

a. Yes, it's very complicated.
b. Sure, I love pizza.
c. Let's go ahead and buy it.

Track 146

(Man) I'd love to try that new Caribbean place for lunch today. I hear they have amazing food.

(Woman) I read a great review of them in the newspaper but I don't really know much about Caribbean cuisine. Is it vegetarian?

(Man) I've never tried it either, but I understand that it's rather spicy. I think there are some meat dishes and some vegetarian meals.

(Woman) I love spicy food, so I think I'd like to try that new place. I love to try new foods, but since I've been a vegetarian for five years I need to make sure any new restaurant has vegetable dishes.

Track 147

How much do the speakers know about Caribbean food?

Track 148

What specific diet does the woman follow?

Track 149

Overall, how open are both speakers to trying new foods?

Track 150

(Man) I just read the best book. It was the true story of a British man who lives in France for a year and starts a new life there. He learns to cook French food and buys a French house.

(Woman) Really? That sounds so romantic. I love to read about people who follow their dreams, no matter what.

(Man) Well, what I really love about the book is that it does not focus too much on the romantic. It really shows the man's struggle to make a new life for himself.

(Woman) Oh, then maybe it's not the book for me. I like to read true stories that are uplifting and not about hardship.

Track 151

What does the woman like to read?

Track 152

What does the man like about the book he has just read?

Track 153

What is the book the man read about?

Track 154

We are pleased to welcome author Emma Hardy here today to speak to our book club about her novels and to read an excerpt from her latest work. As many of you know, Emma Hardy has had a very successful career. She was born and raised in London, England, before moving to Los Angeles as a teenager. She began to write and publish in her early twenties, first in underground horror fiction magazines. When she was 28, she published her first novel, *Mysteries of the Gory Hand*, a book that went on to win the American Horror Writers' Prize for Best Horror Novel of the Year. Since then, Emma Hardy has published 20 more novels, many of them award-winning, and has earned a reputation as one of the best horror writers in our community. Her latest work, *The Gory Stranger*, will be made into a film next year. We're very excited to have her here today at our book club to read from this exciting novel, and without further ado, please help me welcome Emma Hardy.

Track 155

What sort of novels does Emma Hardy write?

Track 156

Where does this short talk take place?

Track 157

How would you best characterize this talk?

Track 158

Hello, travelers, and welcome to the Halifax ferry. Before stepping on board today, please listen to the following safety procedures, provided for your security. When entering the ferry, please note that life jackets are located in the bins above each seat as well as in the storage boxes at the end of each row of seats. In the unlikely event of an accident, please remove life jackets from their storage places and put them on before proceeding to the nearest emergency exit. Emergency exits on the boat are clearly marked with red circles. Life preservers are located near the life jackets. Please note that there is no running permitted on the deck or the ramp leading to the ferry.

Track 159

Where is this announcement taking place?

Track 160

What should passengers do in an emergency?

Track 161

What safety devices are provided?

Chapter 6: Speaking Review

Track 162

Hello, my name is Amar. Several days ago, I put gasoline in my car at your station, and purchased a car wash. I did not have time to go through the wash that day, but kept my receipt and car wash code. Last night, I came back to wash my car. I punched my code into the machine at the entrance to the wash, and was told that the code is invalid. The receipt indicates that the code should be valid for another five days, so it should not have expired yet. Could you please give me a call and let me know what I can do about this? I purchased the supreme wash with wax, so it was rather expensive and I don't want to just lose the money. Again, my name is Amar, and I can be reached at 555-6441.

Track 163

Hello, my name is Jannelle. I'm calling about a package your company was supposed to pick up from my office this morning. I called yesterday and made arrangements for the package to be picked up between 9 and 10 o'clock this morning, and have it shipped to our office in Los Angeles. It is nearly 2:00 P.M. now, and no one has come to pick it up yet. The contents of the package are needed in that office by noon Friday for a very important seminar. I will only be at work until 4:30 today, and no one else will be available to give it to you after that time. It is very important that this package be in Los Angeles on time. The seminar cannot take place without these materials. Please call me and let me know what needs to be done. My number is 555-8790. Thank you.

Track 164

Hello, this is Roderick Jones. I placed an order with you yesterday morning, and neither of the arrangements I paid for have been delivered. Both were supposed to have been sent yesterday. The first was a potted plant with balloons for my secretary, whose anniversary with the company is today. The second was an order of one dozen roses for my wife. She got a promotion at work, and I wanted her to know how proud I am. I don't want either of these important people to think that I forgot about their accomplishments. Today is Friday, and both will be out of their offices over the weekend. I'd really like to have this taken care of today, before they leave work. I use your services often, and have always been happy with your flowers and prompt delivery. Please let me know what can be done about this oversight. Could you please give me a call? My number is 555-9476. Thank you.

Track 165

One of the most difficult aspects of beginning a new job may have little to do with the job requirements themselves. New employees often report that relationships with coworkers and being unfamiliar with office procedures are the biggest hurdles to overcome in the workplace. Obviously, it is important to build a professional relationship with colleagues. But, such relationships often take time to nurture. Maintaining a polite attitude and offering a friendly smile are easy ways to set the right tone with coworkers. Learning office procedures is often a matter of time as well. Employee manuals, observation, and asking colleagues for assistance are likely the best sources of this information.

Track 166

Have you been considering new furniture for your home or office? Well, now is a great time to take advantage of the closeout prices at Seat Yourself Furniture! Our entire stock is on sale from now until the end of the month. We have executive desks, swivel chairs, and file cabinets for the workplace. We have sectionals, ottomans, and recliners for the living room. Whether your style is comfortable or elegant, casual or professional, we have the pieces to suit your life. Buy individual pieces, or buy the entire room. Either way, everything is on sale!

Track 167

As the holidays are approaching, we would like to inform all employees of changes to the work schedule during the next few weeks. Beginning November 15, all employees will have the option of a four-day work week through the end of the year. Employees taking advantage of this opportunity will be expected to report to work one hour earlier than their current eight-hour daily schedule, and stay one hour later each day, Monday through Thursday. This will allow them to continue working 40 hours per week, while being able to take Fridays off. Employees choosing to continue with their current schedules may do so.

Track 168

The salesman and the happy couple are sitting at a desk in the car dealership showroom. There are new car brochures on the table. The salesman is handing the keys to the woman. There is a silver car behind the couple.

Track 169

Several children wearing costumes are on the stage. They are looking at the audience. The children are dressed as bears and other woodland creatures.

Track 170

A female hairstylist is cutting a woman's hair. They are in a salon. The hairstylist is holding scissors, and the customer is wearing a black cape. A row of chairs and a shelf with bottles are in the background.

Track 171

A smiling man wearing a gray suit is presenting at a meeting. He is holding a marker and standing beside an easel with graphs on it. Several people are sitting at a table listening to him. There are cups and papers on the table.

Track 172

I travel for business an average of about four days each month. I take one two-week trip for pleasure each year, as well as several weekend getaways.

Track 173

I prefer to fly on business trips in order to get there and back as quickly as possible. My family and I enjoy driving on pleasure trips.

Track 174

The best pleasure trip we have taken was a Caribbean cruise. The trip lasted seven days, and we visited several beautiful islands. We enjoyed the beaches and snorkeling while in the islands. On the ship, we enjoyed the amazing food and stage shows each evening.

Track 175

I read the newspaper before work. During the day, I often use the Internet to get updates on important news and current events. In the evening, I watch the news on TV.

Track 176

I especially enjoy the newspaper because I can read it at my own pace, and select which articles interest me most.

Track 177

One advantage of TV news is that it is constantly being updated. World events can be reported as soon as they happen, and emergencies can be announced in a timely manner. The disadvantages are that you have to sit through commercials, and you have to watch stories you might not be interested in while waiting for the stories you do want to see.

Track 178

Registration begins at 8:00 A.M. and the conference is scheduled to end around 5:00 P.M., depending on the length of the discussion and questions in the final session.

Track 179

Breakfast will be provided, and attendees will be on their own for lunch. A list of nearby restaurants will be available at the registration tables so you can choose a place to eat.

Track 180

In the morning, you will be able to choose a session offering tips for new agents. In the afternoon, you can choose a session specializing in health policies. General sessions for everyone will discuss changing trends in the business, helping customers choose a policy, and continuing education requirements. These should be helpful to everyone.

Track 181

Classes cost $145 per semester hour. Fees are due by the second meeting of the class.

Track 182
This semester Dr. Diaz will be teaching Writing for Business I on Monday and Wednesday evenings, and Accounting and Marketing on Tuesday and Friday evenings.

Track 183
Writing for Business I is offered on Tuesdays and Thursdays from 5:00 to 7:30 P.M. Advertising and Marketing II is offered on Monday, Wednesday, and Friday evenings from 5:00 to 6:45 P.M. Also, Accounting is offered on Tuesdays from 3:00 to 8:00 P.M. The other classes are in session until at least 9:00.

Track 184
Hello Amar, my name is Logan. I am calling from the gas station and want to apologize for the inconvenience with our car wash last night. I know that must have been frustrating for you. Please stop by the gas station at your convenience, and we will provide you with a new code for the car wash. I would be glad to personally oversee the wash process to be sure the code works properly, and that you are pleased with the outcome when your car is finished. Also, we would like to give you coupons for three free supreme car washes at our station. We appreciate your business, and want to be sure your experience with us leaves you happy. When you stop by, ask for me, Logan, or our manager Terrell. We're looking forward to serving you. Thanks.

Track 185
Hi, Jannelle. This is Adrienne with the delivery service. Let me apologize for the delay in getting your package picked up. Rest assured, we guarantee our work, and will get your package to Los Angeles in plenty of time. I will send a representative to your office right now to pick up the package. If you have to leave before he gets there, let us know. We will have someone pick up the package from your home, or from any other location that is convenient for you. I have upgraded the status of your order, and am sending the package overnight at our expense. It will be in your Los Angeles office by 10:00 tomorrow morning, which will be more than 24 hours before the meeting. We would also like to offer to upgrade your next delivery to priority shipping, at no extra charge. Thank you for your business.

Track 186
Hello, Mr. Jones, this is Aimee from the florist shop. I am so sorry about the oversight with your order. Our computer went down yesterday morning, and unfortunately several orders were lost. I understand your frustration and will make sure that you, your wife, and your secretary are happy with our services. We are delivering your orders right now, and have added a coffee mug filled with chocolate to your secretary's plant. Also, we added an extra dozen roses and some orchids to your wife's vase. Since you have been a valued customer for so long, we had both of these addresses on file. Also, we would like for you to come in and select a potted plant for your own office as our way of thanking you for your loyal business.

Track 187
I think it is a nice idea for bosses to hire their friends and family. It is important to be able to get along with the people you work with. Hiring people you already get along with ensures that this will happen. This can make for a happier work environment for everyone. Also, bosses want employees who are honest and trustworthy. When hiring strangers, it's hard to know that the employee has these traits. By hiring people they already know, bosses can make sure that they have employees who can be trusted. Another advantage of hiring familiar people is that the boss already knows the person's skills. The boss can select friends or family members that he believes are capable, and a good match for the job.

Track 188

I think it is better that current employees be offered positions as managers and supervisors, as long as someone from within the company is qualified. Offering these positions to employees is a way to reward loyalty. It encourages other employees to work hard so that they might be considered for upper level positions in the future. Also, current employees are already familiar with the way the company runs. They can continue current projects with less disruption. They also already know the other employees. Everyone is used to working together, and everyone knows the expectations. Hiring from within can make for a seamless transition.

Track 189

I think taking a job with low pay and good benefits is fine, if the benefits are important to the employee. The rising costs of health care today make insurance a valuable part of an employment package. It could be very expensive to purchase private insurance. Paying for insurance out of one's higher salary still might not provide the employee with much money left over. A low-paying job with benefits could actually give the employee more money in his pocket. Saving for the future is also important. A low-paying job with retirement benefits may provide security for the employee. It may also provide more money in the long run, if he or she has enough money to live on later in life.

Chapter 8: Practice Exam 1

Track 190
  a. The device is broken.
  b. He's on a flight.
  c. They're waiting for a bus.
  d. He spilled the coffee.

Track 191
  a. She forgot the check.
  b. She is ordering dinner.
  c. The restaurant is closed.
  d. She is paying with a credit card.

Track 192
  a. The shelves fell.
  b. The man is checking the inventory.
  c. The woman has an injury.
  d. The boxes are damaged.

Track 193
  a. The children are having fun in the pool.
  b. The children are having a picnic.
  c. This hotel has good rates.
  d. Do not run near a swimming pool.

Track 194
  a. The curtain is closed.
  b. A child is on the examining table.
  c. The doctor is checking his blood pressure.
  d. Nobody is inside the examining room.

Track 195
  a. The women are cooperating.
  b. She likes to exercise at the gym.
  c. They play soccer for exercise.
  d. She is preparing a healthy meal.

Track 196
  a. She's preparing for the meeting.
  b. She's closing her book.
  c. She's ironing her suit.
  d. She's giving a presentation.

Track 197

a. The receptionist is on the phone.
b. The woman hung up the phone.
c. She is turning off the computer.
d. The appointment is cancelled.

Track 198

a. They're shopping for a sofa.
b. They're having a family dinner.
c. They're playing a game.
d. They're putting away the toys.

Track 199

a. The woman is in a department store.
b. The woman is in a grocery store.
c. The woman is buying furniture.
d. The bananas are spoiled.

Track 200

Are you comfortable in that seat?

a. It's near the window.
b. Yes, I am fine here.
c. I don't want to bother him.

Track 201

How do I get to the post office from here?

a. The assistant usually takes the mail.
b. I will buy stamps.
c. Turn left at the stoplight.

Track 202

Will the manager be back soon?

a. He usually returns from lunch at 1:30.
b. I'm about to leave for lunch.
c. It's very nice to meet you.

Track 203

Where did you leave the tickets?

a. From the director.
b. They're on your desk.
c. To the ballet.

Track 204

How long did it take you to get here?

a. I drove.
b. It was very crowded.
c. Half an hour.

Track 205

The bank closes in 30 minutes.

a. We had better hurry and prepare the deposit.
b. I am making a deposit.
c. I'll call back tomorrow.

Track 206

Have you been to Chicago before?

a. I haven't ever met him.
b. I was there two years ago.
c. I have three.

Track 207

The meeting went well, didn't it?

a. Yes, it was definitely a success.
b. No, but I can do it tomorrow.
c. Yes, it is very warm.

Track 208

Did anyone call while I was out?

a. He explained it very clearly.
b. Yes, it's at 4 o'clock.
c. You have two messages.

Track 209

The flu is terrible this year.

a. Does she have a fever?
b. Yes, a lot of people have been sick.
c. I prefer to take the bus.

Track 210

Is the copier working yet?

a. He'll be here tomorrow.
b. Yes, it's very heavy.
c. No, it's still broken.

Track 211

Was the traffic bad today?

   a. I usually leave about 7:30.

   b. Yes, the freeway was pretty slow.

   c. I've never taken the train.

Track 212

How was your trip?

   a. It was wonderful.

   b. I prefer this one.

   c. Six days long.

Track 213

When did your flight arrive?

   a. It was very long.

   b. Flight 319 to Detroit.

   c. This morning at 5:30.

Track 214

Would you rather wait in the lobby or the bar?

   a. Let's stay in the lobby.

   b. Not right now, thank you.

   c. The reservation was cancelled.

Track 215

There will be a parade downtown this weekend.

   a. The mayor is not celebrating.

   b. I would like to see that.

   c. How many would you like?

Track 216

Did I leave my purse in here?

   a. I haven't seen it.

   b. It was very interesting.

   c. I am missing several.

Track 217

May I borrow this book?

   a. No, I probably won't.

   b. I can't tell from this.

   c. Of course, but please return it.

Track 218

Do you like sushi?

   a. I've never tried it.

   b. Fish and rice.

   c. It is from Japan.

Track 219

This data is confusing, isn't it?

   a. I rarely use it.

   b. No, I keep it current.

   c. Yes, it's difficult to analyze.

Track 220

When did you finish the report?

   a. I used to, but I don't anymore.

   b. Yesterday afternoon

   c. It's about our sales.

Track 221

Would you like to join us for lunch?

   a. I left it at the restaurant.

   b. It was very rainy this morning.

   c. No, thanks, I brought mine from home.

Track 222

Can I help you find something?

   a. I'm looking for a black skirt.

   b. I'm not going to make it.

   c. I'm not sure how far it is.

Track 223

This new printer is very fast.

   a. I can lend you mine.

   b. Paper and toner.

   c. Yes, it is much better than the old one.

Track 224

Where is the train station?

   a. It leaves in two hours.

   b. It is faster than the bus.

   c. Across from the park on MLK Street.

Track 225

What are you going to wear to the party?
- **a.** Everyone there was dressed elegantly.
- **b.** I bought a new jacket to wear.
- **c.** I hate to iron.

Track 226

How much do tickets to the game cost?
- **a.** They cost $60.00.
- **b.** I don't know the rules of baseball.
- **c.** I would love to go, thanks.

Track 227

Has the mail come today?
- **a.** Not yet, it's a little late.
- **b.** I haven't heard of that before.
- **c.** It has insufficient postage.

Track 228

I am having trouble with the Internet.
- **a.** Have you called a doctor?
- **b.** Have you checked the connection?
- **c.** I use it for research and entertainment.

Track 229

Why weren't you at work yesterday?
- **a.** I can't stay too long.
- **b.** I had an appointment.
- **c.** We're looking over the sales figures.

Track 230

(*Man*) Has the new catalog from J&R Supply come yet? I'm putting together our order for March, and I need to make sure that the model number is the same on these fittings.

(*Woman*) Isn't it early for the March order?

(*Man*) Yes, a little. I need to get the order in early just in case anything is on back order. If they don't have everything in stock, I'll have to look for a supplier that does.

(*Woman*) Aren't the other suppliers more expensive? I thought J&R had the best prices.

(*Man*) That's true, but they often run out of stock. For the next project to move quickly, we will need to have all our materials on hand. It is worth paying a little more for some things, if we don't have to wait for them.

(*Woman*) You are right. I'll call about the catalog today.

Track 231

Why does the man need the new catalog?

Track 232

What is the man worried about?

Track 233

When do they decide is the best time to call about the new catalog?

Track 234

(*Man*) I heard that the company is going to hire three new workers.

(*Woman*) That's true; they've already started interviewing for one position. Fred told me that one of the women they interviewed was amazing. She has a lot of experience and has really distinguished herself in the industry.

(*Man*) I am excited to hear that. It's always nice to have new ideas around. How long will they be interviewing?

(*Woman*) They will probably be finished next week.

(*Man*) Do you know when they expect the new worker to start?

(*Woman*) Fred said he hopes to have the position filled by the end of the month.

Track 235

How does the man feel about the company hiring a new worker?

Track 236

When is the company interviewing?

Track 237

Who was present at the interview?

Track 238

(*Man*) I am flying to Denver next month to meet with a new client. Have you been there before?

(*Woman*) Yes, but not since 1997.

(*Man*) Can you recommend a hotel? I've never been to Denver and I don't know anything about the city.

(*Woman*) I stayed in a small independent hotel called The Ridge. It was very nice and scenic, with a great restaurant and beautiful views. I know they have all the major chains there, too.

(*Man*) The Ridge sounds like what I had in mind. How long in advance did you have to book your reservation?

(*Woman*) Just a couple of weeks. I am sure you have plenty of time to make a reservation.

(*Man*) Thanks for the tip. That sounds perfect.

Track 239

What is the woman looking for?

Track 240

What is The Ridge?

Track 241

Why is the woman going to Denver?

Track 242

(*Man*) Have you gotten your paycheck yet? I got mine yesterday and I was overpaid by $200.

(*Woman*) No, I didn't get my check yet. Maybe you got a bonus. Sometimes that happens at this time of year.

(*Man*) Who can I ask about it?

(*Woman*) Why don't you talk to Peter in the human resources department? He is always very helpful.

(*Man*) I thought that Peter was out this week. Isn't his wife having surgery?

(*Woman*) You're right. Peter won't be back until Tuesday. You could also ask Cindy.

(*Man*) That's a good idea. I'll go talk to her right now. Thanks for the help.

(*Woman*) You're welcome.

Track 243

What is the man's concern?

Track 244

Why is Peter out of the office?

Track 245

In what department does Peter work?

Track 246

(*Woman*) Did you see that the new restaurant they have been working on down the street finally opened?

(*Man*) I just noticed that this morning. I would love to try it out.

(*Woman*) Well, would you like to have lunch there with me today?

(*Man*) I am having lunch with a client today, but I could join you tomorrow. We could even walk.

(*Woman*) That sound likes like fun. I'll mark it on my calendar. Let's also see if Sandra and Kristen in accounting want to come; they both seemed excited about the new restaurant.

(*Man*) Don't forget Luke. I bet he'd like to come, too.

(*Woman*) I'll invite all three of them this afternoon.

Track 247

Where is the new restaurant?

Track 248

Why can't they go to lunch today?

Track 249

Who will invite Kristin?

Track 250

(Speaker 1) I haven't seen Meredith all week. Is she away on business?

(Speaker 2) No, Meredith has strep throat. She is running a high fever and is resting in bed.

(Speaker 1) I am sorry to hear that. Have you talked to her?

(Speaker 2) Yes, I called her yesterday. She sounded awful, but she said she was starting a course of antibiotics. The doctor told her that she would probably be better in a few days.

(Speaker 1) And is her husband taking good care of her?

(Speaker 2) Yes, she said that Jim had made her chicken noodle soup and ginger tea.

Track 251

Where is Meredith?

Track 252

How long has Meredith been gone?

Track 253

Which of the following is Meredith not doing to recover?

Track 254

(Woman) The vegetable pastries you brought to the company party were wonderful. Did you buy the vegetables at the grocery store?

(Man) I rarely buy produce at the grocery store. I usually go the farmers' market.

(Woman) I didn't know there was a farmers' market nearby. Where is it?

(Man) It's in the lot across the street from the public library on Thursday evenings. I usually stop in there right after work.

(Woman) That is wonderful to find out. I have been very disappointed with the produce in my grocery store. It looks beautiful, but it doesn't have much flavor.

(Man) I like to shop at the farmers' market. It doesn't have the same variety as the supermarket, but the vegetables are always fresh.

Track 255

Why does the man buy vegetables at the farmers' market?

Track 256

When does the man go to the farmers' market?

Track 257

What did the man bring to the company party?

Track 258

(Man) I was just checking our inventory and I noticed that we were running low on rain suits. With the rainy season just around the corner, we had better hurry up and reorder.

(Woman) Thanks for letting me know. I will call our distributor today. Is there anything else you noticed that we need?

(Man) I made a list and left it on your desk. You can look it over when you get a chance, but the rain suits seem to be the most important thing on there.

(Woman) I probably won't get a chance to go over the full list until tomorrow, but I can call about the rain suits today.

(Man) I'd hate to not have them by the time the rain comes.

(Woman) Me, too. Thanks for the heads-up.

Track 259

What does the company need to buy?

Track 260

Why do the men need to hurry with their order?

Track 261

Where can he look to find out what else the company needs to order?

Track 262

(Woman) Do you know why the database is not showing up on my computer?

(Man) The server is down and Pat has been on the phone with the technical support person all morning trying to get it fixed.

(Woman) I really hope they can solve the problem today. I need some of that information to finish my report. I am working from an archive right now, but I will need the most recent data to finish it.

(Man) Pat says they will send a technician out this afternoon if we can't get it fixed by then. Would that give you enough time to finish?

(Woman) As long as I have access to the data at some point today, I should be able to finish. I don't mind staying a little late if I need to.

(Man) Well, hopefully it will be working soon enough that you won't have to.

Track 263

Who did Pat call to try to resolve the problem?

Track 264

Why might the woman need to work late?

Track 265

What does the woman need in order to complete her work?

Track 266

(Man) Are you going to the conference at the convention center next weekend? The speakers are usually very interesting and know a lot about the industry.

(Woman) I would like to go, but I'm not sure if I can make it. The convention center is a long way outside of town and the conference doesn't end until Sunday evening. I have a meeting early on Monday so I can't stay the night.

(Man) Couldn't you drive back Sunday night? That is what I am planning to do.

(Woman) I prefer not to drive at night.

(Man) You are welcome to ride with me if you like.

(Woman) That would be wonderful. Carpooling is always a good idea.

Track 267

Where is the conference?

Track 268

Why can't the woman drive home on Sunday?

Track 269

How does the coworker solve her problem?

Track 270

For the month of April, everyone needs to mark the following dates on his or her calendar. We will have mandatory staff meetings on the 7th and the 21st. The meetings, as always, will run from 9:00 to 10:30 A.M. Please prepare a brief report on your department's current project for the April 21st meeting. On the 16th there will be a representative here from our insurance provider. He will discuss changes to our health insurance packages. You can sign up to speak with him in person during lunch if you want to make changes to your plan. The deadline to enroll in the regional conference is Friday. Please let me know if you plan to attend. That's everything on the calendar for April.

Track 271

What is the main purpose of this talk?

Track 272

Why is the health insurance representative coming to the office?

Track 273

What will staff need to bring to the April 21st meeting?

Track 274

Attention, staff. The weather service is issuing a severe weather warning for the immediate area, beginning at 4:00 P.M. Due to the impending inclement weather, our offices will be closing at 3 o'clock. The forecast calls for severe thunderstorms with a chance of tornados. Please shut down and unplug all computers and other major electronic equipment. Please take home your laptops, the emergency calling procedures from your employee handbook, and any perishable food you may have in the refrigerators. The office will re-open at 7:00 A.M. tomorrow unless you are otherwise notified. Please drive safely.

Track 275

Where would you be likely to hear this announcement?

Track 276

What is the main message in the announcement?

Track 277

Which one of the following measures are office workers not asked to take?

Track 278

Hello, Mr. Flores, this is Pamela calling from Miller Industrial Supply. Your recent order, reference number PQ276890, will ship ground delivery tomorrow at 8:00 A.M. However, the steel couplings, item number 29971, are on backorder. That item will not ship until the seventh of next month. I am sorry for the inconvenience. We have adjusted your billing statement to reflect this change. Please call me back at 972-772-8301 at your convenience to confirm that you have received this message, and to let me know if you want to cancel the backordered item or have it shipped at the later date. Thank you.

Track 279

Who is the telephone message from?

Track 280

What is the problem?

Track 281

Why does the caller need her phone call returned?

Track 282

Would the owner of a green minivan, license plate number XHB-78S4, please report to the north parking lot immediately? The van is illegally parked. You are blocking a delivery truck and must move your vehicle immediately. The delivery truck cannot pass through to the unloading dock. Failure to move your vehicle in the next ten minutes will result in towing and possible fines. Thank you for your immediate attention to this matter.

Track 283

To whom is this announcement directed?

Track 284

What is the problem?

Track 285

What is a possible consequence of this situation?

Track 286

Hello, you have reached the technical support line of Etherwarecorp Software. All our technical support representatives are busy assisting other customers. We value your call and look forward to the opportunity to serve you. Please do not hang up. Your call will be answered in the order in which it was received. You will be asked for the license number of your product. Please have this information on hand. Your approximate wait time is nine minutes.

Track 287

Who would most likely hear this message?

Track 288

What should the listener have available?

Track 289

When will the listener be helped?

Track 290

Welcome to our 12th Annual Regional Conference on Municipal Water Quality. Before I introduce our presenters, I would like to note a few changes to the printed schedule at the front of your folder. Please take note of the following changes. The workshop entitled the "The Future of Chlorine" has been postponed. Due to the floods in Indianapolis, our presenter's flight was delayed. The "Future of Chlorine" workshop will now take place Wednesday in room 316. Also, the workshop called "Piping Solutions" has changed locations; it will be held in room 201. Please note these changes on your schedule. If you have not yet signed up for your workshops, you may do so in the lobby at the end of the convocation.

Track 291

Where is this talk being delivered?

Track 292

What is a consequence of the floods in Indianapolis?

Track 293

What workshop has changed rooms?

Track 294

As you can see from the graph, our sales were up significantly in November from last year. October sales were down a little, but the boost in November more than makes up for that decline. Looking at the quarter as a whole, our growth remains steady. And we have met our sales goal for the quarter. I want to congratulate all of you on this success. Everyone has worked hard to meet this goal. Our team is strong and dedicated. Thank you for your hard work. To celebrate, the company will provide lunch for the whole staff on Friday.

Track 295

What is the overall tone of this speaker?

Track 296

What is the main topic on which the speaker is reporting?

Track 297

What will happen on Friday?

Track 298

This is an automated message from Main Street Bank concerning your business credit card account ending in 8370. In order to maintain the security of your account, we are calling to inform you of irregular account activity taking place on October 2. Please call our customer service line at 800-999-2900 or visit our website at www.mainstreetbank.com to confirm the purchase. The transaction will not post without your approval. Thank you for your prompt attention to this matter. Please understand that we have taken this measure solely to ensure your account's security. Thanks for this opportunity to serve you. The security of your account is very important to us.

Track 299

Who is the speaker of this message?

Track 300

What is the problem?

Track 301

How can the problem be resolved?

Track 302

Attention, passengers waiting to board Flight 472 to Baltimore. Due to heavy snowfall in the Baltimore area, Flight 472 has been canceled. Weather conditions in Baltimore look to remain snowy throughout the morning and afternoon. The forecast does not indicate that conditions will improve for at least 24 hours. We will be unable to reschedule the flight until the National Weather Service lifts its Winter Storm Advisory. Please turn in your boarding passes at the desk for a voucher that you can use on the rescheduled flight or another flight. We are sorry for the inconvenience. As always, safety is our number one concern.

Track 303

Where is this announcement being made?

Track 304

What is the weather like in Baltimore?

Track 305

What should passengers do with their boarding passes?

Track 306

The annual marketing reports are due on January 12th. You will need to turn in a hard copy and a copy saved to a CD. They should include analysis for the previous year and projections for the coming year. You will need to highlight the areas in which our strategy has improved and pinpoint areas that still need improvement. Please also include any innovations your team has made and success stories. Please do not include any images, or unnecessary graphs or charts. Keep your analysis straightforward and only include graphs and charts that clarify the information. Thanks.

Track 307

Which of the following best describes the talk?

Track 308

Which of the following should be excluded from the report?

Track 309

How should the report be turned in?

Track 310

Hello, this Nancy Boyd. I'm calling because I am having a problem with the online order form on your website. I am trying to place an order online, but when I try to submit my order form electronically, I get an error message. I am not sure if the problem is with my computer or your website. I need to get my order in today for a rush delivery of materials that we need for our current project. Please call me back as soon as possible and let me know how I can resolve this problem. This order is very important for my business. Again, this is Nancy Boyd and phone number is 555-1234.

Track 311

Every day more and more people are changing their lifestyles in minor, and sometimes major, ways to minimize their environmental impact. Such small gestures as bringing reusable shopping bags to the grocery store, turning down the thermostat on the hot water heater, or hanging laundry outside to dry on sunny days can save millions of tons of fossil fuels a year. Some people are even making major investments in a greener future by installing solar panels in their homes or purchasing cars that run on alternative fuels. I am doing my part by switching my investment portfolio to Greensense Investments, where I can choose between several environmentally friendly mutual funds.

Track 312

Could your business stand to save thousands of dollars a year? How would it change your bottom line to hold all your business meetings online? Take our free trial to find out. You have nothing to lose! Business meetings require hours of employee planning, expenditures on food and refreshments, and wasted time in transit. It all adds up. For $55 a month you could cut those costs and save that time. Subscribe to our service and hold unlimited business meetings online for $55 a month. Setup is easy and the savings are huge. Visit netmeet.com for details.

Track 313

The couple is standing outside a home that is for sale. They are waiting while the Realtor talks on the phone. They seem nervous and excited, like maybe they are waiting for news. I think that they probably want to buy the house and the Realtor is calling about the price or to set up a tour.

Track 314

I use a credit card about once or twice a week. I pay for most of my regular monthly expenses with checks, and use cash for most daily purchases.

Track 315

I sometimes put gasoline on my credit card because it is convenient. I also use it for big purchases, like appliances or nice gifts.

Track 316

I don't think it is a good idea to use it so much that I can't pay it off at the end of the month. I think that people can get into financial trouble when they have too much debt. It makes sense to have a little debt if it improves your quality of life or makes important pursuits possible, but having a lot of debt is dangerous.

Track 317

The minimum pledge to become a member is $20. We have four suggested membership levels, but you can donate another amount if you like.

Track 318

Sample Response: We accept checks and major credit cards. We can also bill you later if you prefer.

Track 319

The Care and Share Foundation supports a number of local charities. We have been working since 1978 to help meet the critical needs of our community. We support local food banks, the homeless shelter, after-school programs for children, and many other causes.

Track 320

Hello, Ms. Boyd, this is Mr. Doe returning your call about the problem with our online order form. I am sorry about the inconvenience. We have been having problems with our website all week and are working with our web team to resolve them. I will be happy to take your order over the phone. If it is more convenient for you, you can fax the order in and I will be sure that it posts today. I understand that the order is important and I will be sure that you get a rush delivery. Would you like to place the order with me now?

Track 321

At this point in my life, I would be happy to move around to get ahead in my career. I think it is important to do this when you are young, so you can get a lot of experience before you have a family. Moving can be hard after you have a family. It is also hard to make any real civic contributions in a community if you are always moving, because by the time you know the politics and issues of a place, it's time to move again. At some point you have to settle down and commit to a place even if it means that you can't get ahead in your career as easily. I hope to be settled down by the time I'm 35.

Chapter 9: Practice Exam 2

Track 322
 a. They are eating their dinner.
 b. They are looking at a computer.
 c. They are looking out the window.
 d. They are walking down a hallway.

Track 323
 a. They are talking to each other.
 b. They are sitting at their desks.
 c. They are clapping their hands.
 d. They are listening to a speech.

Track 324
 a. They are all swimming.
 b. They are playing soccer.
 c. They are watching a film.
 d. They are running a race.

Track 325
 a. He is walking.
 b. He is laughing.
 c. He is talking.
 d. He is eating.

Track 326
 a. He is playing golf.
 b. He is watching TV.
 c. He is going on a hike.
 d. He is walking outside.

Track 327
 a. They are inside a house.
 b. They are going shopping.
 c. They are taking a walk.
 d. They are having a picnic.

Track 328
 a. They are laughing.
 b. They are standing up.
 c. They are having lunch.
 d. They are in a meeting.

Track 329
 a. She is riding a bike.
 b. She is walking a dog.
 c. She is singing a song.
 d. She is at a computer.

Track 330
 a. She is sitting at a table.
 b. She is drawing a diagram.
 c. She is waiting in a line.
 d. She is stretching out.

Track 331
 a. He is eating his lunch.
 b. The man is skiing down a hill.
 c. The man is typing a report.
 d. He is sitting at a desk.

Track 332
Where is the meeting room?
 a. Down the hall to the left.
 b. Yes, it is the mailroom.
 c. Are you having lunch?

Track 333
Which is my desk?
 a. Do you want to come?
 b. I am certain it is so.
 c. The one by the door.

Track 334
We are the first ones to arrive here.
 a. I thought we would be a little early.
 b. How far is it to the conference room?
 c. What is your social security number?

Track 335
Did you find the camera you lost?
 a. How far have we gone?
 b. No one knows where to go.
 c. Yes, it was in my briefcase.

Track 336

What supplies are you out of?

a. Where is my training CD?

b. I need more copy paper.

c. I am downloading a program.

Track 337

How long will the meeting be?

a. Probably only an hour.

b. Most employees voted yes.

c. I will remember to buy it.

Track 338

I need my computer upgraded.

a. No, we are out of stamps.

b. Fine, I can do that right away.

c. You can get the elevator here.

Track 339

How do I apply for the position?

a. When can I go to lunch?

b. I left my briefcase in here.

c. Just fill out these forms.

Track 340

When did you start here?

a. Friday was my first day of work.

b. Where can I get a new computer?

c. You can use the elevator on the right.

Track 341

Make sure to keep the door closed.

a. I definitely plan on doing that.

b. I didn't see the presentation.

c. It's downstairs in the basement.

Track 342

When are the trainees returning?

a. We have brand new computers.

b. They will arrive tomorrow at noon.

c. These are not the papers we need.

Track 343

Why are you unable to work?

a. Can I get a ride with you?

b. My computer is down.

c. It's at the end of the hallway.

Track 344

Where do new employees sign in?

a. We are late for the sales conference.

b. The seminar is on a new software program.

c. In the human resources department.

Track 345

The office will be closed on Monday.

a. Thanks for reminding me of that.

b. I must be in the wrong waiting room.

c. I will call Tom after the meeting.

Track 346

Which building is the conference in?

a. No, you don't have the correct manual.

b. The one at the corner of Main and Allen.

c. We are going with Jennifer and Ann.

Track 347

I am not sure where the lunchroom is located.

a. It's on the first floor in Room 22.

b. It's time to leave for the meeting.

c. I certainly will call you later.

Track 348

What papers does the publicity department need?

a. Watch out for errors in the text.

b. Which memo am I supposed to read?

c. The press releases about the new software program.

Track 349

We have a lunch meeting today.

a. Have you listed all your expenses?

b. What time will it be starting?

c. When does your CEO leave for England?

Track 350

Where is your supervisor?

    a. He is out of town for the week.

    b. Can you help me with this project?

    c. Just send me an e-mail about it.

Track 351

The conference is about increasing sales.

    a. I will give you my extension number.

    b. Which weekend are you working?

    c. I thought it might be about that.

Track 352

Are you waiting for an interview?

    a. No, we cannot reschedule the seminar.

    b. Yes, I am supposed to see someone at 2:00.

    c. Please take the mail to the mail room.

Track 353

I need to do some more research for my project.

    a. The personnel department is closed.

    b. Do you want me to help you with that?

    c. Which way is the main conference room?

Track 354

Your supervisor is waiting for you.

    a. We have to work on Saturday this week.

    b. Which meeting are you going to?

    c. Tell her I will be right there.

Track 355

I need to rent a car for the trip.

    a. Do you want me to do that?

    b. The e-mail has been written.

    c. Don't worry about being late.

Track 356

Did I leave my cell phone on your desk?

    a. The meeting will start in a few minutes.

    b. You need to sign up right away.

    c. Yes, I was just going let you know.

Track 357

Can you make a plane reservation for me?

    a. I will do it right away.

    b. Janet is on line one.

    c. Is this my new desk?

Track 358

We need to order more forms.

    a. I will meet you at the restaurant.

    b. I think the plan is well organized.

    c. I will do that first thing tomorrow.

Track 359

What is the name of your supervisor?

    a. Mrs. Martinez is sick today.

    b. His name is James Rhodes.

    c. Don't forget your cell phone.

Track 360

I am driving to the meeting.

    a. I need to restart my computer.

    b. Are they late for the dinner?

    c. Can Jean and I ride with you?

Track 361

Where is the cafeteria?

    a. It's next to the copy room.

    b. I want to ask a favor of you.

    c. Stay here until you are called.

Track 362

(Man) I am going on a road trip next Monday and I need to drop off the car to be serviced. Can you pick me up at the shop?

(Woman) Yes, I'd be happy to. How long will you be gone?

(Man) Three weeks. I need to go to four cities in two different states.

(Woman) That's a lot of driving. What's it for?

(Man) We are launching a new software package next month. I am going to demonstrate the product to my clients.

(*Woman*) Does management feel that the product has been tested enough?

(*Man*) I certainly hope so. They say it has been through 10,000 hours of testing.

Track 363
What are the man and woman discussing?

Track 364
What problem does the man have?

Track 365
How long will the man be away?

Track 366
(*Woman*) Should I call the tech people? I can't seem to log on to our company site.

(*Man*) Did you restart your computer?

(*Woman*) I did. It wouldn't accept my password. I tried three times and now I'm locked out.

(*Man*) Okay, but you can't just call anymore. Now you have to fill out a help ticket first.

(*Woman*) Where do I find a help ticket?

(*Man*) It's online at our site. I will fill one out for you and e-mail it to the help desk. What's your ID number?

(*Woman*) It's 04007219.

Track 367
What is the woman's problem?

Track 368
What does the man ask the woman?

Track 369
Why does the man need the woman's ID number?

Track 370
(*Man*) There are sign-up sheets in the break room for product training.

(*Woman*) I took that training last year. I don't see why I need to take it again.

(*Man*) I know, but you have to keep up with the changes that have occurred.

(*Woman*) Well, I guess you are right. I'll go over and sign up now.

(*Man*) This year will be a bit different. I've arranged it so there will only be six people in a class. Last year there were twice as many.

(*Woman*) That makes sense. It's easier to follow the material when there are fewer people.

Track 371
What are the man and woman discussing?

Track 372
Why does the woman think she doesn't need to take the training?

Track 373
What can you infer about the man?

Track 374
(*Man*) What are you looking for?

(*Woman*) I'm looking for a discount coupon for a rental car. I cut it out and thought I put it somewhere on my desk, but it's not there now. Have you seen it?

(*Man*) No, but why not download one from the Internet?

(*Woman*) I tried that. It was only for a 10% discount. I remember that the discount I had was for 20% off a weekly rental.

(*Man*) Why do you need to rent a car for an entire week?

(*Woman*) I have to see all the managers of our stores in the Tri-City area, so I will be gone a whole week.

Track 375
What is the woman's problem?

Track 376
Why doesn't the woman use the coupon on the Internet?

Track 377

Why is the woman going to the Tri-City area?

Track 378

(Woman) My supervisor wants me to come up with a list of ways that we can save energy and be greener, but I can't think of any.

(Man) Well, I have one idea. We should turn off our computers when we leave for the day. That will save energy.

(Woman) Good idea. Thanks. Do you have any others?

(Man) We could save paper by going more digital. Maybe we could even be paperless after a while.

(Woman) I will add that to the list, too.

(Man) And think of all the gas we could save if we all carpooled.

Track 379

What does the woman's supervisor want the woman to do?

Track 380

What is the woman's problem?

Track 381

What can you infer about the man?

Track 382

(Woman) We are having a meeting at 11:00 tomorrow morning. I heard they are going to introduce a new management team.

(Man) Well, I don't know if I can make the meeting.

(Woman) This meeting is mandatory. You have to attend it.

(Man) I don't think I can.

(Woman) What's your conflict?

(Man) I have to attend a training session on the new regulations that are being put in place. This is my last chance to attend it.

(Woman) Well, you should check with your supervisor and see what you should do.

(Man) I plan on doing that.

Track 383

What are the man and woman discussing?

Track 384

What problem does the man have?

Track 385

What is the man going to do to resolve the problem?

Track 386

(Man) I need you to book my trip for the book marketing conference.

(Woman) When does the conference start?

(Man) It starts Thursday morning at 8:00 A.M. and runs through Sunday afternoon. I really would like to get back Sunday night if possible.

(Woman) Let me see. Okay, I have you all set. You leave Wednesday at 4:30 P.M., and guess what? You are lucky. I was able to book you on the last flight out Sunday.

(Man) Great. Thanks.

Track 387

What does the man ask the woman to do?

Track 388

What can you infer about the woman?

Track 389

Why does the woman say that the man is lucky?

Track 390

(Woman) Have you heard about the new security system that is going into effect?

(Man) No, I haven't. Why are they putting in a new system?

(Woman) The keypad system worries management. They are afraid that some employees might write the code for the keypads down and then lose it.

(Man) That could be a problem. How are they going to prevent that from happening?

(Woman) They are going with an ID card that can be swiped and read. That should put an end to any security issues.

(Man) That sounds reasonable to me. I'm surprised they didn't do it a long time ago.

Track 391

What are the man and woman discussing?

Track 392

Why is the keypad system being replaced?

Track 393

What can you infer about the man?

Track 394

(Man) When did you buy the GPS unit?

(Woman) I picked it up this morning. I've got a promotion but it means moving to Wisconsin, so I thought it would be a good idea.

(Man) They are really great to have. I hadn't heard about your promotion but I am happy for you. When are you going?

(Woman) On Tuesday. With the GPS I won't get lost. I have already found a place to stay. I start work at my new location on Friday.

(Man) You sound excited.

(Woman) Well, I am. But I am also going to miss the friends I have made here.

(Man) You will be missed, too, but good luck. Keep in touch and let me know how it works out.

Track 395

Why is the woman going to Wisconsin?

Track 396

Why did the woman get a GPS unit?

Track 397

What can you infer about the man?

Track 398

(Man) Have you talked to the design company about our new website?

(Woman) They sent me an e-mail yesterday saying that they haven't been able to register our name. It's already been taken.

(Man) That's too bad. I will have to talk to the committee and see what other name they can come up with.

(Woman) Well, the good news is that they will send us the final design choices by the end of the week.

(Man) Good. The committee can review the designs and pick one.

(Woman) I know how important this website is for us. It's going to make a big difference.

(Man) I know. We believe it will help us meet our goals for this year.

Track 399

What are the man and woman discussing?

Track 400

What problem do the man and the woman have?

Track 401

What do the man and woman think about the website?

Track 402

Welcome aboard, everyone, and I hope you are prepared for a great experience. We will be going to Monkey Island, where the snorkeling is absolutely wonderful. We will spend an entire day there so you will have plenty of time to see the many exotic fish and their environments. Lunch is included and will be served in the main cabin promptly at 12:00 noon; it will be over at 1:00 P.M. Check in with the equipment staff before we reach our destination, so you will be ready to set out on your adventure. If you have any questions, just ask any of the crew members. They are all excellent snorkelers and can give you some valuable tips. Again, enjoy yourselves.

Track 403

Where would this announcement be heard?

Track 404

What is the purpose of this announcement?

Track 405

What time is lunch served?

Track 406

Hello. We welcome you here today and hope that your tour of this facility will bring you closer to the history of Native Americans in this country. We suggest that you take the elevator to the top of the building and view the 15-minute film before you walk down the ramps through the many exhibits. Each tribe has its own display area with samples of their traditional dress as well as explanations of their beliefs. On the ground floor there is a cafeteria that has foods that represent the various tribes' food choices. There is also a gift shop on the main floor where you can purchase crafts created by Native Americans, We hope you will learn a bit of the lore and wisdom of our Native American friends. Thank you for visiting us today and come back often.

Track 407

Where does this announcement take place?

Track 408

What is the purpose of the announcement?

Track 409

What does the gift shop have?

Track 410

Good afternoon, ladies and gentlemen, and welcome aboard Amtrak. We will be departing shortly. Our club car, located two cars from the rear of the train, is now open and is serving sandwiches, snacks, soft drinks, beer, wine, and other spirits for your enjoyment. The dining car is located at the rear of the train. It will be open from 6:00 P.M. until 10:00 P.M., serving a full menu with sit-down service. The special today is roast turkey with stuffing and your choice of two vegetables. The conductors will be coming around shortly to collect your tickets. Enjoy the trip, and thank you for choosing Amtrak for your travel needs.

Track 411

What is the purpose of this announcement?

Track 412

How does the dining room differ from the club car?

Track 413

What are the conductors about to do?

Track 414

Good morning, ladies and gentlemen. I will be leading your trip from Boston to Orlando and I look forward to getting to know you all a little bit. We will be leaving in a few moments and we will travel south on Route 95 to our final destination. We will make two overnight stops. Our first will be in our nation's capital, Washington, DC. The second will be in Savannah. You will have a bit of time to yourselves in both cities. During the day, we will make three stops, one for lunch and two rest stops. I hope to make your trip as pleasurable as possible. If you have any questions or problems, please address them during one of our breaks.

Track 415

Who is making this announcement?

Track 416

Which city is the first stop?

Track 417

What should someone with a problem do?

Track 418

Good afternoon. We welcome you today for a tour of our campus. You will get to visit some of our dormitories and the main library as well as the dining facility, where we have arranged to have snacks set up for you and your parents. The tour takes about an hour to complete. Since you have all applied to our school, you will be having personal interviews today as well. You should make sure to be on time for the interviews, which generally last about 20 minutes. I think you will agree that our campus is one of the finest in the state. Before the tour starts, please register in Room 15.

Track 419

Who is making this announcement?

Track 420

What advice does the announcer give the applicants?

Track 421

How long do the interviews take?

Track 422

Thank you for calling our reservation desk. Unfortunately, all agents are busy with other clients, but we appreciate your interest. We offer full services to our guests including housekeeping and, if desired, purchase of groceries so they are already in your kitchen upon your arrival. You can check in any time on Saturday between the hours of 9:00 A.M. and 5:00 P.M. For late arrival, special arrangements can be made. All units have decks and a view of the marina. We can arrange pickup at the airport for a small extra fee. We feel confident that your stay will be one of the most exciting and relaxing that you have ever had. Hang on and we will connect you to one of our customer service representatives.

Track 423

Where does this announcement take place?

Track 424

What is the purpose of the announcement?

Track 425

Where are the units located?

Track 426

According to recent reports, the cold snap will continue throughout the southeast for at least another week. Farmers in Florida are particularly concerned about their citrus crop. Groups up and down the coastline from North Carolina to Florida are also worried about the safety of wildlife, such as turtles. Their lives are threatened by the unusually cold temperatures. This is the coldest recorded time in the last 50 years, so bundle up, stay warm, and remember, your pets need shelter, too. This is Larry Dithers signing off.

Track 427

Who is making the announcement?

Track 428

Why is wildlife threatened?

Track 429

What does the announcer tell listeners?

Track 430

We interrupt this program to let you know that there has been a traffic accident on the Sands River Bridge. Traffic is backed up for miles on Third Street, so it is best to take alternatives routes if at all possible. The Sturgeon Bridge is open and there are no traffic delays there. Also, you can bypass the Sands River Bridge by taking Route 16 to Route 25. We expect that traffic will be backed up for at least an hour. After that the Sands River Bridge should be clear. Thank you for your cooperation in this matter. Now back to regular programming.

Track 431

Where does this announcement take place?

Track 432

What is causing the of traffic to back up?

Track 433

Where is the traffic backed up?

Track 434

Good evening, ladies and gentlemen. We are now approaching the equator and you might say that things are heating up. We have an extraordinary evening planned for you tonight. After dinner, there will be a fun-filled variety show on the main deck, which we call "A Taste of Vegas." Later you can dance the night away to the strains of our talented internationally known band, The Ocean Reefs, in the Neptune Nightclub. Tomorrow after we put in, you will have an entire day to explore the magical island of Dupree. Dinner will be onboard again tomorrow evening, but you will be on your own for lunch. So, let the fun begin!

Track 435

What is purpose of the announcement?

Track 436

Where does the announcement probably take place?

Track 437

What is named Dupree?

Track 438

Attention, passengers. Flight 245 to San Francisco has been delayed. Right now estimates are for that flight to leave in two hours. A maintenance issue must be addressed before the plane can be loaded. For those passengers who are traveling on and will not be able to make their connecting flight, please see the attendant at your gate. Your trip will be rerouted in order for you to reach your destination. We will update you of any new developments in a half hour. Thank you for your cooperation.

Track 439

Who is making the announcement?

Track 440

Why is the plane delayed?

Track 441

When will the information about the delay be updated?

Track 442

Hello. My name is Jessica Anson and I had a massage at your salon this morning. After I returned home, I realized that I had forgotten my necklace. I forgot to put it on after the massage. It's a gold chain and I am worried that someone might take it. Could you please look for it in the dressing room? I think I remember putting it on the small table next to a bench. I hope it is there. Diana was my masseuse. Maybe she found it. Anyway, please call me as soon as you get this message, at 343-3989. I appreciate your help.

Track 443

If you have never experienced the warm waters of Puerto Rico, you should definitely plan a visit to this magical tropical island where the beaches are wide and the surf comforting. At Palmas del Sol you will enjoy every amenity under the sun, including a world-class golf course, tennis courts, a spa, and more. Ride the waves of the Caribbean or lie aimlessly on the beach under your private shade tree. This resort offers five different restaurants, each one more inviting than the next. You will never forget your stay with us, so come play with us!

Track 444

Although the new city law has good intentions, I do not believe it will benefit our fair metropolis. Granting tax exemptions to entice a business to relocate here might help unemployment rates, but the rates in our city—and our state, for that matter—are already very low. What our city needs is to have everyone pay a fair share of the tax burden. Letting a large company pay less means that regular citizens will have to pay more, by comparison. Our city offers many benefits to a company; there's no need to add corporate tax breaks to this list.

Track 445

The photo shows two women sitting across a table from a man. They seem to be discussing something. The man's laptop is open. They all seem happy. He could be selling them something or explaining something to them.

Track 446

I have a Canon EOS Rebel. It's brand new.

Track 447

I use it quite a lot of the time, at least two or three times a week.

Track 448

I use it to take pictures of my family and of animals that I see in the zoo and at the park. I also use it for school since I am studying photography and hope to become a photojournalist.

Track 449

The cost of the seminar is $100 for the whole day or $55 for a half day.

Track 450

Lunch is not included in the price of the seminar, but there are nearby restaurants.

Track 451

There are seminars every hour. At ten you can choose between two seminars about writing ad copy. The last seminar of the morning is about writing your first advertisement.

Track 452

Hello. Is that Jessica Anson? This is Martin Castelli at Ocean Salon. I am sure you must be upset about your necklace, especially since it is gold. I understand completely. But I wanted to let you know right away that Diana found it and put it in a safe place. She said it was sitting right there on the table. She tried to catch you, but you had already driven away. Anyway, we have it here, so any time you want to pick it up just ask for me. We are open every day except Monday, from in the morning until 7 in the evening. If you want, call me first to make sure I am here. The phone number here is 673-9090. Again, my name is Martin.

Track 453

I think builders should be required to use green materials in new construction because it is important to use materials that don't pollute or hurt the environment and the people who live or work in the buildings. The only way you can get builders to comply would be by fining them, so I think that is important as well. Nowadays, there are enough green materials that are reasonably priced, so builders wouldn't be facing higher costs than they would with materials that are not green.

Chapter 10: Practice Exam 3

Track 454
   a. Two people are writing a book together.
   b. They're working on a laptop.
   c. The telephone doesn't work.
   d. The computer is broken.

Track 455
   a. It's time to go home.
   b. The meal is not ready to eat yet.
   c. Three people are forming a team.
   d. They're listening to someone speaking.

Track 456
   a. It might rain soon.
   b. The dirt is turning to mud.
   c. Someone is digging a hole.
   d. Something needs to be fixed.

Track 457
   a. A policeman is going to arrive.
   b. A person is answering a survey.
   c. A mother is unhappy with her daughter.
   d. A new person is moving into the house.

Track 458
   a. There's a traffic jam.
   b. A lot of cars are for sale.
   c. The road is being repaired.
   d. A new sidewalk is going in.

Track 459
   a. Two people are being interviewed.
   b. The couple is being asked to leave.
   c. The waiter is taking their order.
   d. The menus have not arrived yet.

Track 460
   a. The kids are making pizza.
   b. They're wearing their new hats.
   c. One of the kids doesn't like vegetables.
   d. Mother is going to be unhappy about the mess.

Track 461
   a. A boat just sank.
   b. Someone is lost at sea.
   c. The beach is not far away.
   d. The sun is setting behind the ocean.

Track 462
   a. There is no food for the bird.
   b. The bird is cleaning itself.
   c. A cat is about to attack the bird.
   d. A bird is hunting for fish.

Track 463
   a. A woman is paying for her purchases.
   b. The bags are filled with credit cards.
   c. Something is wrong with a lot of jeans.
   d. Two clerks are stocking the shelves.

Track 464
Do you know what time it is?
   a. No, I don't have a watch.
   b. This present is for you.
   c. I don't want to be in a hurry.

Track 465
Do you have this shirt in red?
   a. These pants are nice.
   b. Today is not Tuesday.
   c. Yes, we do.

Track 466
When does the show start?
   a. Here's my best friend.
   b. It should begin in a few minutes.
   c. This chair is very comfortable.

Track 467
This coffee isn't hot.
   a. This cake looks like it's too sweet.
   b. I'm sorry, I'll heat it up for you.
   c. We don't have time for this.

Track 468

Are you ready to go?

    a. I'll be dressed in a minute.

    b. I love going to the movies.

    c. This shirt is too tight for me.

Track 469

I'm going to miss my bus.

    a. It's time for dinner.

    b. I'll give you a ride if you want.

    c. Will you order for me, please?

Track 470

Who is coming for dinner?

    a. The food is going to be ready soon.

    b. My friends don't like to drink tea.

    c. Your parents and their friend.

Track 471

Can I borrow your umbrella?

    a. Thanks, I'll take it.

    b. Sure, if you need one.

    c. It's very hot today.

Track 472

Is that a new tie you're wearing?

    a. It is. I got it as a present.

    b. There aren't any more.

    c. I need to change my jacket.

Track 473

Is the news on yet?

    a. My cat needs to go out.

    b. Those boots look good on you.

    c. It starts in five minutes.

Track 474

Why is there no hot water?

    a. The water heater is broken.

    b. You can't drink that water.

    c. I've never heard of such a thing.

Track 475

Can you figure this problem out?

    a. I need to get my car fixed.

    b. Sure, I can babysit for you tonight.

    c. No. Let's ask Mary for help.

Track 476

This is quite a bargain, isn't it?

    a. When does the sale start?

    b. I'm out of change.

    c. It sure is.

Track 477

I like your new glasses.

    a. Thanks, I just got them yesterday.

    b. I have trouble reading in bed.

    c. Hey, did you just arrive?

Track 478

Do you think we need new car insurance?

    a. No, I just filled up the tank.

    b. No, I think we're getting a good deal already.

    c. No, the children can walk home from school.

Track 479

Have you seen my backpack?

    a. You should take a water bottle.

    b. Did you talk to your teacher yet?

    c. It's over by the door.

Track 480

Did you hear something downstairs?

    a. But I'm already up here.

    b. I think it was just the wind rattling the windows.

    c. Why, are we having company tomorrow?

Track 481

Can we take a break?

    a. Good idea. I'm tired, too.

    b. I'll call to get it repaired.

    c. Thanks, I'm full.

Track 482

Where is your sister going for vacation?

a. I think she's going to Hawaii.

b. Is she finally quitting her job?

c. School doesn't start for another week.

Track 483

This is too spicy.

a. No, I don't want to watch the game.

b. Oops, I thought I used too many peppers.

c. Where did you say you got that again?

Track 484

Does Carol have a new boss?

a. She does look a little sick.

b. Yes, I do enjoy my job.

c. No, he's just out of town this month.

Track 485

Do you know whether it's supposed to snow today?

a. My new sweater doesn't fit right.

b. Can we have Christmas dinner at our house?

c. No, I haven't looked at the weather report.

Track 486

Did we just miss the turn?

a. No, it's right up here.

b. It's too far to walk.

c. We never get lost.

Track 487

How did your interview go?

a. She won't talk to me anymore.

b. Really well. I think I got the job.

c. I might have time for a cup of tea.

Track 488

Do we have enough money to buy the tickets?

a. I think so, but I'll check.

b. The show starts in less than an hour.

c. My bank is just around the corner here.

Track 489

Do you have a dentist appointment today?

a. Thanks, my teeth feel great.

b. Sure, I can give you a ride.

c. No, I went yesterday.

Track 490

How much longer until dinner?

a. I need to buy a new pair of shoes.

b. We're expecting a package.

c. It'll be ready in twenty minutes.

Track 491

Basketball is my favorite sport.

a. Really? Mine, too.

b. I can never remember.

c. There are only four teams left.

Track 492

Are you having problems with your computer?

a. Yes, I do know that program.

b. No, it's working just fine.

c. I wasn't planning on going.

Track 493

Are you planting a garden this year?

a. Yes. I'm going to grow tomatoes.

b. Yes, I can make it at five o'clock.

c. Yes, it is hard to reach that.

Track 494

(Woman) Can you pick up the kids from school today and take them to soccer practice at 3 o'clock?

(Man) I thought you said yesterday that you were going to pick them up.

(Woman) I did, but I just got an e-mail from my boss. I have a 3 o'clock meeting that I can't reschedule.

(Man) I was supposed to get my hair cut at 3 o'clock, but I can cancel the appointment.

(Woman) Great. I'll make sure I bring home dinner after my meeting so you don't have to cook.

Track 495

What are the man and the woman trying to figure out?

Track 496

Why can't the woman pick up the kids from school?

Track 497

What was the man supposed to be doing at 3 o'clock?

Track 498

(*Woman*) Professor, I have some questions about the exam on Monday.

(*Man*) Sure, what are they?

(*Woman*) You said that there would be one essay question. Will we have any options for which essay to write?

(*Man*) Yes, there will be three questions you can choose from, and you only need to write an essay on one of the questions.

(*Woman*) If we write two essays, will you give us the grade for the better one?

(*Man*) No. I'll grade whichever one you write first.

(*Woman*) Okay, thanks. See you on Monday.

Track 499

What is the relationship between these two people?

Track 500

What does the woman want to know about?

Track 501

What is going to take place in class on Monday?

Track 502

(*Woman*) How can I help you, sir?

(*Man*) I would like to return these pants, please.

(*Woman*) Certainly. Is there something wrong with them?

(*Man*) My sister gave them to me as a gift, but they're too small.

(*Woman*) Would you like a refund, or would you like to exchange them for a pair that fits?

(*Man*) Can I exchange them for something else, like a shirt?

(*Woman*) Certainly. We'll give you the purchase price of the pants towards any new item.

(*Man*) Great. I guess I'll look around then.

Track 503

What is the relationship between these two people?

Track 504

What does the man want?

Track 505

What does the man decide he is going to do?

Track 506

(*Woman*) We need to make space on the shelves for these new books that just arrived.

(*Man*) Where are we going to put them?

(*Woman*) They're all novels, so we can make room in the fiction section. Let's go through and remove any second copies of the same novel.

(*Man*) Good idea. We can shift things over and make room for the new books.

(*Woman*) Okay. I'll start at the beginning of the alphabet and you start at the end.

Track 507

What describes the situation of these two people?

Track 508

What task do these two people have to accomplish?

Track 509

How do they decide to approach their task?

Track 510

(Woman) Can we finish packing later? I have to meet my friend to help her pick out wallpaper for her living room.

(Man) I won't have time later. I have a meeting until right before we have to leave for the airport. I'll just put my clothes in the suitcase and leave you enough space. You can finish by yourself later.

(Woman) Don't forget to pack your black suit. You don't have anything else to wear to the formal dinner on Saturday.

(Man) Thanks for reminding me. What tie do you think I should wear?

(Woman) I think your blue one is best. Okay, I have to go. I'll see you later.

Track 511

What are these two people doing?

Track 512

Why does the woman want to finish packing later?

Track 513

What is one thing they will be doing during their trip?

Track 514

(Man) I'm having a problem with my car. Can you take a look at it today?

(Woman) Certainly. Let me ask you a few questions first. What kind of problem have you been having?

(Man) It's difficult to start, and when I do finally get it started, I have to let it sit and run.

(Woman) Do you have any problems with stalling once you're driving?

(Man) No. If it drives off without stalling, it's fine.

(Woman) Okay. Leave the keys and your cell phone number at the front desk, and we'll call you in a few hours once we've had a chance to look at it.

Track 515

What does the man want?

Track 516

What is the woman's job?

Track 517

What is one problem the man has with his car?

Track 518

(Man) Your son has been having some difficulty in school.

(Woman) What kind of difficulty?

(Man) He hasn't been doing all his homework, and his test scores have dropped over the past few weeks. Are there any problems at home that might be affecting his work?

(Woman) My mother—his grandmother—died two weeks ago, and he's been pretty upset about it.

(Man) It's pretty common for a death in the family to impact a student's work in class. I'll keep an eye on him, but I'm sure it'll straighten out in a few weeks.

(Woman) Okay. I'll talk to him at home, too. I'm sure everything will be back to normal soon.

Track 519

What is the relationship between these two people?

Track 520

What does the man tell the woman?

Track 521

Why do they think the student hasn't been doing all his homework?

Track 522

(Man) I'm thinking about getting a new cell phone, but I want one that's more powerful than the one I currently have.

(Woman) What would you like your new phone to do that your old one doesn't?

(Man) I want to be able to keep track of my schedule. My old phone has a calendar feature, but I can't sync it up with the calendar on my computer, and it's very difficult to add new appointments.

(Woman) We have a new model that has a very user-friendly calendar that can sync up with your computer either online on through a wireless connection if you're within range of your own network.

(Man) That sounds good. Can you show it to me? I want to make sure the screen is big enough. That's another problem with my old phone—the screen is too small.

(Woman) This model has a good-sized screen. I'll go get you a demo model to look at.

Track 523

What is the relationship between these two people?

Track 524

What does the man want to buy?

Track 525

What is the man looking for in a new cell phone?

Track 526

(Woman) Excuse me, sir. I noticed that you're buying Brussels sprouts. Do you have a good recipe? I've always wanted to eat more Brussels sprouts because they're so healthy, but I never know how to cook them.

(Man) I usually cut them in half first and then fry them in butter over a high heat. Then I add garlic and turn down the heat. When the garlic is cooked, I add a little water and simmer for about five minutes until the Brussels sprouts are tender but still crunchy.

(Woman) That sounds delicious. About how long does it take?

(Man) You only cook the Brussels sprouts for about six or eight minutes. It take a few minutes to cut them up and chop the garlic, so it's only about fifteen minutes total.

(Woman) Thanks so much. I'm going to try that tonight.

(Man) Good luck. I hope you like it as much as I do.

Track 527

Where are these people speaking with each other?

Track 528

What does the woman want to know?

Track 529

About how long does the man say it will take to prepare his recipe?

Track 530

(Woman) How can I help you today, sir?

(Man) I want to return this camera I bought last week.

(Woman) Is there a problem with it?

(Man) Yes. The flash takes a really long time to recharge. I'm missing a lot of good pictures waiting for it.

(Woman) Did you try putting a new battery in? Sometimes even with a new camera, the battery gets worn down just sitting in the box on the shelf.

(Man) I did try a new battery, and it didn't help. I think I want to try a different brand.

(Woman) Very well, then. You can leave this here with me while you shop for a new camera, or I can process a refund to your credit card if you'd rather do it that way.

(Man) I think I'll get the refund right now. It might take me a while to figure out which other one I want.

Track 531

What is the woman helping the man do?

Track 532

What is the problem here?

Track 533

What does the man decide to do in this situation?

Track 534

You have reached the main switchboard at Portland Community College. Please listen carefully to the following options before making your selection. If you know the extension of your party, please dial it now followed by the pound key. If you would like to look up a name in our name directory, please press one. If you would like to reach student services, press two. If you need to speak to an academic advisor, please press three. If you need help directing your call, press zero or stay on the line and an operator will be with you shortly.

Track 535

When would someone hear this message?

Track 536

What is the purpose of this message?

Track 537

What happens if the caller does not press any number?

Track 538

Thank you for coming to our open house tonight. We're very proud of the new offices for our educational foundation, and we're glad to be able to showcase our space. We have a few events planned throughout the evening, which you can see here on this board. Feel free to look around our offices at any time and speak with our knowledgeable staff about what goes on in each area. For those who are interested in the architectural history of this building, our chief architect will be giving a talk at 8 o'clock here in the lobby. A reception will begin at 9 o'clock, at which time we will be giving out our annual employee achievement awards. Again, thank you for coming,

and I hope you have an enjoyable and informative evening.

Track 539

Where would this talk be heard?

Track 540

What is the purpose of this announcement?

Track 541

What should someone who is interested in attending a particular event do?

Track 542

Welcome to the Rotunda of the United States Capitol building. The Rotunda, which is 96 feet in diameter and 180 feet high at its peak, is the main circulation space in the Capitol. It connects the House and Senate sides and is also used for important ceremonial events. It is visited by thousands of people each day. As you see it today, the Rotunda was created by two separate building campaigns. In 1793, Dr. William Thornton won a competition for the design of the Capitol, and he conceived of the idea of a central rotunda. However, construction on the Rotunda was not begun until 1818 because of a shortage of funds and materials and the fire set by the British in 1814. The Rotunda was completed under in 1824 the direction of Charles Bulfinch.

Track 543

This talk is most likely a part of what?

Track 544

Why is the Rotunda the main circulation space in the Capitol?

Track 545

Why was the Rotunda not completed until 1824?

Track 546

You're about to watch a documentary about credit card companies and the kinds of practices they employ. As credit card companies face rising anger among the public, high rates of default and bankruptcy, and new efforts to put in place strong federal regulations, this program examines the future of the massive credit card industry and how these companies impact the fragile national economy. In this program, our correspondents interview industry insiders, lobbyists, politicians, and consumer advocates, exploring their different viewpoints on the recent attempts to reform the way credit card companies have done business in recent decades.

Track 547

What is the purpose of this message?

Track 548

What will the program this message describes do?

Track 549

Who will ask most of the questions in this program?

Track 550

As you plan your family's meals, it's important to keep in mind several basic principles. The first is that diversity is one of the biggest keys to health. Human beings need a variety of sources of nutrition to reach optimal health. Second, certain foods, such as meat, dairy, and sugar, should be eaten in moderation. A well-rounded diet will consist of a variety of foods but will be heaviest in fruits and vegetables and basic starches such as potatoes, rice, or oats. Finally, try to avoid processed foods as much as possible. While cooking from scratch is time-consuming, it is both less expensive and healthier for your family.

Track 551

Where would this message most likely be heard?

Track 552

Which of these foods should people eat least?

Track 553

What advice does this speaker give?

Track 554

The penguins you see behind me are emperor penguins. The emperor is the world's largest penguin. The adults can be up to 4 feet tall and weigh as much as a hundred pounds. Like all penguins, the emperor penguin is actually a flightless bird. What would normally be wings on a bird are stiff and flat like flippers, making all penguins well suited to a marine habitat. The diet of the emperor penguins consists mostly of fish, although they also eat squid and krill. The emperor penguin is best known for the long journeys the adults make each year to feed their offspring. The adults travel up to 75 miles through the antarctic winter to bring food to the breeding colonies from the sea.

Track 555

Where would you most likely hear this talk?

Track 556

What kind of animal is the emperor penguin?

Track 557

What are emperor penguins best known for?

Track 558

This is the planned site for our new city hall building. The site is currently occupied by an empty strip mall. The current building will be torn down, but much of the material will be reused in the new building, including all the electrical wiring and much of the plumbing. Environmentally friendly building techniques will be used throughout the project. This site was chosen for several reasons. It is centrally located in our town, providing easy access for all residents. It is also an area that has undergone an economic decline in recent years. Locating the new city hall here will help revitalize this area and bring more customers to those businesses that have survived.

Track 559

Where is this talk being given?

Track 560

What is the purpose of this talk?

Track 561

What is one reason this site was chosen?

Track 562

Tonight we are proud to bring you a new exhibition by local artist, Mark Gunderson. Mr. Gunderson is a local artist in many senses of the word. He was born in the area and has lived most of his life here, but that's not the only way in which he is local. For two decades, he has been creating three-dimensional paintings and sculpture using local materials, and his work focuses on themes drawn from our region's history, geography, and culture. For this exhibition, Mr. Gunderson worked with another local artist, a Native American who is familiar with the lore of the peoples who lived in this area long before the white settlers arrived. The results of this collaboration are striking in their beauty as well as educational. The town arts council is proud to sponsor this exhibition. We hope you enjoy the show.

Track 563

Who would have given this talk?

Track 564

What is this talk introducing?

Track 565

What kind of art will appear in this exhibition?

Track 566

This is a prerecorded message. Today's movie is Disney's *Beauty and the Beast*. Show times are 12:30, 3:15, 5:00, and 7:40. Tickets are $4 for adults and $2 for children over five. Children five years old or younger are free. We are located at the corner of Third and Ash streets. Our box office opens at noon every day. For future movies and showtimes, please consult our website at www.ashtheater.com.

Track 567

When would someone hear this message?

Track 568

What is the purpose of this message?

Track 569

What is the earliest that someone can buy a ticket to one of these movies?

Track 570

Due to snowy conditions, some schools in the Multnomah County School District will be closed today. Please listen carefully to the following message as some schools will remain open and some will open late. All schools downtown, in northeast, and north Portland are closed for the day. Schools in southwest Portland with the exception of those schools downtown will open three hours late. All schools in southeast Portland will open at their regular time. Snow routes will be used for all buses. Check the district webpage for details if you are not familiar with our alternative snow route stops. Please check back at this number throughout the day for updates.

Track 571

Who would hear this message?

Track 572

What is the purpose of this message?

Track 573

Schools in which part of the district will open late?

Track 574

Hi, Mrs. Barnes, this is Willow. I know I'm supposed to be at your house to babysit in half an hour. Usually I'm never late for babysitting jobs, but I was going to get a ride from my brother and his car wouldn't start. I would've had time to get there on the bus, but the bus was leaving the bus stop just as I got there. I called the bus schedule hotline, and the next bus won't be coming for another 30 minutes, and now that it's rush hour, the bus is going to take longer, so I'm probably going to be an hour late. I know you're going to a surprise birthday party, and I don't want you to be late, but I can't get there any faster on the bus, and I can't get in touch with anyone else who might be able to give me a ride. What should we do?

Track 575

Improvements in communication have enabled and stimulated global economic growth. Improved communication networks facilitate the coordination of transportation and logistics, making transport chains flow much more smoothly. The cost of communications has dropped substantially in recent decades. Developments like fiber optics and the Internet make communications smoother and more useful as well as less expensive. The rise of outsourcing has contributed to a rapid expansion in the international trade of labor services, such as technical consulting and call center services. As a result, international trade includes a widening variety of services that were previously fixed to regional markets.

Track 576

The beauty and size of the Grand Canyon is humbling, but the Grand Canyon you visit today is more than just an awe-inspiring natural formation. It is a gift from past generations that have preserved it and helped develop it in a sustainable way. As you visit the canyon, take time to enjoy this gift, but always keep in mind that this gift must continue to be passed on. We all have the responsibility to ensure that future generations have the chance to experience the same Grand Canyon that we can see today.

Track 577

There is a large snow-covered mountain in the background set against a clear sky. In front of the mountain is a large barn surrounded by a fence. The fence also encloses a pasture. Behind the barn is a row of tall evergreen trees.

Track 578

I don't pay much attention to politics. I don't feel like the things politicians do have much impact on my life. I do pay attention to current events, though, because I like to know what's going on in the world around me.

Track 579

I'm mostly satisfied because I feel like the country is doing pretty well, but of course I have some problems. I think political leaders are sometimes too distant from the people. They need to know more about what it's like to live like the rest of us.

Track 580

I think the economy needs to be turned around. The unemployment rate keeps going up, and that's hurting a lot of people. The government should do something about it, but so should big companies. They're the ones firing and laying off people just to save money. Companies need to know that they're hurting real people just to get a little boost in their profit margin.

Track 581

There are two exams that are each worth 25% of the grade, so the two exams together are worth half of the course grade. The midterm exam has multiple-choice and short answer questions. The final exam only has essay questions, no multiple-choice or short answers.

Track 582

Students are expected to attend all the classes, and class attendance is 20% of the grade. There are also three short papers that must be turned in on time.

Track 583

It is never good to miss too many classes, and you will lose some points for the classes you miss, but one week won't kill your grade. It's very important that you don't miss any paper deadlines because of your trip. You should also check the course schedule to make sure you won't be gone during the midterm or final. A business trip is not a medical excuse or a personal emergency, so you won't be given a makeup or extension because of this trip.

Track 584

I appreciate that you're concerned about our missing the beginning of a surprise birthday party. I would like to avoid being late, but these things do happen. If you want, I can drive down to the bus stop and pick you up. That will probably save some time. I can leave immediately, but I may not get there before your bus arrives. If you bus does arrive before I get there, don't get on it. I'll call you on your cell phone when I'm almost there. See you soon.

Track 585

I do think that technological gadgets make our lives more hectic and stressed. Just because we're able to be in constant communication with everybody, people expect that you'll be available whenever they call, text, or e-mail, and they often get upset if you don't answer immediately or get back to them quickly. Employers are particularly demanding. You're not just at work when you're in the office. Because you can always be reached, they think they can ask you to do more work outside the office. But even with all of that said, I still wouldn't want to do without technology. A simpler life might be less hectic, but I also think it would be more boring. I'll take the stress of a gadget-filled life over the boredom of a simpler life any day.

ADDITIONAL ONLINE PRACTICE ▶

Whether you need help building basic skills or preparing for an exam, visit the LearningExpress Practice Center! On this site, you can access additional practice materials. Using the code below, you'll be able to log in for additional TOEIC practice. This online practice will also provide you with:

- **Immediate scoring**
- **Detailed answer explanations**
- **Personalized recommendations for further practice and study**

Log in to the LearningExpress Practice Center by using URL: **www.learnatest.com/practice**

This is your Access Code: **7571**

Follow the steps online to redeem your access code. After you've used your access code to register with the site, you will be prompted to create a username and password. For easy reference, record them here:

Username:_____ Password:_____

With your username and password, you can log in and answer these practice questions as many times as you like. If you have any questions or problems, please contact LearningExpress customer service at 1-800-295-9556 ext. 2, or e-mail us at **customerservice@learningexpressllc.com**.